Narcissism and the Interpersonal Self

Personality, Psychopathology, and Psychotherapy: Theoretical and Clinical Perspectives

Henry Kellerman, *Series Editor*

Psychopathology and Differential Diagnosis: A Primer
Volume One: History of Psychopathology
by Henry Kellerman and Anthony Burry

Psychopathology and Differential Diagnosis: A Primer
Volume Two: Diagnostic Primer
by Henry Kellerman and Anthony Burry

The Transference-Countertransference Matrix: The Emotional-Cognitive Dialogue in Psychotherapy, Psychoanalysis, and Supervision
by Robert J. Marshall and Simone V. Marshall

An Interpersonal Approach to Child Therapy: The Treatment of Children and Adolescents from an Interpersonal Point of View
by Stanley Spiegel

Theories of Object Relations: Bridges to Self Psychology
by Howard A. Bacal and Kenneth M. Newman

Group Psychotherapist's Handbook: Contemporary Theory and Technique
Edited by Irwin I. Kutash and Alexander Wolf

Character Structure and the Organization of the Self
by Lawrence Josephs

NARCISSISM AND THE INTERPERSONAL SELF

John Fiscalini
Alan L. Grey
Editors

Columbia University Press
New York

Columbia University Press
New York / Chichester, West Sussex

Library of Congress Cataloging-in-Publication Data

Narcissism and the interpersonal self / edited by John Fiscalini and Alan L. Grey.
p. cm. -- (Personality, psychopathology, and psychotherapy)
Includes bibliographical references and index.
ISBN 0–231–07010–1
1. Narcissism. I. Fiscalini, John. II. Grey, Alan L., 1919– .
III. Series: Personality, psychopathology, and psychotherapy (New York, N.Y.)
RC553.N36N33 1993
616.85'85--dc20 92-35506
CIP

∞

Casebound editions of Columbia University Press books are printed on permanent and durable acid-free paper.

Printed in the United States of America

c 10 9 8 7 6 5 4 3 2 1

To Barbara and Kate
J. F.

For Carolyn
A. L. G.

Contents

PART II
THE SELF AND NARCISSISM: THEORETICAL PERSPECTIVES

PART III
CLINICAL NARCISSISM

PART IV
THE THERAPEUTIC RELATIONSHIP

Foreword

Earl G. Witenberg

In this volume, John Fiscalini and Alan Grey give us a comprehensive view of the status of narcissism in this, the last decade of the twentieth century. Narcissism as a notion, as something treatable, was ignored by traditional analysts until Freud died. A few brave souls such as Fromm, Fromm-Reichmann, Horney, Sullivan, and Thompson developed new approaches in the theory and practice with them. They were treated as "deviationists" because of their beliefs in the influence of culture and society. Since World War II and particularly since Kohut a burgeoning interest has developed in these people. Since the notion of self is intimately connected with the concept of narcissism and with the concept of others being necessary to development, the title *Narcissism and the Interpersonal Self* is particularly appropriate.

Can we know the nature of the development of self without others? The question that remains, namely, whether an aspect of self exists independent of interaction, is one that cannot be answered now or perhaps ever.

In this volume the editors have gathered together writings by the most accomplished theoreticians and clinicians. All the authors (and the editors) are candid about their positions and revealing about their attitudes and thinking. As one who has followed intently all the work about narcissism and the self, I had some misgivings about the publication of yet another volume on this topic. Happily, my misgivings are not justified. I found this volume an excellent review with increments in knowledge in the subject. It is well balanced between theory and practice. Comprehensive, inventive, and immensely readable, this volume can be recommended to practitioners, scholars, and students. This is an eminently praiseworthy endeavor.

Acknowledgments

This book offers a collaborative exploration of the Interpersonal psychoanalytic understanding of narcissism and the self. For the gift of their insightful and scholarly contributions, we thank Drs. Bacciagaluppi, Condrau, Feiner, Havens, Hirsch, Levenson, Ortmeyer, Salzman, Schimel, Tatara, and Wolstein, and, for his incisive foreword, Dr. Witenberg. The array of viewpoints they provide about problems of the self is representative of the most recent thinking of contemporary Interpersonal analysts. It indicates, too, how present-day formulations draw upon the earlier contributions of Fromm, Sullivan, Horney, Thompson, and other seminal analysts of the American school.

From the first this book has been a cooperative enterprise, stimulated by the discussions and debates inevitably accompanying our regular Monday morning breakfast meetings. We hope that the printed pages retain some of the spirit of those meetings by serving as a stimulus for further inquiry, rather than by offering final pronouncements. If so, they will have reflected a salient characteristic of the Interpersonal perspective. It is to arrive at a series of successively better approximations to the appreciation of how people deal with their ever-changing psychological worlds.

We wish also to acknowledge our debt of gratitude for the editorial contributions of Gioia Stevens, Anne McCoy, and Bob Mobley of Columbia University Press.

In addition to those acknowledgments shared with Dr. Grey, I would like to express my personal indebtedness to the many students, teachers, friends, and patients who, in various ways, have helped shape my understanding of narcissism and the self. I am especially grateful to Dr. Benjamin Wolstein, whose original analytic perspective has been deeply informative of the uniquely individual aspects of self experience and process. I thank him for his ever-generous encouragement of my ideas. Very special thanks are also due my wife and colleague, Dr. Barbara Suter, for her insightful critiques, kind suggestions, and always helpful advice. And to her and my daughter Kate, my gratitude for their patience during this often preoccupying work.

J.F.

Many teachers, patients, colleagues, friends, and relatives have contributed, directly and indirectly, to my efforts in this volume. There is one person, however, whom I very much wish to thank explicitly. That is my wife Carolyn Grey, whose perceptiveness has helped me in many ways.

A.L.G.

Contributors

Marco Bacciagaluppi, M.D.
Fellow of the American Academy of Psychoanalysis. Member of the Erich Fromm International Society. Training and Supervising Analyst, Instituto Erich Fromm, Bologna, Italy.

Gian Condrau, Prof. Dr. med. et phil.
Member (Switzerland), International Federation of Psychoanalytic Societies.

Arthur H. Feiner, Ph.D.
Chairman, Council of Fellows, Training and Supervising Analyst, Teaching Faculty, William Alanson White Institute. Editor, *Contemporary Psychoanalysis;* Editor, *Contemporary Psychoanalytic Books.*

John Fiscalini, Ph.D.
Training and Supervising Analyst, Supervisor of Psychotherapy, Teaching Faculty, William Alanson White Institute. Faculty and Supervisor, Manhattan Institute for Psychoanalysis. Supervisor, Institute for Contemporary Psychotherapy.

Alan L. Grey, Ph.D.
Professor Emeritus of Psychology, Fordham University. Supervising Analyst, Supervisor of Psychotherapy, William Alanson White Institute. Faculty and Supervisor, Westchester Center for the Study of Psychoanalysis and Psychotherapy. Faculty and Supervisor, Manhattan Institute for Psychoanalysis. Supervisor, Institute for Contemporary Psychotherapy. Advisory Board, *American Journal of Psychotherapy.*

Leston Havens, M.D.
Professor of Psychiatry, Cambridge Hospital and Massachusetts Mental Health Center, Harvard Medical School.

Irwin Hirsch, Ph.D.
Director, Manhattan Institute for Psychoanalysis. Professor of Psychology and Supervisor, Postdoctoral Program in Psychoanalysis and Psychotherapy, Adelphi University. Editorial Board, *Psychoanalytic Dialogues.*

Edgar A. Levenson, M.D.
Director of Training, Fellow, Training and Supervising Analyst, Teaching Faculty, William Alanson White Institute. Clinical Professor and Supervisor, Graduate School of Arts and Sciences, New York University.

Dale H. Ortmeyer, M.D.
Fellow, Training and Supervising Analyst, Teaching Faculty, William Alanson White Institute. Clinical Professor, Adelphi University. Supervisor, Westchester Center for the Study of Psychoanalysis and Psychotherapy. Instructor in Psychiatry, Columbia University. Editorial Board, *Psychoanalytic Psychology.*

Leon Salzman, M.D.
Professor of Psychiatry, Georgetown University School of Medicine. Past President, American Academy of Psychoanalysis. Former Professor of Psychiatry, Tulane University Medical School.

John L. Schimel, M.D.
Associate Director, Fellow, Training and Supervising Analyst, William Alanson White Institute. Clinical Professor of Psychiatry, New York University Bellevue Medical Center. Past President, American Academy of Psychoanalysis. Past President, American Society for Adolescent Psychiatry.

Mikihachiro Tatara, Ph.D.
Professor of Psychology, Hiroshima University, Hiroshima, Japan.

Earl G. Witenberg, Ph.D.
Director, Fellow, Training and Supervising Analyst, Teaching Faculty, William Alanson White Institute. Past President, American Academy of Psychoanalysis.

Benjamin Wolstein, Ph.D.
Training and Supervising Analyst, Teaching Faculty, William Alanson White Institute. Clinical Professor Emeritus, Adelphi University, Postdoctoral Program. Clinical Professor, New York University, Postdoctoral Program.

Narcissism and the Interpersonal Self

INTRODUCTION

Narcissism, the Self, and Interpersonal Psychoanalysis

Alan L. Grey and John Fiscalini

I

All papers in this volume address the theme of narcissism. Understood as the concern of the self with defending the self, narcissism as a subject of psychoanalytic investigation inevitably leads to the study of the self. The self, in turn, is a term employed for viewing any one individual in relationship to others. Clearly, then, to understand narcissism as a psychological defense by one self against others requires scrutiny of what happens to evoke such defense. It turns attention to the sphere of the interpersonal as well as the personal. Once psychoanalysts undertake to penetrate the mysteries of narcissistic processes, their focus expands beyond purely intrapsychic matters to include the contexts in which these processes transpire. This therapeutic perspective has characterized the work of those analysts who have succeeded best with narcissistic problems.

The Interpersonal approach was not at all obvious, however, during the 1920s when analysts dismissed as impossible the treatment of those diagnosed as narcissistic, but it was the route chosen by Harry Stack Sullivan at that time, when he undertook psychotherapy with schizophrenic patients (the so-called narcissistic neuroses). A few other psychoanalysts—pioneers like Erich Fromm, Karen Horney, and Clara Thompson—also became curious about how social experience affects personality. They, too, turned their attention to issues of narcissism and selfhood. In Great Britain as well, somewhat similar issues aroused the curiosity of Melanie Klein and her followers, stimulated by therapeutic endeavors with children. But for the most part, interest in the world of human relationships did not come into the purview of most analysts until after World War II.

The story has been very different since then. In the past two decades, narcissistic patients and disorders of the self have elicited extraordinary attention from analysts of all schools, including new schools brought into being by the topic itself. Disturbances of the self are the dominant theme of an expanding literature. And their study now stimulates a considerable part of the theoretical, diagnostic, and therapeutic imagination and energy of contemporary analysts. Why this new discovery of an old problem? Are we now in an age of the self and its discontents? Is self-preoccupation a new and increasingly prevalent pathology brought about by contemporary cultural and familial factors? Or is narcissism and the disordered self old trouble seen with a new awareness, opened through the accumulated impact of clinical experiences?

Whatever the answers to such questions, we are inevitably confronted by even more raised by the intellectual heritage of psychoanalysis itself. They are questions about whether to understand these psychological phenomena in terms of the autism of unrelated drive, as Freud would see it; or of failed symbiotic merger, as Kohut or the British Object Relationists propose; or of failed integrations between the child and significant others, as Sullivan and the American school describe it. And, of course, clinical problems about treatment of disorders of the self must be addressed. They concern the optimal therapeutic role of the analyst's own private and public self, the uses and misuses of empathy, the nature of mutative processes, the optimal approach to narcissistic resistances and urgent self-esteem needs, and myriad other issues.

Answers have become ever more elusive because narcissism as a construct has come to mean almost all things to all analysts. Some suspect that as a diagnosis it threatens to absorb all patients. Theoretical and clinical complexities, ambiguities, and abuses of the concept of narcissism have seeped into professional discourse everywhere. Because it is conceivably the dominant focus of analytic thought today, it has attracted the application of a heterogeneity of improvised analytic tools, most of them originally designed for very different metapsychological missions. Clearly pertinent, therefore, is any effort to bring some order into the situation by fresh consideration of a conceptual system specifically designed to address disorders of the self, one that has proven useful for the task.

II

The papers in this collection address the topic of narcissism from an Interpersonal perspective. Part 1, the overview section, consists of two articles, one by each of the editors. The first paper, "A Spectrum of Psychoanalytic Self Theories," by Alan Grey, offers a frame of reference from which the Interpersonal theory of self can be understood in relation to other psychoanalytic Self theories. It calls attention to the fact that selves are shaped by more than parent-child dyads and triangles and by more than the first few years of life. Field theory is shown to provide empirically useful guides to the many significant relationships that compose relevant social fields.

In the second essay in the overview, "Interpersonal Relations and the Problem of Narcissism," John Fiscalini focuses more specifically on narcissistic orientations of the self. How they are understood by Interpersonalists in comparison with certain other well-known theories of narcissism is described, and an Interpersonal analysis of conceptual flaws in the traditional psychoanalytic construct of narcissism is offered. Then a verbal portrait is provided of the self-respecting child, and its developmental experiences are differentiated from those of three developmental routes to clinical narcissism.

Part 2 addresses theoretical perspectives on the self and narcissism through five contributions from a variety of perspectives, all of them associated with Interpersonal thought. The assignment of papers to this or any other section is somewhat arbitrary, in that all these discussions focus on clinical and treatment matters, as well as on theory. That state of affairs reflects an important aspect of the Interpersonal-Relations approach. Interpersonal thought tends to be couched in operational terms, close to clinical observation. And in the case of some Interpersonal writers, theory is also anchored in social science research.

The first article in part 2, "Fromm's Views on Narcissism and the Self," by Marco Bacciagaluppi, reflects a continuing and lively interest in the work of

Erich Fromm, one of the pioneers of Cultural-Interpersonal thought. It also illustrates one of four viewpoints described by Fiscalini in his summary categorization of varieties of Interpersonalists (see paper 15). This paper might be regarded as written from the perspective of the *relationists,* "those Interpersonalists who have attempted to build theoretical and clinical bridges between ego psychology, object relations theory, self psychology and traditional and modern Interpersonal theory."

The fourth paper is entitled "The Lost Uniqueness of Kohut's Self psychology: An Instance of Narcissism." By Benjamin Wolstein, it is more than simply a theoretical critique of the conceptions of another psychoanalyst widely known outside Interpersonal circles. This paper states basic convictions about the nature of the self and the centrality of its uniquely personal aspects in analytic inquiry by a leader of what Fiscalini calls the *radical empiricist,* or *experientialist,* group of Interpersonal thinkers. In raising questions about traditionally truncated analytic conceptions of the self, this paper expresses one of Wolstein's cardinal themes: the need for the analysts' own unique personality and self-experience to inform their analytic coparticipation with the patient.

Wolstein's theoretical discussion is followed by a lively examination called "Character, Personality, and the Politics of Change: Implications for an Interpersonal Understanding of Narcissism." Written by Edgar Levenson, one of the best known of the contemporary Interpersonalists, this paper examines some connotations of the concept of character as a construct compared with the idea of personality. It argues that the fixity of structure implied by constructs like character exaggerate the imperviousness of the human personality to change. This paper and the one that follows it (by Grey) might both be regarded as illustrative of what Fiscalini calls the *radical preservationist* viewpoint in Interpersonal theory, or what could also be termed the *radical constructionist* position.

The sixth paper, "The Interpersonal Self Updated," is by Alan Grey. It represents an effort to revise the Sullivanian version of the self in terms of a more consistent employment of constructionist principles coordinated with contemporary empirical findings in the social sciences.

The seventh paper, "The Daseinsanalytic–Phenomenological Approach to Narcissism," is a contribution from a distinguished representative of Swiss Daseinsanalysis. Although the intellectual roots of Daseinsanalysis are derived from sources other than Interpersonal theory in the philosophically oriented writings of thinkers like Heidegger and Boss, many of their emphases bear a striking resemblance to ideas typically associated with the Interpersonal viewpoint. For one thing, they question the utility of fixed diagnostic categories. For another, they urge that analysts look to how their own personalities participate in the treatment interaction. Characteristically, too, Daseinsanalysts are especially concerned with the here-and-now aspects of the patient's life. This paper concludes the theoretical section.

Part 3 explores clinical narcissism and consists of four papers that address psychological phenomena typically associated with disorders of the self. Primarily focusing on clinical description, these papers represent no one theoretical subset of Interpersonal perspectives very distinctly, though some of them might be regarded as illustrative of a more *traditional Interpersonalist* approach.

In the eighth paper, "The Concept of Narcissistic Interactions," Leston Havens proposes some observations that might well serve as a more frequent model in psychoanalytic discussions. Rather than define the normal in terms of the absence of pathology, he suggests criteria for well-functioning self-esteem, or "nonnarcissistic orientations." Borrowing from Craig, he speaks of "a shy acceptance of having been at once entrusted and exposed to this singular existence of one's own," as such a nonnarcissistic attitude. A noteworthy Interpersonal observation of his is that narcissistic attitudes do not simply reside in an individual. They are contextually determined. For example, such attitudes may emerge or recede when one changes one's marriage partner.

Expanding on the theme of intimate relationships, the ninth paper, "Love and Sexuality in Narcissistic Personalities: A Clinical Report," by John Schimel deals with issues very close to the core of what is amiss in narcissistic relationships, although he expresses discomfort with clinical descriptions that are constricted by diagnostic labels.

The tenth essay, "An Interpersonal Approach to Idealization in the Narcissistic Personality," by Dale Ortmeyer, is of interest on several counts. It presents a thoughtful discussion of certain tendencies often observed among those called narcissistic. It is also a persuasive espousal of a pluralistic viewpoint that takes account of the rich history and diversity of psychoanalytic ideas. The pluralistic position has earned considerable popularity in recent years.

Of particular interest, too, is Mikihachiro Tatara's study "Patterns of Narcissism in Japan." In an especially vivid way, it demonstrates the cross-cultural flexibility and fluidity of the Interpersonal approach to problems of clinical observation and nosology. More explicity, this article illustrates that general guidelines and principles are better suited to understanding the wide range of so-called narcissistic phenomena than ethnocentrically bound diagnostic and treatment categories are. Along with Professor Condrau and Dr. Bacciagaluppi, Dr. Tatara is one of the triumvirate of foreign authorities contributing to the present collection.

While references to treatment methods have already appeared in the preceding papers, that task is addressed more explicitly in the four papers constituting part 4, on the therapeutic relationship, the final section of this book.

In paper 12, "Narcissism and Obsessionalism: An Interpersonal Psychoanalytic Approach," Leon Salzman expresses reservations about the misleading nature of nosological entities. Well known for his studies of obsessionalism, here Salzman points to the considerable overlap between supposedly distinct syndromes, such as obsessionalism and narcissism. In the detailed presentation of his *traditional Interpersonal* analytic approach to the treatment of narcissism and obsessionalism, Salzman provides a reference point for examining the *radical preservationist* or *constructivist* perspective of the next two Interpersonal writers.

In essay 13, "The Relation of Monologue and Dialogue to Narcissistic States and Its Implications for Psychoanalytic Therapy," Arthur Feiner approaches the treatment process in a thoughtful and meditative fashion. Taking the communication process as the essence of the therapeutic experience, he ingeniously explores the influences analyst and patient have on each other for their implications about how mutative processes are induced.

Next, "The Ubiquity and Relativity of Narcissism: Therapeutic Implications" by Irwin Hirsch calls attention to several key propositions of an Interpersonal approach to psychoanalysis. Among them is the observation that what is being treated is not simply one person, the patient, but rather the relationship between analyst and patient, which includes how the analyst is contributing to what occurs. Because each relationship is unique, varying with the combined tendencies of both participants, treatment prescriptions must remain flexible to allow for the range of variations. Hirsch notes, too, the historical tendency of analysts to justify their radically new ideas as necessary to accommodate the particular requirements of atypical populations, like those called narcissistic. Through this device many Interpersonal ideas have been absorbed into mainstream psychoanalysis without benefit of explicit acknowledgment.

The final paper, by John Fiscalini—entitled "The Psychoanalysis of Narcissism: An Interpersonal View"—is a unique statement but at the same time shares certain ideas of the *radical empiricist,* or *experientialist,* group of Interpersonal theorists. Going beyond any one particular viewpoint, however, this article offers an overview of various Interpersonal and other approaches to the treatment of narcissistic problems. Thus it provides a measure of closure for this broad survey of Interpersonal thought.

III

Collections of papers can offer a broad range of perspectives on the topic addressed; they are also vulnerable to the possibility of leaving readers without an adequate synthesis of the ideas that they cover. When it is considered that Interpersonal theory itself encourages independence and flexibility in the theories and practices of its adherents, no representative statement of its position can be completely devoid of unresolved questions and differences of viewpoint. At the same time, as a meaningful psychoanalytic position, the Interpersonal standpoint necessarily excludes certain propositions and requires others. In order to identify those tenets of the system, not only does this volume conclude with Fiscalini's synthesis but also the first paper of the collection provides an overview of self theories by Grey.

As further orientation to the contents of this volume, we offer the following summary of some central themes that recur in many of the papers.

1. Human personality, including self-reflexive awareness (i.e., the personified self) and narcissistic experience, develops through relationships between people (see the checklist of ten implications of the interactional perspective in paper 1 of this collection).
2. For human beings no circumstances exist in which personality is free from interpersonal influence. (Some disagreement has arisen about this proposition between *traditional Interpersonalists* and *radical preservationists,* on the one hand, and *radical empiricists* and *relationists* on the other. The first two groups support this proposition, while the latter two, in different ways, place an additional emphasis on what has variously been called a personal, intrapersonal, or intrapsychic dimension of personality, understood as a psychic selfness that is not socially determined.)
3. The human personality, including its self-esteem or narcissistic concerns, is most meaningfully understood through observation and study of interpersonal interactions in both their subjective (i.e., experiential) and behavioral aspects.
4. The clinical psychoanalytic inquiry is most meaningfully conceived of as a process of participant or coparticipant observation. The inevitability of experiential participation in interpersonal or intersub-

jective social fields is a principle that applies to the analyst's role in the psychoanalytic treatment situation as well as to all other life situations. Thus adequate understanding of narcissistic processes requires analysts to recognize that their own presence makes them participants in the observed situation in ways that affect understanding and that can benefit from consensual validation.

5. Especially significant in interpersonal participation in social fields is how the self-esteem of each participant is influenced through mutual interaction. Manifestations of narcissistic concern are responses to social fields, both in everyday life and in psychoanalytic treatment.
6. Self-esteem or interpersonal security needs, even in their more childlike aspects, continue to be an important consideration for each of us throughout life. In that sense, no sharp division exists between those whose narcissistic concerns are more intense and those whose concerns are milder. Narcissistic difficulties in living exist on a continuum.
7. Consequently, nosological categories, like the diagnosis of "narcissistic personality disorder," are of limited utility for the understanding of individual patients, especially given the variation manifested by those with urgent self-esteem concerns. Fixed diagnostic syndromes in the medical model are a cultural artifact of questionable scientific or clinical value. When reified, they function as stereotypes that obscure the actual diversity and individuality of "narcissistic" patients. In this, they inevitably present impediments to effective therapeutic understanding of narcissistic processes and experiences.
8. Distinctly different treatment methods for those patients called "narcissistic" are unnecessary. The psychoanalysis of narcissism does not require a specialized technique. The most effective therapeutic approaches are those sensitive to the infinite possible variations in the interactions between patient and analyst.

Readers, in their exploration of the papers that follow, will find other common themes that typify the approaches and findings of Interpersonal theorists. Useful to remember, however, is that although the Interpersonal perspective in psychoanalysis is demarcated by a unique analytic sensibility and set of conceptions, it is also marked by a broad diversity in thought and practice. This last observation is an invitation to the rich variety of perspectives reflected in the papers of this volume, all engaged in the common mission of understanding and treating narcissism and the interpersonal self.

PART I

Overview

1

A Spectrum of Psychoanalytic Self Theories

Alan L. Grey

"Self" and the "self-regarding sentiment" were ideas central to the theories of Harry Stack Sullivan, as long ago as the 1920s, the decade of his earliest publications. His interest in these matters was anticipated by Adler and Jung, and it was shared also in the United States by some contemporaries, including Horney and Fromm. From another perspective, attention to the self was pioneered in Britain during the 1930s by Klein, Winnicott, and others. As the fame of all these names may suggest, concern with the self, and with how one self relates to another, has moved steadily from the fringes to the focus of psychoanalytic attention. Now the topic is characterized as "the central conceptual problem within the history of psychoanalytic ideas" (Greenberg and Mitchell 1983:4).

This enthusiasm is actually reflective of a much wider tendency in the generic field of psychological literature, resulting in *several hundred times* as many references to self in the past forty years as in the preceding half century (Smith 1988). Sociologists find that "modernization produces a more self-oriented individual" (Westen 1985:345). Some see this trend as "a narcissistic defense against dependence" evoked by "realistic awareness of the insecurity of contemporary social life" (Lasch 1979:102). Others, like Inkeles (1983:312) perceive the growth of individualism as bringing with it changes most of us nowadays would regard favorably: "independence from control by parents, village elders, or other traditional authority figures, especially as concerns intimate associations, as in the choice of spouse or jobs." Such differences in coloration carry over into psychoanalysis. There the more conservative schools first spoke of selfhood largely in the context of narcissism, of social insecurity, and of early childhood needs. Cultural–Interpersonal writers are also interested in those phenomena but start from premises that treat interest in oneself and in one's fellows as normal aspects of adulthood.

Whether or not increased signs of narcissism are indications of actual social trends, and whether or not such trends are ominous, they have led to distinct alterations in what analysts do. Modifications of theory and techniques have expanded the range of treatment practice to include the "narcissistic," a diagnosis that previously had indicated unsuitability for psychoanalysis. These innovations have also brought a plethora of fresh Self theories where previously one orthodoxy dominated. The new individualism has invaded psychoanalysis itself. An increasingly frequent response to this embarrassment of riches has been the espousal of eclecticism, using whatever formulation seems best to fit the particular patient.

In justification, some point to modern physicists, like Stephen Hawking, who notes that "we have made progress by finding particular theories that describe a limited range of happenings." Yet he reminds us that "Ultimately, however, one would hope to find a complete, consistent, unified theory that would include all these partial theories as approximations, and that did not need to be adjusted to fit the facts" (1988:155). In my opinion, psychoanalysts can best build such a unifying theory on foundations constructed by Sullivan, who formulated a conception of selfhood, not as a part theory to explain a limited range of infantile or pathological phenomena, but as applicable to the entire life span.

The intention here is to assess the current array of Self theories as a background for understanding the special contributions of the Interpersonal approach. Discussion is organized under the following headings:

I. Two Perspectives on the Self
II. The Interactional Progression
III. The Neo-endogenous Pattern

IV. The Dyadic or Infantile Dependency Paradigms
V. The Cultural and Interpersonal Positions

I. Two Perspectives on the Self

The idea of a "self" is one particular way of regarding the person psychologically. The concept increases in popularity because of its utility and threatens to displace other terms with longer psychoanalytic histories, like "ego" or "character." To soften the disruptive note, some have suggested that Freud's "*ich*" (or ego) includes the notion of selfhood. But other orthodox writers, like Hartmann, Kris, and Loewenstein, have sought to reconcile the two concepts by "a sharper definition of 'self' in contrast to 'ego'" (1964:131). Despite the mutually opposing stratagems inevitably elicited by this patchwork project, Hartmann and his collaborators did produce an accepted guideline. As it was recently summarized: "The ego was operating within the context of interaction among [internal] substructures, specifically id and superego; the self, however, functions within a context of relationship with [external] objects" (Meissner 1986:381).

That is to say, the subject matter or content for which the term *self* is ordinarily reserved is that of social transactions. Another feature of the self, as generally understood, is that it includes the individual as the object of one's own reflective consciousness, that is, as self-aware and self-evaluating. In going beyond that to underlying assumptions upon which theoretical conceptualizations of the self are based, however, it becomes very useful to recognize a major distinction between two quite dissimilar sets of premises. All the best known psychoanalytic theories draw upon one or the other of these foundations. My thesis is that the principal strengths and weaknesses of each of these theories depends less on minor variations between them than on which of the two foundations is its basis.

The first orientation, introduced by Freud, uses ideas he found in biology. In that discipline it was usually sufficient to focus explanations around anatomical structures and physiochemical processes without attention to psychological phenomena, like behavior or learning. That *Endogenous perspective,* concerned with genetically determined attributes, is carried over by Classical metapsychology to account for many important features of psychological development. The alternative orientation, called *Interactional* is "a theoretical perspective that assumes that a considerable portion of the variance in [subjective experience and] social behavior is due to the interaction of personal dispositions with situational factors" (Snyder and Ickes 1985:895). An earlier and broader statement of this same idea is to be found in "field theory," which Sullivan borrowed from Kurt Lewin: "personality is to be taken as hypothetical. That which can be studied is the pattern of processes in particular recurrent situations or fields which include the observer" (1953:368). Integral to the "personal disposition" part of the equation is the human capacity to learn how to think and behave from experiences in social fields.

Thus the sharpest distinction between the Endogenous and Interactional perspectives lies in the extent to which some sort of learning is considered in explaining psychological phenomena. Obviously, all psychoanalytic theorists from Freud onward accord a place to learning from life experiences. Nevertheless, at least three significant characteristics are attributed to the self from the Endogenous perspective that are regarded as universal and therefore as genetically determined aspects of the human organism, attributes deemed to be manifested independently of learning. They include:

1. Each person has one self, coterminous with the body.
2. A universal unilinear pattern of normal development exists for the self. Although various theorists differ about what it is, they all refer to an Oedipus complex, for example.
3. This developmental pattern is thought to lead normally to maturity, also defined in terms of certain universal characteristics. Most frequently posited are qualities like individuation, adherence to the exercise of choice or autonomy, a sense of individual responsibility, consistency with an endogenous core or true self, etc.
4. Implied by these invariances is a fourth characteristic that the self is an entity with an endogenously set form, almost palpable or anchored in a reified entity like ego. It is not recognized as a construct.

Some quotations from two analysts within the Endogenous group, but usually regarded as among the boldest departures from Freud, may convey the flavor and persistence of Endogenous enthymemes. First, Kohut, who asserts that he can prove the occurrence of "the several constituents that make up the self—its two poles (ambitions and ideals)" and so forth. While he concedes that we can know only the manifestations of the self, he claims that there is an "essence of the self as differentiated from its manifestations" and that "the self is not a concept of an abstract science" (1977:311). Fairbairn, too, has his own conviction that there is "an endopsychic situation of a classic order" that is "the paradigm of all endopsychic situations," and he provides a diagram of the endopsychic ego, which normally includes no less that five component substructures (1952:105).

From the Interactional position, however, to speak of the self is to use constructs, in at least two respects. For one thing, it is a theoretical construct, a "hypothetical," a conceptualization (Sullivan 1953:368). At another level it is a *personal* construct, achieved by each individual through what is learned from interaction with others. Therefore, its organization and features normally vary from one person to another, and from one situation to another, so that the same individual is likely to have more than one subjective self construct, and what is a normal developmental sequence for the self can also be expected to vary with cultural and other circumstances. For instance, individuation and autonomy are very far from the mature ideal for Buddhists, including Buddhist psychotherapists, who favor "no self" (Kolm 1987; Reynolds 1989). In fact, the mature ideal espoused by Endogenous psychoanalytic writers is amazingly like Protestant thinking about the virtues of being true to oneself or one's soul. As G. H. Mead observed "Soul has been the word for distinguishing between the self and the [biological] organism" (1960:149–50).

Even more striking examples of the extent to which self and soul are personal/cultural constructs can be found in the work of investigators like Westen, who reports that

> Something is going on that is clearly in need of explanation when one is confronted with an Australian [aborigine] who is convinced that he is, in every ontological sense, a turtle. . . . This itself is not a phenomenon peculiar to members of less complex societies; individuals in every culture internalize schemas about the nature of reality, though a more stringent empiricism [like that of the Western world] appears to be a historical development unparalleled in any preliterate society.

In an investigation with Lambe of sixty preliterate societies, Westen found that "most cultures either posited multiple souls that do not together form some complete 'self' or they saw the soul as a diffuse quality frequently not co-extensive with the empirical individual" (1985:250–51). Thus, empirically speaking, the Endogenous perspective on self cannot account for the actual range of self-reflexive images of which human beings are capable, but the Interactional position readily does so.

The Endogenous–Interactional distinction does not rest primarily on differentiating types of motivational theories, like drive-versus-relationship postulations. Although this criterion is proposed in some critiques (e.g.,

Greenberg and Mitchell 1983; Gill 1988) it will become more apparent in subsequent discussion that the motivational criterion is too limited a perspective and is therefore substantially misleading. This issue, however, takes us too far ahead in the story right now. The persistence of Endogenous thought may be better understood if we look again at the history of psychoanalytic ideas. An important fact was recalled by Hartmann when he noted that "the process of coming to terms with the environment—except for a few pertinent problems which played a role in psychoanalysis from the beginning—did not become the subject matter of research until a later stage of our science" (1958:7).

By the time that mainstream analysts did turn their attention to "the environment," they encountered a whole series of metapsychological parameters already set in the Endogenous perspective. Those parameters constituted serious obstacles against ideas like a self influenced by actual human relationships. To begin with, Freud saw infants as existing first in a state of "primary narcissism" in which they were virtually uninfluenced by others around them. Later their reactions are limited largely to parental figures and to how those adults function as agents of physiological gratification. How others interact with the child, whether empathically or judgmentally, whether playfully or pedantically, and so forth, is not seen as germane and is not incorporated into the conceptual system. The very gratifications themselves are set by the Endogenous course of psychosexual development. Although the child is seen as somewhat affected by quantitative considerations of excessive or insufficient gratification, even those experiences are regarded as no longer of much consequence after about the age of five, when the Oedipus complex is resolved.

Since the child's personality is no longer very amenable to influence after the age of five, orthodox Self theories must seek explanations for the nature of the self pre-oedipally. So much is fixed biologically, including the universal Oedipus deadline, that mainstream analysts would be hard pressed to deal with the kinds of cross-cultural variations actually encountered. Despite those difficulties, a surprisingly large proportion of analysts uphold the Oedipus doctrine to the present. For instance, Wax (1990) concedes the neglect of parental influences as a Freudian shortcoming but believes it to be remediable within Classical metapsychology. As he says, "the possibility of such a drama [Oedipus] presupposes successful achievement of self-organization." While this is true, a genetically predetermined Oedipus complex rules out Interactional explanations as of little consequence. On this score Freud was quite clear. He expected the crisis to occur quite independently of life events like seductive parents, castration threats, or even living in a nuclear family. "If they have occurred in reality, so much to the good," he said, "but if they have been withheld in reality they are put together from hints and supplemented by phantasy" (1916–1917:370). Small wonder, then, that Freud, with his emphasis on "psychical" or subjective reality, had little need for a concept like "self," which functions within a context of external objects.

In overlooking the full implications of orthodox metapsychology, Wax exemplifies a waffling between Interactional and Endogenous perspectives that has become a frequent phenomenon among those who maintain adherence to the Oedipus idea. But again, this gets a bit ahead of the story. Returning to what happens after early childhood, and after the genetically set repetitions associated with adolescence, adults fall into two basic categories. Those who have successfully achieved an anaclitic (i.e., object seeking) resolution to their oedipal experience relate to significant others primarily as targets for the discharge of libidinal energies. Far from recognizing the psychologically nurturant aspects of adult social intercourse, classical theory regards the fixity of anaclitic structures as useful, as protection against the assaults of inimical external stimuli, much as a turtle shell protects the animal within.

For those who fail to achieve anaclitic internal structuring, the alternative is an even more inaccessible narcissistic defensiveness. It is geared only to self-love, thereby impeding the transference connection and ruling out the possibility of psychoanalytic treatment. Because working with "narcissistic" patients contradicts Classical metapsychology, Object Relations theory has emerged to resolve the contradictions. Illustrative of its efforts has been the introduction of concepts like "self" into mainstream usage to refer to processes involved in dealing with others. That is because problems of relating, which figure prominently in narcissistic symptomatology, had occupied so incidental a place in Classical analysis as not even to merit special terminology. It can even be said that attention to material reality is counter to the canons of orthodox metapsychology.

Whether those contradictions can be resolved validly, short of abandoning the Endogenous perspective, is a major question for us here. Approaching it in terms of underlying philosophical premises, Robbins concludes that "Sullivan and Freud represent two mutually exclusive viewpoints which stem from their differing intellectual heritages." Freud's assumptions "are based on the ideas of European writers like Kant—who tried to understand the individual by starting inside his head and working his way out." By contrast, Sullivan "was influenced by American writers, social thinkers who took the integrated individual in a social setting as a given and who endeavored to understand him from without as derivative rather than a constitutive entity." Consequently, attempts to put the Endogenous together with the Interactional must result in "confusion and inner contradiction," according to Robbins (1989:639). This does not imply that what is inside the head must remain separated from social behavior but rather that if they are to be put together theoretically, they had best be put together from the start.

The reasons must be quite compelling then that have led analysts strongly tied to orthodoxy to insist nevertheless on inserting an interacting self into a theoretical system that works so much better without it.

II. The Interactional Progression

In this age of science, it would be very plausible to expect that the compelling reason for shifts in mainstream psychoanalysis to a more Interactional or "relationship" orientation has been the sheer weight of scientific evidence. Data justifying such a shift have been with us for most of the twentieth century. A brief overview might begin with reexamination of the fundamental orthodox belief in "psychic reality," in contrast to "material reality," as determinative of human psychology (Freud 1916–17:368). Much of metapsychology and its applications have rested on the assumption that the experiences of childhood register like nursery rhymes, as unchanging guides for our thinking and acting thenceforward. Thus transference has been understood as fixedly repetitive from childhood onward.

The most obvious consequence is that the patient's current circumstances are seen as little more than triggers that reactivate early childhood conflicts that are played out essentially as replications of the original instances. Moreover, these conflicts are understood as focused only around sex and aggression. This belief has been exploded by attributional bias research (e.g., Brown 1986:ch. 5) revealing how sensitively the words and actions of experimental subjects are guided by current behavior and other characteristics of apparently neutral experimenters. Even more germane are contemporary studies of the impact of countertransference (e.g., Wallerstein 1986:236–44). Moreover, current neurological research indicates that even "Memory is not an exact repetition of an image in one's brain, but a recategorization" shaped by the context of recall (Rosenfield 1988:192). In short, to postulate a sharp boundary between what goes on "inside" the mind as opposed to "outside" it is to erect a false dichotomy that obscures a continuing interaction.

Another premise integral to the Endogenous perspective is that "development is linear and cumulative—that is that certain personalities are more adult than others on a cross-cultural basis." It, too, rests on "little empirical evidence for such orderly and progressive change" according to systematic developmental researchers (Datan, Rodeheaver, and Hughes 1987:162; see also Carson, 1989, pp. 228–29). Instead, it has been proposed that at least three different sorts of development occur over the life span, only one of which is "age-graded" and influenced greatly by the biology of childhood growth and of aging. Another kind of trend is "history-graded" and much affected by prevailing social processes, with a third "non-normative" influence of idiosyncratic biological and social events (Baltes, Reese, and Lipsitt 1980:75 ff.).

A major implication of such social science research is to dispel the orthodox belief in an Oedipus complex that is endogenously determined and therefore occurring in all societies. Among the increasing number of cultures in which exceptions have been found to this alleged universality are Papua, New Guinea (Lidz and Lidz 1989:197); Japan (Tatara, 1982; Roland 1988:78 ff.); India (Grey 1973); Polynesia (Kardiner 1945). From his study of Amerinds, particularly the Navajo, Proskauer (1980) noted at least three factors that could affect so-called oedipal phenomena, including whether families are (1) nuclear or clan oriented, (2) matrilineal or patrilineal, and (3) structured to connect or to separate incestuous and competitive motivations. That the Oedipus myth is only a fable implies the need for substantial revision in analytic understanding of how the self develops. It means that narcissistic (pre-oedipal) and anaclitic (post-oedipal) selves need not be regarded as categorically different, nor does their treatment need to be so regarded.

In short, the major thrust of social science evidence is quite like what biologists say, when they tell us that "a human being or any other living organism is very far from being a closed system" (Holt 1989:134). While that message may have been less obvious when the endogenetic postulates of orthodoxy were first laid down by Freud, by now it is not a new idea. It was long known, for instance, by 1959, when P. B. Medawar, Nobel laureate in medicine and physiology, wrote of "the two systems of heredity enjoyed by man: *endosomatic* or internal heredity for the ordinary or genetical heredity we have in common with other animals; and *exosomatic* or external heredity for the nongenetic heredity that is peculiarly our own—the heredity that is mediated through tradition, by which I mean the transfer-of-information through nongenetic channels from one generation to the next" (p. 92). To this he added a most unambiguous warning that the view of social behavior as governed by "an overriding authority . . . imposed by agencies beyond man's control—all those are biological judgments, but I assure you, judgments based upon a bad biology" (1959:94–95).

As an alternative that takes account of the kinds of research findings just cited, the Interactional perspective integrates the contributions of mainstream psychoanalysis with the discoveries of psychologists, sociologists, and anthropologists. In their review of the history of Interactional thought, Snyder and Ickes mention not only Cooley and Mead, among others, but also Kurt Lewin's "dictum that behavior is a function of both the person and the environment" (1985:896). They go on to recognize "an obvious intellectual debt to Sullivan's interpersonal theory of psychiatry" (1985:934). Coming a bit more recently than the pioneers, Berelson and Steiner's inventory of more than a thousand consistently replicated research findings pulled together what constitutes a robust empirical basis for the Interactional approach. "Nearly all of these findings," they concluded, "all except a few that deal with near-physiological aspects of behavior, lead the individual directly to other people—not only for facts and beliefs about the nature of the world, but also for what he has learned to want, to value, to consider right and good, to worship . . . and his very picture of himself stems in large measure from how others regard him" (1964:665–66).

Far from dismissing biology or "intrapsychic" processes, Interactional formulations are intended to eliminate unreal conceptual barriers between subjective experience and the interpersonal contexts in which they occur. For convenience in further discussion, key features of psychodynamic Interactionism are presented herewith. Summarizing in terms of ten generalizations is arbitrary, of course, but research citations are included to indicate that their content is not arbitrary and to offer sources for additional information on the statements made.

The Interactional Perspective: A Checklist of Ten Implications to Distinguish It from the Endogenous Perspective

A. Concerning Human Development

1. *Need for social contact and learning.* The development of a human personality (including a self) requires interaction between the biopsy-

chological predispositions of the neonate and others who are already socialized human beings (Berelson and Steiner 1964; Stern 1985).

2. *Extrafamilial social learning.* The environments that significantly affect the self extend beyond the infant–mother dyad and the nuclear family to include more nearly comprehensive social fields—friends, neighbors, teachers, coworkers, spouses, the entire society, and its contexts (Segall 1986; Honess and Yardley 1987).
3. *Continuing change.* Significant changes in personality (including the self) continue past early childhood and throughout the life span via interaction between personal predispositions and social circumstances (Baltes, Reese, and Lipsitt 1980; Chess and Thomas 1984; Lerner 1990). Even memories of the past are affected by current circumstances (Rosenfield 1988; Pillemer and White 1989).

B. Concerning Psychological Norms

4. *Relativity of norms.* Because fulfilling and effective modes of functioning vary in different social fields, it follows that useful optima and models of normality for organization of the self will also vary (Segall 1986; Gollin, Stahl, and Morgan 1989).

C. Concerning Motivations

5. *Culturally shaped motivations.* What motivates any person, and how satisfying any experience proves to be, is shaped through interaction between flexible human predispositions and socialization contexts (Kornadt, Eckensberger, and Emminghaus 1980).
6. *Three major motivations.* Besides their culturally guided needs for physiological satisfactions, human beings are impelled toward self-affirming social contacts and toward the exercise of competencies, both variously defined in differing social contexts (White 1959; Seligman 1975).

D. Concerning Treatment:

7. *Inevitability of treatment interactions.* Each person in the treatment setting inevitably affects and is affected by all others currently present as well as by experiences in relevant past situations. The effects always include involuntary as well as voluntary reactions, influenced by the person's role and observational standpoint (Wallerstein 1986; Strupp 1989).
8. *Varied treatment methods.* Operationally, the most effective treatment is what most enhances the particular person's ability to cope with his or her situation. Insofar as situations vary, the best treatment procedures will vary from one case to another, even extending beyond the feasible range of dyadic models to preventive strategies (Brenner 1973; Heller 1990).

E. Concerning Tests of Psychoanalytic Hypotheses:

9. *Systematic data testing.* Consensual validation principle. Since they are so influenced by the perspective of the therapist's role, clinical conclusions about the treatment situation require corroboration from other sources. Only when clinical and theoretical propositions can be either confirmed or modified with attention to all relevant evidence does the self-corrective process of scientific research allow us to trust our theories as more probable than available alternatives (Cohen and Nagel 1934; Weick 1985).
10. *Testable language.* Thus the value of definitions and hypotheses is reduced when they are insufficiently explicit for their consistency with each other and with relevant information to be assessed (Cohen and Nagel 1934).

Necessarily this selection of hypotheses is guided by its concern primarily with matters pertaining to the self. The selection is not meant to be exhaustive or to imply that Interpersonal theory provides no further ideas, for instance, about communication processes or creativity. Nor does it include important propositions shared with the Endogenous perspective, since the immediate purpose is to distinguish between them. This difference rests on at least one clear common theme implicit in all the propositions.

The field theory or Interactional premise is that human personality is inherently interconnected with the environing milieu and, as part of that principle, that any adequate study of personality calls for multiple observational standpoints, whether in the treatment context or in research. More explicitly, both therapists and researchers are affected along with the patients or study samples with whom they are engaged. To control for observational limitations introduced by one's participatory role, the phenomena under study had best be examined from multiple observational standpoints. Both therapist and researcher are well advised not only to be observant participants but also to seek consensual validation.

The internal coherence of the ten implications seems to suggest that Interactionists are closely in accord and also that they are concerned with social research. This is hardly the case. For instance, implications numbered 2 (extrafamilial social learning), 4 (relativity of norms), or 9 (systematic data testing) might well be challenged by some Interpersonalists. What the challengers do not always realize is that if the Interactional thrust of any of these propositions is reversed, it automatically introduces internal contradictions into the system. As flexible as the perspective is in some respects, it cannot accommodate all divergences and still be meaningful. The same limitation holds for the Endogenous perspective, a guideline often honored in the breach by Self theorists, as we will see. For instance, many introduce propositions like those in numbers 1 (need for social contact and learning), 6 (three major motivations), or 7 (inevitability of treatment interactions). Indeed it has been the fate of many Interpersonal ideas to turn up in the orthodox literature, whether through parallelism or as a result of unacknowledged borrowing. But whatever the source, when an Interactional principle is introduced into an Endogenous system, it unavoidably brings inner contradictions to what classically had been the relatively harmonious Freudian theoretical structure.

Thereby hangs the tale that runs through all Self theories welded to Endogenous foundations. The self, a construct dealing with the effects of me–you interaction, is inserted into a theoretical universe that scarcely allows for the relevance of such processes. Mainstream theorists dealing with Interactional phenomena too often proceed like jigsaw puzzle enthusiasts confronting a partially incomplete picture. They are each supplied with an official box of pieces consisting of Endogenous concepts and terms and also have available an unofficial canister of Interactional ideas. Sometimes the official box fails to yield a piece that fits some clinical phenomenon important to depict. Then the venturesome analyst locates a conceptual segment, perhaps concerned with the self or with relationship style, available in the unofficial container and well suited to the immediate task even if not to the larger orthodox picture on the official box cover.

Once Interactional shapes have been added, the official conceptual pieces no longer conform well to new configurations. Nevertheless, a prevailing preference for those familiar segments of orthodox language requires that their contours be mutilated so that they can continue in the picture. The result is an overall effect replete with discordant images, wherein, among other strange portrayals, infants normally cogitate beyond their symbolic ability and adults normally are rather infantile. Such consequences understandably escape notice in the puzzle fans' intentness on solving the immediate task. As Winnicott said about his own innovative ideas, "I am not an intellectual and, in fact, I personally do my work very much from the body-ego, so to speak" (1965:161).

This remark provides a clue concerning the still pending question about why mainstream analysts insert an Interactional self into their Endogenous theoretical system, a system that works so much more smoothly without it.

They are taking account of their own empirical experience, if not of the increasing research evidence cited earlier here. Not only research, but clinical data, too, lead toward Interactional ideas. Back before Winnicott, Karen Horney put it plainly that "My desire to make a critical reevaluation of psychoanalytic theories had its origin in dissatisfaction with the therapeutic results" (1939:7). Almost fifty years later her daughter, Marianne Eckhardt, was still finding that "Theory and practice have always been at odds. But the present trend of observations suggests the poorness of fit between experience and theory is becoming more irksome" (1988:424).

Not one but two major discrepancies divide contemporary psychoanalysis, according to Gill (1988). One is on the treatment level "between those who believe the analyst inevitably participates in a major way in the analytic situation and those who do not" (p. 305). The other "between the interpersonal paradigm and the drive–discharge paradigm" has also been used elsewhere to classify on the theoretical level (Greenberg and Mitchell 1983). While ideas about motivation are involved in the split between the orthodox and the Interpersonalists, to focus the division around drive theory misses the bull's-eye. The pertinent connection between both treatment and human development is that both are interactionally determined. Consequently Gill fails to recognize the close link between theoretical and treatment debates around Interaction issues.

If Classical ideas about motivation differ from the Interpersonal view, it is not specifically because Freud employs a drive–discharge model. Drive is a very loose term (see, e.g., Shaw and Costanzo 1982:29–31). Thus a theory may employ the notion of the discharge of drive as tension reducing and still be Interpersonal as is the case with Sullivan, or Classically analytic as with Freud, or even Behaviorist as with Clark Hull. Moreover, a paradigm may identify personal relationship as a central need and yet allot very little causal significance to it. For example, consider Melanie Klein's idea of infants, who are powerfully drawn to the mother but respond to her in terms of their own preset genetic fantasy programs, and not in response to the actual quality of the mothering. Here the infant is conceptualized as psychologically like a honeybee or other social insect.

The core distinction is one that has already been considered at some length. It concerns whether the remarkable human proclivity toward interactional social influences is adequately recognized, not only in the context of motivating drives. The principle also pertains to development over the life span, to what is normal psychologically, and to the nature of treatment interaction among other matters. The place accorded to our exosomatic heredity, as Medawar called it, to our inevitable bond with social fields composed of other human beings, is what distinguishes the Interactional perspective from the Endogenous. By contrast, the latter relies on endosomatic or biologically determined explanations for human acting and thinking, drawing on our own civilization for universal norms.

As the core ideas of Classical metapsychology have been established—ideas like a linear sequence of developmental stages, the Oedipus complex, libido theory, tripartite personality structure, and others—the consequence is that compromises between the two theoretical standpoints are impossible without substantial internal contradictions (Grey 1988; Robbins 1989). These classical building blocks need only to be reconsidered alongside the ten Interactional hypotheses stated earlier to see why that is the case. In other respects, as psychoanalytic positions, both schools share many ideas. Both take account of an endogenetic endowment and also of the significance of early experience, unconscious motivation, the emotional impact of the treatment dyad, and so forth. But these shared convictions are set into very different schematic foundations for the understanding of social living and the nature of the self.

The irreconcilability of Classical metapsychology with an Interactional approach, and with biological and psychological research as well (see, e.g., Holt 1989), has not deterred many talented analysts from holding fast to the aegis of orthodoxy in their efforts to attach it to innovative Self theories and related treatment efforts. If we wish to assess such theories, it is convenient to imagine them arrayed along a continuum between that Classical aegis as one pole and the Interactional as the other. This scheme is heuristic, of course, and does not imply that midway positions are logically or scientifically tenable.

When a Self theory is placed at any point on the continuum, its position becomes a relative approximation of how closely it adheres to the precepts of orthodox metapsychology or how nearly it approaches the guidelines of the Interactional perspective. To note how they are distributed is also to locate the mix of inner inconsistencies underlying their Self theories. At the same time it testifies to the widespread concern for more effective treatment that has impelled many analysts to venture beyond the constraints of their theoretical roots, despite the reluctance reflected in their conceptual language (see, e.g., Wallerstein 1986:section IX).

For present purposes those writers who share many beliefs are considered as a group, and their common feature is identified primarily to assess the extent to which they become concerned with Interactional matters linked to selfhood. The progression begins closest to the conservative pole, with the *Neo-endogenous* position, which includes the Self theories of Ego psychologists like Hartmann, Mahler, Kernberg, Jacobson, and Erikson, all of them rather orthodox. The next grouping, to be called the *Dyadic or Infantile Dependency* position, moves somewhat closer to an Interactional model. Winnicott, Kohut, Guntrip, and Fairbairn sit at this locus. A third orientation, generally known as the *Cultural* school, will continue to be given that designation here. It includes names like Fromm, Horney, Schachtel, not to forget Adler. These people all make a substantial leap toward Interactionism, abandoning most of the conceptual language of Classical metapsychology. If they are to be distinguished from those at the Interactional position, it is only because the latter more thoroughly and consistently apply field theory or Interactional guidelines, people like Sullivan, Thompson, and their past and current associates.

III. The Neo-Endogenous Pattern

Analysts like Hartmann, Mahler, Erikson, and Jacobson are best known as Ego psychoanalysts. They are discussed here because they did employ the term *self* in describing how people relate to the "object world," that is, to other people. The very term *object world* depersonalizes references to other people and thereby vitiates the implications of relatedness. Mindful of the mechanistic flavor of words like ego used to describe intrapsychic structures, Hartmann (1950) employed the term "self" for reference to persons interacting. But that very paper was dismissed by Kernberg (1984:229) as one in which "Hartmann, in effect, removed the 'self' from metapsychology." It adds little to the present discussion to try to decide whether Kernberg also fits best here as a more radical Neo-endogenous thinker or whether as a conservative Kleinian linked to the Dyadic group discussed next. In any case, Jacobson credits Hartmann with having introduced "self" into analytic discourse in that 1950 paper (Jacobson 1964:6n.). Perhaps those mutually contradictory judgments by Kernberg and Jacobson sum up the Neo-endogenous contribution to psychodynamic theories of the self, as an innovation without any real changes.

Actually the self had already been brought into psychodynamic discourse in the two previous decades by Cultural–Interpersonal writers like Horney and Sullivan. They replaced Freud's intrapsychically oriented tripartite version of personality with discussions of socially interacting selves. Hartmann, too, recognized social learning as an important aspect of personality much neglected by Freud. Therefore, he brought consideration of learning and adaptation into mainstream writing through his invention of "the conflict-free sphere" of ego, but at the same time, he and his colleagues were committed to protecting the Master's conceptualizations of id, ego, and superego. If the idea of a "self" was to be included in the metapsychological armamentarium, it could not be allowed to displace or disrupt any of those three interlocking agencies. This was accomplished by presenting self as appended to a superordinate ego, a device generally accepted by all Neo-endogenous writers.

In dealing with the series of problems introduced by the new interest in adaptation, this treatment of the self was far more satisfactory for defending doctrine than for clarifying how human beings relate to each other. The doctrinal impediments lay in premises that accorded relevance to only a very restricted range of rudimentary biological needs and environmental interactions. Over time, as Freud developed his system of internal structures, metapsychology more and more dismissed learned adaptations in favor of intrapsychic solutions. Hartmann reminds us that "Freud started from the idea . . . [of] the ego [as] storehouse of what has been learned. Freud reversed his view explicitly [1937, Analysis Terminable and Interminable] when he pointed to the fact that there was no reason to assume that the ego was not built on hereditary predispositions" (1964:131).

If the ego is preset through heredity rather than learning, then to what extent can a self subordinated to that ego perform adjustively? The impasse is quite obvious upon consideration of what is usually implied by the idea of adaptation. The *Psychiatric Dictionary* (1973:14), for instance, says that it means a fitting together of person and environment "typically achieved through a combination of alloplastic maneuvers (which involve alteration of the external environment) and autoplastic maneuvers (which involve a change in the self)." Changes, whether alloplastic or autoplastic (ergo, adaptation in its usual sense), were not possible for an Ego psychology in which personality structures were largely determined endogenously and were essentially unchanging after the resolution of oedipal issues in early childhood. Indeed, the self and the environment are hardly in sufficient contact with each other for significant mutual effects to transpire. As Schachtel summed it up, "For ego psychology, the world remains, as it was in Freud's thought, a need-object for man which he uses merely for the discharge of tensions in order to return, directly or by detour, to a tensionless state or to gain the pleasure of a decrease of excitation" (1959:12).

The most apparent aspect of Schachtel's statement is his well-founded rejection of drive–discharge theory as an adequate model for human motivation. According to that theory, animals strive toward a state of quiescence, and when satisfied they are inactive. Instead, Schachtel called attention to phenomena rather like what Robert White, the academic psychologist, termed "competency motivation" when he published essentially similar conclusions in the same year, 1959. A principle now solidly established on the basis of intensive observation and research, it describes how all mammals, especially more intelligent species, actively seek to expand their skills and experiences and do so particularly in states of well-being, as when they play. But actually it is another aspect of Schachtel's message, and not the drive–discharge model per se, that first separated orthodox analysts from the Cultural–Interpersonal school.

The fact is that Sullivan shared the drive–discharge or tension reduction model with all other analysts and with most other psychologists functioning in his day. Where he departed from Freud's paradigm long before 1959 was in the much wider range of motivations he recognized as essential to human well-being, a biological endowment also implicit in Schachtel's descriptions of "openness to the world." It includes a need for interpersonal contact and for all the varied forms of mutual interaction required to develop what each society recognizes as its particular version of normality. The crucial distinction, then, is between that Interactional version of mutual autoplastic and alloplastic social influences versus the orthodox idea that people deal with each other almost solipsistically largely as objects for the discharge of tensions.

The "self" and the "object world" of Jacobson's book title are both terms referring to people, that is, to the experiencing person and the significant other in any given situation. In Neo-endogenous discussions, the situation usually considered is limited either to mother and child or to patient and analyst parallels of that dyad. In looking at those accounts, the question is how much their orthodoxy permits inclusion of alloplastic and autoplastic personality changes implied in the idea of adaptation. The answer that emerges is that, whatever the quality of actual descriptions of people, Neo-endogenous formulations about them are of human beings not unlike lizards in a terrarium. Men and women satisfy their limited range of instinctual requirements within a predictable ecology, protected against turbulence in the surrounding social climate by neglect to consider it. The real world of people is transformed into that limited perspective by three principal devices. These are: (1) concepts blurred by referential drift; (2) the self conceived as epiphenomenon, lacking real impact; and (3) the social worlds of normal people reduced to an "average expectable environment."

It was referential drift, or the obscuring of meanings, that led Eagle to remark that "Hartmann's contribution can be viewed essentially as a politico-theoretical one" in which deviations were evaded by wordplay (1984, p. 16). Drift also prompted Kernberg's dismissal of Hartmann's views on the self, a concept especially germane here for assessing this sort of definitional vagueness. To begin with, Hartmann's employment of the word *self* was usually restricted to the same colloquial usage it had found in Freud's writing. At those times it did not refer to a structure or a function but was simply a noun to distinguish between me and others. Or it was an adjective chosen for similar purposes in terms like *self-representation* or *self-evaluation.* In another connotation, he and Jacobson spoke of "self-representations" as "unconscious, preconscious and conscious endopsychic representations of the bodily, and mental self in the system ego" (Jacobson 1964:16). In this sense, the self was reduced to an epiphenomenon, merely subjective experience not affecting the function of the classical ego as regulator of social adaptation (Hartmann 1964:160).

Noteworthy, too, is the implication inherent in the idea of an "average expectable environment" that it is sufficient to consider the central or general qualities characterizing a milieu. Small variations are not regarded as particularly important for influencing personality, a conclusion that is very dubious, to say the least. Indeed, the most recent research into "Human Behavioral Genetics" (Plomin and Rende 1991) indicates that even within a single family each member experiences a significantly different environment: "For personality and psychopathology there is continuing consensus that shared rearing environment is of negligible importance, that environmental influence is nearly exclusively of the nonshared variety" (p. 160). More than that, the Neo-endogenous conception is of a "representation" fixed in the individual's early past and not of a direct and current interaction with others that allows for new and modifying experience.

These practices eased acceptance of the "new" entity on the same basis by still other Neo-endogenous writers. In that group are Hartmann, his collaborators Kris and Loewenstein (e.g., 1964), and Erikson (1968). If Mahler's empirical contributions to infant research sometimes took her beyond Hartmann, she sedulously avoided recognition of any serious differences, explicitly reaffirming her commitment to the "pillars of psychoanalytic metapsychology" (1972:333). Despite direct experience with infants, for instance, she supported Freud's impression of infantile unrelatedness and "primary narcissism," one of the ways in which she continued "to squeeze object relations and self into instinct theory . . . [and into] nearly incoherent jargon" (Eagle 1984:26).

Much the same might be said of Erikson, who informally expanded the range of psychoanalytic cultural observations but still managed to cancel out potential theoretical departures. For instance, he seemed to approve of his own talent for referential evasiveness when he wrote that

> so far I have tried out the term identity almost deliberately—I like to think—in many different connotations. . . . Identity in its vaguest sense suggests, of course, much of what has been called the self by a variety of workers, be it in the form of self-concept, a [Sullivanian] self-system, or in that fluctuating self-experience described by Schilder, Federn, and others. (1968:208–9)

A remarkable gift for vagueness is suggested by this linking of "identity" with Sullivan's ideas about the self-system—especially so in light of Erikson's' espousal of the idea that identity develops according to an "epigenetic principle which is derived from the growth of the organism *in utero*" (1968:92). Like other Neo-endogenous theorists, Erikson saw identity as primarily governed by the ego, with influences from the superego. As for how identity functions in relation to id, ego, and superego, Erikson is remarkably obscure but still essentially in accord with Hartmann. At first it may seem that Kernberg does not belong with this Neo-endogenous group, for he explicitly elevates the self into a "psychic structure." At the same time he insists that the self "is clearly embedded in the ego" (1984:232), which still entitles him to claim a position "well within the Freudian metapsychology" (1984:190). That does not speak very well for the lucidity of the metapsychology.

For lucidity's sake, it may be well to review what has emerged about Neo-endogenous perspectives on the self and its role in social adaptation. How is this role understood by these theorists? "Vaguely" is the most tempting reply, given the prevalence of referential drift. But I will resist this temptation and, instead, say something in behalf of the Neo-endogenous approach. For one thing, these theorists do make an effort to increase attention to reflective awareness by espousing the reference frame of a self. But they are not yet ready to accord significant influence to that subjective awareness or to the window it opens on the world and its varied attractions. To do so would seem to diminish the importance of Freud's discovery of the unconscious and its inexorable power. The credibility of that position cannot be dismissed lightly by any clinician who has worked with patients trapped in the bog of their own repetitive self-defeating behavior.

If the self has so limited a role in Neo-endogenous thought, that may be because it tends to be discussed by them largely in terms of conscious and preconscious self-representations, with more deeply buried images assigned to ego or superego. But this is not the only reason for the neglect. The self is also associated with "external" social experiences, many of which are not deemed to be important unless they are linked to our putative animal nature. What are emphasized are hidden themes of destructiveness and of libidinal pleasure or unpleasure associated with biological functions of an oral, anal, or genital nature. Unfortunately Neo-endogenous thought overlooks the ways in which the nature of human animals differs significantly from the nature of other animals.

For one thing, at birth human beings have far fewer highly focused innate reaction patterns. Many aspects of themselves and of the world about them can become important to them, depending on how experience guides them. As Schachtel observed, "in the growing child and in the adult man almost any activity can assume consummatory character, that is to say, become an end in itself" (1959:73). The wide diversity of life-styles from one family to another, from one subculture to another, from one society to another attests to that variability. Because of the dissimilarities between life stories, it is best for one to cover a wide field before concluding that the key facts have been located. Some of them lie in the vocational history, in early or later schooling, sleep and sleep functions, games and sports, friendships, and so forth, as well as in the usual areas of orality, toilet habits, and genitality. The contrast is between a Neo-endogenous narrowly defined early environment and a broad sweep of past and ongoing experiences, both conscious and unconscious. Moreover, people retain a capacity for flexibility and change in dealing with all kinds of experience that have not yet proven unduly damaging. The metapsychological model rests far too heavily on the clinical evidence of crippled functioning instead of on the normal range of psychological performance.

Neo-endogenous analysts may well explore beyond the prescribed focus, but if so, their theories do not afford them adequate conceptual tools. On the contrary, they are deterred by such doctrines as Hartmann's postulation that psychological normality is the result of an "average expectable environment" with respect to early psychosexual experiences. And despite his exposure to a wide array of cultures, Erikson happily accepted that idea. He even applauded it as "a more truly ecological as well as inescapably societal formulation" (1968:222). Very similar implications arise from Mahler's references to "an ordinarily devoted mother" and from Jacobson's blurred references to parents as the "object world." This notion of a universal neutrally facilitative environment rests on at least three misconceptions about human psychology:

1. It neglects significant interpersonal experiences other than those linked to our putative animal nature.
2. It fails to recognize that "ordinarily devoted parents" do not merely provide a milieu for epigenetic emergence. Inevitably their interactions with the child influence it in particular ways and so do significant others (e.g., peers).
3. Psychological well-being itself varies according to the requirements of one culture or another, and so do the socializing environments that lead to it.

In summary, while Neo-endogenous writers recognize a need to expand orthodox theory, they pursue that undertaking in a timorous and confused fashion. Of Mahler, it has been said that those of her writings that "are closer to actual observation are most useful and most fully supported by other data, while the formulations derived from traditional theory are more likely to be suffused with virtually undecipherable jargon" (Eagle 1984:28). Although Erikson commands a more graceful jargon, almost the same might be said of him. That still leaves the question of how often these and other Neo-endogenous contributors venture beyond doctrine to data. Measured against the Interactional checklist, it becomes apparent that those ventures are infrequent. Erikson, Kernberg, and Mahler sometimes take account of social learning (checklist item 1) or the relevance of systematic data testing (checklist item 9), but they can hardly be accused of consistency in these matters. Hartmann's ideas about conflict-free learning are based more on jesuitical ingenuity than on actual modes of socialization. The self does not get beyond being an incidental kind of mental activity within a mechanistic ego, geared to myth about an average expectable environment.

IV. The Dyadic or Infantile Dependency Paradigms

The names of Balint, Fairbairn, Guntrip, and Winnicott are best known as representing British Object Relations theory, while Kohut and Wolf are leaders of American Self psychology. Putting them together under the Dyadic rubric allows for the identification of basic commonalities across the two schools, in the hope of helping to untangle a literature now overly complicated. One controversial distinction they share is that of breaking with Freudian metapsychology, at least around issues of the self in relationships. Perhaps for this reason, they are sometimes regarded as more akin to Sullivan, even within their own ranks, than the facts warrant. What Guntrip saw as the common ground was that "Harry Stack Sullivan's clear rejection of instinct theory as an adequate concept for human psychology, and his adoption of interpersonal relations experience as his basic concept, I believe as early as 1925, was the first absolute breakthrough of object relations theory" (1971:20–21).

The thesis to be discussed here is that while Dyadic theorists moved in the same general direction as Cultural-Interpersonal thinkers did, they did not make "an absolute breakthrough" in the sense of appreciation of the implications of field theory. The result is a view of relationships caught between two paradigmatic horses pulling in different directions, a conceptual plight illustrated in its most obvious form by the work of Melanie Klein. She, far more than Sullivan, served as an important source for Dyadic thinking. On the one hand, Klein stressed the significance of relationship, of the tie between the mother and her infant during its early postnatal life, and even prenatally. At the same time, this relationship was seen as endogenously determined, evolving essentially within the mind of the child in an inevitable sequence. She is not a Dyadic theorist then, like her successors who went a major step beyond to insist that the relationship with the mother is influenced by her as a real person. But the fact remains that Klein showed the way within her circle to important new psychodynamic paths and pitfalls, both of which were pursued vigorously by her followers.

The shift in theory was a major one, leading away from the orthodox emphasis on oedipal conflict with a fantasied father as the key to adult intrapsychic life. Now the primary consideration became how the self is shaped through early experience with a real pre-oedipal mother. Integral to the shift were new therapeutic approaches with a more personal, even maternal, regard for those treated. These methods were found to expand the range of the treatable to so-called narcissistic conditions previously deemed inaccessible. By implication, at least, these innovations challenged Classical metapsychology on many fronts. That is not to imply a rejection of the Oedipus complex. These writers still retained at least token loyalty to a genetically determined Oedipus complex subsequent to early shaping of the self by mother-child interactions.

While those included here in the Dyadic group actually functioned similarly in most respects, they did vary among themselves in how directly they acknowledged departures from the fold. Some, like Winnicott, insist that their ideas supplement rather than contradict orthodoxy. Others, like Fairbairn, forthrightly reject classical analysis. Still others follow Kohut's example and straddle questions about whether their views on the self are in contradiction to Freud's metapsychology. If this state of affairs is a tribute to the liveliness and flux of contemporary analytic discourse, it also contributes to endemic ambiguities and confusions in Dyadic metalanguage. In this respect Melanie Klein's intellectual heirs follow not only her insights but also her blind spots, which stem from unawareness of the requirements for psychological theory building.

As a consequence their theories are seriously flawed in several ways. For one thing, many hypotheses are inconsistent with each other, as in acceptance of the Oedipus complex. Beyond that, little attention is given to stating propositions clearly enough for testing, nor is much effort made to check assertions against empirical evidence other than personal clinical impressions. Reminiscent of this naiveté is Fairbairn's conviction that he has advanced radically from Classical thinking when he replaces Freud's concept of the ego with his own equally unprovable reifications.

One major confusion besetting these theorists is their failure to appreciate the methodological and psychological implications underlying their practical understanding of the effects of human interactions in a clinical context. The accumulated evidence clearly cautions against reliance on those clinical observation alone as sufficient for reliable psychological generalizations. The roots of that evidence go back to 1929 when Werner Heisenberg called attention to how the measuring instruments introduced into an experimental field, and the particles being measured in quantum mechanics research, interactively influence each other. Since then, what is true for inanimate particles has been found also to apply to animate human beings. Support for this proposition extends beyond the testimony of the many analysts of diverse theoretical persuasions who find both members of the treatment dyad inevitably participant in the process (Gill 1988). It is also the conclusion of research psychologists that "it is difficult to imagine *any* situation into which a social psychological investigator enters that would not involve some kind of demand characteristics or experimenter effect" (Sampson 1971:83). More recent researches (see, e.g., Brown 1986:183 ff.) continue to support and expand the pioneering studies in this area by Orne (1962) and Rosenthal (1966), among others.

What transpires in the experimental milieu is at least equally true of less controlled circumstances. Everywhere, observation involves participation and consequent mutative effects for the participants, to varying degrees and in sundry ways. Whether or not "growth" occurs, in the sense of desired or advantageous outcomes, the fact remains that to be engaged in living is to be involved in changing, psychologically as well as in other respects. What holds for researchers, and for the everyday world, must also affect analysts, a phenomenon again attested to in systematic research (see, e.g., Wallerstein 1986:236–61). To spell it out more concretely, each participant in a social field must arrive at an orientation to those circumstances, an observational standpoint, in order to function at all. As an aspect of becoming oriented, "human beings can engage in highly effective and influential unprogrammed and unintended communication with one another" (Rosenthal 1967:365). The resulting observational standpoints guide *both* patient and analyst in their roles and in their perceptions of what is most pertinent. Thereby they are also guided away from what can be ignored. This selective attention is inevitable, since it is impossible for any one person to perceive or to integrate effectively all possible viewpoints and data simultaneously. Even if no barriers were posed by personal defensiveness, selectivity is inevitable. Reliability of findings, then, requires looking beyond any single observer or mode of observation to all pertinent sources for consensual validation.

Because they are integral to human relatedness, how adequately these Interactive influences are recognized in Dyadic formulations becomes germane to appreciating Dyadic understanding of human relationships. It seems best to divide the assessment into two parts. First we can review their methodological approaches, or how information is acquired and processed, to be followed by an overview of the resulting information itself. Here again, Melanie Klein set the model, or perhaps more accurately, she preserved orthodox research traditions, in confining her evidence largely to the treatment situation. She went beyond that only insofar as she described prenatal and neonatal ideation without having studied even the external behavior of any child below about age three (Greenberg and Mitchell 1983:123 n.).

Aware that her portrayals of early fantasy life implied intellectual capacities well beyond available evidence, Winnicott nevertheless defended that approach. Suggesting that analysts are privy to deeper truths, he cautioned that "The direct observer of infants must be prepared to allow the analyst to formulate ideas about very early infancy which may be psychically true and yet which cannot be demonstrated" (1965:112). He seems confident here that analysts will not disagree among themselves and also that their standpoint is bias free. It is reminiscent of his view of the analyst's "hate in the countertransference" as "objective," that is, as unaffected by the analyst's own needs (1949).

A similar claim is made by Balint, this time on behalf of patients rather than analysts, that their communications are uncontaminated by the situation itself. He begins by raising the question of whether "the different analytic atmospheres created by the analyst's personality would exercise a decisive influence upon the actual transference situation . . .," and then dismisses the problem as of no real import. "Curiously enough, this does not seem to be so. Our patients, with very few exceptions, are able to adapt themselves to most of these individual atmospheres and to proceed with their own transference, almost undisturbed by the analyst's countertransference" (1986:218–19).

For another illustration, we might turn to Heinz Kohut who seeks "a more broadly based scientific objectivity than that of the nineteenth-century scientist—an objectivity that includes the introspective–empathic observation and theoretical conceptualization of the participating self" (1977:68). As Kohut sees it, then, his observations are not affected either by his history as a person, his theoretical investments, or his responsibilities as a therapist. While this Dyadic analyst has gone beyond his Neo-endogenous cousins in perceiving that he serves as an "object world" whose warmth or lack of it will powerfully affect the patient, he has not gone far enough to recognize the reciprocal nature of the interaction. That is, the patient serves as an object world too, whose mode of relating does affect the analyst. Some Dyadic analysts are so unmindful of the prevalence of countertransference influences that they neglect to discuss the issue. Others are quite aware of those processes, but their inconsistent grasp of field theory is reflected in other methodological procedures as well as in their conclusions.

Interactional effects are also overlooked in conceptualizing how patients reconstruct their own histories. There is a failure to recognize it as a process influenced not only by the presence of the analyst but also by adult patients as observers of their childhood selves. If we continue with Kohut, he regards early childhood recollections as permitting a more differentiating grasp of the meaning of the psychological experience than is offered by the direct approach to the child since (a) the original experience emerges with undiminished vigor and (b) verbal communication concerning it is vastly facilitated (1971:33 n.).

Here Kohut innocently confuses convenience with conformity to fact. As summarized by Pillemer and White, the thrust of systematic studies is that "memories that were originally filed in the preschool years are hampered by early limitations in organizing and understanding," interfering with adequate retrieval. Moreover, memories recovered "may lose some of their child-like characteristics" distorting the nature of the subjective experience in other ways besides the demand characteristics evoked by the presence of the analyst (1989:336). The unwitting distortions resulting from misunderstanding these matters are readily traced in Dyadic Infantile Dependency schemata. It means that, divested of terminological intricacies and metaphors, *portrayals of how the self emerges are often little more than imaginative extrapolations from relationships with patients as experienced by their analysts.* Observations of patients' behavior in the consulting room, blended with what they now recall from early childhood, are converted into conclusions about mother (the analyst) and baby (the patient). These dubious conclusions then serve as the basis for interpretations emphasizing the infantility of what might better be understood as adult reactions. Thus a tendency is observable in the clinical literature to blur distinctions between the infant's need for the mother, the tenderness between marriage partners, and realistic appreciation of a patient toward a helpful analyst.

Another methodological holdover from metapsychology that is quite characteristic of this group of writers is the retention of orthodox terminology. Even when redefined, it preserves Endogenous perspectives. Such language leaves "the great world of humankind to things with which commerce of specifiable kinds permits the discharge of psychic energies" rather than human transactions (Holt 1989:195). Thus Fairbairn, often seen as a most radical innovator, even as an Interpersonalist, still employs body metaphors to indicate modes of relating—anal, breast, penis, castration, genital—not to mention internal structures such as his "inclusion of the id in the ego" (1952:88) as well as an "internal saboteur," a "libidinal ego" and so forth. It prompts Eagle to object to "the vagueness and murkiness of certain basic concepts. For example, what precisely is meant by such concepts as internalization and internalized objects" (1984:79)? The tendency to reify processes as if they were anatomical components obscures and neglects their interactional nature.

Before we trace the consequences of these methodological survivals from the old orthodoxy, due note must be taken of the fruitful new ideas and practices welcomed in many quarters through the influence of the British and American heirs to Melanie Klein. If the Dyadic analysts only partially sweep out the intrapsychic constraints of id-ego-superego machinery, at least they relegate that machinery to a post-oedipal era where it rests, ignored as beyond the level of personality development being treated. This allows a distinct expansion from the Neo-endogenous portrayal of parents as instinct releasers at best and of analysts as vaguely benign plumbers who relieve clogging in the psychic pipes with penetrating insights. Now the model is of infants who have a basic need for human contact with a mother (object) whose capacity or incapacity for tenderness significantly affects the adequacy of the infant's self-realization. And yet these new insights into the human thrust for engagement with a world of people and things run aground not very far from where they are launched, lured by those flawed methodological marker buoys, those orthodox modes of thought held over in the minds of Dyadic analysts.

Resultant limitations can be summed up largely in terms of three tendencies. For one thing, while the person is now recognized as importantly affected by real relationships, virtually all significant influences are seen through the single prototypical model of the dyad. Even the oedipal triad recedes from center stage. The patient's early history becomes the mother-child dyad, and it is assumed to be determinative, with the patient–analyst dyad as a present-day analogue. From that perspective, the treatment relationship becomes centrally important, but the influence of the analyst's actual personality may not be too closely examined. Nor do other current influences of work or friendship get great attention any more than past experiences outside the home do. Important as early mothering is, it cannot provide adequate explanation for all the consequential social patternings that shape one's personality and fate. Whether or not there is continuity of relatedness with parents after early childhood and the quality of that later relatedness also make a difference. Moreover, many others have significant roles to play in socialization:

> People do not simply "maintain relatedness" in some generic sense, but must learn to cope with a range of relationships—with Dyadic peers (e.g., friends, competitors), with kin (i.e., extended families, clans, etc.), with mateships (including post-pubertal sexual motivations), with coalitions (i.e., nonkin groupings like fellow workers, other groupings) as well as with dyadic hierarchical arrangements (e.g., mother, father, child) and so forth, each capable of variations in pattern and in consequences. (Buss 1991:468)

An equally repetitive second characteristic is that the significant phases in the shaping of the self are described as not extending beyond the first few years of childhood. Cooper summarizes both this conviction and the research methods behind it: "It is central for Kleinian theorists, self psychologists and at least some object-relational psychoanalysts to maintain that the crucial events of neurosogenesis are pre-Oedipal in nature and are reconstructible within the psychoanalytic situation" (1985:13).

That early childhood determinism fails to stand the empirical test. Chess and Thomas (1984) report that: "As the field of developmental studies has matured, we now have to give up the illusion that once we know the young child's psychological history, subsequent personality and functioning are *ipso facto* predictable" (p. 293). This is based on their New York Longitudinal Study of the origins and evolution of behavior disorders from infancy to early adulthood and also on other studies they cite. They add that "The emotionally traumatized child is not doomed, the parents' early mistakes are not irrevocable . . .," nor are these the only factors in the equation. The brief time span allotted to the forming of personality by Dyadic writers is more reminiscent of how long their treatment contacts may last than of how long it takes the child to reach some sort of maturity.

A third commonality is the tight focus on the themes of dependency, in its various aspects, as the essence of the developmental experience. The centrality of the separation–individuation process follows from the persisting conviction that all other influences shaping the personality normally are preset *in ovo* and not through interaction with qualities of the mother or significant others. The "good enough" mother does not intrude on the nature of the child but serves only as a "holding environment" offering basic essentials of tender care. In this sense, the neonate is like a tulip bulb whose inherent qualities will bring forth the same flower in any greenhouse that fulfills the "good enough" provision.

Only psychopathological manifestations derive from the nature of the mother. Only bad objects are internalized (Fairbairn 1952:178). "It is the innate tendencies toward integration and growth that produce the health, not the environment" says Winnicott (1965:68). Therefore if we wish to understand the socialization experience of the British empire builders, we must look to nannies changing nappies in the nursery and not to the competencies learned on the playing fields of Eton, to the chumships, adventurousness, and curiosity engendered along with less glorious attributes in the course of engagement with the larger world.

In sum, these theories (1) reduce the wide variety of significant human relationships to a single sort of dyadic model, (2) restrict mutative experience to a brief early segment of the total life span, and (3) limit the range of developmental tasks, so that ultimately little is considered other than the Dyadic Infantile Dependency experiences of child with mother as a model for all significant subsequent relationships, including the treatment experience. It leads to an absurdly narrow perspective on all the experiences that influence each person's selfhood. In terms of the ten guidelines of the Interactional checklist, Dyadic writers go beyond the old orthodoxies with respect to only one or two of them and to parts of two more. On a theoretical level, they clearly insist on the innate human need for social contact (item 1) and on a necessity for self-affirmation, if not for the competencies related to self-affirmation (item 6). Some of these writers, like Kohut, even show passing concern for data testing (item 9). Their discussions of theoretical matters are, however, too ambiguous and incomplete to qualify as well-realized theories and are better described as Dyadic Infantile Dependency *prototypes.* Their ideas are better realized on the clinical descriptive level where therapeutic empathy and concern are introduced and allowance may even be made for individual variations in treatment method (item 9).

V. The Cultural and Interpersonal Positions

The two schools to be reviewed last here are the Cultural and Interpersonal, usually seen as belonging to the same club. In the early days of their mutual contact, that was true in a literal sense. After Karen Horney came to New York City in 1934, she joined regularly with three kindred spirits for refreshment and talk. This trio included Harry Stack Sullivan, Clara Thompson, and William Silverberg who had been friends since their Washington–Baltimore days. "On a whim of Sullivan's the group took to calling itself the 'Zodiac,' " as Quinn describes it (1987:286). She also recounts the lively story of their split with the New York Psychoanalytic Society and, eventually, their further separation into an American Institute (Horney), and a White Institute (Sullivan, Thompson, Fromm), which it is unnecessary to recount here. It may be clarifying to note, however, that their separation was more political than ideological. Thus, while they all shared many fundamental views, Fromm joined the White group despite the fact that his ideas are closer to Horney's than to Sullivan's.

Since their intellectual beginnings extend back more than half a century, this group of Cultural thinkers is described last here, not because they are the most recent, but because their pioneering ideas about the social origins of selfhood still stand as the most innovative departures from classical doctrine. Those labels have misled some into the impression that the perspective is primarily sociological. Actually it is Interactional, very much addressed to the interplay between social transactions and subjective experience.

It will be recalled that the ten key Interactional hypotheses distinguishing this newer perspective from Classical metapsychology explicitly introduce previously neglected considerations far beyond social custom alone. Those ten criteria point to the human need for contact and for learning, to a complexity and flexibility of motivations besides sexuality and aggressiveness, to the significance of extrafamilial influences, to the human capacity for change over the whole life span, to treatment implications and so forth. Because all those criteria are most consistently recognized and built into Interpersonal theory, for present purposes they can serve as a summary of Sullivan's position. Not the least of his achievements is the winnowing out of most of the obscure jargon of metapsychology while still preserving the useful discoveries of psychoanalysis. This, too, might be said of Horney and Fromm (Horney 1939: 7–36). Their language is directly linked to an observable world, but they do not implement the Interactional checklist as consistently as Sullivan does.

Among the tenets held by all three is recognition that personality is shaped, not only in early childhood and within the nuclear family, but also in response to the whole broad range of societal interactions. But here, for instance, some distinction is required between Sullivan, on the one hand, and Horney and Fromm on the other. While all reject an Endogenous Oedipus complex, neither of the latter two presents an elaborated developmental theory. If we move on to motivational matters, all of them as a group decidedly move beyond Eros and Thanatos in their understanding of human needs as including loving and self-affirming relationships. All of them, too, stress the negative effects of anxiety and insecurity aroused by disapproval (checklist items 5 and 6).

These thinkers are also well aware that human psychological ills, if they are to be alleviated in any fundamental way, can and probably must be addressed not only through reparative therapies but also via modifications in society (checklist item 8). Here Fromm is especially explicit, notably in *The Sane Society* (1955), and in *The Revolution of Hope* (1968). Toward the end of his life, Sullivan also turned his attention to encouraging collaboration between anthropologists and personality development experts for "uncovering significant details" to improve the social organizations contributory to interpersonal functioning (1953:380), and he devoted time to the World Health Organization. Other names that might be added to the list of those sharing most, if not all, of these interactional tenets are Fromm-Reichmann, Kelman, Levenson, Schachtel, and Witenberg.

In short, the preceding survey indicates substantial consensus among these writers on most of the Interactional checklist criteria. They include the social contact need (item 1), the influence of extrafamilial contexts (item 2), the cultural shaping of motivations (item 5), social competencies as affecting selfhood (item 6), the utility of varying treatment approaches (item 8), integrating theory with social science data (item 9), and the need for explicit language (item 10). Then why separate these mutually harmonious thinkers into a Cultural and an Interactional group? It is that Cultural theorists like Fromm and Horney meet the foregoing seven of the checklist criteria while Sullivan, the first psychodynamic Interactionist, also meets the other three criteria, as Clara Thompson also does.

In her comparison of Fromm and Sullivan some years ago, Thompson made essentially the same observation about Sullivan's surer grasp of field theory (1950, 1964). That is, unlike Cultural writers, Interactionists see the self as changing over the entire life span (item 3). Beyond that, they recognize that the type of self that is normal or optimal in one social context will necessarily differ from what functions best in another status group or society (item 4). It also follows that as persons move from one situation to another, their self-orientation is modified (item 7). Whether the expert thinks in terms of absolutes or of relative standards in these matters can seriously affect diagnosis, treatment, and the development of preventive and ameliorative mental health measures.

Cultural writers like Fromm and Horney warn against blind acceptance of outmoded bourgeois conventions about work or gender role and other forms of ethnocentricity but then, with equal fervor espouse other myths of Western culture that they share with the Dyadic Infantile Dependency school. That is, they all believe in the existence of a "real self," an inner core that allegedly arises in a spontaneous and unexplained way very early in life, enduring inwardly ever afterward. Like Dyadic analysts, too, they warn that violations of this supposedly veridical self are undermining to psychological well-being. Winnicott, for example, speaks of an inner core that "must never be affected by external reality" (1965:133). And for Fromm, "I am 'I' only to the extent . . . to which I have achieved an integration between my appearance . . . and the core of my personality" (1968:87). Moreover, he postulates a "productive personality," beyond social influences, someone who "transcends himself as a creature, raises himself beyond the passivity and accidentalness of his existence" (1947:37) to achieve "norms postulated by the great spiritual teachers of the human race" (1955:69).

Here Fromm forgets that his enthusiasm for selfhood is definitely *not* shared by all great spiritual teachers, not even by the Zen Buddhists whom he very much admired. The fact is that their doctrine of "no self" (e.g., Kolm 1987) runs directly counter to his humanistic emphasis on autonomy and is widely accepted in the East, where it serves as the basis for Japanese Morita therapy. In Morita therapy, clients rely on conformity "to what reality brings them to do" (Reynolds 1989:11) and learn that "Constructive Living teaches only how to be 'nothing special' " (1989:21).

The Dyadic and Cultural schools find apparent confirmation for a "true self" in clinical experience filtered through poorly understood preconceptions traditional in our own culture. That tradition has an amazingly long history, traced by Bertrand Russell, from Plato to Christianity, to Locke among other English philosophers, and also to the German Romantic movement where "self development was proclaimed as the fundamental principle of ethics" (Russell 1945:682). This emphasis makes poor sense to Russell who noted that "Man is not a solitary animal, and so long as society survives, self-realization cannot be the supreme principle of ethics" (1945:684). Nor was the self glorified by Freud with his Hobbesian view of human nature as nasty and brutish. In their embracing of selfhood, however, the Dyadic and Cultural theorists substituted a romantic Rousseauian image of humanity as innately noble unless corrupted by the sickness of the social environment.

Clinical support for ideas of a true self derive from the inevitable manifestations of defensiveness in the course of any analysis, when the patient insists on pursuing repetitive self-defeating modes of functioning. If the patent hollowness of these defensive tactics is recognizable, that seems to indicate the existence of a standard of genuineness against which the falsity is exposed; a "true self" is being violated. Thus Horney speaks of a "real self" that is "the original force toward individual growth and fulfillment with which we may again achieve full identification when freed of the crippling shackles of neurosis" (1950:158).

Such reasoning approaches the magical in its reification of a fixed true self as infallibly sensing from its "original" emergence where fulfillment lies. It implies that the very young child has a godlike anticipation of its own future possibilities. But human potentialities depend so much on how they are nurtured through social contacts that effectiveness requires an orientation that shifts in accordance with the state of the environment in which one functions. Would Freud's true psychoanalytic sensibilities have emerged if he had been born in a Neanderthal cave, or would Gandhi's pacifism have flowered in ancient Sparta? The idea of a human organism that is not modified continuously through interchange with an environment is scientifically indefensible.

Yet other considerations besides cultural traditions and phenomena of defensiveness and resistance persuade present-day analysts that the self merits their attention. Most convincing of all the evidence is probably our own direct experience of inner continuity and differentiation from others. This evidence is vividly conveyed by what Erikson calls the "acute identity confusion" that occurs when the sense of self is gravely shaken. To convey the quality of this emotional trauma, Erikson quotes at length from William James' autobiographical report of a horrendous nightmare. While asleep one night, James could no longer discern whether his dream thoughts had been generated in his own mind or belonged to someone else. "Whose? Whose? Whose? Unless I attach them, I am swept out to sea with no horizons and no bond, getting lost" (Erikson 1968:206). What Erikson failed to note was James' recognition that the *sense* of continuity does not constitute factual proof of a self that stops changing. Rather, James regarded the idea of "a sort of metaphysical or absolute Unity" as a bit absurd. Instead, in a manner anticipatory of Sullivan, he spoke of "a stream of selves" whose continuity "like the unbrokenness in an exhibition of 'dissolving views' in no wise implies any farther unity or contradicts any amount of plurality in other respects" (1950:335). His opinion is echoed in current philosophical inquiry, which finds "a range of significantly different cases" with respect to selfhood (Hirsch 1982:310).

In setting aside subjective convictions as definitive proof of immanent selfhood, James evinces greater philosophical and psychological sophistication than one finds in the Cultural school. Fromm and Horney, as its representatives, manifest a scientific fuzziness, reflected in an inconsistent grasp of field theory. This separates them from the Interactional position more basically than specific differences about the self do. Other issues as well might be chosen to illustrate the consequences of that lack of clarity, for instance, their neglect of the impact of countertransference interactions. Here again is the hidden belief that just as the "real self" can escape influence by the social fields of daily life, so, too, can the analyst's self be unaffected by the patient.

These ideas of a real or best self untouched by life experience are implausible to Clara Thompson from her Interactional position. For one thing, she regards immutability as likely to indicate defective functioning of the self and notes that Sullivan shares her view. As Thompson understands it, "most people have a more or less extensive rigid portion [of personality] which has been developed in response to intense anxiety" (1964:38). It is this traumatized aspect of self that "tends to remain unchanged throughout life" (1964: 39). For another thing, universal norms like Fromm's "productive personality" make little sense to her. For instance, primitive societies could not have given their members the varied means of dealing with nature or with other human societies that are possible today. Therefore, they could not provide the kinds of competencies or experience found in contemporary selves. "Just as the unfertilized ovum will never become a human being, potentialities which are not developed through the interest and activities of others acting on the young self will never become anything which could be called a contribution to the self" (1964:42).

But it is possible to go beyond the relative plausibility of various theories to empirical research for exploring the role of external contexts in affecting selfhood not only in childhood but also in later years, when analysts do not usually expect change. It would seem, for instance, that the very sense of inner continuity is a matter of little import to six-year-olds. Aboud and Ruble report that "it is clear from this research that continuity is not a salient feature of the young child's self-concept" (1987:96). Youngsters seem to rely not so much on internal cues as on adults for their sense of secure orientation. The very criteria for judging continuity and differentiation are derived not from within so much as from the social context. Thus a sample of a thousand fifth- through twelfth- grade boys and girls confirmed the prediction that "one perceives self and others not as they are in themselves but insofar as one is different and in terms of those peculiarities" (McGuire and McGuire 1989:136). That is, the idea of an "inner direction" misleads if it does not remind the clinician that the very criteria for that orientation are developed in relation to others.

Again, Fromm's incomplete grasp of the principle of interactional fields is revealed when he asks "how then can we understand that the child who—at least in our culture—has little contact with the life of society, is molded by it" (1941:287). Implicit in the question is his assumption that only during childhood is the personality molded by experience. And, in fact, the question does make us aware of how difficult it is to account for the rapid, contemporary modifications in customs and life-styles without recognition of mutative capacities in adulthood. Answers to Fromm's question emerge when adult personality is studied in relation to social contexts (see, e.g., Grey 1989). In one study, for example, West, Nicholson, and Arnold (1987:298) found that "patterns of personal change and role innovation following work role transitions do appear to be systematically related to role requirements and personality." Another investigation, of a sample of women, indicated that, even more than work roles, motherhood can bring major changes in identity (Rossan 1987:317). Findings like these tend to bear out William James' view that the sense of unchanging selfhood is a subjective orientation rather than a fact.

While no sampling of psychological studies can be conclusive in itself, the preceding illustrations are part of an accumulating body of clinical and research evidence favoring consistency in application of the field theory principle. Because they stray from that standard in significant ways, Cultural writers seem not to have grasped the principle fully. On this basis it is meaningful to separate them from Interactionists, even though our earlier tally of the Interactional checklist clearly indicated that the two groups share many important premises. This similarity of understanding includes views on problems of the self popularly called "narcissism," usually referring to pronounced overvaluation of oneself. With respect to self-evaluation a cardinal premise of both Interactionists and Cultural theorists is that human beings are powerfully impelled toward self-affirming social experiences and that serious threats to this motivation arouse anxiety and other disruptive emotions (checklist item 6).

In his early work with acute schizophrenic adolescents, Sullivan demonstrated clinically that so-called "narcissistic" disorders were not indications of excessive self-love, as Freud had believed, in labeling them. Rather they were associated with profound self-rejection, which could be relieved by appropriate therapeutic measures, bringing improved functioning (Sullivan 1962, especially chapter 11). Along with him, Cultural analysts like Horney led the field in their recognition that concern with positive self-regard is normal. It is not intrinsically narcissistic, they insisted, and they perceived exaggerated forms as defensive disguises. The pioneering contributions of the Cultural–Interpersonal analysts in this area have been widely adopted if seldom acknowledged by other analytic schools, where metapsychological baggage still inspires oxymoronic circumlocutions like "normal narcissism" (Kernberg 1975:315 ff.).

Although Sullivan's use of the field theory principle marked a major advance in analytic thinking, his own writings did not fully realize the implications of Interactionism. For instance, he did not spell out his developmental schema beyond young adulthood, nor did he explicitly consider other developmental sequences normal under altered conditions. Then too, his descriptions of the "personified self" were so sketchy as to permit an impression that Interpersonal theory deals with little beyond the influence of anxiety. Unquestionably Sullivan left a legacy of vehement objections and misunderstandings concerning his views about the uniqueness of the individual self.

Yet it would distort the thrust of Sullivanian thinking to overlook that his therapeutic methods introduce the possibility for great flexibility for shaping the interaction to the particular needs of the individual. Although he never succeeded in developing a satisfactory alternative to Kraepelinian diagnosis, whose disease-model rigidity he so disliked, Sullivan emphasized approaching each patient with the aim of identifying and understanding that particular person's particular recurrent self-defeating patterns of living. The feasibility of a more systematic interactional diagnosis was later demonstrated by Eric Berne (1964), whose idea of "games" suggests a promising solution to the task. Sullivan's discussions of clinical practice also introduce the possibility for a far more active and varied role for the analyst than that of a "mirror." At the same time, he only began to explore the potential range of therapeutic strategies. This increased flexibility is counterbalanced by far greater alertness to the *inevitable* influences of the analyst's own personality. Consequently, Interpersonal analysts are trained to be self-observant participants.

If this résumé of Sullivan's work seems inappropriately brief for a presentation of the "Interpersonal self," perhaps that impression can be remedied. For one thing, there is the checklist of ten Interactional guidelines that appeared earlier in this paper and that has been used throughout for assessing other Self theories. The checklist sums up major respects in which Interpersonal theory has advanced beyond orthodox metapsychology in ways reflective of empirical social science findings. This is not to obscure some instances where the checklist propositions take the implications of field theory beyond Sullivan's own thinking.

In another paper written for this volume, "The Interpersonal Self Updated," there is further exploration of the strengths and weaknesses of the Interpersonalist perspective. Evaluation is in terms of more recent clinical and research evidence, much of which calls attention to the significance of contextual influences on personality. For this reason, modifications are proposed in conceptualizing the self that afford a more thorough implementation of field theory. Therein lies an operational indication of the continuing robustness of the premises underlying Interpersonal theory.

References

Aboud, F.E. and D.N. Ruble. 1987. Identity constancy in children: Developmental processes and implications. In T. Honess and K. Yardley, eds., *Self and Identity: Perspectives Across the Lifespan,* pp. 95–107. New York: Routledge and Kegan Paul.

Balint, M. 1986. *Primary Love and Psychoanalytic Technique.* New York: DaCapo Press.

Baltes, P.B., H.W. Reese, and L.P. Lipsitt. 1980. Lifespan development psychology. In M.R. Rosenzweig and L.W. Porter, eds., *Annual Review of Psychology.* Palo Alto, Calif.: Annual Reviews, Inc.

Berelson, B. and G.A. Steiner. 1964. *Human Behavior: An Inventory of Scientific Findings.* New York: Harcourt, Brace and World.

Berne, E. 1964. *Games People Play: The Psychology of Human Relationships.* New York: Grove Press.

Brenner, M.H. 1973. *Mental Illness and the Economy.* Cambridge, Mass.: Harvard University Press.

Brown, R. 1986. *Social Psychology,* 2d ed. New York: Free Press.

Buss, David M. 1991. Evolutionary personality psychology. In M. Rosenzweig and L.W. Porter, eds., *Annual Review of Psychology.* Palo Alto, Calif.: 42: 459–91.

Carson, R.C. 1989. Personality. In M.R. Rosenzweig and L.W. Porter, eds., *Annual Review of Psychology.* Palo Alto, Calif.: Annual Reviews, Inc.

Chess, S. and A. Thomas. 1984. *Origins and Evolution of Behavior Disorders: From Infancy to Adulthood.* New York: Bruner/Mazel.

Cohen, M.R. and E. Nagel. 1934. *An Introduction to Logic and the Scientific Method.* New York: Harcourt, Brace.

Cooper, A.M. 1985. A historical review of psychoanalytic paradigms. In A. Rothstein, ed., *Models of the Mind: Their Relationship to Clinical Work.* New York: International Universities Press.

Datan, N., D. Rodeheaver and F. Hughes. 1987. Adult development and aging. In M.R. Rosenzweig and L.W. Porter, eds., *Annual Review of Psychology.* Palo Alto, Calif.: Annual Reviews, Inc.

Eagle, M.N. 1984. *Recent Developments in Psychoanalysis: A Critical Evaluation.* Cambridge, Mass.: Harvard University.

Eckhardt, M. 1988. Psychoanalysis is alive and well: Meeting the challenges of diversity. *Journal American Academy of Psychoanalysis* 16:417–30.

Erikson, E.H. 1968. *Identity: Youth and Crisis.* New York: Norton.

Fairbairn, W.R.D. 1952. *Psychoanalytic Studies of the Personality.* London: Routledge and Kegan Paul.

Freud, S. 1916–1917. Introductory lectures on psycho-analysis. *Standard Edition* 16. London: Hogarth Press.

Fromm, E. 1941. *Escape from Freedom.* New York: Rinehart.

——. 1947. *Man for Himself: An Inquiry into the Psychology of Ethics.* New York: Rinehart.

——. 1955. *The Sane Society.* New York: Rinehart.

——. 1968. *The Revolution of Hope: Toward a Humanized Technology.* New York: Harper & Row.

Gill, M.M. 1988. The interpersonal paradigm and the degree of the therapist's involvement. In B. Wolstein, ed., *Essential Papers on Countertransference,* pp. 304–38. New York: New York University Press.

Gollin, E.S., G. Stahl and E. Morgan. 1989. On the uses of the concept of normality in developmental biology and psychology. In R.W. Reese, ed., *Advances in Child Development and Behavior,* vol. 21. New York: Academic Press.

Greenberg, J.R. and S.A. Mitchell. 1983. *Object Relations in Psychoanalytic Theory.* Cambridge, Mass.: Harvard University Press.

Grey, A. 1973. Oedipus in Hindu dreams, in Ghandi's life, and in Erikson's concepts. *Contemporary Psychoanalysis* 9:327–55.

——. 1988. Sullivan's contribution to psychoanalysis: An overview. *Contemporary Psychoanalysis* 24:484–97.

——. 1989. The analytic career: identity change through adult work role. *Contemporary Psychoanalysis* 25:641–62.

Guntrip, H. 1971. *Psychoanalytic Theory, Therapy, and the Self.* New York: Basic Books.

Hartmann, H. 1956. Comments on the psychoanalytic theory of the ego. In *Essays on Ego Psychology* New York: International Universities Press.

——. 1958. *Ego Psychology and the Problem of Adaptation.* New York: International Universities Press.

——. 1964. The function of theory in psychoanalysis. *Psychological Issues* 4:117–43.

Hartmann, H., E. Kris, and R.M. Loewenstein. 1964. Papers on psychoanalytic psychology. *Psychological Issues* 4(2): 5–206.

Hawking, S.W. 1988. *A Brief History of Time from the Big Bang to Black Holes.* New York: Bantam.

Heller, K. 1990. Social and community intervention. In M.R. Rosenzweig and L.W. Porter, eds., *Annual Review of Psychology.* Palo Alto, Calif.: Annual Reviews, Inc.

Hinsie, L.E. and R.J. Campbell. 1973. *Psychiatric Dictionary,* 4th ed. New York: Oxford University Press.

Hirsch, E. 1982. *The Concept of Identity.* New York: Oxford University Press.

Holt, R.R. 1989. *Freud Reappraised: A Fresh Look at Psychoanalytic Theory.* New York: Guilford Press.

Honess, T. and K. Yardley. 1987. *Self and Identity: Perspectives Across the Lifespan.* New York: Routledge and Kegan Paul.

Horney, K. 1939. *New Ways in Psychoanalysis.* London: Routledge and Kegan Paul.

——. 1950. *Neurosis and Human Growth.* New York: Norton.

Inkeles, A. 1983. *Exploring Individual Modernity.* New York: Columbia University Press.

Jacobson, E. 1964. *The Self and the Object World.* New York: International Universities Press.

James, W. 1950. *The Principles of Psychology,* 2 vols. New York: Dover (authorized republication of 1890 edition published by Henry Holt.)

Kardiner, A. 1945. *The Psychological Frontiers of Society.* New York: Columbia University Press.

Kernberg, O. 1975. *Borderline Conditions and Pathological Narcissism.* New York: Jason Aronson.

——. 1984. *Severe Personality Disorders: Psychotherapeutic Strategies.* New Haven: Yale University Press.

Kohut, H. 1971. *The Analysis of the Self: A Systematic Approach to the Psychoanalytic Treatment of Narcissistic Personality Disorders.* New York: International University Press.

——. 1977. *The Restoration of the Self.* Madison, Conn.: International University Press.

Kolm, S. 1987. The Buddhist theory of "no self." In J. Elster, ed., *The Multiple Self.* New York: Cambridge University Press.

Kornadt, H.J., L.H. Eckensberger and W.B. Emminghaus. 1980. Cross-cultural research on motivation and its contribution to a general theory of motivation. In H.C. Triandis and W. Loner, eds. *Handbook of Cross-cultural Psychology,* 6 vols., vol. 3. Boston: Allyn and Bacon.

Lasch, C. 1979. *The Culture of Narcissism.* New York: Norton.

Lerner, R.M. 1990. Plasticity person-context relations and cognitive training in the aged years: A developmental contextual perspective. *Developmental Psychology* 26(6):911–15.

Lidz, T. and R.W. Lids. 1989. *Oedipus in the Stone Age: A Psychoanalytic Study of Masculinization in Papua, New Guinea.* Madison, Conn.: International Universities Press.

Mahler, M. 1972. On the first three subphases of the separation–individuation process. *International Journal of Psycho-Analysis* 53:333–38.

McGuire, W.J. and C.V. McGuire. 1989. Developmental trends and gender differences in the subjective experience of self. In T. Honess and K. Yardley, eds., *Self and Identity: Perspectives Across the Lifespan.* London: Routledge & Keegan Paul.

Mead, G.H. [1934] 1960. *Mind, Self, and Society.* Chicago: University of Chicago Press.

Medawar, P.B. 1959. *The Future of Man.* New York: Mentor Books.

Meissner, W.W. 1986. Can psychoanalysis find itself? *Journal of the American Psychoanalysis Association* 34:379–401.

Orne, M.T. 1962. On the social psychology of the psychological experiment: With particular reference to demon characteristics and their implications. *American Psychologist* 17:776–83.

Pillemer, D.B. and S.N. White. 1989. Childhood events recalled by children and adults. In R.W. Reese, ed., *Advances in Child Development and Behavior,* vol. 21. New York: Academic Press.

Plomin, R. and R. Rende. 1991. Human behavioral genetics. In M. Rosenzweig and L.W. Porter eds., *Annual Review of Psychology.* Palo Alto, Calif.: Annual Reviews, 42: 161–90.

Proskauer, S. 1980. Oedipal equivalents in a clan culture: Reflections on Navajo ways. *Psychiatry* 43(1):43–50.

Quinn, S. 1987. *A Mind of Her Own: The Life of Karen Horney.* New York: Summit.

Reynolds, D.K. 1989. *Flowing Bridges, Quiet Waters.* Albany: State University of New York Press.

Robbins, A.D. 1989. Harry Stack Sullivan: Neofreudian or not? *Contemporary Psychoanalysis* 25(4):624–40.

Roland, A. 1988. *In Search of Self in India and Japan: Toward a Cross-cultural Psychology.* Princeton, N.J.: Princeton University Press.

Rosenfield, I. 1988. *The Invention of Memory: A New View of the Brain.* New York: Basic Books.

Rosenthal, R. 1966. *Experimenter Effects in Behavioral Research.* New York: Appleton-Century-Crofts.

——. 1967. Covert communication in the Psychological experiment. *Psychological Bulletin* 67:356–67.

Rossan, S. 1987. Identity and its development in adulthood. In T. Honess and K. Yardley, eds., *Self and Identity: Perspectives Across the Lifespan,* pp. 304–19. New York: Routledge and Kegan Paul.

Russell, B. 1945. *A History of Western Philosophy and Its Connection with Political and Social Circumstances from the Earliest Times to the Present Day.* New York: Simon & Schuster.

Sampson, E.E. 1971. *Social Psychology and Contemporary Society.* New York: Wiley.

Schachtel, E.G. 1959. *Metamorphosis: On the Development of Affect, Perception, Attention, and Memory.* New York: Basic Books.

Segall, M.H. 1986. Psychology in global perspective. In M.R. Rosenzweig and L.W. Porter, eds., *Annual Review of Psychology.* Palo Alto, Calif.: Annual Reviews, Inc.

Seligman, M.E.P. 1975. *Helplessness: On Depression, Development, and Death.* San Francisco: W.H. Freeman.

Shaw, M.E. and P.R. Costanzo. 1982. *Theories of Social Psychology.* New York: McGraw-Hill.

Smith, M.B. 1988. A semi-aquarian view of (mental) health planning. *Contemporary Psychology* 33:490–91.

Snyder, M. and W. Ickes. 1985. Personality and social behavior. In G. Lindzey and E. Aronson, eds. *Handbook of Social Psychology.* 3d ed. Hillsdale, N.J.: Lawrence Erlbaum Associates.

Stern, D.N. 1985. *The Interpersonal World of an Infant: A View from Psychoanalysis and Developmental Psychology* New York: Basic Books.

Strupp, H.H. 1989. Psychotherapy: Can the practitioner learn from the researcher? *American Psychologist,* 44 (4):717–24.
Sullivan, H.S. 1953. *Interpersonal Theory of Psychiatry.* New York: Norton.
——. 1962. *Schizophrenia as a Human Process.* New York: Norton.
Tatara, M. 1982. Psychoanalytic psychotherapy in Japan: The issue of dependency pattern and the resolution of psychopathology. *American Academy of Psychoanalysis* 10 (2):225–39.
Thompson, C. 1950. *Psychoanalysis: Evolution and Development.* New York: Thomas Nelson.
——. 1964. *Interpersonal Psychoanalysis: The Selected Papers of Clara M. Thompson.* Maurice R. Green, ed. New York: Basic Books.
Wallerstein, R.S. 1986. *Forty-two Lives in Treatment: A Study of Psychoanalysis and Psychotherapy.* New York: Guilford Press.
Wax, M.L. 1990. Malinowski, Freud & Oedipus. *International Review of Psychoanalyses* 17 (1):47–60.
Weick, K.E. 1985. Systematic observational methods. In G. Lindzey and E. Aronson, eds., *Handbook of Social Psychology,* 3d ed. New York: Random House.
West, M., N. Nicholson and J. Arnold. 1987. Identity changes as outcomes of work-role transitions. In T. Honess and K. Yardley, eds., *Self and Identity: Perspectives Across the Lifespan,* pp. 287–303. New York: Routledge and Kegan Paul.
Westen, D. 1985. *Self and Society: Narcissism, Collectivism and the Development of Morals.* New York: Cambridge University Press.
White, R.W. 1959. Motivation reconsidered: The concept of competence. *Psychological Review* 16:297–333.
Winnicott, D.W. 1949. Hate in the counter-transference *International Journal Psycho-Analysis* 30:69.
——. 1965. *The Maturational Processes and the Facilitating Environment: Studies in the Theory of Emotional Development.* Madison, Conn.: International Universities Press.

2

Interpersonal Relations and the Problem of Narcissism

John Fiscalini

"A clash of doctrines is not a disaster—
it is an opportunity. . . . The clash is a sign that
there are wider truths and finer perspectives."

Alfred North Whitehead

"The concept of narcissism has not played the important
role it deserves in the clinical investigations of psycho-analysts. . . .
This role can be fully understood only if narcissism is freed from
the restricting frame of reference of the libido theory."

Erich Fromm

Narcissism has become a central theme in contemporary psychoanalytic thought and practice. The past two decades have witnessed a geometric, if not exponential, growth in papers and books on narcissism and such related subjects as symbiosis, individuation, empathy, idealization, shame, and the self. Narcissism is in the theoretical air and omnipresent in the clinical ground as well. Without question, the narcissistic personality has become a dominant focus of analytic attention.

Why this flurry of interest? Where does this psychoanalytic centering on self-centered Narcissus come from? Where lie its origins, its roots? Are contemporary cultural conditions producing a new form of patient, a new strain of psychopathology? Is it a new patient, however, or psychoanalytic consciousness itself that is being raised? Is the current interest in narcissism a result of changes within psychoanalytic thought and awareness, a shifting of paradigmatic attention, a new awareness of phenomena previously treated as theoretically or clinically marginal now seen in other ways or now treated in other terms? Perhaps the current focus on Narcissus is largely a matter of analytic fad or fashion. Is the topic of narcissism then to be dismissed as mere analytic trendiness or as the misbegotten child of psychoanalytic politics?

The current prominence of this complex, controversial, and often confusing subject is, of course, like many things in life, multidetermined and complicated in its roots. Clearly, our contemporary culture in many ways fosters the development of narcissistic values and attitudes. As well, signs of shifts or changes are evident in fundamental psychoanalytic models. And unquestionably, the concept of narcissism has become fashionable and even faddish. Nonetheless, the popularity of narcissism as a psychoanalytic concept rests, fundamentally, upon the centrality of the human questions that it addresses. For whatever else it may be, the psychoanalytic concept of narcissism is an attempt to understand or explain the fundamental problems of (1) *human singularity,* matters of self, identity, individuality, and individuation; (2) *human relatedness,* matters of union, love, separateness, symbiosis, dependency, and community; (3) *human significance,* the core issue of self-esteem and self-love—in other words, the matter of personal worth or, more generally, of human value; and (4) *human limitation,* questions of human ideals, perfectibility and finiteness (or, in clinical terms, omnipotence, idealization, and grandiosity). In its very richness and complexity as a concept, however, lies one of narcissism's most problematic features, its susceptibility to misuse and overuse. If it is one of psychoanalysis' more germane concepts, it is also one of its more confusing ones.

The current and relatively new popularity of the concept of narcissism rests upon a further foundation—the paradigmatic shift among post-Freudians from a drive psychology to an emphasis on object relations and on the self. The unifying thematic of narcissism, as a contemporary psychoanalytic concept, is, most broadly, the self. This shift in mainstream psychoanalysis, long presaged and deeply influenced by the work of the Cultural–Interpersonalists, is what has given new recognition to this concept and made it an essential one in the contemporary Freudian vocabulary. This shift in psychoanalytic models has also led to a rediscovery and new appreciation of the theoretical and therapeutic insights of the American school of Interpersonal Relations, particularly about pivotal issues of self-esteem, self-illusion, and self-alienation. The study of narcissism has, in recent years, been associated primarily with the Self psychology of Kohut and the Object Relations concepts of Kernberg, Masterson, Modell, and other Ego psychologists. Yet, the American school, pioneered by the work of Sullivan, Fromm, Thompson, and Horney, among others, has made a significant and original contribution to the understanding of those phenomena that today we call narcissistic. The theoretical and clinical contributions of the Interpersonal-Relations theorists have, in many ways, antedated conceptions and therapeutic approaches mistakenly thought by many to have originated with contemporary Freudians. Interpersonal-Relations theorists have, of course, brought their own particular psychoanalytic stamp—a rich amalgam of pragmatism, pluralism, and field theory—to the study and treatment of narcissism. The American school does not, however, represent a uniform or unitary metapsychology or methodology. Rather, it defines a complex and diverse set of psychoanalytic ideas and practices, with a common Interpersonal sensibility and tradition. However much alike they may be, Interpersonalists also differ, at times profoundly so. This rich diversity is reflected in their understanding of narcissism and in their work with narcissistic patients and problems.

The study of narcissistic processes, in whatever metapsychological language it has been framed, has led to considerable controversy, both within and between psychoanalytic schools. The topic, touching, as it does, upon such central and vital human issues, has led quite naturally to a significant diversity of thought and practice. Broadly considered, the myriad controversies about narcissism concern three areas of analytic thought and practice: diagnosis, etiology, and treatment. Each area of concern has been approached from a wide variety of viewpoints, both within and across theoretical boundaries. As Whitehead reminds us, however, conflicting ideas represent an opportunity to discover, or even create, wider truths and new perspectives. This paper, in examining the Interpersonal understanding of the problem of narcissism, is an effort to realize that opportunity.

Before turning to a discussion of the central subject of this essay—the diagnosis and etiology of clinical narcissism, I briefly examine some theoretical and terminological ambiguities of the psychoanalytic concept of narcissism.

Narcissism: Conceptual and Terminological Ambiguities

A commonsense meaning to the term narcissism is shared by most people. As an everyday term in the world of ordinary discourse, narcissism refers unambiguously to self-rapture, in all its many phenomenal forms. The consensual understanding is that this is a pejorative "self-love," and in our ordinary speech, when we use the term narcissism we always refer, explicitly or implicitly, to one or both of the two human attributes or dimensions fused in its meaning—introversion and overvaluation, or in the language of the self, self-centeredness and self-inflation.;[1]

As a psychoanalytic term, however, narcissism has proven to be a problem. In the world of psychoanalytic discourse, the meaning of narcissism becomes more complex and more confusing. Narcissism has been an extensible psychoanalytic term, one that has been expanded to explain or define, at different levels of conceptualization, a broad manifold of psychic processes or phenomena that are seen as significantly involving some facet of the self. Narcissism has been used by analysts to refer variously to any or all of the following: a sexual perversion; a developmental stage, so-called primary narcissism; a mode of object choice, patterned on some identity with the self; an immature or pathological self-centered or grandiose way of relating to others; a character disorder, the so-called narcissistic personality; the psychoses, or "narcissistic neuroses," historically considered psychoanalytically inaccessible; and the complex psychological process or state of self-esteem.

Narcissism has a long history in psychoanalytic theory. The term reaches back to Freud's early concept, and beyond, and its usage is deeply etched in psychoanalytic convention. The wild popularity of Kohut's ideas and those of other post-Freudians writing in the vernacular of narcissism may have cemented this concept even deeper in our theoretical and clinical imaginations. Nevertheless, the contradictory and inconsistent ways in which it has been used over the years have made its use problematic or at least fraught with difficulty. Both Pulver (1970) and Moore (1975), in their critiques of the concept, observe that narcissism is one of the most confusing, as well as one of the most important, contributions of psychoanalysis. It has been used by different theorists in so many different ways about so many different things, which are "often related to each other only in vague and obscure ways" (Pulver 1970:320), that it is often difficult to know what we are talking about when we use the term. The conceptual and terminological complexities and confusions that now inhere in this term have prompted many theorists to propose various reforms in its use—either to limit or narrow its use (see, for example, Joffe and Sandler 1967; Pulver 1970; Teicholtz 1978) or to redefine it (see Horney 1939; Fromm 1955; Stolorow 1975). Paradoxically, these proposals, whatever their respective merits, have added even further semantic complexity.

The theoretic and semantic difficulties that now characterize this concept stem from three sources: (1) inherent problems in Freud's original libido concept of narcissism; (2) the effort by post-Freudian Ego and Object-Relational theorists to cling to the libido metaphor, and their inability to specifically redefine the concept in terms congruent with the emerging interpersonal thrust of their ideas; and (3) narcissism's spread of meaning, in which it has come to mean or be linked with almost everything under the psychoanalytic sun. Freud, for example, used the concept of narcissism to partially explain hypochondriasis, homosexuality, sleep, primitive thought, autoeroticism, resistance, exhibitionism, masochism, sadism, the war neuroses, group formation, hypnosis, jealousy, superego formation, repetition compulsion, secondary gain, and humor, among a number of other processes. These phenomena, as Moore (1975) observes, "encompass such diverse elements as clinically observable aspects and attributes of human behavior (biological as well as psychological, individual, social, normal, and pathological), pathological syndromes, and abstractions, i.e., theoretical concepts of genetic, structural, dynamic, and adaptive significance."

This broad use of the concept of narcissism derives directly from the nonspecific nature of Freud's original concept and from his effort to use it to unify a diverse group of clinical processes, states, and entities in libidinal terms. And as Pulver (1970) points out, as the terms of Freud's libido concept were increasingly elaborated with developments in psychoanalytic theory, the definition of narcissism and its theoretical applicability expanded too.

Further difficulty derives from the tendency to think that extremely complex states or processes are somehow explained or understood once labeled narcissistic. Consider, for example, the attempt to understand the complex interpersonal and intrapersonal processes that characterize the infant's earliest relationship with its interpersonal world in terms of the concept of primary narcissism. A complex subject is made all the more complicated by trying to understand it in inherently simplistic terms and in terms, moreover, that mean different things to different people. Those who use the concept often use it in very different ways to signify very different constructions of the infant's psychic experience. Some theorists, for example, use it to refer to antenatal experience or to the neonate's supposedly autistic and deeply self-absorbed relationship (or nonrelationship) with its environment, whereas others use the term to refer to symbiotic-like forms of primitive relatedness that are much more akin to what Balint (1968) meant by "primary love."

The difficulties with the concept of narcissism briefly noted here in terms of primary narcissism also characterize its other uses. One of the most striking of these is the use of the term to denote the process or state of self-esteem. Consideration of this use takes us into the very heart of the problem with the psychoanalytic concept of narcissism—Freud's formulation, in which the ordinary meaning of narcissism was stretched to encompass both "normal" and "abnormal" self-love, leading to unending confusion.

Freud's (1914) paper on narcissism was a polemic against Jung and an argument for Freud's libidinal metapsychology. Nevertheless, Freud's concept of narcissism, as Moore notes, "played a pivotal role in the development of the structural theory. Narcissism was the seed which germinated into ego psychology" (1975:243). In his 1914 paper, Freud, in transition from the topographic to the structural model, struggled to encompass his beginning ideas about the self and its interpersonal relations within an outmoded theory of energic (drive) distributions—the economic model. Freud, as Moore observes, "was still holding steadfastly to his earlier ideas while he moved on to new ground. The result is an admixture of the old and the new, with both semantic and conceptual confusion" (1975:245). Narcissism was a problem birth. As Freud himself put it, "the narcissism was a difficult labor and bears all the marks of a corresponding deformation" (Jones 1955:304). Though elegant, comprehensive, and logical, Freud's libido theory of narcissism is fundamentally flawed.

Freud's hydraulic metaphor of narcissism is inherently flawed in two ways. First, it assumes a fixed quantity of libido that flows in U-tube fashion from one psychic pole to another. There is an assumed inverse relationship between ego libido—libidinal cathexis of the self—and object libido, libidinal cathexis of the other; the more one loves oneself, the less so others, and vice versa—logically consistent but clinically indefensible. In real life, self-love and love for others are, in fact, indivisible. The Cultural–Interpersonalists Horney (1939) and Fromm (1947) were the first of Freud's critics to point this out. Fromm, in several of his writings (1955, 1964, 1973, 1980), has commented on how narcissism is the *opposite* of both love of others and love of self. It is, in other words, the antithesis of loving relatedness. As Thompson (1950) notes, "narcissism as clinically observed is not self-love but self-hate." And it is hate of others too.

These Interpersonal critiques have been echoed in the more recent criticisms of some post-Freudians (Pulver 1970; Kernberg 1975; Stolorow 1975). This problem, in fact, led Kohut, who in his early theorizing struggled to hold on to the libido metaphor while remaining true to the clinical facts, to postulate two *kinds* of libido, narcissistic libido and object libido: "Narcissism . . . is defined not by the *target* of the instinctual investment . . . but by the *nature* or quality of the instinctual charge" (1971:26, italics mine).

Kohut's insight, like those earlier of Fromm and Horney, acknowledges that self-centeredness defines a form, not a direction, of relatedness. Interestingly, Kohut's bifurcated libido parallels Sullivan's division of the interpersonal goals of man into those of security and satisfaction, respectively the pursuits of self-esteem and of intimacy and sensual gratification, or, in Freudian terms, object love. Though Kohut saw the problem with Freud's conception of narcissism, his allegiance to the libido metaphor forced him to adopt, as Stolorow (1975) notes, the metapsychologically untenable hypothesis of two kinds of psychic energy. Eventually, of course, Kohut solved the problem by dropping the libido concept in his later work and restating narcissism in new terms—those of the self and its selfobject relations. Thus, he more openly declared himself for the interpersonally oriented Self theorist that he, in fact, had become. Of course, Kohut clung to the libido in one final way, by assigning it to the so-called oedipal dynamic. And in doing this, paying obeisance to Freud's metapsychology, he freed himself enough to develop his personal version of a psychology of an interpersonal self.

There is a second, and interrelated, flaw in Freud's concept—the economic model's inability to differentiate quality from quantity. The definition of self-love in solely quantitative terms makes it impossible for the model to distinguish realistic, self-generated self-esteem from defensive pride or megalomaniacal self-inflation or delusion. Since Freud used narcissism to include self-regard as well as self-inflation, his model required additional terms. Thus arose the somewhat bewildering proliferation of different types of narcissism such as "primary," "secondary," "healthy," "pathological," "normal infantile," and so on. The inherent confusion of quantity and quality—good and bad self-love—is still responsible for much of the confusing use of the term narcissism. Thus, for example, one can, in one sentence, refer to narcissism in such a way as to indicate "normal" strivings for self-esteem, pathological self-centeredness or grandiosity in the adult, and the naive egocentricity and "grandiosity" of the child. Now this is possible to understand, but it is, I think, unnecessarily complicated.

Freud's theory of narcissism, as noted earlier, was an attempt to theoretically fit emerging ideas about the self and interpersonal relations into an older drive framework that simply could not house them without conceptual and terminological difficulties. These complications and confusions have been compounded by the efforts of later Freudians—Ego psychologists and Object Relations theorists—to do the same thing: to force-fit interpersonal and self ideas and sensibilities into a framework not built for them. Witness, for example, Kohut's theoretical gymnastics before he relinquished the libido formulation of narcissism. Recognizing these problems, some post-Freudian theorists have proposed Ego-psychological redefinitions of the concept (e.g., Stolorow 1975; Rothstein 1980a). Though these efforts have much to recommend them, they tend, paradoxically, to confuse the issue even further, adding even additional meanings to the concept.

Stolorow, a Self psychologist, has proposed a contemporary Ego-Psychological elaboration of the concept of narcissism, offering the following functional definition: "Mental activity is narcissistic to the degree that its function is to maintain the structural cohesiveness, temporal stability, and positive affective coloring of the self-representation" (1975:179).

Stolorow offers a persuasive argument for his concept, demonstrating its helpfulness in eliminating many of the ambiguities and difficulties of the drive concept. Stolorow's ideas have a definite Interpersonal character. In fact, many of his insights reflect those of Interpersonalists of earlier generations. For example, Stolorow's thesis that sexual perversions may be attempts to restore self-esteem or to shore up a faltering self-representation is strikingly similar to the Interpersonal-Relations theorists' fundamental insight that sexuality (perverse or otherwise) often reflects the pursuit of security or self-esteem—i.e., the avoidance of anxiety, rather than the pursuit of lust.

Stolorow's formulation of narcissism is strikingly similar to Sullivan's concept of interpersonal security. Security, for Sullivan, defines the sector of psychic life that characterizes the human striving for self-esteem, for reflected interpersonal approval—exactly what Stolorow calls narcissism and Kohut called narcissistic libido. Stolorow's "narcissistic activity," thus, is almost identical to Sullivan's pursuit of security—both are psychic actions directed toward the protection and organization of the self-representation, or, in Sullivan's preferred Interpersonal term, *self-personification.*

The term *narcissistic* may also cover aspects of the personality other than the interpersonal self, the need for security, or self-esteem. As used by Kohut, Stolorow, and contemporary Self psychologists, the term may also refer to aspects of what I refer to as the personal, personalized, and relational selves—the inherent human needs and strivings for personal self-realization, personalized order and organized representation, and relational intimacy (cf. Fiscalini 1990a, 1991). I am sympathetic with the thrust of Stolorow's ideas, and his functional approach to narcissism is a vast improvement over Freud's concept. Nevertheless, Stolorow ends up like most other Freudians—using narcissism as a way of talking about the self (although in a clearer and more limited way than is usual). And he, too, runs into semantic problems. Though he thoughtfully attempts to delineate a clear and precise semantic of narcissism, Stolorow ends up using the term in ways that contradict his very own definition of it. Such is the beguiling complexity of the concept. It weaves its confusing spell even on those who attempt to reform its usage.

Interpersonal-Relations theorists have not had to follow this confused and confusing path. Since they, from the beginning, rejected the libido theory and advanced an explicit psychology of the self and its interpersonal relations, Interpersonalists, unlike Freudians, have not needed narcissism as a theoretical concept or construct to refer to the self, self-esteem, or to intrapsychic or interpsychic relations of self and other. Using a different conceptual system, and not constrained by a theoretical allegiance to a libidinal metapsychology, Interpersonalists have been free to use narcissism in its everyday meaning, as a descriptive term for a particular set of pathological attitudes, and they have been able to account for other processes and phenomena called "narcissistic" by Freudians in other, and ultimately clearer, simpler, and less confused or confusing terms. Though one might recommend that all psychoanalysts follow the Interpersonalists' lead and restrict their usage of the term *narcissism* to its ordinary, everyday meaning, there is little likelihood of this happening, at least in the near future. The term is simply too deeply rooted in analytic tradition and convention. Despite its flaws, narcissism is a central analytic concept and is extensively used. To be sure, the term is an evocative one, and as Fromm foretold, it draws attention to an important set of problems in many, if not all, patients (and analysts). Even if one chooses to follow the lead of the Interpersonalists and delimit use of the term, one must, for purposes of scientific communication, be aware of its major uses by the wider analytic community.

So how do post-Freudians use the term? I have reviewed this already, but in brief outline, the concept of narcissism is used generally to refer to the following dimensions of the self or self-experience: *self-esteem* or self-respect; *self-extension,* in which others are experienced symbiotically as part of one's self, vis-á-vis Kohut's concept of the selfobject; *self-centeredness,* in which others may be seen as separate but, unimportant (actually self-extension and self-centeredness may simply represent points on a continuum of self-absorption); self-aggrandizement or *self-inflation,* i.e., grandiosity; and *self-perfection,* feelings or attitudes of symbiotic bliss, euphoria, and perfection.

To summarize: there seem to be two major ways in which the term *narcissism* is used in contemporary psychoanalysis: (1) what we may call a *broad* use, which refers most widely to processes related to self-esteem and self-organization; and (2) a *narrow* use, which refers, more delimitedly, to various degrees of self-inflation and self-centeredness, which may (a) universally characterize "normal" early childhood psychic functioning or (b) be represented in adulthood, or childhood, as "abnormal" or pathological development

Whatever our theoretical perspective or semantics, we might all agree that the concept of narcissism, however defined, broadly or narrowly, touches upon central dimensions of the human psyche. So let us turn to some clinical issues—to a consideration of clinical narcissism and questions about its diagnosis, psychodynamics, and etiology.

The Narcissistic Personality: Interpersonal and Freudian Views

The diagnostic picture of narcissism is both complex and ambiguous. Clinically, narcissism has come to signify an ever-broadening manifold of psychopathological phenomena. Both a diagnostic spread and an increasing frequency in use characterize the nosology of the so-called narcissistic personality. Moreover, this term is used by different theorists with different diagnostic implications or to refer to clinically dissimilar phenomena. And conversely, many theorists use a variety of different diagnostic terms to refer to the same clinical phenomena that others call narcissistic. This diagnostic complexity raises some interesting questions. Does it mean, first of all, that "narcissistic" problems are a new, and increasingly prevalent, form of pathology brought about by contemporary cultural and familial factors? Or is narcissism an old form of psychic disorder newly conceptualized? Second, are narcissistic individuals, like those called schizoid or borderline, uniquely self-disordered, unlike other neurotics? Or is all neurotic suffering fundamentally a disorder of the self? And, third, is there a specific diagnostic entity, the narcissistic personality, or is narcissism a fundamental dimension of all psychopathology—a type of problem rather than a type of person? A look at the ways in which analysts have defined their patients and their problems as "narcissistic" may help us answer these questions and delineate similarities and differences in Interpersonal and Freudian clinical and diagnostic conceptions of narcissism.

Perhaps not since the time of Freud's work with hysteria or that of Sullivan's with schizophrenia has a form of psychopathology been so identified with the work of one theorist as narcissism has been with Heinz Kohut. It was Kohut who, in 1968, coined the term *narcissistic personality disorder*, and it was the popularity of his ideas on narcissism that gave the initial impetus to its rapid rise in diagnostic use.

Until the time of Kohut's work, there were but a handful of clinical papers on narcissism in the Freudian literature: Jones' (1913) study of the "God complex"; Abraham's (1919) review of "narcissistic" resistances; Freud's (1931) and Reich's (1933) delineations of a "narcissistic character type"; Riviere's (1936) study of the negative therapeutic reaction and of the narcissistic resistances of controllingness, contempt, and self-inflation; Annie Reich's (1950, 1960) two classics on the inconstant self-esteem of "narcissists" and its attempted regulation or repair via idealized object choices; and the more recent work of Murray (1964) and Rosenfeld (1964) who are prominent among the few pre-Kohutian Freudian contributors to the clinical understanding and definition of narcissism.

In contrast, the Cultural–Interpersonal clinical literature, drawing heavily on this school's traditional focus on problems of the reflected self, has, from its very beginnings, devoted considerable attention to those personality problems that are called narcissistic in mainstream literature. This work has sometimes been phrased in the language of narcissism but more often has not. Sullivan studiously avoided the term. Though he extensively addressed the central problems of clinical narcissism, both in its broad and narrow senses, Sullivan (1940, 1953, 1954) framed his formulations of these problems in the preferred language of the interpersonal self. Fromm and Horney, too, made seminal contributions to the clinical understanding and definition of "narcissistic" processes. But they, unlike Sullivan, framed many of their observations in the explicit language of narcissism.

For those unfamiliar with her work, Horney's (1937, 1939, 1945, 1950) ideas on narcissism, when first encountered, seem strikingly modern. Though she first wrote on the subject more than fifty years ago, her ideas foreshadow much of what is now written on the subject. And in her last work (Horney 1950), she, like Kohut nearly thirty years later, recast nosology in terms of "narcissistic" dynamics. In an early work, Horney (1939), defining clinical narcissism as self-inflation, had noted that

> The bewildering number of contradictory qualities attributed to narcissism . . . results in part from a failure to recognize that narcissism is but one specific *trend within a personality structure.* It is the combination of trends which gives a personality a certain coloring. . . . narcissistic trends . . . may be entangled, for example, with perfectionistic, masochistic, and sadistic trends (p. 97, italics mine).

Fromm (1947, 1955, 1964), too, was an early student of narcissism. He detailed the clinical features and psychodynamics of a "narcissistic orientation," which, in his view, ranged from mild self-centeredness to profound solipsism and grandiosity (Fromm 1964). Earlier, Fromm (1947) had described a "marketing character" whose clinical features overlap, in many ways, with current descriptions of narcissistic personalities.

Both Horney and Fromm saw the essence of narcissism as self-alienation, and both, like Winnicott (1960), spoke of a real or true self whose development was arrested or crippled in the pathological narcissistic process, which, in their view, is one that is greatly fostered in pathological societies such as our own. Though creative psychoanalytic thinkers with original neo-Freudian viewpoints, both Horney and Fromm were influenced by their early training in Europe as Freudian analysts. And both, particularly Fromm, tended to shape their thought in terms of Freud's metapsychological categories, recasting many Freudian concepts in Culturalist–Interpersonal terms. It is not surprising then, that both Fromm and Horney explicitly formulated clinical theories of narcissism, reinterpreting Freud's libidinal formulations from a Culturalist perspective.

The native American Sullivan, on the other hand, was not trained in Freudian psychoanalysis, and though influenced by Freud's ideas, he developed his own in relative independence of Freud, following out the shape of his own individuality, instead of shaping his ideas in contrast to those of Freud. Sullivan, as noted previously, did not use narcissism as an explicit category of psychopathology, although his theory of the interpersonal self and its vicissitudes and his ideas on the psychodynamics of "customarily low self-esteem" are thoroughly consistent with most modern clinical concepts of narcissism and bear a close affinity to the ideas of Kohut. Though Sullivan did not speak of a narcissistic personality, he did describe a "self-absorbed" personality syndrome in which there is a "a cosmic centering in the person" and experience is largely bifurcated in terms of the primitive early childhood pattern of "good mother" and "bad, or evil, mother." Sullivan (1940) described these persons as particularly apt to become "disappointed, wounded, or misunderstood" in their relations with those whom they cannot idealize. He sardonically added that "one cannot but marvel at the failure of learning which has left their capacity for fantastic, self-centered illusion so utterly unaffected by a life-long series of educative events" (p. 80).

Sullivan further held that this "deviation of growth" was of early developmental origin, coming from "the time of predominantly autistic verbal behavior." He also delineated three other syndromes—the ambition-ridden, the inadequate, and the chronically adolescent—that all overlap in their major characteristics with what is now called the narcissistic personality.

Until recently, however, very few contemporary Interpersonal papers have been published on narcissism. But this has not been because attention has been focused elsewhere, as in the case of the Freudian literature. The central clinical "narcissistic" issues, such as problems of self-regard, archaic needs for empathic understanding, self-alienation, "self-love," and defensive grandiosity, idealization, and detachment, and so on, are clinical themes that appear and reappear throughout the Interpersonal clinical literature. But it is seldom expressed in the language of narcissism. For most Interpersonal theorists narcissism has been an uncomfortable clinical idiom and an unnecessary one. Since the vicissitudes of the interpersonal self and its object relations have traditionally formed the central focus of Interpersonal-Relations theory, analysts of this school have been free to frame their clinical and therapeutic studies of "narcissism" in the simpler and clearer language of the self, a step that Kohut, the popularizer of narcissism, eventually found necessary in his metamorphosis from an orthodox Freudian to a self-named "Self psychologist."

Interpersonalists have tended, in practice, to regard "narcissistic" problems or trends as constitutive of all the traditional nosological categories, and thus they have, until recently, tended to diagnostically fit such trends into one or another of the major neurotic syndromes or "dynamisms of difficulty," according to their particular mix with other character trends.

In recent years, however, a more explicit discussion of clinical narcissism has taken place among Interpersonalists (cf. Bromberg 1979, 1983, 1989; Blechner 1987; Epstein 1981; Field, 1987; Grey 1987; Imber 1984; Mitchell 1986, 1988; Ortmeyer 1987; Spiegel 1987; Tauber 1982; Tenzer 1987; Witenberg 1974; and Wolstein 1981, 1986, 1987). This development reflects the increasing cross-fertilization of ideas and practices that characterizes contemporary clinical psychoanalysis. The Interpersonal school, perhaps more than any other psychoanalytic school, has been open to a pluralism of metapsychological perspectives and, as such, is particularly sensitive to new developments or trends in other psychoanalytic quarters. Thus, the recent explicit attention to "narcissism" among Interpersonalists represents a recognition of new nosology, rather than new pathology, and it is an attempt at dialogue with those who frame their clinical observations in a broadly Freudian (i.e., Ego-psychological, Self-psychological, Object-Relations) vernacular.

It is, in other words, an effort by Interpersonal-Relations theorists to articulate and communicate some pertinent clinical insights and Interpersonal therapeutic conceptions about core problems of self-esteem, self-illusion, and self-alienation in an idiom that is perhaps more congenial to the wider psychoanalytic community. It is hoped that such efforts will lead to a greater sharing of therapeutic insights about this ubiquitous human problem.

Kohut's description of a narcissistic character type, the narcissistic personality disorder, in terms of persisting childhood longings, or archaic "preoedipal" needs, to be ideally "mirrored" by idealized others, and his delineation of its core pathology in terms of early, severe defects in self-esteem and self-definition, reflect his Interpersonal sensibility, and bear a striking similarity to the theoretical formulations of both Sullivan and Horney. Kohut's therapeutic conceptions, however, differ radically from those of these theorists, and particularly from the confronting therapeutics advocated by Fromm.

Kohut's work on narcissism, along with that of such post-Freudian coevals as Gedo (1981), Giovacchini (1979), Kernberg (1975), Masterson (1981), Miller (1981), Modell (1975, 1976), and Rothstein (1980a), among many others, represents a development in what Wolstein (1984) has termed the Ego–Interpersonal paradigm in psychoanalysis—what Greenberg and Mitchell (1983) call the "Relational" model, and in aspects of what I have termed the "Interpersonal" model of psychoanalytic inquiry (Fiscalini 1990b). This work builds upon and continues the earlier work of Object-Relational Ego psychologists such as Hartmann (1939, 1950), Jacobson (1964), and Mahler (1963, 1968), and it reflects the sharpening focus on the dynamics of the representational self and its interpersonal relations (particularly their developmentally earlier aspects) that has centrally characterized the paradigmatic shift from a drive theory and oedipal focus to a self–other and pre-oedipal psychology in mainstream psychoanalysis.

Kohut and other contemporary Freudians write about narcissism in terms of a specific narcissistic personality. Study of their case examples and clinical vignettes suggests, however, that these theorists are addressing a core dimension of psychopathology that cuts across diagnostic categories, rather than a circumscribed and separate clinical entity—or at least, they are referring to a clinical entity that overlaps considerably with other, more traditional diagnoses. Many of Kohut's narcissists, for example, could legitimately fit into other diagnostic categories. Today an increasing tendency is evident among analysts influenced by the work of Kohut and Kernberg and other contemporary Freudians to diagnose many patients as narcissistic personalities whom analysts of other schools of thought would classify as obsessionals, depressives, hysterics, and so on.

Clinical narcissism, whether thought of in terms of a psychopathological dimension or a personality type, comprises a set of clinical features that define what may be called the *core narcissistic constellation.* All other associated symptomatology derives from the following primary dynamics: (1) grandiosity; (2) self-centeredness and lack of empathy for others; (3) cyclic contempt and idealization of both oneself and others; (4) thin-skinnedness, or abnormal self-esteem vulnerability; (5) thick-headedness, or psychological inaccessibility and imperviousness; (6) attitudes of entitlement—assumed special rights or privileges; (7) other-directedness, or the ceaseless search for the approval, admiration, attention, and acceptance of others; and (8) power orientation—controllingness and coerciveness. This narcissistic constellation bears a striking similarity to many of the central clinical features of Thompson's (1938) detached, Sullivan's (1956) hysteric, Guntrip's (1969) schizoid, Salzman's (1980) obsessional, and Bonime's (1982) depressive and paranoid personality.

The nosology of the narcissistic personality is complicated in at least two major ways. Not only does this diagnostic term cover the same nosological territory as other diagnostic terms do, but also, paradoxically, it is used by different theorists to cover what seem to be fundamentally different diagnostic territories. Not everyone's narcissist is the same. Consider, for example, those patients described by Kohut (1971) and Kernberg (1975) as narcissistic personalities. As Ornstein (1974) and others have noted, Kernberg and Kohut seem to use the same diagnostic label to refer to quite different patients. Some overlap is present in Kohut's and Kernberg's diagnostics, but many of Kernberg's narcissistic patients seem far more disturbed than those of Kohut. Moreover, Kernberg views his narcissists as borderline, whereas Kohut regards the narcissistic personality disorder as pathologically and developmentally intermediate between borderline and neurotic functioning. Kernberg would most likely classify many of Kohut's narcissists, particularly the less disturbed ones, as neurotics. Such, then, is the complexity of this diagnostic term, and the phenomena to which it refers. The same term means different things to different theorists, and different theorists use different terms to mean the same thing.

Contemporary Freudian analysts have become increasingly aware of the clinical significance of problems of the interpersonal, or reflected, self and its defensive illusions. This growing awareness among mainstream analysts, in combination with their wish, for reasons of metapsychological loyalty, to circumscribe this core "narcissistic" dimension of psychopathology within the rubric of a specific clinical entity, the narcissistic personality (and thus preserve the "oedipal" patient as a primary drive disorder), has contributed significantly to the diagnostic spread and frequency of use of this nosological category. An increasing number of patients and an increasingly wider range of them are being diagnostically squeezed into this category. More and more patients, often with quite varied clinical features, are now defined as narcissistic personalities on the basis of the inevitable presence of "narcissistic" dynamics, in either the broad or narrow sense. Inevitably, diagnostic homogeneity results—everybody becomes a narcissist. The nosological "blurring" inherent in this expansion of the diagnostic range of narcissistic personality has led, as might be expected, to counterbalancing efforts to recreate diagnostic heterogeneity. Hence, the proliferation of narcissistic "subtypes" (for example, see Bursten 1973). As Meissner (1979) and Masterson (1981) note, we now have the arrogant or phallic narcissist; the ambition-ridden narcissist; the Nobel-prize-winner type; the manipulative psychopathic narcissist; the needy and demanding dependent, clinging narcissist; and the timid and shy closet narcissist. One could continue this until one had, in effect, stood traditional nosology on its head and redefined it in terms of narcissism. And, in fact, this is exactly what Kohut does when he revises nosology in terms of "selfobject" dynamics.

Kohut's new nosology was foreshadowed in Horney's work. In her final schema of neurotic character structure (Horney 1950), all neurosis is seen as narcissistic. All neurotics are seen as developing self-contradictory defensive character trends. This leads, in turn, to inner conflicts and a comprehensive neurotic solution by compensatory processes of self-idealization involving an *idealized image*, a *search for glory*—the attempt to actualize the defensive *idealized self*, and hatred and contempt toward the *real self*. This psychodynamic schema, which bears a formal similarity, though very different metapsychological sensibility, to Kernberg's theory of borderline/narcissistic dynamics, outlines various neurotic forms of the search for glory, including a specific character type that is similar to Kohut's narcissistic personality disorder. Thus, Horney, impressed with the clinical centrality of defensive self-idealization, envisions all neurosis as "narcissistic"—as self-alienated and compensatorily grandiose. Horney's work has not, however, received the attention it deserves, and its influence has been relatively limited, largely because she and her followers have worked outside the psychoanalytic mainstream and form a relatively small and less influential psychoanalytic tributary. Kohut's work, on the other hand, lies largely within mainstream psychoanalysis (though it has required complex theoretical gyrations to maintain its metapsychological ties to orthodoxy), and thus it has had a much broader, if not necessarily more original, impact on the wider psychoanalytic community.

Kohut and Wolf (1978), increasingly attuned to the clinical significance of disordered archaic needs for self-esteem and self-definition, broadened Kohut's earlier concept of narcissistic disorder to include, with the possible exception of the oedipal "neurotic," all patients, who were now defined as various kinds of selfobject- or self-disorders. And soon thereafter, Wolf (1984) included Oedipus, too, as a disorder of selfobject relations. Thus, in the Kohutian framework, all disorder had become one of disordered selfobject relations—i.e., narcissism. In other words, Kohut had moved toward an Interpersonal conception of neurosis—pathology was of the self; and Kohut's self, like Sullivan's, was an interpersonal self—the "me," a reflection of other reflected selves.

So, where does all this leave us? How are we to understand the diagnostics of narcissism? Let us return to our three questions—first, the question of the recent diagnostic popularity of the "narcissistic personality." Does it reflect changes in cultural trends or in theoretical paradigms? Are we simply looking at an old form of psychic disorder that has been newly recognized (or cognized)—old whine in new diagnostic bottles? Or are we looking at a rise in the actual incidence of clinical narcissism?

Narcissism is an ancient form of human suffering. Mankind undoubtedly has struggled with narcissism since time immemorial. The themes of destructive self-involvement and self-aggrandizement reach far back, beyond Greek mythology, and have figured prominently in all the world's literature. As Dyrud (1983) notes, themes of narcissism and its perils may be seen in the sacred writings of all the major human religions. Though narcissism may not be new, the question remains whether it is on the rise, at least in contemporary Western culture. Are we seeing more narcissistic patients and pathology today than earlier? Do we live in a culture and time that is fostering more and more narcissism? Much about our culture certainly seems to foster, or highlight, pathological narcissism. Nevertheless, our current "culture of narcissism" (Lasch 1979), with all its greediness, competitiveness, materialism, and psychic emptiness, seems not so very different, in significant outline, from Western culture of the first half of the twentieth century—that "insane society," to paraphrase Fromm, so criticized as alienated and unloving by such Interpersonal analysts as Horney (1937), Fromm (1947, 1955), and May (1950, 1953). A comparison of Horney's patient of the 1930s and Lasch's of the late 1970s suggests that Lasch's "narcissistic personality of our time" is, in many ways, Horney's "neurotic personality of [her] time"—unduly sensitive to rejection, anxious, searching for unconditional love, insatiable, hostile, and striving ceaselessly for power, prestige, or competitive victory. Perhaps the clinical face of narcissism has in some way changed in recent years, assuming different manifest features, but if our patients have changed in their basic form of pathology, I think that it has not happened within the past twenty years, or even the past fifty years. Consider what Horney (1939) had to say more than fifty years ago:

> Narcissistic trends are frequent in our culture. More often than not people are incapable of true friendship and love; they are egocentric . . . they feel insecure and tend to overrate their personal significance; they lack judgment of their own value because they have relegated it to others (p. 98).

Look even further back in time, to Freud's patients of the late nineteenth century. Far more narcissism and character disorder are present here than is often acknowledged. Today, many of Freud's neurotics—his hysterics, for example—would most likely be diagnosed as narcissistic or borderline, depending, of course, upon whom they sought for consultation. In my opinion, the recent psychoanalytic attention to narcissism seems fundamentally to reflect a change in nosology (i.e., in psychoanalytic paradigm), not in pathology. The change has been, in other words, primarily in our perceptions of our patients, not in our patients. And this change in perception, as I have noted previously, has been mainly among mainstream analysts.

Some Interpersonal analysts with a psychosociological sensibility—notably Fromm (1947, 1955); Grey (1975); and Dyrud (1983)—who have examined narcissism in its broader historical–cultural sweep, point to an important and neglected area of research—the sociopsychological analysis of the historical and cultural factors that foster narcissistic pathology in the individual and those that may mitigate or militate against such development. Fromm, in his concept of "social narcissism," addresses the social psychology of narcissism from yet a different perspective. Fromm discusses the process by which "individual narcissism is transformed into group narcissism [in which] the clan, nation, religion, race, etc, become the objects of narcissistic passion instead of the individual" (1964:73). Fromm details the historical role of social narcissism in cultural pathology and its significance as a root cause of social and religious violence. As psychoanalysts, we often see social narcissism close at hand—in our own internecine battles and rivalries, and in our metapsychological conceits, or as Rothstein (1980b) puts it, in our "narcissistic investment in our paradigms."

Analysts' theoretical perspectives and allegiances have played a determining role in their understanding of the nature of narcissism. Let us examine this in relation to our second question: is narcissism a unique self-disorder, fundamentally unlike other forms of neurosis?

Many contemporary post-Freudian theorists view the narcissistic personality as a disorder of the self, a uniquely "pre-oedipal" problem that can be sharply distinguished from the presumably healthier neurosis of the oedipal patient, who supposedly is drive disordered rather than self-disordered. Contemporary Interpersonal-Relations theorists and Self psychologists, on the other hand, tend to view *all* neurosis, including the so-called oedipal neurotic, as fundamentally a disorder of the self and its interpersonal (or self object) relations. I believe that these theorists would all concur with the statement that "all personality disorder is . . . disorder of the self, at all levels of psychic organization" (Fiscalini 1988:129)—from the conflicted self of the anxious neurotic to the fragmented self of the terrified schizophrenic.

The concept that two types of patients exist—the oedipally conflicted neurotic and the pre-oedipal self-disordered (narcissist, schizoid, etc.)—does not hold up clinically. It is a false dichotomy required as a theoretical necessity by those analysts who have tried to remain loyal to drive theory and somehow preserve its centrality, by grafting their emerging self and Interpersonal sensibility onto a libidinal metapsychology. And so the bifurcated diagnostics: self-disorder for Narcissus; drive disorder for Oedipus. Interpersonal-Relations theory, rejecting a psychosexual or libidinal model of development, focuses instead on an evolving developmental series of increasingly mature interpersonal relationships and self-experiences. Personality disorder is viewed in terms of a continuum of disturbance. From this theoretical perspective, diagnostic classification does not require a dichotomy between "neurotic" and narcissistic; self or narcissistic processes (in both the narrow and broad sense) are recognized in all personalities and in all personality disturbance.

We now approach our third question: does narcissism represent a dimension of psychopathology, or is it a personality type—a specific entity. I view it as both: a type of problem and a type of person. What do I mean by this?

I believe that all people are "narcissistic" in three different, though interrelated, senses: (1) In the broadest sense, all people, to one degree or another, have problems with self-esteem. (2) This problem with self-esteem inevitably involves, for everyone, some early damage, i.e., deficits in so-called "normal narcissism." All of us have persisting archaic needs for self-esteem that are grandiosely based and express themselves in what Kohut calls "mirroring" and "idealizing" needs. (3) Moreover, all people develop "pathological" narcissism or, in other words, narcissistic defenses of grandiosity, self-centeredness, imperviousness, etc., at various levels of consciousness. Thus, all our patients have problems with "narcissism." To say it in another way, the *core narcissistic constellation* refers collectively to a set of processes, dynamisms, and ways of relating that, in variable form and severity, characterize all people—"normal," neurotic, and the even more severely disturbed. Some people, however, are so predominantly or singularly characterized by these traits that we may properly refer to them as narcissistic personalities. In other words, all patients have narcissistic issues, some pervasively so. Thus, we can speak of the analysis of narcissistic processes in every patient's treatment, as well as the analytic treatment of the narcissist—that person or personality who presents a predominance of narcissistic dynamisms and traits. In sum, what we are talking about are two things: a dimension of psychopathology that cuts across the spectrum of disorders and a group of patients with a predominance of such problems.

A range or continuum of "narcissistic" problems or personalities exists, in terms of: (1) *Severity*—narcissism (in all its senses) ranges from more primitive and severe to milder forms: (2) *Patterning*—all people have mixed narcissistic features, and often patients present some narcissistic issues, but not others. The particular pattern of narcissism is always highly individual, and often it is mixed with other significant clinical features—e.g., obsessionalism, hysterical theatrics, depression, masochism, etc. (3) *Chronicity*—narcissistic functioning may be chronic and continual, or it may be episodic and only occasional. (4) *Breadth*—narcissism may characterize all, or most, of a person's interactions with others or manifest itself only in a few areas of functioning where the individual is narcissistically vulnerable. To summarize: all narcissists, and all patients in their narcissism, vary in the severity, frequency, extensiveness, and individual patterning of their narcissistic concerns and problems.

Narcissists, like each individual with narcissistic features, tend to be consistent in their behavior and experience. But character has complexity as well as consistency. We are all much more complex than otherwise—in our narcissistic facets as well—and our relatedness to others and to ourselves, narcissistic and otherwise, varies to some degree with its interpersonal context—with the situation, time, and person(s) with whom we are integrated.

It seems to me that in clinical actuality all patients are complex and individual integrals of various personality trends. All the various dynamisms that characterize the various diagnostic categories—e.g., obsessionalism, hysteria, paranoia, narcissism, etc.—represent processes, capacities, or ways of being or relating that are universal, and they typify us all in some aspect of our living, even if only in very minor ways. Each of us represents a unique category, a certain individual pattern, of these various dynamisms, though we may be predominantly this or that sort of person or personality. We are all mixed neurotics, even those of us who appear to more nearly approximate a pure type. Diagnostic categories are not truly discrete, nor are they real entities; they are simply names given to certain identified clinical features.

Even though we may be more simply human than otherwise, as Sullivan (1940) reminds us, we are also very individual in our humanity. Even in our narcissism—the very antithesis of our unique individuality—we are all uniquely configured. And just as hysterics, obsessionals, depressives, etc., represent a heterogeneous lot—among themselves, and in their overlap with other categories—so too with narcissists. Patients may be more narcissistic than otherwise, but always, their narcissism is uniquely patterned. Great heterogeneity exists among narcissists—in the nature, pattern, dynamics, and pathogenetic paths of their characteristic narcissistic features. With narcissists, as with all patients, therapeutic understanding requires that these individuals be grasped in his or her true singularity—in his or her specific and unique psychic necessities and experiences.

The Interpersonal Etiology of Narcissism

How does one become narcissistic? We may ask ourselves whether some specific developmental path exists for the narcissist. Is there, in fact, a particular set of early, or later, interactions that predispose the individual toward narcissistic ways of being and relating? The answer is both yes and no. No, in that each person's narcissism is always individually configured or patterned. And so is its interpersonal birth and development. Nevertheless, notwithstanding the inevitable Procrustean implications of such typology, three etiological patterns of narcissism may be delineated. We may call them: (1) the *shamed child,* (2) the *spoiled child,* and (3) the *special child.*

These patterns represent broad dimensions of childhood experience and parent–child interaction that, in my view, are significantly implicated in the development of vulnerable self-esteem and narcissistic relatedness. These patterns are sketches of ideal types; they do not exist in pure form, only in complex combination. The narcissism of any person is always a complex and unique integral of his or her shamed, spoiled, and special selves.

This typology is a heuristic, offered as a way of examining some significant aspects of the interpersonal development of narcissistic processes and problems. These three etiological patterns, as outlined here, are highly abstract, schematic representations of what, in actuality, are complex sets or series of interpersonal interactions and personal experiences that are lived out in a multitude of individual ways. The shamed, spoiled, and special child each refer to myriad interpersonal interactions that involve complexly intertwined integrating tendencies (motives) of both parent and child. The development of narcissism always involves the interpersonal participation of at least two people in complex interaction; it is never simply a matter of just what one person does or of just what one person dreams up. Narcissism, in other words, is inevitably interpersonal and interactional.

A comparative analysis of psychoanalytic theories of narcissism, or even a full discussion of an Interpersonal developmental theory of narcissism, goes beyond the scope of this brief outline and is a subject for a more extended study. I offer here simply an introductory outline of those interpersonal relations and self experiences that I think are most central in the development or formation of narcissistic pathology—an abstract, as it were, of some important developmental vicissitudes of the interpersonal self. This etiological abstract or schema is premised largely on the Interpersonal principles of Sullivan's (1940, 1953) theory of personality, though it also reflects the influence of Kohut's (1971, 1972, 1977, 1984) and Kernberg's (1975) ideas on narcissism and Stern's (1985) developmental observations and conceptions.[2]

Before considering the developmental origins of clinical narcissism, let us review what would represent a healthy developmental sequence with respect to the evolution of a strong and centered sense of self-esteem or interpersonal security.

The Self-Respecting Child

The child who develops a solid, realistic, and personally grounded sense of security or self-esteem—so-called healthy narcissism—requires an interpersonal environment, a home, in which both unconditional and conditional love and approval are given appropriately by the parenting figures. The child's activities, states of being, or experiences that are reflectively appraised and approved (i.e., "mirrored") undergo an optimal developmental progression characterized by a gradual disillusionment of the child's egocentricity, naive "grandiosity," and "idealization" of others.

The infant's or child's mind is immature: egocentric, naive about the constraints (or possibilities) of reality, limited in its grasp of the world. Infants or children, in their developmental immaturity, "expect" immediate and (from an adult's perspective) immoderate response. Children simply know no better, at least not in the beginning. They have but a rudimentary grasp of their own limitations or of the characterological or situational constraints of their caretakers. Hence, young children inevitably experience others in "idealized" terms, and their archaic needs for interpersonal approval and acceptance are inevitably experienced in terms that are egocentric and naively "grandiose." This, then, is the early nature of the interpersonal self. Though interpersonal security, or self-approval, is a lifetime need, the nature of its conditions—what constitutes security or approval—changes with maturation and experience. And in the very beginning for the young human being, approval and security are based on the infant's or child's *egocentricity* and *naive grandiosity*—on what has been called "childhood narcissism," or early needs for "mirroring" and "idealizing."

Very young children require mirroring or loving approval, which from an adult perspective may seem extravagant or extreme, for activities or being-states that later on in their development will be responded to in a more modulated way. For example, parents may adore or admire their children for some seemingly ordinary action or interaction—a smile, a spoken word, a state of exuberance or enthusiasm, an expression of some desire, an impetus to share an experience or emotion—or cherish them for simply "being," i.e., being alive. This early "unconditional" cherishing or adoring of infants or young children, this beaming approval, in conjunction with the parent's enjoyment and acceptance of the child's reciprocal admiration and expectation of "perfect parenting" is laid down as the wordless foundation of all later self-esteem. It forms the nonverbal core of the interpersonal self.

If this early cherishing and mirroring approval is appropriately and consistently related to actual children—as they are, not as desired to be—it becomes internalized as their own strong and primal sense of confirmed personal worthiness, which persists throughout life as the core of all self-respect. Its absence, what Balint might call the "basic fault" and what we observe in patients as a vague, difficult to describe, sense of "wrongness" or "badness"—of being somehow defective or no good, harkens back, I think, to early deficits of "mirroring" in this preverbal time. This difficulty is often refractory to verbal intervention and needs to be worked though analytically in what I have called the "living through process" (Fiscalini 1988).

As children mature, and develop in cognitive and emotional capacity, respectful parents' reflective approval—their "mirroring" and openness to being "idealized"—becomes conditional, consciously or unconsciously. Though some of the early "unbounded love" continues to characterize the parent's interactions with the child, approval becomes both more tempered and more selectively offered or received. There is, in other words, a gradual limiting or disillusioning of the previously "unbounded self"—the egocentric and naively grandiose child—and, reciprocally, of the primitively idealized parent. Optimally, this process allows for the continued, never to be withdrawn, unconditional approval of children *for themselves*—in their unique being—but not of some of their behaviors or ways of being, which are progressively shaped to the contours of their maturing capacities.

Children feel truly accepted only when parental approval is attuned to their developing abilities and needs. Approval must be empathically attuned to the developmental significance of their behavior or experience. And it must be related to the psychological meaning of an activity or accomplishment (e.g., the joy in an endeavor, effort put forth in an activity, risk taken in an action, or desire implicit in an act), not simply to the external action or achievement. When the socialization or child-rearing process, including the setting of limits, is consistently applied and commensurate with the maturational and developmental capacities of children and their personal abilities and limitations, it will result in a more realistic, less grandiose, basis for self-esteem; increased awareness of and empathy for others; and internalized and autonomous standards of self-evaluation.

To summarize, the building of a robust interpersonal self—a realistic, internally guided sense of self-worth—requires the following process of optimal "illusioning" and "disillusioning" reflected appraisals by parents and significant others: (1) conditional approval of increasingly more "mature" capacities and more "realistic" behaviors or states-of-being; (2) continuing unconditional, or "idealized," approval of the child's "core being" as singularly significant; along with (3) a realistic appreciation and unconditional approval of the child's increasingly apparent limitations (of talent, intelligence, appearance, ability, etc.). Respectful (and self-respecting) parents foster both realistic limits of what is approvable and approval of real limitations (both in their children and in themselves). Such parents gradually deidealize their children as, reciprocally, they encourage the children to gradually deidealize them. They see their children (and themselves) for who they are, while continuing to boundlessly cherish them in their imperfect and idiosyncratic being. There is, in other words, a continuing "tender" unconditional approval of their children's singularity and uniqueness simultaneous with a "tougher" conditional approval based on their developing abilities—e.g., having better self-control, better tolerance of stress, greater patience and forebearance, greater ability to be alone or do things alone, greater attention span and ability to contain feelings, and increased capacity to do more complex things. In this way, the children move from an egocentric and naively grandiose basis of self-esteem—security based on the "exaggerated" appraisal of idealizing and idealized parents—toward a more realistic and autonomous basis of self-esteem, both expecting of themselves what they can realistically attain and respecting themselves regardless of their personal limitations or potentialities. Simultaneously, their self-respecting children move toward an increasingly more mature and realistic appraisal and approval of the singularity of their parents and significant others. This constitutes healthy self-respect and respect for others.

The Shamed Child

When children experience chronic disapproval, and premature disillusionment, of significant aspects of their developmentally appropriate attaching (loving), depending, asserting, expanding, or individuating needs, because of parental anxiety, envy, jealousy, or hate, they will grow up feeling shamefully and fearfully inadequate in these areas of their being and relating. Even their very need for approval, or "mirroring," based on their "grandiose" yardstick, and their need to approve of, or idealize, their parents may become shamefully unacceptable. These "shameful," anxious aspects of the psyche are dissociated and become part of the "not-me" self-personification or self-representation. Sometimes they are deeply buried and never shown; more often, they are manifested or shown but not consciously experienced.

Shamed children's relationships with their parents are characterized by an unempathically harsh and excessive setting of limits. The parents anxiously or angrily demand, consciously or unconsciously, that the children be more mature or "grown-up" than the children can be. There is, in other words, a premature disillusioning of the children's egocentricity and naive grandiosity—of their need to be mirrored in "grandiose" terms and to experience others in similar idealized terms. Too much is expected, or demanded, of these children in various aspects of their living.

These children's self-hatred and self-repudiation is always accompanied by the development of "narcissistic" dynamics. Shamed children develop grandiose or unrealistic self-expectations that somehow they *should,* or *could,* or even *must,* be more, or better, or different than their rejected actuality. Such children feel "bad" or "wrong"—in some way that is often hard to verbalize, just not good enough: too babyish, too "big for one's britches," too needy, not needy enough, too willful, too willing, what have you. These spurned children also become self-centered, in direct proportion to their experience with anxiety or shame. This self-centeredness or preoccupation with interpersonal security—i.e., "selfobject" relations—may be hidden in seeming (object) relatedness to others and not present itself in its more obvious narcissistic forms. If the injury to these children's interpersonal self, i.e., self-esteem, is broad and deep, they may later spend most of their adult lives searching for security rather than for satisfying, fulfilling, or loving experiences, however disguised this effort may be. What in the children incurs parental disapproval varies from parent to parent, family to family, and situation to situation. The envelope or limit of shame is, of course, that of human possibility; any human capacity or need may be subject to interpersonal rejection and repudiation. Parental disapproval varies, of course, in both breadth and severity. It may be mild and limited to relatively peripheral aspects of a child's functioning, or it may be severe and addressed to central aspects of the child's psyche.

The persisting unmirrored needs of children, whether dissociated or selectively inattended, are often found in symptomatic activity—e.g., compulsive or addictive behaviors, defensive searches for glory—or in an aching, hard to voice sense of unworthiness that may be experienced at varying levels of consciousness. Shamed children's conscious or unconscious experience is marked by a residual longing or need for approval of the rejected aspects of their psyches. This can be as specific, for example, as an unconscious longing to have their athleticism or artistic talent appreciated; or it can be more general, as in unconscious longings for interpersonal affirmation and confirmation of their states of desire; enthusiasms; feelings of accomplishment; experiences of pleasure, expansiveness, effortfulness; caring feelings; or dependent wishes to be "babied" and tenderly cared for. Most primitively and nonspecifically, there may be persisting needs for approval of one's self, one's very aliveness—to simply "be" and to be cherished for that "being."

The substitutive security operations, or character defenses, of shamed children are those modeled or permitted in the home, be it masochism, depression, obsessionalism, sadism, or whatever. Manifest narcissism—such as overt grandiosity, demandingness, self-centeredness—or expansiveness of any kind is not acceptable in this home, and thus it is not manifested, for it, too, would lead to anxiety or hostility.

The etiological pattern of the shamed child, when it is the predominant one in the developmental mix, fits the clinical picture of the shy or timid narcissist. These are the patients who might be diagnosed by some analysts (certainly by Kohutians) as narcissists but would more likely be diagnosed as obsessives, depressives, schizoids, or paranoids, depending on their characterological style. The defensive narcissism, before treatment, tends to be covert, hidden behind other character defenses, as are the persisting aspects of the personality that remain unmirrored and unloved.

The Spoiled Child

Not infrequently, parents will indulge their children, cherish them, but fail to modify their approval to their children's developing maturity and growing ability to accept limits, handle more complex tasks, and tolerate greater separation and autonomy. This excessive approval and "protracted illusionment" of children's egocentricity and naive grandiosity expresses itself in two different ways, or subpatterns: *uncivilized children* and *infantilized children.*

Parents of uncivilized children are overly lenient and fail to set appropriate limits or expectations for them. Often the children are treated as though they were young princes or princesses. Also, the parents overpraise the children and fail to establish realistic conditions for approval that are tied to the children's real abilities. In contrast to the situation of shamed children, spoiling parents, for a variety of neurotic reasons, do not expect enough of their children. There is much "untamed" grandiosity and idealization in this situation, and it leads, in childhood and later on in adulthood, to demanding and self-centered despotic behaviors, which are often rationalized as being assertive; feelings of anxiety, anger, and frustration when such individuals are treated as ordinary persons, since there is the expectation that they should be able to command a greater deference or latitude from nonfamily others; and feelings of inadequacy, shame, or anxious inferiority when the individual runs into realistic difficulty, reversal, or failure, since grandiose self-expectations have been built up by parents' inflated appraisals. These children, in other words, are not properly prepared for life.

Indulgence, of course, always implies deprivation. When children are overadmired, some "real" aspects of the children are neglected. These unmirrored or disapproved needs, parts of the actual self, become repressed, part of the "not-me," and persist unconsciously as "childhood narcissism" into adulthood. Spoiling or indulgent overvaluation of children implies a parental inability to tolerate their needs to be independently effective. It also implies a rejection of both the children's real limitations and their developmental needs for limit and realistic appraisal. Parental spoiling of children is invariably neurotic and self-centered. It may be born in the parents' low self-esteem, possessiveness, hostility, fear of the children, guilty overcompensation, or desire to live out unresolved narcissism, to name but a few of the motives that may push parents to spoil their children.

The pattern of the infantilized child is substantially similar in its "narcissistic" dynamics to that of the uncivilized child but with a different, and less aggressive, emotional tone, and a somewhat different manifest clinical picture later on. Narcissism is created here by parental fearfulness, overprotection, and overly "sensitive" and indulgent treatment of the "fragile" and precious child. Parental problems in affirming and accepting the child's expansive, assertive, and autonomous strivings often spring from the parent's anxiety about separation. And this often coexists with parental controllingness and domineeringness, which is denied and often rationalized as caring or loving concern. Spoiling parents, particularly when infantilizing, tend to foster their children's defensive idealization of them, which, coupled with explicit or implicit interference with the children's asserting and individuating needs, cripples the development of the children's ability to define themselves—i.e., value themselves by autonomous standards. This, then, is the infantilized child: dependent, timid, and fearful of autonomy and separation. This child is cherished and generally approved of but is not released to a larger living.

The spoiled child, unlike the shamed child, manifests both overt and covert characterological narcissism. This manifest narcissism may be accompanied, particularly in the infantilized child, by conscious feelings of inferiority and inadequacy, which have a defensive aspect. In contrast to the uncivilized child, the "overly sensitive" infantilized child's defensive narcissism may be more masked or covert, less openly extractive, angrily demanded, or consciously entitled, and more idealizing. What is unacceptable to the spoiled child, as an adult, are persisting anxious and shameful "not-me" longings to be accepted, or mirrored, for oneself (and similarly to accept and adore significant others in their imperfect actuality). And, for the spoiled child, there is always anxiety about defining oneself or using one's own resources.

Clinically, the intertwined subtypes of the spoiled child are always mixed with aspects of the shamed child. Depending on the particular etiological patterning and its "narcissistic" severity, the patient may be diagnosed as a narcissist or as having one of the other neuroses—often as a hysteric, depressive, dependent, or inadequate personality when the "spoiled" picture is predominant, depending, of course, on the nature of the character defenses adopted. In the case of very severe problems with being "civilized," particularly when linked with severe shaming, diagnosis may include acting-out or psychopathic features. In all these clinical pictures, there is overt defensive, i.e., "pathological," narcissism, learned in the faulty interactive patterns of the spoiled child. This defensive characterological narcissism covers over, and is not to be mistaken for, the repressed and unmirrored loving, expanding, and individuating needs of the young child. These repudiated aspects of the psyche may clinically manifest themselves in covert "narcissistic" needs, which may become more conscious as they become more accepted, and eventually lived and worked through, in the psychoanalytic situation.

The Special Child

This pattern of parent–child interaction combines aspects of the shamed child with a variant of the spoiled child. This etiological dynamic typifies many of those patients who are most commonly, or unequivocally, diagnosed as narcissistic personalities. This developmental picture characterizes, for example, the ontogeny of many of Kernberg's narcissists and Kohut's "noisy" or "demanding" narcissists. One may recognize it in Kohut's (1979) celebrated case of Mr. Z.

As with shamed children, the parents of special children are often rejecting and neglectful: too busy, moralistic, competitive, envious, angry, anxious, perfectionistic, or otherwise self-preoccupied to relate and respond to their children's developmentally appropriate needs for attention, admiration, acceptance, and affirmation in significant aspects or dimensions of their living. But unlike shamed children, special children are also highly prized. At the same time that important aspects of their egocentric and naively grandiose needs for approval are spurned or shamed, these children are "spoiled" in self-centered ways, used narcissistically, by their parents. In this situation, the parents, because of their uncentered selfness and narcissistic self-centeredness, treasure or prize the children for ways of being that are construed by the parents as bringing glory or reflected self-esteem to themselves. Thus, "special" or superior qualities, achievements, abilities, or talents are "over-mirrored" and become the selective basis for the children's self-esteem. These "special" qualities may be real or illusory; in either case, there is a rewarding of a "false" self and simultaneous disparagement of a "real" self—the child's actuality—which, to a greater or lesser extent, remains unloved and unadmired.

The developmental experience of special children leads, in varying pattern, to compulsive strivings for success of one sort or another; feelings of specialness; demands for praise and special treatment; and manifest arrogance and grandiosity, often rationalized by feelings of entitlement. And it leads, inevitably, to secret fears of inferiority and inadequacy.

Parents' narcissistic focusing on their children's "specialness" or superiority goes hand-in-hand with false praise and false relatedness to their developing affectional, anaclitic, and assertive needs. The inherent falseness of the parents' narcissistic approval is often unconsciously discerned by the children, who know that they are props for the parents' shaky self-esteem. Consciously, of course, the children often need to deny this, and they may strive desperately, often out of love for the parents, to meet the parents' narcissistic necessities.

These "mismirrored" special children end up feeling special, yet unworthwhile. The children get what they do not need and do not get what they do need. Unconscious longings for "mirroring" from ideal, caring parents coexist with manifest narcissistic pathology stemming from parental misapproval and overapproval. Loved only for their "special" features, and not for their greater being, these special children grow into archetypal narcissists—only secure interpersonally when experiencing themselves as special or superior, always anxious about their shamed and unacceptable "ordinary" humanity and unique individuality. Rage, aloofness, controllingness, demandingness, and contempt are frequently adopted ways of protecting the narcissistically distorted "good me," the superior self.

In summary, narcissistic problems may be seen to develop from interpersonal interactions, starting in infancy, which (1) promote the development of overt and covert substitutive defensive narcissistic ways of being and relating—so-called pathological narcissism; and (2) fail to meet early naively "grandiose" and egocentric—i.e., "narcissistic"—needs for reflected approval, which persist as repressed aspects of unmet "childhood narcissism."

The defensive, characterological narcissism stems from faulty, anxious (or hostile) relatedness between parent and child in which there is (1) an indulgence or spoiling of the child in various ways—failure to set limits, failure to selectively reward maturing capacities, overprotection, false praise of the child, etc.; (2) explicit or implicit fostering of unrealistic or grandiose self-expectations (on the part of both child and parent), in some way or another making approval contingent on grandiose achievement; or (3) overapproval or selective approval of some real or imagined "special" achievement, ability, or personal or physical feature of the child and selective rejection or ignoring of the child's personal limitations and real attributes. The particular combination of these three pathological factors, their severity, and the particular areas of the self they affect determines the nature of the covert or overt characterological narcissism in each particular case.

Defensive substitutive narcissism always coexists with the persisting unconscious or preconscious "narcissistic" aspects of children's loving, depending, asserting, and individuating needs that have been repudiated in the narcissistic developmental process. The characterological defensive narcissism—that which comes out of neurotic, false relating—may be generally distinguished from the dissociated or selectively inattended childhood "narcissistic" needs of the children, i.e., their appropriate needs to be cherished for themselves, by its characteristic immoderation, insatiability, rigidity, compulsivity, ruthlessness, and haughtiness. Nevertheless, it is not always clear whether some clinical instance of narcissism reflects a wounded childhood need or a requirement of the patient's defensive system, i.e., injured defensive pride. Ultimately, this judgment can come only from the intensive and intimate work with patients in the coparticipatory therapeutic inquiry, that is, from getting to know them in their particularity.

Notes

1. Perhaps introversion or self-absorption is the more basic attribute of narcissism, as is indicated by its Greek root (interestingly enough, also the root for narcotic), *narke,* meaning numbness or stupor.

2. By contrast, most contemporary Freudians (for example, Blanck and Blanck 1974, 1979; Horner 1979; Masterson 1981, 1988) draw heavily upon the developmental theories of Freud, Mahler, Klein, Kohut, and Winnicott for their understanding of narcissism. Winnicott's developmental ideas and Mahler's separation–individuation schema are particularly emphasized in many contemporary Ego-psychological and Object-Relational accounts of the etiology of narcissism.

References

Abraham, K. 1919. A particular form of neurotic resistance against the psychoanalytic method. In *Selected Papers on Psycho-Analysis.* London: Hogarth Press, 1949, pp. 303–11.

Balint, M. 1968. *The Basic Fault: Therapeutic Aspects of Regression.* London: Tavistock.

Blanck, G. and R. Blanck. 1974. *Ego Psychology: Theory and Practice.* New York: Columbia University Press.

——. 1979. *Ego Psychology II: Psychoanalytic Developmental Psychology.* New York: Columbia University Press.

Blechner, M.J. 1987. Entitlement and narcissism: Paradise sought. *Contemporary Psychoanalysis* 23:244–54.

Bonime, W. 1982. The paranoid and the depressive. *Contemporary Psychoanalysis* 18:556–574.

Bromberg, P.M. 1979. The use of detachment in narcissistic and borderline conditions. *Journal of the American Academy of Psychoanalysis* 7:593–600.

——. 1983. The mirror and the mask: On narcissism and psychoanalytic growth. *Contemporary Psychoanalysis* 19:359–87.

——. 1989. Interpersonal psychoanalysis and self psychology: A clinical comparison. In D.W. Detrick and S.P. Detrick, eds., *Self Psychology: Comparisons and Contrasts.* Hillsdale, N.J.: Analytic Press.

Bursten, B. 1973. Some narcissistic personality types. *International Journal of Psychoanalysis* 54:287–300.

Dyrud, J. 1983. Narcissus and nemesis. *Psychiatry* 46:106–12.

Epstein, L. 1981. Countertransference and judgments of fitness for analysis. *Contemporary Psychoanalysis* 17:55–68.

Field, H. 1987. Some idealizing transferential and countertransferential experiences. *Contemporary Psychoanalysis* 23:230–38.

Fiscalini, J. 1988. Curative experience in the analytic relationship. *Contemporary Psychoanalysis* 24:125–41.

——. 1990. On self-actualization and the dynamism of the personal self. *Contemporary Psychoanalysis* 26:635–53.

——. 1991. Expanding the interpersonal theory of self-threat. *Contemporary Psychoanalysis* 27:242–64.

Freud, S. 1914. On narcissism: An introduction. *Standard Edition* 14:67–102. London: Hogarth Press, 1957.

——. 1931. Libidinal types. *Standard Edition* 21:215–20. London: Hogarth Press, 1961.

Fromm, E. 1947. *Man for Himself.* New York: Holt, Rinehart and Winston.

——. 1955. *The Sane Society.* New York: Holt, Rinehart and Winston.

——. 1964. *The Heart of Man* New York: Harper & Row.

——. 1973. *The Anatomy of Human Destructiveness.* New York: Holt, Rinehart and Winston.

——. 1980. *Greatness and Limitations of Freud's Thought.* New York: Harper & Row.

Gedo, J.E. 1981. *Advances in Clinical Psychoanalysis.* New York: International Universities Press.
Giovacchini, P.L. 1979. *Treatment of Primitive Mental States.* New York: Jason Aronson.
Greenberg, J. and S.A. Mitchell. 1983. *Object Relations in Psychoanalytic Theory.* Cambridge, Mass.: Harvard University Press.
Grey, A.L. 1975. Modern alienation and the good old days. *American Journal of Psychoanalysis* 35:123–33.
——. 1987. Entitlement: An interactional defense of self-esteem. *Contemporary Psychoanalysis* 23:255–63.
Guntrip, H. 1969. *Schizoid Phenomena, Object Relations and the Self.* New York: International Universities Press.
Hartmann, H. 1939, 1958. *Ego Psychology and the Problem of Adaptation.* New York: International Universities Press.
——. 1950. Comments on the psychoanalytic theory of the ego. *Psychoanalytic Study of the Child* 5:74–96.
Horner, A. 1979. *Object Relations and the Developing Ego in Therapy.* New York: Jason Aronson.
Horney, K. 1937. *The Neurotic Personality of Our Time.* New York: Norton.
——. 1939. *New Ways in Psychoanalysis.* New York: Norton.
——. 1945. *Our Inner Conflicts.* New York: Norton.
——. 1950. *Neurosis and Human Growth* New York: Norton.
Imber, R. 1984. Reflections on Kohut and Sullivan. *Contemporary Psychoanalysis* 20:363–80.
Jacobson, E. 1964. *The Self and the Object World.* New York: International Universities Press.
Joffe, W.G. and J. Sandler. 1967. Some conceptual problems involved in the consideration of disorders of narcissism. *Journal of Child Psychotherapy* 2:56–66.
Jones, E. 1913. The God-complex. In *Essays in Applied Psycho-analysis, II,* pp. 244–65. London: Hogarth Press, 1951.
——. 1955. *The Life and Work of Sigmund Freud,* vol. 2. New York: Basic Books.
Kernberg, O. 1975. *Borderline Conditions and Pathological Narcissism.* New York: Jason Aronson.
Kohut, H. 1971. *The Analysis of the Self.* New York: International Universities Press.
——. 1972. Thoughts on narcissism and narcissistic rage. *The Psychoanalytic Study of the Child* 27:360–99.
——. 1977. *The Restoration of the Self.* New York: International Universities Press.
——. 1979. The two analyses of Mr. Z. *International Journal of Psychoanalysis* 60:1–27.
——. 1984. *How Does Analysis Cure?* A. Goldberg and P.E. Stepansky, eds. Chicago: University of Chicago Press.
Kohut, H. and E.S. Wolf. 1978. The disorders of the self and their treatment: An outline. *International Journal of Psychoanalysis* 59:413–25.
Lasch, C. 1979. *The Culture of Narcissism: American Life in an Age of Diminishing Expectations.* New York: Norton.

Mahler, M. 1963. Thoughts about development and individuation. *The Psychoanalytic Study of the Child* 18:307–24.

——. 1968. *On Human Symbiosis and the Vicissitudes of Individuation.* New York: International Universities Press.

Masterson, J.F. 1981. *The Narcissistic and Borderline Disorders: An Integrated Developmental Approach.* New York: Brunner/Mazel.

——. 1988. *The Search for the Real Self.* New York: Free Press.

May, R. 1950. *The Meaning of Anxiety.* New York: Norton.

——. 1953. *Man's Search for Himself.* New York: Norton.

Meissner, W.W. 1979. Narcissistic personalities and borderline conditions: A diagnostic differential. *Annual of Psychoanalysis* 27:171–202.

Miller, A. 1981. *Prisoners of Childhood.* New York: Basic Books.

Mitchell, S.A. 1986. The wings of Icarus: Illusion and the problem of narcissism. *Contemporary Psychoanalysis* 22:107–32.

——. 1988. *Relational Concepts in Psychoanalysis: An Integration.* Cambridge, Mass.: Harvard University Press.

Modell, A. 1975. A narcissistic defence against affects and the illusion of self-sufficiency. *International Journal of Psychoanalysis* 56:275–82.

——. 1976. The "holding environment" and the therapeutic action of psychoanalysis. *Journal of the American Psychoanalytic Association* 24:285–307.

Moore, B.E. 1975. Toward a clarification of the concept of narcissism. *The Psychoanalytic Study of the Child* 30:243–76.

Murray, J.M. 1964. Narcissism and the ego ideal. *Journal of the American Psychoanalytic Association* 12:477–511.

Ornstein, P.H. 1974. Discussion of the paper of Otto F. Kernberg, "Further contributions to the treatment of narcissistic personalities." *International Journal of Psychoanalysis* 55:241–47.

Ortmeyer, D.H. 1987. Idealization in the transference and countertransference. *Contemporary Psychoanalysis* 23:221–29.

Pulver, S. 1970. Narcissism: The term and the concept. *Journal of the American Psychoanalytic Association* 18:319–41.

Reich, A. 1953. Narcissistic object choice in women. *Journal of the American Psychoanalytic Association* 1:22–44.

——. 1960. Pathological forms of self-esteem regulation. *The Psychoanalytic Study of the Child* 15:215–32.

Reich, W. 1933, 1945. *Character-Analysis.* New York: Orgone Institute Press.

Riviere, J. 1936. A contribution to the analysis of the negative therapeutic reaction. *International Journal of Psychoanalysis* 17:304–20.

Rosenfeld, H. 1964. On the psychopathology of narcissism: A clinical approach. *International Journal of Psychoanalysis* 45:332–37.

Rothstein, A. 1980a. *The Narcissistic Pursuit of Perfection.* New York: International Universities Press.

——. 1980b. Psychoanalytic paradigms and their narcissistic investment. *Journal of the American Psychoanalytic Association* 28:385–95.

Salzman, L. 1980. *Treatment of the Obsessive Personality.* New York: Jason Aronson.

Spiegel, R. 1987. Reflections on entitlement and idealization. *Contemporary Psychoanalysis* 23:272–77.

Stern, D.N. 1985. *The Interpersonal World of the Infant.* New York: Basic Books.

Stolorow, R. 1975. Toward a functional definition of narcissism. *International Journal of Psychoanalysis* 56:179–85.

Sullivan, H.S. 1940. *Conceptions of Modern Psychiatry.* New York: Norton.

——. 1953. *The Interpersonal Theory of Psychiatry.* New York: Norton.

——. 1954. *The Psychiatric Interview.* New York: Norton.

——. 1956. *Clinical Studies in Psychiatry.* New York: Norton.

Tauber, E. 1982. Preoccupation with immortality. *Contemporary Psychoanalysis* 18:119–32.

Teicholtz, J.G. 1978. A selective review of the psychoanalytic literature on theoretical conceptualizations of narcissism. *Journal of the American Psychoanalytic Association* 26:831–62.

Tenzer, A. 1987. Grandiosity and its discontents. *Contemporary Psychoanalysis* 23:263–71.

Thompson, C. 1938. Development of awareness of transference in a markedly detached personality. *International Journal of Psychoanalysis* 19:299–309.

——. 1950. *Psychoanalysis: Evolution and Development.* New York: Grove Press.

Winnicott, D.W. 1960, 1965. Ego distortion in terms of true and false self. In *The Maturational Processes and the Facilitating Environment,* pp. 140–52. New York: International Universities Press.

Witenberg, E.G. 1974. Some notes on narcissism. *Contemporary Psychoanalysis* 4:465–68.

Wolf, E.S. 1984. Selfobject relations disorders. In M.R. Zales, ed., *Character Pathology,* pp. 23–38. New York: Brunner/Mazel.

Wolstein, B. 1981. The psychic realism of psychoanalytic inquiry. *Contemporary Psychoanalysis* 17:595–606.

——. 1984. Book review: Psychiatrist of America: The life of Harry Stack Sullivan. *Psychoanalytic Psychology,* 1:165–72.

——. 1986. Transference neuroses and resistance neuroses. *Contemporary Psychoanalysis,* 22:202–17.

——. 1987. Experience, interpretation, self-knowledge. *Contemporary Psychoanalysis,* 23:329–49.

PART II

The Self and Narcissism: Theoretical Perspectives

3

Fromm's Views on Narcissism and the Self

Marco Bacciagaluppi

When I first started working on the subject of this essay I turned to Cooper's chapter on narcissism in vol. 7 of the *American Handbook of Psychiatry,* 2d edition (Cooper 1981). Next to the classical views of Freud and those of recent Freudian writers such as Kohut and Kernberg, Cooper also mentions neo-Freudian authors such as Horney and Sullivan, but Fromm's name is missing. This is a familiar occurrence. As Greenberg and Mitchell (1983) remark, Fromm anticipated certain psychoanalytic concepts by decades but receives little recognition for his contributions. One aim of this paper is, therefore, to establish Fromm's priority on the subject of narcissism and the self.

Fromm, in turn, seems to have paid scant attention to other developments in psychoanalysis. In the index of the complete German edition of his works—the only one in existence to date (Fromm 1980–81)—the names of Kohut and Kernberg do not appear, and Fromm makes only a brief, albeit appreciative, mention of the British school at the end of part one of the *Anatomy of Human Destructiveness* (Fromm 1973). The isolation among different psychoanalytic writers and groups may itself be an expression of narcissism. In this paper I compare some of Fromm's concepts with recent developments in psychoanalysis and in other areas. By establishing connections, I hope this paper may be a contribution toward the overcoming of the "narcissism of minor differences" in our field, to which Werman (1988) has called attention.

Third, I hope this paper may contribute to a wider circulation of Fromm's ideas in the psychoanalytic community. I think it has always been true that Fromm's ideas were more familiar to the general public than to psychoanalysts. This can be confirmed with reference to the Italian situation. When in the early 1960s a group in Milan started introducing neo-Freudian ideas into Italy, they were particularly interested in the therapy of the psychoses, and therefore the authors most often quoted were Sullivan, Fromm-Reichmann, and Arieti. Psychoanalytic groups with a specific interest in Fromm started to appear in Italy only in the 1980s.

The aspects of Fromm's work that are stressed in this paper are his emphasis on the impact of real-life events, his discussion of self-love, his concept of social character, and, among his more clinical contributions, his concept of secret family narcissism.

The Self

As the title of this book implies, the pathology of narcissism is tied up with the pathology of the self, and especially with the regulation of self-esteem. Kohut (1971) writes: "In the narcissistic personality disturbances . . . the principal source of discomfort is thus the result of the psyche's inability to regulate self-esteem" (p. 20). The self, according to Kohut, "is a content of the mental apparatus but is not one of its constituents, i.e., not one of the agencies of the mind" (p. xv).

The self and its pathology are currently most commonly associated with the work of Kohut and his followers, but he was preceded by several other writers. Kohut (1971) himself credits Hartmann with "the conceptual separation of the self from the ego" (p. xiii) and then goes on to quote other authors in the area of American Ego psychology, such as Erikson and Mahler. He does not quote either American neo-Freudians or the British school.

In the chapter already cited above, Cooper (1981) points out that both Sullivan and Horney were using the concept of self before the war. It is also a central concept in the British school, as exemplified by the title of Guntrip's collected papers: *Schizoid Phenomena, Object Relations, and the Self* (1969). Guntrip says that "the primary fact about human beings" is "their experience of themselves as that significant and meaningful 'whole' which we call a 'person' " (p. 10).

As regards Fromm, consider this passage from *Man for Himself* (1947):

> The scars left from the child's defeat in the fight against irrational authority are to be found at the bottom of every neurosis. They form a syndrome the most important features of which are the weakening or paralysis of the person's originality and spontaneity; the *weakening of the self* and the *substitution of a pseudo self* in which the feeling of 'I am' is dulled and replaced by the experience of self as the sum total of others' expectations. (p. 161, italics added)

Here Fromm expresses very clearly a holistic view of personality and anticipates Winnicott's distinction of the true and false self by several years (Winnicott 1960). Horney, as quoted by Cooper (1981), had anticipated it even earlier when writing about the "loss of the 'real me' " (p. 302). In this passage from Fromm, in contrast with Kohut's overly cautious theoretical jargon, there is also a strong sense of real-life events affecting the child's self. Fromm also discusses the loss of a sense of self and its compensation through a "secondary sense of self" in *The Sane Society* (1955:143).

Another convergence between Kohut and Fromm, unacknowledged by Kohut, concerns the productiveness of the self. In *The Restoration of the Self* Kohut (1977) writes of the "creative-productive-active self" (p. 76) and of the self as an "independent center of initiative" (p. 80), yet no mention is made of Fromm's highly relevant discussion of productiveness of thirty years before (Fromm 1947:91–98).

It is interesting to speculate why Kohut does not acknowledge these priorities. In the preface to this book (1977:xix–xxi) he explains that the integration of different viewpoints would be too difficult. In view of his concern for the preservation of the (Freudian) psychoanalytic "group self" (p. 85, footnote), it is possible that another reason for not making an extensive review of the literature was to avoid quoting heretical writers like Horney, Sullivan, and Fromm, who would have been very relevant to, but embarrassing for, the "group self."

Narcissism

The subject of narcissism features prominently in Fromm's writings. He worked on this concept over a span of forty years, from a paper on self-love published in *Psychiatry* in 1939 to his last book, *Greatness and Limitations of Freud's Thought,* originally published in German (1979). His main presentation of the concept is to be found in chapter four of *The Heart of Man* (1964b). It is also discussed at some length in *The Anatomy of Human Destructiveness* (1973) and in a series of unpublished seminars held in Locarno (1974:171–92). In the following discussion, in addition to referring to published and unpublished works by Fromm, I also rely on Rainer Funk's *Erich Fromm: The Courage to Be Human* (1978, 1982), a very useful systematic account of Fromm's thinking.[1]

In Fromm's writings we may distinguish three levels of discussion of narcissism: (1) the theoretical level; (2) the level of social pathology, in which narcissism is considered as a character structure; and (3) the clinical level. Because of the scarcity of clinical contributions in Fromm's published work, I shall have to rely mainly on unpublished material for point 3.

Theoretical Level

In relation to Freud, Fromm takes sharp issue with the idea that love for other and love for oneself are alternatives. In *Man for Himself* (1947:132–36) he writes that, on the contrary, "the attitude toward others and toward ourselves, far from being contradictory, are basically *conjunctive.*" "Love of other and love of ourselves are not alternatives." "*Love,* in principle, *is indivisible.*" "*Selfishness and self-love, far from being identical, are actually opposites.* The selfish person does not love himself too much but too little; in fact he hates himself." "*It is true* [as Freud says] *that selfish persons are incapable of loving others, but they are not capable of loving themselves either*" (all italics in the original).

These conceptual clarifications are important objections to the retention of the term *narcissism,* which implies, both in the broader cultural tradition and in the narrower context of Freudian psychoanalysis, that self-concern is equivalent to self-love. Kernberg (1975) also agrees that the self-love of the narcissist is only apparent.

On the other hand, Fromm never seems to have disputed the fact of a primary self-centeredness of the infant. In chapter 4 of *The Heart of Man* (1964b:65) he begins his description of narcissism with the primary narcissism of the newborn infant and says: "The infant is not yet related to the outside world." Fromm only started questioning this assumption in a footnote to *The Anatomy of Human Destructiveness* (1973:227). In retaining the concept of primary narcissism, Fromm follows the tradition of Freud and of Freudian authors such as Kohut and Kernberg who have addressed the same issue more recently. Kohut (1971:25), for instance, states very clearly that the narcissistic structures he describes (the grandiose self and the idealized parent) are means by which "the child replaces the previous perfection."

This tradition had already been challenged by some authors of the British school, for instance, by Fairbairn, who claimed that the infant is "object-seeking" from birth. This critique on the part of British authors is reviewed by Bowlby in the appendix to *Attachment* (1969:371–75). Guntrip (1969) is another British author who criticizes the concept of narcissism. He says of the schizoid that "his love-objects are all inside him . . . so that his libidinal attachments appear to be to himself." "Narcissism is a disguised internalized object-relation" (p. 42). More recently, Stern (1985) has provided empirical evidence that there is no such thing as a normal autistic or symbiotic phase, thus giving support to these earlier critiques.

In Fromm's main presentation of narcissism—in chapter 4 of *The Heart of Man* (1964b)—he distinguishes between two forms of narcissism, one *benign*, the other *malignant*. He writes: "In the benign form, the object of narcissism is the result of a person's effort" (p. 77). But then he adds: "The very fact that the work itself makes it necessary to be related to reality constantly curbs the narcissism and keeps it within bounds." Thus, beneath the distinction between two forms of narcissism, the concept of primary narcissism still lurks.

Fromm was misled by Freudian theoretical residues in his own thinking. Although he had already transcended the Freudian position by his concept of self-love, he never fully worked out the consequences. The Freudian fallacy lies in the idea that man at birth is unrelated. Within Bowlby's ethological framework, we may consider that there was survival value in the prehistorical environment for babies to be related from birth and that such a trait would therefore have been selected in the course of evolution. Stern (1985) has provided the empirical evidence for primary relatedness. A primary state of unrelatedness is only pathological, due either to inborn defects or to unnatural environmental circumstances—ranging from an unresponsive mother to the extreme case of feral children. The normal situation is a loving relationship with the mother, leading to self-love and love for others in the child.

Although Fromm distinguished narcissism from self-love, he still thought that primary narcissism was a normal phase. He did not take the further step of viewing narcissism as always pathological. Instead, he retained the term *narcissism*, accompanied by the adjective *benign*, to designate self-love. It seems to be more appropriate to do away with both the concept of "primary narcissism" and its specification of "benign narcissism" and to distinguish between the capacity for love toward self and others—the normal situation—and narcissism—always a pathological development, however widespread.

A further clarification concerns cognitive development. According to Hoffman (quoted by Friedman 1985:515), a child in the second year of life may be "egocentric" (in the Piagetian sense) at a cognitive level and yet experience empathy for the distress of others. More primitive manifestations of empathy are even present at birth.

The Character Structure

According to Fromm, narcissism is one of the nonproductive orientations in the process of socialization, i.e., one of the nonproductive forms of interpersonal relatedness. As Funk (1978) points out, although Fromm repeatedly elaborated on these concepts in all his work, these orientations consistently range between two extremes: symbiosis and withdrawal (see table 3.1).

Narcissism lies at one extreme of the range and is characterized by the greatest degree of withdrawal. For the narcissistic person, "only he himself and what pertains to him has significance, while the rest of the world is more or less weightless" (Fromm 1973:228). "The narcissistic person achieves a sense of security in his own entirely subjective conviction of his perfection. When others wound his narcissism . . . a narcissistic person usually reacts with intense anger or rage."

The narcissistic orientation is also found at the level of groups. Fromm discusses group narcissism, e.g., in *The Anatomy of Human Destructiveness* (1973:230–31). He points out that in a group this orientation is shared; it furthers the cohesion of the group, makes manipulation easier, and provides substitutive gratification. Wounds to group narcissism are also reacted to with rage and are important sources of violent conflicts between groups.

Although Freud's characterology is one of the sources of Fromm's, for which Fromm repeatedly gives Freud credit, Funk (1978:307) states that "how Fromm arrived at these orientations is not an easy question to answer. He simply deduced them from all the conceivable possibilities of a nonproductive relation to the world." At this level, therefore, Fromm's primary source is not clinical, and the main function of his characterology is as a conceptual tool in social psychology.

This conceptual tool was already clearly defined in a paper written in 1932 and reprinted in 1970 in *The Crisis of Psychoanalysis*, where Fromm

TABLE 3.1 *Relationship of the Orientations in the Process of Assimilation and Socialization*

Orientations	In Assimilation Process	In Socialization Process	
Nonproductive	Receptive	Masochism	Symbiosis (authoritarian)
	Exploitative	Oral (Sadism)	Symbiosis (authoritarian)
	Hoarding	Anal (Sadism)	Symbiosis (authoritarian)
	Marketing	Indifference	Withdrawal
	Necrophilic Destructive	Necrophilic Destructiveness (narcissism)	Withdrawal
Productive	Working	Loving, reasoning	

SOURCE: Reprinted with permission; from R. Funk, *Erich Fromm: The Courage to Be Human* (New York: Continuum, 1982), p. 47.

writes: "The task of social psychology is to explain the shared, socially relevant psychic attitudes and ideologies—and their unconscious roots in particular—in terms of the influence of economic conditions on libido strivings." After his rejection of the libido theory, Fromm referred to the shared psychic attitudes as the "social character" (1941).

One example of this use of characterology is Fromm's Mexican study (Fromm and Maccoby 1970). In that study, three main character types were found, and each was related to a sociohistorical structure. The nonproductive–receptive character was related to the feudal society that both preceded and followed the Spanish conquest. The productive–hoarding character was considered typical of the peasant mode of production when peasants possess their own land. The productive variants of the exploitative character type "are the modern entrepreneurs."

As regards the narcissistic character, Fromm repeatedly stressed its widespread occurrence in our own society, for example, in the organization man (1964a) or among political leaders (1964b). This subject has been discussed more recently by Christopher Lasch (1979). Even more recently, attempts have made to verify empirically the occurrence of narcissistic traits in the population (Richman and Flaherty 1988). Fromm's hypothesis of a prevalence of the narcissistic character structure in our society (although its connection with Fromm is often not acknowledged) thus seems to be shared and may be subject to verification.

As regards group narcissism, Fromm considers it the result of a transformation of individual narcissism (1964b). This subject has been viewed in very different terms in more recent discussions. Group narcissism has been considered the result of *cultural revolution*. Boyd and Richerson (1985), for example, regard ethnocentrism as an example of cultural group selection. Group narcissism may even have its roots in *biological evolution*. According to Tinbergen (1981) it originated in group territorialism.

Clinical Level

Fromm's description of the narcissistic character orientation, reported above, coincides with certain items of the DSM III-R description of the narcissistic personality disorder, namely (1), (3), and (8) (see table 3.2), and with one major feature of Kernberg's account ("I do not need anybody else": 1975:231).

In what follows, further contributions of Fromm's are reported, drawn from unpublished sources.

In a series of unpublished seminars held in Locarno, Switzerland, which are closer to the clinical level (1974), Fromm adds: "a narcissistic person needs and lives on the feeding of his narcissism" (p. 175). This corresponds to item (7) of the DSM III-R criteria. Fromm (1974) also describes the tendency to follow an overidealized leader, which corresponds to item E3 of DSM III (this item is no longer present in DSM III-R). Finally, when Fromm (1974) says "the narcissistic person is a terribly insecure person" (p. 181), his description shares another feature with Kernberg's (1975). We may conclude that, at a clinical level, Fromm's description of the narcissistic personality corresponds fairly closely to that prevailing in the literature.

In his unpublished Locarno seminars, Fromm also stresses the general relevance of narcissism: "Narcissism is a crucial problem of human development" (1974:176) and it is "a life work to overcome one's narcissism" (1974:177). And in these seminars, Fromm also discusses one form of group narcissism that is of clinical relevance, namely, *family narcissism:* "There is a secret narcissism of families. Think of these families where the mother comes from . . . a step up the social ladder and will feel forever that her family is better than that of the husband, or vice versa" (1974:192).

In an unpublished lecture given in New York on "The Causes for the Patient's Change in Analytic Treatment" (1964a, designated in the Fromm Archives as u1964c), Fromm makes a distinction between *benign* and *malignant neuroses.* This is not a central concept in Fromm's writings, but it is useful both clinically and in order to establish connections with other authors.

TABLE 3.2 *Diagnostic Criteria for 301.81 Narcissistic Personality Disorder*

A pervasive pattern of grandiosity (in fantasy or behavior), lack of empathy, and hypersensitivity to the evaluation of others, beginning by early adulthood and present in a variety of contexts, as indicated by at least *five* of the following:

1. reacts to criticism with feelings of rage, shame, or humiliation (even if not expressed)
2. is interpersonnally exploitative: takes advantage of others to achieve his or her own ends
3. has a grandiose sense of self-importance, e.g., exaggerates achievements and talents, expects to be noticed as "special" without apprpriate achievement
4. believes that his or her problems are unique and can be understood only by other special people
5. is preoccupied with fantasies of unlimited success, power, brilliance, beauty, or ideal love
6. has a sense of entitlement: unreasonable expectation of especially favorable treatment, e.g., assumes that he or she does not have to wait in line when others must do so
7. requires contant attention and admiration, e.g., keeps fishing for compliments
8. lack of empathy: inability to recognize and experience how others feel, e.g., annoyance and surprise when a friend who is seriously ill cancels a date
9. is preoccupied with feelings of envy

SOURCE: Reprinted, with permission, from American Psychiatric Association, DSM III-R (1987).

By benign neurosis Fromm means the neurosis of personalities who have reached the genital level, whose neurosis is mainly due to traumata, and whose prognosis is therefore more favorable. In this he says he agrees with Freud's final views set forth in *Analysis Terminable and Interminable.* In these patients the nucleus of the character structure is intact. In the malignant neuroses the nucleus of the character structure is damaged. It is characterized by "malignant passions" such as (1) destructiveness, (2) narcissism, and (3) incestuous fixation. "Here the job of cure would be to change the energy charge within the nuclear structure" (p. 23).

Fromm seems to be referring to the whole area between neurosis and psychosis, characterized (in terms of Bowlby's attachment theory) by attachment and multiple binds to bad and/or weak objects and requiring a shift in attachment (what Freudians call the cathexis) onto alternative objects. Here, narcissism converges with other "malignant passions" into the wider category of malignant neuroses.

In using this single category for all the intermediate conditions between the neuroses and the psychoses, Fromm may be likened to Guntrip and Kernberg. Guntrip (1969) also considers only one category, that of the "schizoid personality," which includes various features, among which are narcissism and a basic fixation to the womb. Likewise, Kernberg also considers only one category, that of the borderline conditions, within which the narcissistic personality represents a subgroup (Kernberg 1975). The schizoid personality, according to Kernberg, also belongs to the borderline group. Kohut, instead, regards the narcissistic personality and the borderline personality as distinct groups, the latter lying nearer to the psychoses, while he views the schizoid personality as a subgroup of the borderline conditions (1971).

Kohut and Kernberg also differ in the way they conceptualize these entities. According to Kohut (1971), psychoses are characterized by the fragmentation of self and object, borderline conditions by fragile self and object images, and the narcissistic personality by stable narcissistic structures (the grandiose self and the idealized object). According to Kernberg (1975), psychoses are characterized by the fusion of self and object. In borderline conditions, the differentiation of self-images from object images is attained, but not the integration of good and bad aspects. Splitting is the essential defensive operation of the borderline personality organization. Finally, the narcissistic personality is characterized by an integrated grandiose self.

DSM III-R is content with merely listing the schizoid, the narcissistic, and the borderline personalities side by side, without attempting any hierarchical organization. Table 3.3 compares Fromm's categorization with the others I have discussed.

We may conclude that the concept of malignant neurosis makes it possible to establish connections between Fromm and the other authors who have studied severe nonpsychotic pathology.

Case Material

I briefly present some clinical material in which narcissistic traits are not traced back to "primary narcissism" but in which use is made, instead, of Fromm's notion of "secret family narcissism."

TABLE 3.3 *Intermediate Conditions Between Neuroses and Psychoses*

Fromm	Guntrip	Kohut	Kernberg	DSM III-R
malignant neuroses	Schizoid personality	Narcissistic personality Borderline personality	Borderline personality of which the narcissistic personality is a subgroup	The Sschizoid (301.22), narcissistic, (301.81) and border-line (301.83) person-alities are listed side by side

This male patient did not present any specific symptoms. His work situation was stagnant, and he had spells of apathy. Traffic delays would make him furious. He had masturbatory fantasies with a girlfriend of the past who resembled his mother. He had never succeeded in establishing a satisfactory long-term heterosexual relationship.

His father was authoritarian and sadistic. The mother was a submissive housewife. In his preschool years the mother kept the patient close to her and involved him in her practical activities. When school started, a younger brother was born and the patient passed under his father's control. Although the patient hated his father's authoritarian ways, he appreciated his intellectual interests and identified with them.

One remarkable feature of this therapy was that for a long time not the slightest mention was made of the younger brother. The matter only started to surface in the third year of analysis. The patient mentioned being disappointed when the mother failed to appreciate his adult interests. He remembered his preschool years as an "earthly paradise." He described himself in that period as a "little prince." In particular, he used to assert his will by saying in a threatening tone: "You know how nervous I am." To that he associated his maternal grandfather, who was even more tyrannical than the patient's father. He expected complete submission from his daughter and even required her to peel his grapes for him. The patient then added that the mother used to say he was like his grandfather. I pointed out that an archaic paternal model had come to the surface, mediated by the mother, and existing prior to the patient's identification with his father.

He later said that, in his relationship with a woman, he used to "lose himself" in the woman, he felt the woman was an extension of himself. Then he brought a dream in which he masturbated the girlfriend of the past, and she had a few pubic hairs. He associated hearing his mother say that when she got married she was "a little girl." I told him

> he had been involved in his mother's incestuous fantasies with her own father, but this implied that she saw him as someone else and did not appreciate him for what he really was.

The patient's behavior in his first five years of life could certainly be described as "narcissistic," the birth of the brother as a "narcissistic wound," and his reaction, persisting into adult life, as "narcissistic rage." However, instead of using the concept of primary narcissism, I suggest the following interpretation.

When the patient was born, the mother did not recognize his potential true self and help its development. Instead, she had a distorted view of the patient as her own father and offered him ready-made models of himself as the tyrannical grandfather and herself in an abject ancillary position, ready to obey every whim of his, including presumably sexual ones. Instead of helping him to develop his true self, she offered the patient a drugged surrogate (this patient at one time took amphetamines), which gave rise to a narcissistic false self. It was this false self that was disappointed by the brother's birth. When later the mother was not interested in the patient's more autonomous identification with his father, we may presume that the disappointment resided in the true self.

This interpretation dispenses with the concept of primary narcissism but takes into account early traumata, Bowlby's concepts of parent–child inversion and models of self and others, and family dynamics spanning three generations, incorporating Fromm's concept of "secret family narcissism." Also, Kernberg, despite his predominantly Freudian orientation, admits the possibility of this sort of dynamic when he writes of the mother's "narcissistic use of the child which made him 'special' " (1975:235).

From the cultural point of view, I believe this kind of situation stems from the family structure of the peasant adaptation, in which children are kept bound to the family (Bacciagaluppi 1984).

As regards the inflated self-concept, which is a hallmark of narcissism, it is generally regarded either as the residue of a hypothesized normal phase (e.g., by Kohut) or as a compensation for dependence (e.g., by Guntrip). My own clinical experience, as in the case reported here, suggests a more interpersonal origin of the inflated self-concept. I find it is generally due to a distorted image that the parent has of the child and that the child is forced to assimilate. This image is often a compensation for real love, or, more accurately, for love of the child's real self. It originally comes from outside: the child is loved because he or she is viewed as someone else—an idealized object of the parent. The child is thus impelled to develop a false self, which not merely is a necessary means for survival but also has gratifying aspects.

Fromm's concept of "secret family narcissism" is reflected in more recent interpersonal views such as Mitchell's (1988) notion of the "parental induction" of narcissistic problems. Mitchell writes: "Such a parent insists on specific overvaluations of the child or herself or both. These illusions have become addictive for the parent, and they become a dominant feature in the possibilities for relatedness which such a parent offers the child" (p. 197). This interpersonal aspect may even be detected in the classical myth. When Narcissus looks into the water, two persons are actually present. The water may be viewed as the symbiotic mother, reflecting back an idealized and gratifying image and thereby keeping the child bound to a lifeless situation.

Treatment

In his unpublished New York lecture, Fromm (1964a) writes that, for these more severe cases, "the problem of cure lies in the following: that the patient confronts the irrational archaic part of his personality with his own sane, adult, normal part; that this very confrontation creates conflict, and that this conflict activates . . . a striving for health" (p. 25). According to Fromm, this confrontation does not take place in Freudian analysis, in which the patient is artificially infantilized and becomes a child.

On the one hand, Fromm writes that "one of the essential conditions to analyze is that the analyst experiences in himself what the patient is talking about" (p. 39) and that "there is no capacity to be judgmental or to be moralistic . . . once one experiences this as one's own" (p. 40).

On the other hand, he speaks of the confrontation with "the child and the irrational person with all sorts of crazy fantasies" (p. 28). Here he sounds, not sympathetic toward the child in the patient but, on the contrary, rather disapproving.

As Guntrip writes in the introduction to his collected papers (1969:10), the schizoid problem "involves a fundamentally different point of view from that of the moral approach. Instead of assuming an individual strong enough to be able to respond to the appeal of moral values and capable of accepting training and education of character . . . the great problem is that *the foundations of an adequate 'self' were prevented from growing in infancy*" (italics added).

Fromm himself takes the same position in the passage on the self quoted here from *Man for Himself.* If Fromm shows some contradiction in his view of severe pathology, it may stem from the residue of Freudian theory in his thinking. Of the three "malignant passions," he no longer subscribes to the instinctual source of destructive aggressiveness, but he does retain belief in primary narcissism and in a natural tendency to regress to symbiosis with the mother (Funk 1978:52). These are certainly widespread phenomena, but they do not belong to the nature of humanity in the environment of evolutionary adaptedness. These Freudian residues may unwittingly have drawn Fromm back into Freud's Augustinian view of the child as a small sinner, which Fromm had previously so vigorously challenged.

The most suitable approach for severe pathology, in my view, is best summed up by a quotation from Guntrip toward the end of Bowlby's *The Making and Breaking of Affectional Bonds* (1979:155): "[the therapist's job] is, as I see it, the provision of a reliable and understanding human relationship of a kind that makes contact with the deeply repressed traumatized child."

Fromm's confrontational and direct approach seems better suited to the "benign neuroses." As I remarked elsewhere (Bacciagaluppi 1989), his approach is reminiscent of certain techniques of short-term therapy. Fromm himself, at the end of his New York lecture (1964a), advocates the use of short-term therapy for the "benign neuroses" (p. 43).

In the treatment of more severe pathology, Fromm's active and committed approach may need to be integrated at a theoretical level with a recognition of the patient's split-off core and, at a technical level, with the use of "participation in"—something that has been conceptualized only in recent years (Bacciagaluppi 1989).

1. At the theoretical level, although Fromm had partly overcome the Freudian position by distinguishing narcissism from self-love, he still retained the concept of primary narcissism and was thus misled in his own thinking by a residue of Freudian theory. I think that it is crucial to distinguish between the capacity for love toward self and others—the normal situation—and narcissism—always a pathological development. Fromm's concept of self-love can be viewed as an important contribution to an alternative framework for the psychoanalytic understanding of narcissism.
2. At the level of social psychology, Fromm's concept of the social character, determined by economic conditions, is a very useful tool for empirical research. The prevalence of the narcissistic character structure in our society is a hypothesis that awaits confirmation.

3. Finally, at the clinical level, Fromm's concept of secret family narcissism is a central contribution, one that converges with some of the most advanced thinking of the Interpersonal–Cultural school.

Note

1. I wish to express grateful thanks to Dr. Rainer Funk, Fromm's literary executor, for valuable advice and for placing at my disposal essential material from the Fromm Archives in Tübingen. I am also indebted to Dr. Mariano Enderle for sending further relevant material from the United States.

References

American Psychiatric Association. 1987. *Diagnostic and Statistical Manual of Mental Disorders,* 3d ed., rev. (DSM III–R). Washington, D.C.: American Psychiatric Association.

Bacciagaluppi, M. 1984. Some remarks on the Oedipus complex from an ethological point of view. *Journal of the American Academy of Psychoanalysis* 12:471–90.

——. 1989. Erich Fromm's views on psychoanalytic "technique." *Contemporary Psychoanalysis* 25: 226–44.

Bowlby, J. 1969. *Attachment and Loss: vol. 1, Attachment.* New York: Basic Books.

——. 1979. *The Making and Breaking of Affectional Bonds.* London: Tavistock.

Boyd, R. and J.R. Richerson. 1985. *Culture and the Evolutionary Process.* Chicago: University of Chicago Press.

Cooper, A.M. 1981. Narcissism. In S. Arieti and H.K. Brody, eds., *American Handbook of Psychiatry,* 2d ed., vol. 7. New York: Basic Books.

Friedman, M. 1985. Toward a reconceptualization of guilt. *Contemporary Psychoanalysis* 21: 501–47.

Fromm, E. 1939. Selfishness and self-love. *Psychiatry* 2: 507–23.

——. 1944. *Escape from Freedom.* New York: Farrar & Rinehart.

——. 1947. *Man for Himself: An Inquiry into the Psychology of Ethics.* New York: Rinehart.

Fromm, E. 1941. *Escape from Freedom,* New York: Rinehart.

——. 1955. *The Sane Society.* New York: Rinehart & Winston.

——. 1964a. The causes for the patient's change in analytic treatment. Unpublished lecture given in New York. Tübingen: Erich Fromm Archives.

——. 1964b. *The Heart of Man: Its Genius for Good and Evil.* New York: Harper & Row.

——. 1970. *The Crisis of Psychoanalysis: Essays on Freud, Marx and Social Psychology.* New York: Rinehart & Winston.

——. 1973. *The Anatomy of Human Destructiveness.* New York: Holt, Rinehart & Winston.

——. 1974. Ten unpublished seminars held in Locarno, Switzerland. Tübingen: Erich Fromm Archives.

——. 1979. *Sigmund Freud's Psychoanalyse—Grosse und Grenzen.* Stuttgart: Deutsche Verlags-Anstalt, 1979. American ed.: *Greatness and Limitations of Freud's Thought.* New York: Harper & Row, 1980.

——. 1980–81. Gesamtausgabe, vol. 1–10, R. Funk, ed. Stuttgart: Deutsche Verlags-Anstalt.

Fromm, E. and M. Maccoby. 1970. *Social Character in a Mexican Village.* Englewood Cliffs, N.J.: Prentice Hall.

Funk, R. 1978. *Mut zum menschen: Erich Fromm's denken und werk, seine humanistische religion und ethik.* Stuttgart: Deutsche Verlags-Anstalt. American ed.: *Erich Fromm: The Courage to Be Human.* New York: Continuum, 1982.

Greenberg, J.R. and S.A. Mitchell. 1983. *Object Relations in Psychoanalytic Theory.* Cambridge, Mass.: Harvard University Press.

Guntrip, H. 1969. *Schizoid Phenomena, Object Relations and the Self.* New York: International Universities Press.

Kernberg, O. 1975. *Borderline Conditions and Pathological Narcissism.* New York: Jason Aronson.

Kohut, H. 1971. *The Analysis of the Self.* New York: International Universities Press.

——. 1977. *The Restoration of the Self.* New York: International Universities Press.

Lasch, C. 1979. *The Culture of Narcissism: American Life in an Age of Diminishing Expectations.* New York: Norton.

Mitchell, S.A. 1988. *Relational Concepts in Psychoanalysis: An Integration.* Cambridge, Mass.: Harvard University.

Richman, J.A. and J.A. Flaherty. 1988. "Tragic man" and "tragic woman": Gender differences in narcissistic styles. *Psychiatry* 51:368–77.

Stern, D.N. 1985. *The Interpersonal World of the Infant. A View from Psychoanalysis and Developmental Psychology.* New York: Basic Books.

Tinbergen, N. 1981. On the history of war. In L. Valzelli and L. Morgese, eds., *Aggression and Violence: A Psychobiological and Clinical Approach.* Saint Vincent, Italy: Edizioni Saint Vincent.

Werman, D.S. 1988. Freud's "Narcissism of minor differences": A review and reassessment. *Journal of the American Academy of Psychoanalysis* 16:451–59.

Winnicott, D.W. 1960, 1965. Ego distortion in terms of true and false self. In *The Maturational Processes and the Facilitating Environment.* London: Hogarth.

4

The Lost Uniqueness of Kohut's Self Psychology: An Instance of Narcissism

Benjamin Wolstein

The problem of narcissism is the problem of the self. Traditionally, the notion of the self received short shrift in the therapeutic corpus of Freud and his followers. In classical diagnostic metapsychology, the narcissistic neuroses were, in fact, defined as being unpsychoanalyzable across the board, primarily because they were believed incapable of establishing a clinical transference. In other words, the narcissistic neuroses were actually treated as nothing but the clinical resistance neuroses, as distinct from the transference neuroses, only raised from direct psychoanalytic inquiry to the level of diagnostic metapsychology, and named after the Narcissus myth of ancient Greek culture. Resistances, arising at the level of clinical psychoanalysis, were also considered unpsychoanalyzable in the traditional Freudian corpus. They could not be interpreted; they had, instead, to be overcome or conquered (Wolstein 1986, 1987), for they got in the way of Freud's interpretive metapsychology—which, in his view, was the main therapeutic event. In short, the narcissism of diagnostic metapsychology, not unlike resistance in therapeutic psychology, proved refractory to the traditional psychoanalyst's interpretive method. This category of patients was, therefore, long excluded from the domain of clinical psychoanalytic inquiry.

Only after such clinical researchers as Reich (1933), Anna Freud (1936), Hartmann (1939), Sullivan (1940), Thompson (1950), Fairbairn (1952), and Klein (1964) developed new empirical methods of relating to resistance in its various forms, especially during the 1930s, could these patients be welcomed into psychoanalytic therapy, even though they were still diagnosed as narcissistic. They were considered treatable by direct relational methods now, precisely because their armor, defense mechanisms, or security operations could be explored and made conscious in their character, ego and object, or interpersonal relations, respectively. That is to say, in their relations to the other, as distinct from the self. All resistance, it became increasingly clear, was designed to defend against the other, so the patients termed resistive or narcissist were concerned, not with cultivating the subjective sense of a unique self, but with projecting whatever reflection they would create of themselves in the minds of others. That, as a result, was where they generally found themselves, out of their own minds. They may, therefore, be described as being overly adapted or consensual, overly egoic, objectified, or interpersonalized. For in psychic transit, I am suggesting, they lost track of the first-hand experience of their own selves and topped it off with a strong aversion to the uniqueness of their own individuality.

Against the background of this history I place my discussion of Kohut's Self psychology. First, I posit a brief historical note to point to the similarity I see between Kohut's view of the self in Self psychology and Sullivan's view of the self in Interpersonal Relations. Considerations of metapsychology aside, they both refer to the same sector of the psyche in analysis. The self as object is the self of reflected appraisal: the self that is seen always from the standpoint of its external surroundings, not from the standpoint of its internal resources; always as done behavior from without, not as experience had from within.

These views are both one-sided, however. They empty the self of direct personal experiences, of its subjective side, by means of deconstructing the statements made about its uniquely individual psychic resources, as though the language of psychoanalysis is about language itself rather than some subject matter other than language—namely, the life experience of feeling, thought, and imagination undergone in clinical psychoanalytic inquiry. In a parallel vein, Ferenczi and Rank were, by 1923, already opposing the impersonal didactic analysis for psychoanalysts in training in favor of a personal therapeutic analysis. The first they found interpretive in the extreme, the second experiential in the first person—from which it follows for psychoanalytic psychology: you cannot tell the difference between the subjective and the objective sides of the self, if you have not, so to speak, been there and back yourself.

To return to Kohut: among his major works are *The Analysis of the Self* (1971), then *The Restoration of the Self* (1977), and finally, the text from which all quotations from his work are taken in this chapter, *How Does Psychoanalysis Cure?* (1984). These writings, in my view, represent a progressive effort to reconstruct the conceptual and clinical terms of traditional psychoanalysis so as to make credible the treatment of patients he actually carried out, though they were once placed beyond the range of any possible psychoanalytic treatment. He did that, to my best knowledge, without openly suggesting that Freud's therapeutic view of the narcissistic—or, as termed above, resistance—neuroses was no longer tenable, and then making a clear and clean break with classical Freudianism on that point. For he still believed the basic technique of psychoanalysis was nothing more, or less, than the interpretation of transference—even though he, in fact, consistently joined the resistance of his patients with an empathic, supportive confirming stance as selfobject, not unlike Alexander and French's (1946) proposal to join their transferences toward a corrective emotional experience. It is of more than passing interest that the two procedures are often closely compared. Kohut, in his last work, was keenly aware of this, recognized its unfortunate implications for his own innovative effort, but failed, in my view, to disentangle his joining with the resistances of patients from Alexander's joining with their transferences. I return to this point below.

What follows is a consideration of why Kohut lost track of the uniqueness of the self—both clinically in that he took an empathic, supportive stance as selfobject with patients regardless of their diversity and conceptually in that he did not allow for bringing that objective stance into balance with its subjective origins in the uniqueness of each individual therapist as well. As a result he never found the uniqueness of the self, his Self psychology blurred its claim to uniqueness, and his combined perspective and procedure became an instance of the very syndrome he sought to cure. There is something circular in the coordination of theory and practice—not limited, I suspect, to Kohut alone—that deserves further attention and inquiry. But the generality of that topic would take us far beyond the specific theme of this chapter.

Kohut's views of psychoanalysis set forth in his final volume hold no surprises for those readers who have followed the statements of his evolving ideas in his two previous major efforts. Most important of all, of course, is the theoretical centrality he continues to confer on the outer social and interpersonal side of the self, what he terms the selfobject, as both the real and internalized, and the practical deemphasis on the inner psychic and individual side, the selfsubject in his term, as both imagined and externalized. Difficult though this may be to comprehend about his recently announced innovation in contemporary psychoanalysis, it is, nonetheless, still true that the psychic self as a dynamic point of origin, or source of its own uniqueness, still fails to receive the attention it deserves in his work or, of course, in general psychoanalytic inquiry. So his version of Self psychology proves, in the end, to be insupportably one-sided. It provides for no more than a truncated psychology of the self, lacking as it does a point of dialectical tension for psychic movement toward both connectedness and separateness from within. Curiously enough, not unlike Hartmann's (1939) Ego psychology and Sullivan's (1940) Interpersonal Relations of the late 1930s, this Self psychology of the 1970s unfortunately lacks a developed perspective of inner experience on adaptation or consensual validation. So this Chicago school of Self psychology may be said to lack the dimension of uniqueness in two senses: for the individual experience of the self and for the overall domain of psychoanalysis.

But its lost uniqueness, difficult though that may be to realize, is not the most troubling thing about the conceptual and clinical scheme Kohut proposes to the psychoanalytic community for daily use in therapeutic inquiry. The core of it lies not so much in its limited reference to the unique dimensions of the psychoanalytic self as, surprisingly enough, in its limited response to the unique situation in contemporary psychoanalysis. He did, of course, attempt to articulate a notion of the self that, let it be emphasized at the outset, has no antecedents in traditional or mainstream psychoanalysis, and that is his most outstanding strength. One certainly looks in vain for any substantial consideration—barely a passing mention, if that—in Freud or the Ego psychologists. Among those who pioneered beyond the mainstream, Sullivan and the Interpersonalists not only deprived the interpersonal self of uniqueness and individuality but also conceived it as made up of reflected appraisals. During their tenure as the major spokesperson for psychoanalysis, one must look elsewhere for full statements of the psychology of the self: in American philosophical psychology, to, for example, James above all, and later, to Mead and Dewey. Yet Kohut, belatedly, thought he could introduce Self psychology into psychoanalysis without a critical overhauling of the empirical and systematic foundations of that inherited clinical inquiry. Instead, he sought arbitrarily to carve up the multidimensional phenomenon of the self and simply pass over such of its aspects as would not fit into the established conceptions of psychoanalytic inquiry, and that is his most profound shortcoming.

The theme of lost uniqueness takes on added and unanticipated dimensions. The unique individuality of patients, as already noted, is not a matter for Kohut's palpable concern, empirical or interpretive. Not only is the immediacy of direct clinical interaction hardly noticed, but the pluralism of interpretive myth and metaphor is fully ignored. Nor are we told what happens to those of his patients who may follow an interpretive perspective about their own and their psychoanalyst's experience quite different from his special type of Self psychology ambiguously linked to the instinctual–libidinal metaphors of Classical metapsychology. The question is how the "Self psychologically informed" (p. 107) psychoanalyst responds to patients who may be quite otherwise informed. Are they beyond the analysts purview? All the recommended empathy, understanding, and compassion inexplicably fall short of modifying the unidirectional slant of one's interpretive outlook during actual clinical inquiry.

There is a second sense in which his Self psychology manifests its lost uniqueness. Less obvious than the loss of uniqueness of the individual self, perhaps, is the ambiguous uniqueness of self psychology as a whole in relation to current developments in psychoanalytic inquiry. It is less obvious, I believe, mainly because Kohut and his students have devoted such enormous energies to establishing the public impression that self psychology represents a new departure from traditional psychoanalysis, when, in the crunch, even he would not say it was—nor could it be, committed as they all are to putting a new face on old notions. Thus, "the interpretive approach . . . (is) the *ultima ratio* of the analyst" (p. 74), and "self psychology relies on the same tools as traditional analysis" (p. 75). When, in addition, he becomes with patients the empathic sustaining selfobject above all, he sinks into a mire of internal contradictions of feeling and thought from which he does not extricate himself. I discuss them briefly next.

Though aspiring to be a new school of Self psychology, he comes down foursquare on the side of the traditional "basic psychoanalytic technique" (p. 107 and foreword). That means, of course, the interpretation of transference—"the primary analytic tool of therapy" (p. 75) and the archetectonic of his metapsychology for doing it. But is interpretation, alone, the critical mutative factor in psychoanalytic therapy? Since 1915–1917, when the basic technique was first laid out, have we learned nothing beyond interpretation, nothing about the empirics of resistance and anxiety or the psychic center of the self, not to mention transference? But these are not his questions. He would, instead, squeeze a new Self psychology into the old technique, the long-established interpretation of transference with its traditional myth and metaphor. No further does he go on the procedural level of technique, no closer to the immediacy of directly felt experience, holding firm, instead, to the basic technique established in Id psychology and elaborated in Ego psychology.

The glimmerings of change that first appear at the order of interpretation soon fade away. Though Kohut struggles in his last book, unlike his two previous ones, to free himself from the singularity of Freud's instinctual–libidinal metaphor, his struggle is, in my judgment, finally unavailing of his goal. The best he offers, in the end, is "the self psychologically informed" psychoanalyst who interprets transference only, who excludes all other exploratory interests from the "basic psychoanalytic technique," and who follows a relatively unmodified classical point of view. Toward this end, he also lops off the immediate and private aspects of the psychic self that extend beyond that procrustean bed of clinical theory and practice he prefers. Therefore, he finally concludes, psychoanalysts should continue doing what they have always done, except that he would urge them to become "self psychologically informed" according to his lights. But not in a clear and consistent way: he cautions against any selfic activity that interferes with the thought and practice of the "basic psychoanalytic technique."

He does not, in sum, dedicate his perspective on Self psychology to forming and formulating a rounded psychology of the self, adequate for the empirical, systematic, and interpretive requirements of contemporary psychoanalytic inquiry. Hesitating to push very firmly against the constrictive pressures of his inherited tradition, he cannot discover what lies beyond it. Nor, as a result, can he envision the merits of a pluralistic over a monistic outlook on the perspectives of interpretation. So he is forced into many unfinished and inherently contradictory positions about the nature of his psychoanalytic participation with patients. What follows is a discussion of some selected topics from which I derive these conclusions.

I

A most striking instance of this egregious and unresolved difficulty in Kohut's thinking about the basic psychoanalytic technique is his description of the psychoanalyst's participation with a patient as an empathic confirming selfobject. It does not suffice for him to say quite simply and directly, as others do in other schools of thought, that psychoanalysts should be empathic, understanding, and compassionate toward the psychic sufferings of patients or, lacking such qualities, to assume them as their adopted "analytic attitude" (p. 80). Though the claim he stakes out for the value of empathy is rather large, even suggesting some monopolistic interest, empathy is not enough for him. Surprisingly, he also describes the psychoanalyst as a confirming selfobject, or a sustaining selfobject. Consider, now, the difficult position he puts his Self psychology into by pointing the psychoanalyst's activity toward becoming the patient's object. That is, I infer, in contradistinction to remaining a subject with the patient as well. The self whose object the psychoanalyst is urged to become belongs, of course, to the patient. The psychoanalyst, now become object, is then urged to participate in two very specific yet conflictual ways, as both empathic and confirming or sustaining.

How does a psychoanalyst accept this unusual counsel: to both become a selfobject and, as such, remain capable of interacting with a patient? How does a psychoanalyst, as selfobject, follow the suggested agenda of being both empathic and confirming? The intended meaning is, I think, that the psychoanalyst take an analytic attitude, that is, actively turn the self presented in therapy into a selfobject, recommending that the psychoanalyst show but a partial self and let the patient with the intuitive interest get to the psychoanalyst's still undisclosed selfsubject. Did he believe it desirable—or even possible—for the psychoanalyst to remain a closed and anonymous subject in any long-term therapy? Or did he believe that with the notion of selfobject he was, probably unawares, introducing a special form of countertransference—controlled, contrived, attitudinized—since it was his general rule no matter what a particular patient's transference might be? But he is unfortunately burdened, here, with an unworkable congestion of contradictory ideas.

Recall Alexander and French's (1946) recommendation made back then in the name of "corrective emotional experience." Kohut did (p. 78), aware, I suggest, of the therapeutic proximity of their views, and hoping, if possible, to disentangle the phrase from Alexander's innovative short-term experiment, namely, that the psychoanalyst present patients with a self-consciously controlled attitude taken specifically to run counter to their unconscious transference expectation, with the therapeutic intention of providing them with the sort of experience that, in the psychoanalyst's judgment, they did not get with their parents. So Alexander, here, literally performed the surrogate emotions of corrective parenting, as though to supply under clinical conditions the experience originally absent or distorted. He probably thought that patients would not, as a rule, become aware that their psychoanalysts were trying to act *in loco parentis,* intending to give them a different experience of parenting, or that they could not become aware of the psychoanalysts' glossing over their own psychic reality, that is, the actual feelings and thoughts their psychoanalysts may have, though unexpressed, no matter the actual historical experience they made evident in transference—but agree with the analysts or not, so far understood.

When Kohut, however, also proposes that the psychoanalyst become both empathic and confirming or sustaining in one and the same selfobject attitude with a patient, we need more direction from him. He never tells us how one manages to accomplish that. I think he could not—any more, incidentally, than his followers can, for it seems practically impossible to accomplish both at a single point of experience. Empathy is, everyone agrees, neither confirming nor disconfirming; Kohut defines it as "vicarious introspection" (p. 82), that is the capacity to feel and think one's way into the inner experience of another, and I see it, rather, as an unselective—what Freud meant, perhaps, by an evenly distributed—mode of attention. Now empathy, as unselective attention, may be readily distinguished from both sympathy, which is confirming, and antipathy, which is disconfirming. It is, in itself, neither. To sustain another is not empathy but an act of sympathy; not to sustain, but disdain, is an act of antipathy. In raising the standard of empathic confirming selfobject to the level of therapeutic policy, Kohut is, therefore, proposing a practically undoable task: so twist one's inner psychology into special attitudinal shape as to hold a position so internally contradictory.

Besides, when the direct expression of empathy is attitudinized into a therapeutic stance, it becomes a grotesque distortion of its psychic reality. Comparing it with the expression of spontaneity may illumine the point here. "Act" spontaneously and you convey the very opposite of the required spontaneity you consciously know is, in fact, lacking—because if you are spontaneous, you do not have to "act" it. Spontaneity is primarily felt and gone through. It is not an "act" but a sense of being one's self expressed in the qualitative mode. We first have it in the active and first-personal experience of "I" as origin and then behave it in the reactive and third-personal relations of "me" and "you" as outcome—certainly not the other way around, where the outcome precedes its origin—unless, of course, Kohut still had in mind something quite different from the ordinary usage of the terms of empathy, sympathy, and antipathy, as well as those of experience and behavior.

However, even if it were suggested that he ascribed to the psychology of empathy a less generally accepted sort of meaning, another issue that follows from his procedural view of empathy is not as easily disposed of. That conjoint standard of being both empathic and sustaining or confirming, which he urges "self psychologically informed" psychoanalysts to enact, is still problematical. It calls into serious question the source of his very strong emphasis in his writings on empathy. His Self psychology requires this overemphasis, I suggest, precisely because he also found it practically impossible to extend himself in unencumbered empathy toward a patient while, at the same time, having to sustain that patient as well. It is overemphasized, then, because empathy is not enough, but sustenance is too much. On the one hand, he does not strike a true empathic note, nor, on the other, does he take the freedom to pursue a more naturalistic course of empirical and systematic inquiry directly with his patients without confirmation or sustenance during the exploratory phases of their therapeutic effort. Instead, he raised to the level of policy for all psychoanalysts a contradictory mode of procedure that appears somehow to satisfy him. But realistically, now, do all "self psychologically informed" psychoanalysts have to follow that procedure, even when it fails to express the uniqueness of their individualities?

So the question remains: how to proceed with this internally contradictory proposal? I suggest two ways. First, for him, is that he sought to present with patients an idealized selfobject version of himself, as a "self psychologically informed" psychoanalyst who appears indefinitely removed at a distance from the real—that is, other than psychoanalyst—selfsubject version of himself. Then, for others, is that he sought to generalize at the level of procedure—or, indeed, theory of technique—for the psychoanalytic community in general a stance with patients that undoubtedly suited the deeply private turnings of his own particular psychology, about which I propose not to speculate here, his intuitively gifted patients probably doing that far better than anyone else. He is, it goes without saying, entitled to the desires, attitudes, and aspirations of his own personal psychology, even to express them in his preferred form of psychoanalytic discourse. Yet further comment is needed. If he truly meant to be both empathic and sustaining, he would have to be straightforward with patients whose desires, attitudes, and aspirations diverge from his preference for empathy with sustenance, not to mention his colleagues and students, or work with them only as selfobject, the selfsubject never in the open. Perhaps the principle of individuality for all who take part in clinical psychoanalytic inquiry, patients as well as psychoanalysts, their modes of clinical interaction as well as their interpretive metapsychologies, is a principle whose acceptance is overdue.

Again, here as in various approaches to object relations, the uniqueness of the self remains unfound. Lacking this subjective sense of self, Kohut froze his formulation into a formula: the emphatic confirming psychoanalyst as selfobject with patients, to the exclusion of the rest of the personality, especially the selfsubjective side, whether or not the particular patient requires so self-distorting a transformation of the psychoanalyst. Seek it or not, then, the "self psychologically informed" patient, willy-nilly, receives both empathy and sustenance, regardless of how misleading and confusing this conflict of attitudes may become for the two participants. No doubt Kohut was, somehow, personally able to amalgamate qualities that appear so contradictory on their face. He relied on some undescribed, perhaps personally impenetrable, private means unique to him and, in the measure of that uniqueness, unavailing to others who would realize those contradictory qualities without suffering from internal congestive breakdown.

I intend this to apply, not to Kohut only, but to him as well, for when it comes to accepting the uniqueness of all psychoanalysts and patients, no one can claim supremacy in therapeutic inquiry for a preferred mode of procedure—which, in the final analysis, remains radically individual. So long as we deal with the cosmic and the general, we deal only with the symbols of reality, but as soon as we deal with private and personal phenomena as such, we deal with realities in the completest sense of the term. That is, in contemporary psychoanalytic terms, the unique experience of the private and the personal yields the only true psychic reality, which is, in turn, the domain of unconscious psychic experience as distinct from the many highly speculative symbols about its meanings.

II

Kohut's position is, literally, unregenerate. It leads him into a most difficult, if not impossible, program of attempting to influence psychoanalysts of various persuasions to adopt an ambiguous view of empathy similar to his, yet unique to him. That program has unending conflict written into it from the start. Consider, instead, the unique subjective side of the psyche as an ineradicable feature of every psychoanalyst's clinical inquiry, copresent and emergent with the objective consensual side. Consider, also, that both sides are secured in personal alignment with one another according to the natural capacities and developmental limitations that each psychoanalyst brings to therapy with each patient. Kohut's proposed perspective of Self psychology would, curiously enough, require a more nearly comprehensive definition of the self, enlarged to encompass the private individual side, in order to get a clearer view of empathy.

Even more important for clinical procedure, a psychoanalyst is free to drop Kohut's attitude of sustaining empathy, from the outset an internal contradiction. A psychoanalyst need not, in fact, adopt any single attitude at all, and certainly not anyone else's, since the conduct of psychoanalytic inquiry is, finally, a matter of following one's deeply personal individual requirements, including the directness of spontaneity as well. The practical and viable recommendation to each psychoanalyst is: discover personal ways to best participate in clinical psychoanalytic inquiry without having to move into, or out of, any such proposed attitude as emphatic sustaining selfobject—which, I am suggesting, most likely suited Kohut's own psychic alignment of personal capacities and limitations best. An enlarged psychology of the self is open to the uniquely individual development of each psychoanalyst's therapeutic procedure.

This issue dates Kohut back to the 1930s. During that decade, psychoanalysts were being encouraged to adopt a wholly objective technique, the "basic psychoanalytic technique," and apply it independently of their private and personal input. Recall Sullivan in this connection, as another example from that period. His misprision of operationism, it is now clear, enabled him to invoke that philosophy of scientific method to support his consensual reading of basic psychoanalytic technique as participant observation. He prepared the ground for a relativity perspective on the gathering of psychoanalytic data, which was its source of strength. But he too, however, did not formulate it in personal terms, which was its major weakness. He saw participant observation arising from the inevitably interpersonal character of the therapeutic field of inquiry and proposed that psychoanalysts treat the data gathered through their participation with patients from their own particular standpoint of observation. Yet they were, he also held, the experts in the study of difficulties in living; so construed, his psychoanalytic field of inquiry remained, I suggest, only half-interpersonal. Psychoanalysts still were, of course, the participant observers, but they never became observed participants, keeping the structure and function of their own personalities outside their interactive field with their patients. In this way, their therapeutic field of inquiry was one-sidedly interpersonal, the first person left unapparent and undefined.

That too, by the way, is my view of Crowley's (1952), Tauber's (1954), and Thompson's (1956) exploration of countertransference with patients in the early 1950s. Missing from their discussions, innovative though they were in their time, is a naturalistic and unselfconscious recognition that, in spite of their trained experience (which is, after all, the root meaning of expertise), psychoanalysts are human-psychic beings no different in kind from patients. When, therefore, psychoanalysts appear without their first-personal experience in interpersonal therapy, they do so as a matter of choice. However, a consistently participant approach to therapeutic observation and inference would have required them to acknowledge their own unique selves, each with their own unique perspectives becoming actively involved in experiential fields of inquiry with patients. That is to say, the early 1950s work on countertransference fully accords with Sullivan's 1930s notion of participant observation, extending its application to the data of countertransference. This meant, in clinical effect, that the interpersonal inquiry was geared to the patient's interpersonal psychology, now including the data of countertransference for operational statement, insofar as those data (reported to the patient or not) facilitated the patient as observed participant, but never the psychoanalyst. More recent Interpersonalists recommend that psychoanalysts resist transformation on principle, yet they end up in the unavoidable quandary: how to escape transformation. It seems practically self-evident that in the very act of having to resist it, they are automatically transformed by that resistance. These Interpersonalists seek to accomplish the Sullivan ideal of participant observation and avoid the counterpoint of observed participation, but they only restate a peculiarly American development of Freud's original view, derived from hypnocathartic therapy, that all evidences of countertransference be kept out of the interactive field of clinical psychoanalytic inquiry—as though that ideal were possible, or that he himself had lived up to it.

And read Kohut on this point, in his own terms coming to this same traditional conclusion: "the expansion of analytic theory that self psychology considers the unavoidable consequence of its clinical discoveries does not per se imply a change in the way self psychologically informed analyses are being conducted . . . it does not lead to a change in basic psychoanalytic technique" (p. 107). Here again, a psychoanalyst proposes a reconstructed point of view concerning the empirics and the systematics of clinical psychoanalytic inquiry and—despite "some inner reluctance" (p. 107)—concludes with a strong affirmation of the status quo ante. The struggle long undergone with this issue is, patently, neither conceptual nor clinical, since one might expect him to manifest greater self-confidence and take his new perspective into new psychoanalytic technique as well. But the issue is, finally, deeply private and personal. Between what he believes about his clinical practice and what he writes for the record lies a rich soil for self-distortion, at the expense of what he privately knows to be the case. Otherwise, why mention the "inner reluctance" to offer any change in the basic psychoanalytic technique? He may not have meant what he wrote, but a reader can only take what he wrote to be his meaning.

This recurring peculiarity in the history of psychoanalysis derives from the language and thought in which each theorist chooses to state a unique response to that technique. The private aspects of experience are not readily stated in the public domain with an assured degree of consensual power. Perhaps theorists write for theorists, while clinicians talk to patients. The tendency is to edit out the purely private and personal from the published statements about technique, glossing over the plain ubiquity of individual differences among psychoanalysts. However, it is not a basic technique but a shared structure of inquiry, a common set of definitions, postulates, and theory, that confers unity on this field. Even Sullivan, whose changes in technique follow his special version of operationism, nonetheless precluded from direct clinical study the evidence for unique individuality, implying, in this way, the animadversion to countertransference, no less than Freud who first made it explicit, or Kohut who did not change the basic technique.

The boundaries of a truly interactive field between psychoanalyst and patient should be opened to their unique aspects of self, both conscious and unconscious. Since they are present anyway, acknowledged or not, it is useful to explore them, not that psychoanalysts or patients can, or even wish to, say everything they feel or think, but that they may, rather, do therapy with greater freedom, imagination, and directness. Those traditional and Interpersonal psychoanalysts, who undergo the psychic pressure to resist on principle being transformed by their patients, put themselves into a state of unavoidable anxiety about being influenced. In the very decision to resist transformation, they are already transformed by the resistance. Why do they become anxious about being influenced by their patients? They have basic insecurity, I think, about manifesting some unique aspect of self without inhibition.

III

The basic psychoanalytic technique disguises the impersonal exercise of authority, which is less clearly evident to the clinical ear than the personal authority exercised behind the classical mirror. Less clearly evident, it becomes more subtle—therefore, more easily overlooked. Yet it, nonetheless, has clinical effects. When, for example, Freud characterized the role of the psychoanalyst as a mirror, surgeon, or catalyst, that served to acknowledge the psychoanalyst's effective personal relation to the patient. Those carefully chosen metaphors depict his personal participation in the therapeutic experience and suggest a treatment of patients at once very professional and very direct, yet very interpretive in the biological metaphor most personal to him, for he considered the psychoanalyst a sort of messenger transmitting the truth of a metapsychology with putative universality, and that parameter of interpretation still holds into the present for all traditional psychoanalysts. Between him and them, however, are some noteworthy differences, ordinarily neglected though they may be. He could, alone among them, claim that the instinctual–libidinal metaphor derived from the development of his own personality, portray it as emblematic of his own deep-seated neurotic problems, and use it to liberate his own unconscious psychic striving and imagination in felt and thought experience. For he, quite literally, earned that metapsychology from the guts and genitals of his own life, suffered and undergone. Can we do less than follow his lead in this matter and each seek to earn our own perspectives from our own psychic realities? In the hands of traditionalists like Kohut, however, the authority of modern expertise no longer has the personal touch. Refer, above, to sections I and II on this point. Does it account for his enormous yet conflictual emphasis on empathy?

Freud, as is well known, found the grid of his own interpretive metapsychology in the familial experience he deeply felt and thought and lived through in the first person. He rediscovered the child in the adult first and foremost in himself, romantic that he was, which gave him the interpretive strength to articulate that dimension of himself to patients uncompromisingly. From this unique experience of personal knowledge, he found ingenious ways to move into myths and metaphors general enough, abstract enough, compelling enough to appeal to the apperceptive consciousness of his patients, colleagues, students, readers, and, it goes without saying, himself. But he left no room for others to present any myth or metaphor contrary to his own: recall, for example, Adler and Jung, Ferenczi and Rank, not to mention the patients of his major case studies. The authoritarianism of the current traditionalists is new, by way of contrast, precisely because their working myth and metaphor are closer to Freud's than to their own experience lived at first hand. It was he, not they, who truly earned the personal value of selected Greek mythology combined with the instinct or libido metaphor of nineteenth-century biology through extraordinary original means, and it is they, not he, who learned a so-called basic technique by adopting an analytic attitude impersonally arrived at. So their use of his overall perspective on metapsychology is, for them, a far less deeply rooted personal striving.

Now, it seems, their agreement that his metapsychology, or some close variant of it, is the only one admissible, even, in fact, that interpretation itself is the only legitimate parameter of psychoanalytic therapy as a whole, may be more clearly understood. The interpretive terms of the Ego-psychological, Object-Relational, and other such traditionally oriented biological approaches down to the present, if only because they are not personally derived, constitute a new but impersonal exercise of authority. Psychoanalysts who adopt them have to take an analytic attitude in support of them, and, by that move, lose the interpretive power still dormant in their own psychologies. The personal aspects of their psychic realities that transcend the biologically oriented myths and metaphors of Freud's original approach remain untouched in their personal analyses and unassimilated into their basic procedures. This new authoritarianism is, of course, deeply embedded in an analytic attitude toward procedure that remains inflexible and unyielding to individual experience. The unique self is countertransference, they say, and therefore not discussable as new metapsychology—or, if discussed, not capable of changing the old. The appearance of dogmatism, here, also comes from the fact that experiental inquiry fails to affect the preestablished parameter of the basic technique: interpretation of transference.

Kohut does not clearly distinguish himself from the biological model of psychoanalysis. Nor, despite all the new interpretive construction of his self psychology, does he free his striving to speculate in other directions. The more he would free himself from the biological base of classical metapsychology, to which he appears to have unbreakable commitments, the more complex his thinking becomes. For example, he asserts that such traditional goals of psychological development as Freud's post-oedipal genitality or Klein's postparanoid–depressive object love are "in error" (1984:7). Yet he does not, in asserting that, also see how the surrender of their postulated goals also involves the surrender of the instinctual–libidinal archetectonic on which they are based. In my view, he remains committed to the perspective of instinct, libido, or drive, or what I term the biological model. Thus, when he later discusses weaknesses of the self from the standpoint of his own Self psychology, he considers them primarily functions of drives and distinguishes those that "lead to drive phenomena" from those that lead to the "isolation of drives" (p. 10). It is his ambiguous response to the powerful hold of historical authority that, I think, causes all this conceptual complexity.

Take another example. He ascribes psychological primacy to affection and assertiveness, which are traditionally considered secondary, and a secondary position to lust and destructiveness, traditionally considered primary (p. 12). If he had truly dropped the biological metapsychology, he would not have felt obligated to give it a secondary position, or any position at all, before actual inquiry in the particular case. His interpretive effort at reversal is, indeed, superfluous for those psychoanalysts of the self who have no prior historical allegiance to the biological model. They do not, as he does, have to reverse the classical relationship between the biology of the id or drives on one side and the psychology of the ego or self on the other. Nor do they have to decide before empirical psychoanalytic inquiry which to designate primary and which secondary, within the Freudian dualism, or which tertiary and so on, outside that dualism. Consider, also, what his formulation does not include: that the biological concern may, a priori, not be primary as Freud first held, nor secondary as Kohut later holds; that it may, indeed, have no direct relevance to actual clinical conditions for conducting a particular psychoanalytic inquiry; and that it should, therefore, be treated as being no more, no less, significant than any other environing feature of the psyche, ego-interpersonal or social, political or economic, educational or religious, and so on. Let the patients decide where they stand, about which issue, at what level of significance, with what strength of commitment.

A final comment about classifying Kohut's perspective on Self psychology, to conclude this section. I suggest the rubric of the sociological model—more precisely, the biosocial model—as a wide enough umbrella for grouping a number of perspectives on metapsychology developed during the 1930s, especially those of character analysis, Ego psychology, Object and Interpersonal Relations, and now, added to them, his Self psychology. In spite of the numerous philosophical, terminological, and dispositional differences among these perspectives, they fixed upon certain widely held themes in various measures. They all shared a serious and reconstructive interest in the environing goals, values, and ideals of the patient's psychological life. They covered a wide gamut: social, cultural, and economic, in addition to familial (oedipal), and object and interpersonal (pre- and post-oedipal), and now the selfobject. All—including Self psychology, belatedly—took part in that widespread movement of thought and practice of that radical decade, from the standpoint of the internalizing (in Sullivan's term, personifying) processes by which, and the internalized (in Sullivan's term, again, personified) to which, patients and psychoanalysts became adapted in a functional consensus with their significant others (in Kohut's term, selfobjects) in the more proximate, and with their generalized others in the more distant, environments. Those perspectives were diverse in vision yet convergent in procedure. All joined in opening to clinical psychoanalytic inquiry the selfsame sector of personality, variously named character armor, defense mechanism, and security operation. Most generally termed resistance, it had never before been explored on a par with transference. As distinct from the classical perspective of the id, or the biological model, I group these perspectives under the sociological model, to point up the basic change from the instinctual–libidinal to the ego–interpersonal, or social–cultural, approach to the analysis of the psyche.

I do not see what clarity comes of distinguishing the two groups as drive and relational models. It is, for example, beyond question that the character–analytic and the ego–psychological, as well as the many approaches of object relations, belong as much to the drive as to the relational models; even Freud's id psychology falls, in some sense, under both. Those I group under the sociological model may, if one so wishes, more traditionally be named id–ego instead of biosocial perspectives. This holds especially for the varieties of approach to Object Relations because they are usually stated in the metaphorical language and thought of instinct and libido. On the other hand, those of Interpersonal Relations take a far less speculative position: they set forth the category of biological needs (a subject matter for the biological and physiological sciences) side by side with, yet empirically distinct from, the category of social and interpersonal security operations (a subject matter for the social–psychological and psychoanalytic sciences)—a most useful distinction for the purposes of clinical psychoanalytic inquiry, into the present.

However, the problem with using drive and relational to distinguish the first (1915–1917) from the second (1930s) model is insurmountable. These terms gloss over the critical historical differences between the two. In fact, all models of direct psychological inquiry from their roots in Mesmer and Puységur onward, in whatever interpretive perspective, toward whatever therapeutic objectives, work, strictly speaking, with relational experience, while no putatively relational model of the 1930s does without some reference to the drives of the biological organism, such as id, instinct, libido, drive–discharge, or need–satisfaction. It is preferable, therefore, to subsume the classical perspective under biology (instinct–libido or id) and the modern perspectives under sociology (biosocial or id–ego). Against the background of this discussion, consider for inclusion in this group Kohut's Self psychology. Combining as it does the instinctual–libidinal within itself, his Self psychology remains a rather traditional perspective; it is no more conceptually adequate for exploring the private and the personal as immediate experience than Hartmann's ego structure or Sullivan's self system; it does not refocus beyond the id and the id–ego to include the psychic center of the psychoanalytic self as the origin of its own becoming the other's selfobject.

IV

Individuality "is founded in feeling; and the recesses of feeling, the darker, blinder strata of character, are the only places in the world in which we catch real fact in the making, and directly perceive how events happen, and how work is actually done. Compared with this world of living individualized feelings, the world of generalized objects the intellect contemplates is without solidity or life." During actual psychoanalytic inquiry, the feeling of individuality arises in the passage of unconscious to conscious psychic experience, undergone in the first person, singular and active. It is the active movement of transference in its primary sense of immediate experience moving from inside outward that holds the personal disposition toward individuality—as distinguished from the reactive movement of resistance in its primary sense of reflective experience moving from outside inward that holds the Ego–Interpersonal disposition toward consensual adaptiveness.

While it is true, as already mentioned, that Kohut falls back on the traditional parameter of interpreting—which is, of course, manipulating symbolic representations of—transference according to the basic psychoanalytic technique, it is also true, as another instance of ambiguity, that he mentions the "spontaneous mobilization of the transference" (p. 4). These ideas neither fit nor support but confound one another. Here again, he is unfortunately burdened with an unworkable congestion of contradictory ideas. To treat the spontaneity of transference by that technique, as though symbols of interpretation have the therapeutic value, is like following a recipe without eating the pudding. While, to catch hold, the symbols of interpretation must meet the standards of critical intelligence, yet the proof of the interpretation is still in the experience overall. From this point of vantage, Sullivan's sardonic reaction to the plethora of interpretation, that the supply far outstrips the demand, takes on its full sense and adequacy. The excess of unfelt interpretation, curiously enough, makes it irrational as well.

In that context, Kohut also postulates a "tension arc" as the "dynamic essence of the complete, nondefective self" (p. 4–5). The attainment of that state is how he defines cure. Recall, here, Fromm-Reichmann's (1950) view of the human psyche inherently striving toward mental health—that is, toward self-completion—or Thompson's (1950) clinical version of it, that patients find their way toward psychic well-being, however their psychoanalysts may define it, as long as psychoanalysts remain alert to the effects of countertransference and stand clear of their patients' striving. Though he may seem to aspire to something more complex—mainly, I suggest, because he finally retained the basic traditional metapsychology—his systematic intention is most likely the same as theirs. He also observes that "the defective self of the patient with a narcissistic personality disturbance will mobilize its striving to complete its development, that is, that it will try again to establish an uninterrupted tension arc"; I think they would most likely have agreed with him about that, albeit in other interpretive terms. Now, if he had enlarged this point of view beyond the category of narcissistic personality disturbance, to include all human psychology, diagnosed or not, psychoanalyzed or not, I think we could all agree with him about that, too.

Kohut's tension arc so resembles Sullivan's self dynamism that psychoanalysts schooled in the classical Interpersonal tradition may readily accept it, but stripped, however, of the unbearable burden of his Self psychology cum instinctual–libidinal archetectonic. It is when he proceeds to discuss the metapsychology of narcissism that the contradictions arise; here, most contemporary Interpersonal Relationists will follow him only with great difficulty. For example, is he suggesting the need for basic changes in Freud's diagnostic metapsychology (in which, unequivocally, narcissistic disturbances are not psychoanalyzable), and does he, for unspecified reasons, have trouble making them? Or is he, through restatement, trying to affirm the basic tenets of instinctual–libidinal metapsychology, now reversed as secondary but unreconstructed as pluralistic, without acknowledging how severely they limit the open study of narcissism, even his own? Once again, he seems locked into holding incompatible ideas. His thinking casts both ways for no palpable point intrinsic to the thought itself: walking a tightrope, as it were, to gain acceptance from both sides. First, with the more recent Self psychology: he supports the instinctual–libidinal metapsychology by making its nontreatment of narcissism more acceptable to the post-Freudians. Then, with the older instinctual–libidinal metapsychology: he supports Self psychology by making its belated treatment of narcissism more acceptable to the traditional Freudians. Because this issue is, finally, not substantive but political in origin, he failed, not unexpectedly, to resolve it on empirical and systematic grounds—an instance of the very narcissism he would treat.

There is a self-fulfilling symmetry of ideas that cuts a deep swath through his last major effort. In a very obvious sense, the question he poses (How does analysis cure?) appears superfluous to the task he actually accomplishes. For, he concludes, even the "self psychologically informed" psychoanalyst must fall back on the "basic psychoanalytic technique." His answer is, then, it now cures the way it has always cured since the basic technique was first developed. All traditional psychoanalysts, among whom Kohut obviously includes himself, define their therapeutic technique as being no more, no less, than the interpretation of transference. Any aspect of the clinical psychoanalytic experience unencompassed by transference interpretable from the perspective of traditional metapsychology, original or reversed, stands outside the defined parameter of Kohut's basic technique. That specifically excludes from his technique of interpretation, among other things, resistance and anxiety; countertransference, counterresistance, and counteranxiety; a patient's direct experience from session to session in the first person, singular and active; and, of course, a patient's interpretation of the traditional interpretation to make room for his or her own.

This conclusion points up the lost uniqueness of Kohut's Self psychology. It finally requires no basic changes in the inherited traditions of psychoanalysis, coming down firmly on the side of the basic psychoanalytic technique and obliquely on the side of its metapsychology. He turned a blind eye, moreover, to the unique self that extends beyond that approach: a psychic center of origin that moves itself outward from within, striving for completion no matter how the empathic sustaining selfobject may environ it.

It is fitting, therefore, to end with a brief comment comparing what he and others term the "basic technique" of traditional psychoanalysis, a newly adopted convention appearing with greater frequency in the current literature, with a statement of the actual technique in the literature of classical psychoanalysis. Students of the field now tend to designate as traditional that past which provides the historical context for their own view of the present and put aside the rest. The fusion of the classical Id and the later Ego or Self psychologies into one lumped-together past as traditional, without conceptual or clinical distinction among them, gives rise to confusing side effects. Mainly, I suggest, the current innovative efforts become blurred and lose the distinctiveness of their original vision. Recall Freud (1917), in the *First Introductory Lectures,* describing his clinical work as on the battlefield of transference where *all* the contending forces must meet, including his own; for, he held that we must master the symptoms then, dissolve them. The means to do this he sow in the relationship to the physician, which evokes—new editions of those early conflicts, in which the patient strives to behave as he originally behaved, while one calls upon all the available forces in his soul to bring him to another decision.

This original procedure has obviously undergone many changes over the years. But, as stated in 1917, Freud was deeply, squarely, irrevocably involved with the patient. The measure of his involvement clearly differs from that of the Ego and Self psychologists who arbitrarily limit their technique to the interpretation of transference. They scale down to a false sense of neutrality the extraordinary degree of involvement to which Freud, by far their leading traditional precursor, informed us he had committed himself. From the statement above about his psychoanalytic technique it is clear beyond question that he sought clinical knowledge through a directness of experience unfettered by the interpretive parameters of sacrosanct tradition. So, instead of merely admiring his daring forays into Greek myth and metaphor and repeating his patterns of interpretive outlook, why not follow the path of this self-analyzed psychoanalyst as a therapeutic coparticipant, instead? Why not, as he did, each seek the truth of their own individual metapsychologies and exercise the unique freedom to offer them with equal authenticity, conviction, and thoroughness to patients? Every psychoanalyst must seek a perspective and create a technique that allow for the deeply private gift of talent to show itself, the inner voice that gives a psychoanalyst the uniqueness of self and the wholeness of personality.

In the contemporary psychoanalytic study of transference, resistance, and anxiety, why not also recall the guideline Breuer first took with Anna O., as well as Freud's with his various patients? They each traveled their own individual ways toward enlarging a patient's scope of awareness in the interactive field of inquiry they shared. Merely interpreting transference as such, in symbols of myth and metaphor very speculative at best, and in patterns of discovery no longer original or fresh, should not be considered the basic psychoanalytic technique. Obviously, in light of the above, technique consists in a psychoanalyst's meeting transference directly with patients, feeling and thinking through it in depth, living and working through it over time, toward enlarged awareness and toward a shared recognition of this new experience against the backdrop of previous resistance and anxiety about that now enlarged awareness. A technique of interpreting transference alone, unrooted in direct psychoanalytic experience, is not genuinely therapeutic. Unlived, unfelt, unthought through, such interpretation inevitably falls on deaf ears.

V

Breuer and Freud, Adler and Jung, Ferenczi and Rank—indeed, all research metapsychologists down to the present—were baffled by the great unmet challenge cutting across their overall structurings of psychoanalytic inquiry: that is, how to establish beyond controversy some universal connection between their particular interpretive myth or metaphor at one level and their unconscious psychic experience becoming conscious as first-personal event at another? Is the connection between experience and interpretation itself a matter of empirical and systematic knowledge, a matter interpretive and speculative? Or is it a matter of something else still unexplored? Is it perhaps a matter of the original creative resources all coparticipants—here including, I suggest, patients as well as psychoanalysts—each bring to the clinical psychoanalytic inquiry? Or is the gap in psychoanalytic knowledge between experience and interpretation ultimately unbridgeable, except as a matter of deeply held personal belief, value, or ideal?

References

Alexander, F. and T.M. French. 1946. *Psychoanalytic Therapy* New York: Ronald Press.

Crowley, R. 1952. Human reactions of analysts to patients. *Samiksa* 6:212–19. Reprinted in B. Wolstein, ed., *Essential Papers on Countertransference*, pp. 84–90. New York: New York University, 1988.

Fairbairn, W. 1952. *An Object Relations Theory of Personality*. New York: Basic Books.

Freud, A. 1936. *The Ego and the Mechanism of Defense*, pp. 1915–17, New York: International Universities Press.

Freud, S. 1917. Introductory Lectures on Psycho-analysis. *Standard Edition* 16 London: Hogarth.

——. 1943. *A General Introduction to Psychoanalysis*. Garden City, N.Y.: Garden City Press.

Fromm-Reichman, F. 1950. *Principles of Intensive Psychotherapy.* Chicago: University of Chicago Press.

Hartmann, H. 1939, 1958. *Ego Psychology and the Problem of Adaptation.* New York: International Universities Press.

Kohut, H. 1971. *The Analysis of the Self.* New York: International Universities Press.

——. 1977. *The Restoration of the Self.* New York: International Universities Press.

——. 1984. *How Does Psychoanalysis Cure?* Chicago: University of Chicago Press.

Klein, M. 1964. *Contributions to Psychoanalysis, 1921–1945.* New York: McGraw-Hill.

Reich, W. 1933, 1945. *Character Analysis.* New York: Orgone Press.

Sullivan, H.S. 1940. *Conceptions of Modern Psychiatry.* Washington, D.C.: W.A. White Psychiatric Foundation.

Tauber, E. 1954. Exploring the therapeutic use of countertransference data. *Psychiatry* 17:331–36. Reprinted in B. Wolstein, ed., *Essential Papers on Countertransference,* pp. 111–19. New York: New York University, 1988.

Thompson, C. (with Patrick Mullahy). 1950. *Psychoanalysis: Evolution and Development.* New York: Hermitage House.

——. 1956. The role of the analyst's personality in therapy. *American Journal of Psychotherapy* 10:347–59. Reprinted in B. Wolstein, *Essential Papers on Countertransference,* pp. 120–30. New York: New York University, 1988.

Wolstein, B. 1983. Transference and resistance as psychic experience. *Contemporary Psychoanalysis* 19:276–94. Reprinted in D. Milman and G. Goldman, eds., *Techniques of Working with Resistance,* pp. 249–67. New York: Jason Aronson, 1987.

——. 1986. Transference neuroses and resistance neuroses: Notes on classical diagnostic metapsychology. *Contemporary Psychoanalysis* 22:202–17.

5

Character, Personality, and the Politics of Change: Implications for an Interpersonal Understanding of Narcissism

Edgar A. Levenson

Many years ago, I was invited to participate in a two-day conference of psychoanalysts meeting with Jiddu Krishnamurti, a renowned Indian sage. Mr. Krishnamurti had been, in his teens, the darling of the British Theosophist movement and had written a number of highly regarded texts on the meeting of Eastern and Western philosophy. It looked to be a lively idea. The first day, about twenty of us met with Krishnamurti, a very handsome, rather diminutive man. It went something like this: someone would say, "Krishnamurti-ji (or some similar honorific) what do you think about intimacy?" And he would answer, "What is intimacy?" The questioner would try to elaborate, "Well, intimacy is the wish to be close to another." "What is close?" Krishnamurti would ask. And so it went. I suppose this was some variety of the Oxford Ordinary Language approach to philosophy (Grice 1989).

I do not recall learning anything particularly substantive, but the style of inquiry struck a responsive chord: that is, the challenging of our casual presumption of shared linguistic meanings—that we are talking the same language. Words carry with them a penumbra of implicit meanings, which may be different for different speakers. What is even more interesting is that words have a magic archeology; that is, their etymological roots can leach through and tacitly influence the speaker (Thas-Theinemann 1968; Levenson 1981).

Well then, what is character? What is personality? It must be understood that these two terms are often used as though they were cognates—interchangeable—an egregious error from my point of view and a failure to recognize that they represent entirely different vantage points in psychoanalysis with entirely different outcomes. Sullivan, particularly, elaborated the concept of personality and talked not at all of character (except in the Edwardian sense of being of good character); whereas the Object Relations and Self-psychology therapists have developed character—which they may casually misidentify as personality—as a central dimension in their theoretical formulations.

What, then, is character? One notes it derives from the Greek, to incise, or to cut into a hard surface. Personality, in contrast, comes from a Latin or Estruscan word meaning mask or masked player. The implications are very different, and as I have said, the ancient meanings still inform contemporary usage.

Character implies a structure, the rock on which the person's life is built. It is the core of what has been called a "one-person" psychology: this is I (Ghent 1989). Unlike temperament and specific talents, which are presumably genetic givens (an infant is born with specific temperament and talents, but not character), character may be considered the consequence of experience, either developmental or even—as in Fromm and Horney—cultural (Kagan 1989). But however it develops, present character is *not* a dynamic equilibrium. It is a construct, a thing.

Personality has an entirely different set of implications. As Sullivan defined it, "personality is the relatively enduring pattern of recurrent interpersonal situations which characterize a human life" (1953:110–11). Note the wording: "relatively enduring pattern," "recurrent interpersonal situations." The implication is clear. Personality is the sum of personae, of all one is; conscious, dissociated, unattended, rational, irrational, parataxic, autistic, whatever. The self, for Sullivan, is the top of the iceberg, what one takes oneself to be. Unlike character, this is not writ in stone. Personality is simply the sum of recurrent patterns, of persons' experience of themselves in the aggregate of interpersonal situations. It is the patients on the stages of their lives, what William James called "a theater of simultaneous possibilities" (1981:288).

Bear in mind that interpersonal situations are not necessarily limited to real exchanges. What Sullivan called "eidetic imagery," fantasies about the world, or dreams are considered reflections of interpersonal experience. What makes these patterns "relatively enduring" is not that they constitute a structure but that they are instead a matrix of interpersonal experience that has a very powerful homeostatic pull. In other words, patients stay the way they are, not because of the intransigent stoniness of character, but because of a sustained, recursive set of experiences that do not change and do not easily allow for novelty. Patients are recalcitrant to change, not because of the rigidity of character, but because of a powerful interpersonal matrix that does not readily permit new experience to take place—even in the therapy. Patients' infamous resistance to change, the repetition compulsion, may be due—not so much to the hegemony of fantasy, or to the limitations imposed by developmental deficit—but, rather, to their need to recreate, over and over again, a psychologically safe milieu. "Safe" may sound like an odd formulation for the distressed lives most patients lead, but as the psychoanalytic saw has it, whatever the patient does, it is a lot better than something else! A neurosis is a compromise solution.

For Sullivan the dynamism of this system is maintained by anxiety, which is an interpersonal event, a response to interpersonal threat (contagious anxiety, separation and loss, the other's rage, whatever). This seems to me to be the most radical statement of a truly at-least-two-person psychology, one in which one person is not so much impinged upon by another, but one in which a network of people all collude to maintain a homeostatic balance. It is essentially compatible with a systems approach.

To summarize, character is *who* I am. Personality is *how* I am. Character is the most generally applicable, abstract formulation of the person. Personality, in contrast, is the most specific and context dependent. Character tends to tautologize behavior; e.g., the "narcissistic" character will behave in a certain way because that is how narcissistic characters behave. Personality, in contrast, portrays people as constructed and maintained socially, by their circumstances.

Character and personality convey different versions of the self. For Kohut, the self is an internal structure, something the person builds throughout infancy and childhood. A relatively undamaged self is a relatively intact structure or edifice. As Wolf (1988) defined self it is a "coherent and enduring configuration [which emerges] during the interplay of inherited and environmental factors . . . [It is] a unit which endures over time. It is a self-propelling, self-directed and self-sustaining unit" (p. 182).

As I have said, for Sullivan, the self is simply that part of the personality that one can grasp and consciously formulate. It is not a thing. What Sullivan called the "self-system" is something altogether different, an elaborate monitoring system that alerts the person to anxiety in the necessary others and makes possible the avoidance of disruption of relationships. The self-system and the self cannot be considered coterminous or synonymous.

Sullivan, quite famously, rejected the characterological concept of unique individuality. He did not say that he thought it did not exist; rather, he felt it to be outside the realm of psychological investigation and therefore outside his purview. This has given most post-Sullivanians a difficult time; indeed most of them repudiate it. As Wolstein (1987) put it, "[there is] a psychic point of origin, an internal source of agency, a unique sense of self that every participant must place before the other during some phases of their psychoanalytic experience. This is the psychic center of the self, which I distinguish from the interpersonal ego" (p. 632). Yet, the concept of inherent uniqueness as a characterological given, a core, albeit a cherished contemporary conceit, carries with it some serious conceptual limitations.

For example, characterology has a hard time explaining evil. Since character is relatively fixed, evil must be done by evil people. One need only think of the furor provoked by Hannah Arendt's attempt in *Eichmann in Jerusalem* to suggest that evil things are done by ordinary people, or conversely, Fromm's (the archetypal characterologist) not very effectual attempt to reify evil in *The Anatomy of Human Destructiveness* to understand how bankrupt a concept character may be as an explanation for individual behavior in a social context (Arendt 1963; Fromm 1973).

In contrast, if we are the sum of our interpersonal transactions, we very well may be different people in different settings. This allows for elasticity—certainly a desideratum—but also for a social plasticity that can be horrifying. Perhaps that is why a man may be a concentration camp guard and then escape to another country and live an apparently uneventful, conventional life.

If one is willing to entertain my point that character and personality are words that carry with them an implicit set of meanings, then the rest of the set follows rather obviously. If one believes in character, then therapy must be incisive; literally, one must cut into it, either by interpretation as Reich, Fromm, and to some extent, Kohut did, or one must act restitutively, repair the edifice as Self psychologists do. The therapist is acting *upon* an internal structure. If one believes in personality, then, the patient changes when the context, the interpersonal matrix, can be changed. The therapist is not acting upon an internal structure but interacting with the patient. The curing field lies directly between the two, and the therapist cannot change the patient without changing himself or herself at least within the context of the treatment. As Hoffman (1987) has indicated, this postulate leads to a radical use of so-called countertransference. To quote him, "[there is] a perspective that has become the basis for a new treatment model, one that takes the analyst's participation into account in a manner that marks a radical departure, even within the interpersonal movement, where the soil for the development of this model is most fertile. It is a development which is being fueled by and is fueling related developments in many fields of inquiry" (p. 213).

> To use a brief example: a middle-aged man comes into therapy with a presenting problem of intractable jealousy. He is hounded by a voyeuristic interest in his women friends' past lovers. He does not suspect present infidelities, although he has been essentially cuckolded many times with previous women. Otherwise everything is "perfect." He has had one marriage and many relationships, all of which have failed.
>
> Aside from his tortured curiosity, he is a virtual Galahad with women. He is unfailingly kind, generous, solicitous. As a child, he had been adored, idealized by his mother, who told him how handsome, how marvelous, how generous he was. He was the dream of every mother on the block. His psychopathogy, his voyeuristic preoccupations, were the most human thing about this parfait knight. Like the Taoist admonition, "when the Good Man enters, Evil begins!" he drove everyone around him to excesses of misbehavior. This he does not see at all.
>
> All this is characterology, who he is, what impact he has on others. It is only with the transference, the relationship with the therapist, that personality can be brought into focus. He is, of course, a disappointing patient. He tries earnestly, as does the therapist, who increasingly feels he or she is letting the patient down. The therapist strains, the patient hangs on the edge of quitting therapy. The patient hopes for an epiphany, an insight that will "cleanse him"—make it all clear—in a word, perfect his perfection. If one fails to cure him, a very powerful underlying paranoid trend begins to emerge. He is really totally untrusting.
>
> To move from character to personality assessment requires participation with him, reflected appraisals, and according to my version of therapy, a very careful monitoring by the therapist of what it is like to be with him. He is both disappointed and disappointing. For change to occur, both participants may well have to experience frustration and anger. Can you imagine this man with a therapist who has to be the very best therapist?

> The therapist and patient experience together—and struggle through together—what is being talked about in his life. The therapist becomes part of the disease he or she set out to cure. Part of the resolution is seeing this, part is the de novo corrective experience of having something new happen, both different from the women friends and different from his absent father who never intervened in the mother–child dyad.

Psychoanalytic theory is replete with dichotomies: intrapsychic/interpersonal, drive/relational, fixation/regression, deficit/conflict, even the hoariest of all, nature/nurture. One is always tempted to say, "Why not see and use both perspectives?" But these are not different perspectives on the same reality: they are different realities, entirely different pervasive sets about what reality is. They are different philosophies of life. Therapists who talk about character and character disorders see patients, psychotherapeutic devices, and outcomes differently than therapists who talk about personality. As I have said, one should not assume that because we are using the same words, we are using them the same way. We talk to each other across different universes of experience, and to understand each other, we must begin with the assumption of difference. I believe that our particular Tower of Babel is built on the paradoxical illusion that we are all speaking the same tongue.

I must repeat, my insistence on a clear-cut distinction between character and personality may lead to some initial confusion, since, as I have said, these terms are sometimes used as if they were interchangeable. As an example, Akhtar and Thomson (1982), in an overview of narcissistic personality disorder, say, "The diagnosis of narcissistic *personality* disorder has been used with increasing frequency in recent years; DSM III lists it as a distinct *character* disorder. Yet the concept remains poorly defined and controversial" (p. 12, my italics). As I shall elaborate, it is with these most trying patients that the political implications of the character/personality dichotomy are most evident.

Whether "personality" or "character," one cannot deny that a real value resides in having a classification that delineates a group of difficult patients who operate in a similar way in the world and call out in the therapist a similar type of response. Perhaps these patients have always been with us and were, in earlier times, called "borderline" or "pseudoneurotic–schizophrenic." How does it profit us to call them "character" disorders, rather than just troublesome patients? What is the appeal of *any* character diagnosis for therapists? Clara Thompson used to say, if you find yourself thinking about diagnosis after the first week of therapy, look to your countertransference!

Any reader not totally committed to one ideology or another cannot fail to be impressed—and one might hope dismayed—by the total conviction with which prominent analysts proclaim diametrically opposed clinical strategies for what they diagnose as the very same characterological category. Kohut and his cohort, in treating narcissistic disorders, proselytize for an empathic participatory position (Kohut 1979). Kernberg says that Kohut is wrong; "systematic analysis of the positive and negative aspects of the patient's grandiosity from an essentially neutral position better achieves the goal of full activation of the narcissistic transference" (1974:226). Masterson says, "the therapist's challenge in the psychotherapeutic approach is to serve as guardian of the emerging real self by maintaining an emotionally neutral stance" and that if the patient behaves regressively, "the treatment will come to a halt" (1989:1, 26). In the most extreme contrast imaginable, Margaret Little, in her account of her analysis with Winnicott, describes, with evident approval, Winnicott's virtual encouragement of her regressive behavior—so much so that she endured several hospitalizations during the therapy. It is an astounding document. Winnicott's support of Little's regressions was sustained during his marital crisis *and* a coronary occlusion (which Little—the regressed patient—was the first to diagnose). Moreover, all during this period, Little's professional career—writing, teaching, seeing patients, institutional advancement—proceeded famously, One certainly wonders about the possible countertransference in Winnicott's nurturance and the iatrogenic influence in her regressions (Little 1988).

So, if esteemed analysts disagree about the treatment but do agree about the diagnosis, is it unreasonable to wonder whether their clinical successes depend more on the diagnosis than the treatment? Characterological nosology permits us to entertain a certain attitude toward the patients that is essentially political; that is, it permits us to see the patients' problems as in their character, allows us to intervene incisively and makes it possible for us to treat the extreme reactions the patients call out in us, as something they have put into us, as if in our process of repairing the character, a stone chip flew into our eye. We do not see our reaction as *our* problem, but as the patients'. By seeing the disturbance as "in" the patients rather than in their milieu, therapists are powerfully armored against these very intransigent and demanding people.

For example, Paulina Kernberg reported on a thirty-year-old nurse who had severe difficulties in living (Kernberg 1971). Yet, her functioning was not all that exceptionable, and Kernberg diagnosed her as having a psychoneurotic reaction, mixed type, passive–aggressive personality. Only in the course of the treatment when the patient's transference became "regressive," overblown, did the diagnosis change. The effect of changing the diagnosis was for Kernberg to be able to say this is *her*—not *me* with her—and to stand stalwartly fast against the importuning emotional onslaught. There was certainly no suggestion that the therapeutic relationship was so stormy because psychoanalysis, or psychoanalysis with Kernberg, recapitulated, in some way, the extremely oppressive patterns of her life. Her meticulous "empathic" concern with the patient's "psychic reality" permitted her to think of herself as effectively neutral and as nonparticipant as a classical Freudian analyst, although presumably to different ends. Even though the patient left arbitrarily with a minimum of gratitude to the therapist for evident improvements—"Who would call this a treatment," she said derisively on leaving, Kernberg's confidence was not one whit shaken. She was neither angered nor disappointed (Kernberg 1971:467).

There are, of course, other analysts who see themselves much more as impinged upon by the patient, for example, in Grinberg's concept of projective counteridentification, in which the therapist becomes the "passive object" of the patient's fantasies (Grinberg 1979:73). To quote Grinberg, "The specific response of the analyst will depend on his degree of tolerance of the patient's projective input"—not, one notes, in any way on the accuracy or relevance of the patient's assault.

As Feiner put it, "These views still retain the idea that the triggering of its occurrence in the therapist comes *from* the patient. It would lead one to see countertransference 'induced' or 'evoked' in the analyst by the patient. This still falls short of conceptualizing [it] as part of a truly interpersonal, interpenetrating process" (1973:113).

Compare, for example Searles' (a radical Interpersonalist) statement, "she was enormously formidable in her power to mobilize ordinary unconscious guilt in the other person" (1979:309) with Grinberg's (1979) statement that "the analyst may have the feeling of being no longer his own self and of unavoidably becoming transformed into the object which the patient, unconsciously, wanted him to be." There is, in the latter, certainly no implication, as Searles suggests, that the patient is extremely adept at accurately nailing the other person, getting the person where it really hurts.

How does the patient do that? From the point of view of character, it is just a quality of "those" people. They can do it because they are so crazy. But how? Grinberg says, The analyst's reaction stems, for the most part, independently of his own conflicts and corresponds in a predominant or exclusive way to the intensity and quality of the patient's projective identification. In this case, The origin of the process comes from the patient and not the analyst (1979:177).

Who decides that? Of course, the analyst. It sounds to me like a more sophisticated version of "the debbil made me do it." For that matter, all the language of objects and self-objects seems to me a language of evasion. What is an object? A concrete thing? Self-object seems such an oxymoron, like "thunderous silence," a juxtaposition of two incompatible concepts. A self is a person: an object is a thing, by definition.

The dynamic personality view would suggest that these patients are extremely well attuned to certain aspects of the therapists and their participation and that these aspects are there and a problem for the therapists in their own lives. Most traditional patients do not detect them or are too polite or too frightened of rejection to attend to them. These so-called "narcissists" do not respect the privacy of the therapist. How do these self-absorbed people manage to see so much? *Why* must they see so much? Is it merely intrusiveness, a need for symbolic fusion, or could the extreme testing be also a wish to authenticate the therapist and thereby themselves? Life in the anxiety zone is made up of omissions and blind spots. One must not see what is there to be seen because it disrupts the capacity of the caretaking others (including the therapist) to meet one's needs. It is true that I am blurring the distinction between narcissistic and borderline character disorders. But I believe the distinction is blurred. At any rate they can both be subsumed under the rubric of "self-object relations disorders" as Kohut and Wolf would have it (1978).

Why do we treat them? Because they are there? Because it is our job? In truth, there is something very oddly appealing about them. Paradoxically, these "sick" patients are often most engaging. Unlike obsessional patients for whom the therapist barely exists, could be dead in the room and the patient would drone on unperturbed, these folks *demand* one's presence, excoriate one's sore spots, and strangely enough, when they do work out, seem often, at least to me, the most satisfactory people I have worked with although the experience was horrible. I suppose one might say that their interest in the analyst is narcissistic; they are interested only to the extent that they need the analyst. But, oddly, they seem often rather caring—at least, in between the bouts of fury.

I think of a patient who not only gave me a terrible time but also abraded every physician, taxi driver, and functionary she dealt with. She infuriated everyone, but she was not wrong—just exceedingly impolite. She was a master at puncturing all the pretentions we have about our jobs, why we do what we do.

One day, sitting with her and having the usual feeling of my bile rising, my dignity and professional amour propre trashed, I thought to myself—not that I must brace myself against this onslaught of her projective identifications—but more plaintively, "How does she manage to do this to me?" I had a spontaneous association to a patient I had treated many years before, an adolescent boy, a high school dropout whose mother would put on his shoes and socks every morning while he lay abed. One day—I hope in the process of the therapy—he said to her quietly, "Mother, I don't want you to do that anymore." Miracle of miracles, his mother, this engine of implacable invasiveness, looked surprised and said, "Oh, alright" and never did it again. I was very impressed.

So, I said to this woman, "Listen get out of my head. I wish you would stop telling me what I should feel and when I should feel it." She looked surprised and, mirabile dictu, she stopped. Again, I was impressed. The most parsimonious explanation is that I told her what was in *my* head, not hers. Also I asked her to please stop what she was doing because it was upsetting me. I was left with the impression that projective identification is a bit like the Dracula story; the vampire, for all his powers, cannot break into the bedroom, one must open the window and *invite* him in—at least the first time. When I closed my window, she left me alone. I cannot help but feel that what was resolved was not her character defect—it was all too sudden for that—but a dynamic interaction between the two of us, to which I contributed my own operations.

Another brief example with the same patient: she was quite infamous among friends (of whom she had many, by the way) and colleagues for her demands for attention and concern. Any suggestion of a lack of interest in her was greeted with a barrage of furious invective. One session, she was telling me a story. Suddenly, she stopped and said sharply, "Are you paying attention?" In truth, I was not. Instead of sustaining the usual stony but professionally endorsed silence or confronting her with her self-absorbed, narcissistic demands for unflagging attention, I said, "I wasn't paying attention. I'm sitting here trying to remember whether I gave the same hour to two patients." She said, "Well, look in your book and find out." I did. I then listened, and she continued without any further comment. I must say I felt grateful to her.

I am claiming, then, that the concept of "character" is armor for the therapist and that much of the wild, frenetic "transference" one sees with these patients may be iatrogenic, a reaction of enraged frustration at the analyst's imperturbability and an unwillingness to be part of what the analyst observes. As Wyse so eloquently put it, "Just as therapists must patiently await transformation into meaningful personhood in the patient's eyes, so must "borderlines" patients await transformation in the eyes of their therapist [sic] into meaningful personhood rather than being viewed as interesting, challenging, difficult and resistive nosological entities, disorders, syndromes, characters, and personality organizations" (1989:669).

To use another example: Ghent (1989) quotes a "moving" example of Kohut's efforts to hear the patient's complaints as legitimate and his interpretations, however well intended or thoughtful, as merely words. "What I had not seen, however, was that the patient had felt additionally traumatized by feeling that all these explanations on my part came only from the outside: that I did not fully feel what he felt, that I gave him words, but not real understanding, and that I therefore repeated the essential trauma of his early life. The task that the analyst faces at such moments—the crucial moment in which a 'borderline' condition either will or will not become an analyzable narcissistic personality disorder—is largely one of self-scrutiny" (p. 195).

I would agree absolutely. Yet, in the case of Kohut's that I present later, he does precisely the opposite, in spite of the patient's repeated references to a dream, which is a tip-off. Later in the same quote, he says, "Only the analyst's continuing sincere acceptance of the patient's reproaches as (psychologically) realistic." Note the parenthetic "*psychologically* realistic," not simply realistic. The patient is understood to be distorting. On the next page, Ghent concurs with the characterization of the narcissistic patient as being "exquisitely sensitive to humiliation and tends to experience *any* interpretation as humiliating." If patients are to assume agency for their actions, why not therapists? Why should therapists tell patients what is in their minds? How can they know? Maybe therapists are humiliating the patients. As Havens (1989) put it, "[We] need to deflect the preconceptions and projections dominating clinical fields and [move] toward an attitude going beyond respect for the patient, substituting instead a real democracy of relationship between therapist and patient. The old hierarchies are to be dismantled" (p. 139).

To illustrate this point, I want to go briefly to a famous case of Kohut's, the Two Analyses of Mr. Z. (Kohut 1979).

> Mr. Z's analysis took place in two segments, each conducted five times weekly and lasting about four years, separated by an interval of five and a half years. The first analysis was classical; the second represented Kohut's working out of his new vision of Self psychology. It is to be noted that Mr. Z. improved markedly in both therapies. The classical treatment was hardly a failure. Kohut attributes his most significant sign of advance in the therapy to a dream that occurred about six months before termination of the first treatment. The patient was in a house, at the inner side of a door that was a crack open. Outside was *the* [sic!] father, loaded with gift-wrapped packages, wanting to enter. The patient was intensely frightened and attempted to close the door in order to keep the father out. Kohut is perfectly aware of the transference implications of the dream; it refers to "his ambivalent attitude towards the father." But it is not considered that this may be exactly what Kohut is doing—forcing gift-wrapped packages on the patient who is trying to guard his privacy. One notes—with some amusement—that after the successful termination of the first therapy, Kohut's first sign of recurrent trouble was a *Christmas* card indicating that Mr. Z might soon be returning (vide, Mr. Z's dream of "gift-wrapped" presents).
>
> Shortly after the beginning of the second analysis, Mr. Z had another dream, of an idealized powerful man, holding an umbrella in one hand and gloves in the other. Strikingly the figure of the man is very "plastic and prominent" while the background is blurry. Again, the transference note is detected and interpreted, but again, it is not considered that something interactional and real could be taking place, that Mr. Z may be seeing or wishing to see Dr. K clearly. It is considered an idealizing transference. A significant theme in the second therapy was the mother's invasiveness into the boy's privacy. Does this have some relevance to his trying to keep the door closed? Dr. K again provides the patient with an extended exegesis on his life and motivations. The metaphor has changed, but the relationship has not. Dr. K tells Mr. Z what Mr. Z is all about. There are again, in the second analysis, references by the patient back to the father dream, but again this is not heard as a message about anything real.

In the first analysis, the emphasis is Freudian, and in the second Self psychological, but in both the patient is told what he is doing and why. Dr. K can interpret with conviction because character per se is constant, even though his view of character *development* has changed. Transference remains a distortion laid on the therapist. In the second analysis, the metapsychology has changed, but the intent is restitution of characterological deficit. The patient is listened to carefully and empathically, *not* to hear if he may be correct about anything, but to provide him with an experience that will supply the mortar of a restoration (to use Kohut's own term) of characterological deficit. He continues to wrap up the patient's life and hand it to him. The patient's desire to see him clearly is certainly a wish carried over from his father, but it is not an anachronistic repetition of a past need: it is a present need.

Kohut never goes the next step, which is to see his own participation and to see the patient's perception as real. As Ghent (1989) quotes Arnold Goldberg, "Self psychology struggles hard *not* to be an interpersonal psychology not only because it wishes to avoid the social psychological connotations of the phrase but also because it wishes to minimize the input of the analyst into the mix . . . [so] as to allow a thwarted development to unfold. Since self-psychology is predominantly a developmental psychology it is based on the idea of a developmental program (one that may be innate or pre-wired if you wish) that will reconstitute itself under certain conditions" (p. 188).

Analysis A and analysis B seem to me like analysis A and analysis A'—not all that different. The basic premise remains unchanged. The analyst is operating upon something in the patient: who the patient is. This reification makes it possible to avoid the awareness that two personalities with two different agendas are engaging each other. This is not to say that the therapy was not successful. Psychoanalysts, like magicians, depend on contiguous magic. They do a lot of things, all together. Sometimes it works, sometimes it does not. When it does, it is difficult to dissect free the different threads of connection and consequence.

The characterological position holds that it is very difficult for people to change; like the proverbial leopard, they must change their spots. The dynamic personality position posits that it is easy for people to change—they can and do change very suddenly and markedly; the real difficulty is in creating new circumstances, shifting the system sufficiently. In the dynamic personality position, the therapist is a participant, in a real way, and consequently these patients are extremely distressing. Somewhere, Searles has commented that, at a point in the therapy, they may become the most important person in the therapist's life. One must examine very carefully why one is willing to work with so disruptive a partner. I feel that if the therapy works, one is likely to have a radical experience; I think they really change one's life.

Do they represent a new patient, a clearer diagnostic category than the old categories? I really doubt it, nor am I alone in that belief (Cooper 1987). Character is the analysts' Holy Grail, a dream of a solid immutable truth—something they can put a finger on. Personality is a much more elusive and a much more interactive category. What we define as borderline or narcissistic is only an exaggeration of cultural directions in style. We do live in a narcissistic culture and we tend to call our mates and friends "narcissistic" when they do not give us what we want. The personality orientation is simply more wary of diagnosis and its implication for reassuring the therapist by reifying the patient.

I believe that character formulations do not engage some deeper reality. I also think that in another decade or so they will be replaced. I think they are essentially a political solution: one that describes a contemporaneous way of being, which permits analysts to shift the nature of their participation without offending the mandarins of their psychoanalysis establishments or losing their credentials. It is as regressive as it is advantageous. Although it protects the esteem of the therapist, facilitating work with patients who would otherwise easily drive one to despair, it also acts as a leash, preventing the therapist from taking the next step into the unknown, committing to a necessarily ambiguous participation with the patient toward mutual change—what Meltzer (1979) called the "Virgil-leading-Dante" model of analysis, wherein the therapist "risks everything" in the voyage to the underworld.

I would suggest that a reexamination of the premises that underlie concepts of *character* and *personality* reveal vitally different premises about what change is and what part we must play in having it come about.

References

Akhtar, S. and J.A. Thomson. 1982. Overview: Narcissistic personality disorder. *American Journal of Psychiatry* 139:12–20.

Arendt, H. 1963. *Eichman in Jerusalem: A Report on the Banality of Evil.* New York: Viking Press.

Cooper, A.M. 1987. The changing culture of psychoanalysis. *Journal of the American Academy of Psychoanalysis* 15:285.

Feiner, A. 1973. Countertransference and the anxiety of influence. In L. Epstein and A. Feiner, eds., *Countertransference,* pp. 105–28. New York: Jason Aronson.

Fromm, E. 1973. *The Anatomy of Human Destructiveness.* New York: Holt, Rinehart, and Winston.

Ghent, E. 1989. Credo: The dialectics of one-person and two-person psychologies. *Contemporary Psychoanalysis* 25:169–211.

Grice, P. 1989. *Studies in the Way of Words.* Cambridge, Mass.: Harvard University Press.

Grinberg, L. 1979. Countertransference and projective counteridentification. In L. Epstein and A. Feiner, eds., *Countertransference,* pp. 169–91. New York: Jason Aronson.

Havens, L. 1989. *A Safe Place: Laying the Groundwork for Psychotherapy.* Cambridge, Mass.: Harvard University Press.

Hoffman, I.Z. 1987. The value of uncertainty in psychoanalytic practice. *Contemporary Psychoanalysis* 23:205–15.

James, W. 1981. *Principles of Psychology,* vol. 2. Cambridge, Mass.: Harvard University Press.

Kagan, J. 1989. *Unstable Ideas, Temperament, Cognition, and self.* Cambridge, Mass.: Harvard University Press.

Kernberg, O. 1974. Further contributions to the treatment of narcissistic personalities. *International Journal of Psychoanalysis* 55:214–40.

Kernberg, P. 1971. The course of analysis of a narcissistic personality with hysterical and compulsive features. *Journal of the American Psychoanalytic Association* 19:451–71.

Kohut, H. 1979. The two analyses of Mr. Z. *International Journal of Psychoanalysis* 60:3–27.

Kohut, H. and E. Wolf. 1978. The disorders of the self and their treatment. *International Journal of Psychoanalysis* 59:414–25.

Levenson, E. 1981. The rhetoric of intimacy. *GROUP* 5:3–11.

Little, M. 1988. Winnicott working in areas where psychotic anxieties predominate. *Free Association* 3:8–41. London: Free Association Books.

Masterson, J. 1989. Maintaining objectivity crucial in treating borderline patients. *The Psychiatric Times* 6:1, 26.

Meltzer, D. 1979. Routine and inspired interpretations. In L. Epstein and A. Feiner, eds., *Countertransference,* p. 134. New York: Jason Aronson.

Searles, H. 1979. The analyst's experience with jealousy. In L. Epstein and A. Feiner, eds., *Countertransference,* pp. 305–27. New York: Jason Aronson.

Sullivan, H.S. 1953. *The Interpersonal Theory of Psychiatry.* New York: Norton.

Thas-Thienemann, T. 1968. *Symbolic Behavior.* New York: Washington Square Press.

Wolf, E. 1988. *Treating the Self.* New York: Guilford Press.

Wolstein, B. 1987. Anxiety and the psychic center of the psychoanalytic self. *Contemporary Psychoanalysis* 23:631–58.

Wyse, L.A. 1989. Book Review: *The Borderline Patient.* J. Grotstein, M. Solomon and J. Lang, eds., *Journal of the American Academy of Psychoanalysis* 17:667–70.

6

The Interpersonal Self Updated

Alan L. Grey

As a psychoanalytic formulation that has sturdily weathered more than half a century, the Interpersonal conceptualization of the self deserves some effort at review and revision. A useful place to begin is with the Interpersonal premise that the self is not an entity but a construct. That is true in at least two respects. The first consideration is that the selves of individuals are constructs at which they arrive through both self-reflexive and unaware psychological interactions with others. Since no two interactional histories are likely to be identical, it follows that, most probably, neither will any two self-constructs, especially in light of related variations in biological endowment. The second sense in which self is a construct refers to the metalevel at which generalized schemas of self are proposed by theorists. That is, Self theories are constructs to describe constructs and are influenced by the theorist's own prior constructs (see, e.g., Sullivan 1964:217n).

It follows that for formulations about the self to apply to a broad range of persons, times, and places, they must build upon these two considerations.

This means that the wide divergences between circumstances affecting different selves recommend that generalizations about those selves include some specification of the contexts to which they apply. Beyond that, since all theories are generated by human beings who are similarly permeable to the conditions under which they operate, it seems clear that their assertions are likely to benefit from consensual validation, using appropriate external criteria. The cornerstone underlying these tenets of Interpersonal psychoanalysis was called "field theory" in Sullivan's work (1953:367–369). Its sustained vigor is confirmed in current clinical attention to countertransference (e.g., Epstein and Feiner 1979; Wolstein 1988; Levenson 1991), as well as in continuing contributions by cross-cultural researches (e.g., Grey 1975a, 1975b, 1973; Segall 1986), and by constructionist psychologists whose focus is the self (e.g., Bruner 1990; Cushman 1990).

Evidence accumulating from these and other sources urges further extension of the field theory approach to formulations about the self. How that can be accomplished is a leading theme in this paper, and it is examined in three sections. Section I addresses the Interpersonal explanation of self as a personal construct, section II looks at the Interpersonal self as a theoretical metaconstruct, and section III proposes an updating of that metaconstruct.

I. Self as a Personal Construct

For some time now, experienced clinicians have known that blue-collar workers are usually less amenable to introspectively oriented treatment techniques than patients with more intellectual occupational backgrounds are (see, e.g., Grey 1969; Dean, Kraft, and Pepper 1976). A somewhat related observation is that the patient's self in the consulting room is not necessarily consistent with modes of relating elsewhere—say, at home or at work. Where these two phenomena overlap is that both urge the need to consider cultural and subcultural contexts. That principle is relevant for understanding not only the various effects of different cultures but also even the influences on a single individual moving from one setting to another. Complexities of that sort are appreciated and resolved in Sullivan's approach to the self by starting from the more embracing perspective of "situation" as a necessary frame for thinking about matters of identity.

Situations are not "outside" the personality; the intimate connection between private mental processes and transactions in the world is what makes inferences possible about someone else's covert experience. Although reasoning from appearances to their subjective correlates is far from foolproof, clinicians rely on it as a crucial source of data about patients. Social psychologists have demonstrated, too, that even when we seek to understand our own feelings we count on situational cues (e.g., Schachter and Singer 1962). Human psychological life involves a circuit of continuous exchange between the subjective "inner" world and "external" behavioral interactions of oneself with others. There is no private self untouched by outer social experience and no social interaction unaffected by one's subjective orientation.

In more recent decades, psychoanalytic writers (e.g., Kohut, Winnicott) more and more have recognized that early relationships between mothers and children have major impact on the children's sense of themselves. But these object relations theories offer only limited awareness of the pervasiveness of social influences. For one thing they focus almost exclusively on early childhood, and for another, on the mother–child dyad. Even so, the mother's part is understood as if her personality can be abstracted from the cultural web of meanings in which it is immersed. Thus how she serves as culture-bearer largely escapes attention, except perhaps for passing recognition that verbal communication may transmit culture. "It makes far more sense," says Cushman, "to argue that the language and frame of reference of a culture . . . is enacted, taught, and discussed as soon as the parents begin interacting with the fetus through movements, touch and sound" (1991:215).

Besides mothers, many others will also influence the baby's life course from the nursery to the grave and will help to define what become crucial identity markers for that individual. The diversity of possible markers that can become compelling may suggest the potential variety and range of self-organization. One person may feel confirmed by a life of ascetic withdrawal, another by intense sensual experience, a third by careful exegesis of obscure texts, and still another by taking human heads in a state of rage and frenzy. In simpler cultures only a limited variety of life-styles may be available, and although more options occur in complex ones, some choices are not necessarily feasible for any one person confined to a particular subgroup. Fashion designers cannot prosper among the American Amish any more than pacifists would in cannibal New Guinea. These brief illustrations of single criteria are not intended, of course, to obscure that each person (and each society) is defined by many identity markers, including those pertinent to gender, status, occupation, religion, etc.

However the self-reflexive picture is composed, the achievement of that very capacity for self-awareness implies a relatively advanced level of socialization of the child. Long before the child's becoming aware of being one way or another or of wishing to achieve particular qualities, many tendencies have already begun, some of them never to reach consciousness. This distinction between what is self-reflexive and what is not is a hallmark of psychoanalysis since Freud's day. It was he who discovered that self-awareness is a major tool for achieving desired personality changes. Thus it becomes a key conceptual device in formulations about personality for psychotherapeutic purposes. The criterion of access to consciousness has the further advantage that it is applicable cross-culturally since awareness and dissociation of personal attributes can be anticipated to be useful information for observers everywhere. Perhaps for both these reasons, Sullivan adopted it as a central reference point in describing the self.

In Interpersonal terminology, the self of which one is aware is called the "personified self." Its range of sentience is controlled outside of consciousness by processes collectively called the "self-system." They are defensive security operations to protect against exposure to characterizations that threaten to evoke unbearable anxiety. In Sullivan's own words:

> From the time that the self-system begins to emerge, three aspects of the personality process can be rather readily distinguished: first, the waking and thoroughly active self; second, the part of the personality which is not readily accessible to awareness—the rest of the personality which, in another context can be considered as the whole personality with the self as the eccentric part, and finally the period spent in sleep, in which the self is relatively dormant and many things can be done which cannot be done when the self is functioning actively (1956:4).

In sum, the four major subconstructs of personality, for Sullivan, are:

1. *self-system,* including the *personified self*
2. *the rest of the personality*
3. *situations* (referring particularly to others, real and illusory)
4. *sleep*

The fourth of these designated processes, sleep, is regarded by Sullivan as an occasion when the workings of the self are largely suspended. Here he is referring to the protective functions of the self-system, which relax in sleep, allowing dreams to be a useful window into hidden currents of personality. In any case, the point is that during sleep the waking self is set aside, leaving the sleep state outside our immediate focus. But, at least by implication, this reference to sleep brings us again to the important issue of awareness.

When awareness is invaded by serious challenges to any self-personification that serves as a serious source of self-esteem, such a confrontation can evoke intolerably intense levels of anxiety. At that point the function of the self-system is to blur or to dissociate the threatening knowledge through censorship maneuvers called "security operations," lest the personality become seriously disorganized, at least temporarily. Thus far, the description is quite similar to Freud's, in portraying the constraints of conscience on consciousness. The two schools even agree that most psychological activity takes place outside consciousness, as when Sullivan refers to the self-reflexive personified self as the unusual or "eccentric part" of personality.

Beyond this point, however, the orthodox and Interpersonal versions begin to part company. In Sullivan's formulation, it is disapproval or anticipated disapproval from significant others that is threatening, rather than hypothetical intrapsychic energy imbalances. Whatever evokes disapproval is experienced as "bad-me," especially during childhood, and being "bad" jeopardizes the sense of security provided by key human relationships. Worse yet, what is experienced as potentially destructive of that security requires either the achievement of reassurances or self-system intervention to obliterate awareness of terror. Such "not-me" episodes are typically not recalled. In order to sustain psychological security, then, behavior is restricted by the tolerances of a person's essential reference groups, as that person understands them. And if not behavior, at least consciousness, is thus restricted. By such processes, social canons of acceptability become integral to one's personality.

If much of self-definition occurs in this manner, then communications—both verbal and preverbal—clearly play a major role in how we become what we are. But social communication is no simple matter, involving far more than merely the mechanical recording or mirroring of messages. "In developing a theory of personality," cautions Sullivan, "you must remember that [communicated] signs are signs only when there is an interpreter to attach meaning to a body of otherwise physical phenomena" (1953:88). And of special interest for Sullivan about this process is not only the syntaxic conscious level of understanding but also how the message is further shaped outside awareness by security operations of the self-system. Security operations protect the stability of personality, but that stability can be at the expense of self-knowledge and in opposition to the goals of treatment.

So significant are self-system operations to Sullivan that *self-system* is the term used not only for automatic censoring but also as a designation that includes the personified self. Owing to this emphasis, some critics both within and outside the Interpersonal school have regarded the Sullivanian self as dealing with little more than defenses against anxiety. And, indeed, there is some justice to that assessment if we do not venture beyond formal statements and fail to look at his portrayal of human development in a succession of steps toward increasing awareness, relatedness, and competency. The developmental schema does illustrate that despite imbalances in exposition, the key Interpersonal constructs are sufficiently broad and flexible to accommodate substantial expansion.

Consider, for instance, those clinical phenomena widely referred to as "narcissistic." For one thing, even this sketchy outline makes it apparent that concern with self-esteem and with favorable self-personifications is not found to be restricted to one special type of people, marked off from the rest of humankind. Defenses against negative judgments are typical of all of us, and insofar as our self-personifications remain reasonably consistent with actual transactions, their costs in how we mislead ourselves stay within our means. Such defenses "imply nothing more than that the child [or adult] is alive" (Sullivan 1953:224).

Yet, when the nature of what is a privately acceptable self-personification is so discrepant with uncensored experience that very extensive security operations are required, then the resulting loss of orienting information may be great enough to jeopardize effective functioning to the point where the person is labeled "neurotic" or even "psychotic." Not intrinsically infantile or pathological, an *excessive* concern with one's self-image becomes unfortunate when it substantially reduces the ability to live comfortably and adequately in the world. One virtue of this schema is its parsimony. It focuses attention on what is clinically relevant without calling for completely different therapeutic principles for those dubbed "narcissistic." It indicates, rather, that the treatment tasks always involve finding ways for decreasing self-system activity by relieving the *unwarranted* anxieties of patients through reducing their threatening distortions.

In summing up the personified self as a construct, then, it refers to the aspect of the self-system that is reflected in statements pertaining to the subject "I," and "as such it is the source of communicated information, as contrasted with other information about the person's self-system, which must necessarily be inferred" (Sullivan 1954:178). Beyond several statements of this sort and references to a "drive to mental health" (1954:100), all too little was indicated directly about the personified self and about nondefensive functions of personality. Moreover, what he did say referred more to the personified self as mental contents than to how it works as process. What is paradoxical is that his basic postulates conceive of "all that lives" as responsively engaged "in communal existence with its environment" (1972:12), yet he wrote mostly about unresponsiveness and the human resistance to change.

The paradox can be resolved by distinguishing between his clinical discussions of rigidities associated with psychological traumata, in contrast to the theoretical bases of Interpersonal theory, which also vigorously address the human potential for nondefensive awareness, for flexibility, for creativity. Thus Clara Thompson went to some pains to present a more balanced picture of both sides of the Interpersonal self. While it does include "a more or less rigid portion which has been developed in response to intense threat and anxiety," there are also other possible outcomes. "There must be many whose early lives were sufficiently secure to permit the development of large areas of the self without concern for approval or disapproval. . . . The self in interpersonal theory is not identical with the self-system although it includes it" (1964:39–40).

Thompson emphasized that the capacity for change continues throughout life. "Alterations of the self can also occur when significant people in our lives change, and in adapting to the new situation, certain characteristics may be pushed aside and others allowed to emerge" (1964:40). She called attention, moreover, to Sullivan's postulation of "a basic drive in man toward growth and maturation" (1964:88). Although he used the misleading label of "power" for this motive, what he intended is quite close in meaning to White's term "effectance" (see Carson 1969:22).

Discussion thus far has concentrated on core hypotheses about the self as proposed by Sullivan and amplified by others, like Thompson, to indicate the bases on which reformulations will be proposed. What makes those hypotheses worth retaining is that they continue to fit with accumulating evidence from the clinic and from psychological research. For instance, Thompson's statement that human nature is capable of continuing flexibility in adulthood is sustained in current studies of the adaptivity of the aged (e.g., Lerner 1990).

What endures in the Interpersonal version of self is that the individual's perceptions and behavior, whether defensive or otherwise, grow out of an inherent human capacity to learn through inevitable interaction in social fields. And those social fields, Schachtel (1959:14) notes, extend far beyond early dyadic family constellations to peers, teachers, neighbors, lovers, co-workers, leaders, and subordinates, to the larger world. That perspective is a major departure from the ethnocentric and nativist premises still lingering to various degrees in other analytic schools as a survival of Classical metapsychology.

Before we move on to the second section of this paper, Interpersonal premises about the self can be clarified further by looking at an apparent contradiction in Sullivan's formulations. That seeming inconsistency, concerning the question whether each self is unique, results from approaching the topic in two very different ways. On the one hand, he insists that the subjective experience of any two people is never identical, even when they simultaneously participate in the same situation. Each construes reality in his or her own fashion, and thus "The practical impossibility of one-to-one correspondence of mental states of the observer and the observed person should be evident" (1964:55). Nor is he implying that when impressions differ it is because one of the participants is necessarily more accurate than the other. Quite the contrary, he warns that "certainty about interpersonal processes should seldom concern one. Information about any situation should be considered as a formulation of probability" (1964:53–54).

If this position sounds like radical relativism, wherein all versions have equal validity, that is not at all what he has in mind. Rather it is a warning about hazards inherent in observation and communication, and it urges procedures for sifting out more reliable from less reliable information. The detailed attention accorded to possible mutual misunderstandings in the dialogue between patient and analyst is a hallmark of Interpersonal clinical procedures (see, e.g., Sullivan 1954; Epstein and Feiner 1979; Wolstein 1988).

In striving to avoid the Tower of Babel that can emerge from the uniqueness of subjective experience, in one controversial paper Sullivan recommended the use of operational discourse, in Bridgman's sense. That is, communications should draw, as explicitly as possible, upon mutually observable phenomena as the basis for statements. Partly because of its title, "The Illusion of Personal Individuality," this message struck many as dismissive of the very singularity of the subjective self that Sullivan was seeking to address. So sacrosanct is the idea of individuality in the United States that the vehemence of protest led Helen Swick Perry, his loyal editor and biographer, to concede that the title was "unfortunate" (Sullivan 1964:196).

Actually, the provocative paper indicates a clear awareness of "the unique individuality of experience" and notes that when using consensual language to communicate subjective impressions "we forget how strikingly novel the experience was and how peculiarly it had fringes which apply only to us." Granting all that, he warns us not to forget that we also "get great richness from social intercourse" (1964:214). Whatever the loss in relinquishing the autistic, personalities cannot sustain their vigor over the long haul without shared meanings. In a very real sense, self-realization is not only an individual, or dyadic, but also a communal achievement. This observation applies especially in scientific endeavors, like psychoanalysis, whose robustness rests upon consensual validation.

II. The Interpersonal Self as Theoretical Metaconstruct

Sullivan is reputed to have assessed his own contribution to psychoanalysis as "an operational statement within a field theory" (Perry 1982:253). At least one way to understand the reference to field theory is as an intention to preserve and expand psychoanalytic insights in ways that take adequate account of the interplay between person and social context. Moreover, he strove to couch his own views in empirically testable terms. For present purposes we focus particularly on how effectively he applied field theory—where his efforts seem to have succeeded and where they did not. Operational tests of Interpersonal theory will also receive attention, at least to the extent of the citing of some particularly relevant research studies.

As has already been suggested, the field theory premises guiding Interpersonal formulations demonstrate a sustained vigor in how well they fit with contemporary constructionist thought in the social sciences. This thinking goes well beyond obvious generalizations about social custom as a regulator of human behavior. It explores how even the most private of our experiences are shaped through interactions with others. Moreover, it becomes clearer that these influences are pervasive through preverbal interactions from birth onward (see Trad 1990, 1991).

Elsewhere in this volume, I have traced how Interpersonal theory seems unique among psychoanalytic schools in the consistency with which it holds to field theory. One important instance of how Interpersonal formulations permit flexible consideration of the interplay between the social milieu and the individual is in the treatment of questions about what motivates the self. Goals esteemed in Western cultures and in Object Relations theories, such as individuation and autonomy, are not assumed to be equally pertinent everywhere. Rather, it is proposed that the functioning of the self can be examined from the perspective of how effectively one learns to "integrate situations." This phrase refers to the extent to which interactions are conducted in a manner that contributes to the mutual fulfillment of the requirements of the participants, whatever the forms taken by these requirements. Efforts to specify the diverse array of motivations manifested by the self presented Sullivan with a formidable problem inasmuch as he well knew that culture leads to "great differentiation of the goals of behavior and therefore of the integrating tendencies that characterize interpersonal relations" (1956:10). He settled, nevertheless, for two broad categories: "satisfactions," involving biological needs, and "security," concerned with finding acceptance and avoiding anxiety in personal relationships. (As noted previously a third impelling drive reflected in developmental formulations is "power" or effectance). It is a perspective that recognizes that all human psychological needs can become variously expressed and inextricably intertwined. For instance, people continually violate their own biology unknowingly, as health treatises are fond of reminding us, and knowingly as in anorexia or marathon races. Moreover, while contexts exist in which only one person is present, for the socialized human being *no situations are psychologically free of interpersonal motivations and influences integral to the socialized self.*

Despite its elasticity in taking account of the countless variations arising from reciprocal interplay between individual and the wide range of possible interpersonal milieux, this schema for understanding human motivations provides a meaningful focus for the clinical observer. This focus is on security—the urge for acceptance by others and by oneself. It is a consideration that influences how all other drives are pursued, whether for contact and related biologically based requirements or for various types of effectance ("power"). This quest presses one to conform to whatever expectations are believed necessary for being accepted by the significant other. To some extent the expectations attributed to this significant other are particular to those interacting, and to some extent they are canonical in the wider culture.

Useful assessment requires that the observer understand not only generic human nature but also social definitions specific to the circumstances. Thus, in his discussion of the psychiatric interview, Sullivan takes pains to spell out a description of how patients are likely to regard the cultural role of the psychiatrist as an expert (1954:26ff.). Each situation generates its own more or less urgent dialectic of tugs, the one to meet wishes of others versus pulls toward one's own private requirements, where they diverge. How well a person succeeds in integrating the range of situations that compose his or her life is a central focus for the Interpersonal perspective on the self. If we judge by how widely psychoanalysts are coming to recognize the relevance of relationship needs in clinical practice, then the Interpersonal approach has achieved a large measure of practical validation.

With refreshing consistency, the concern for self-esteem as necessary to emotional security is seen as so salient that it serves as an organizing principle for the Interpersonal self, it will be recalled. Thus affirmative, or at least minimally tolerable, self-characterizations compose the entire content of the personified self, while all else is relegated to the rest of the personality through automatic censoring by the self-system, as guardian against intense anxiety. So stated, this paradigm is useful in most treatment situations as a guide to the limitations in a patient's self-report. It also holds important implications for how those limits can be tightened or eased. But since Sullivan's day, further understandings of how to elicit information are emerging from social constructionist extensions of the field theory idea, especially via the use of narrative to provide contexts for both speaker and auditor. On this basis, a proposal for improvement of the personified self as a construct will be described in section III.

Moving ahead to other conceptualizations related to selfhood, we see that the self-system and the rest of the personality have continuing utility, but they can also benefit from a fresh look. Both of those concepts are concerned with nonverbal or nonself-reflexive psychic processes, called the unconscious by Freud. As Sullivan used these terms they continue to have connotations reminiscent of the Freudian emphasis on automatic, primitive, and pathological aspects of unconsciousness. Thus they leave the impression of distinct discontinuity between the maladaptive unaware, on the one hand, and socially adaptive activities of the personified self, on the other.

This impression is contradicted by current clinical experience, such as the utility of countertransference as a source of information, and by psychological research (e.g. Singer 1978; Singer and Kolligian 1987; Lazarus 1991a, 1991b). Actually, a reasonably careful reading of Sullivan also reveals clear clinical descriptions of many adaptive functions carried out through nonverbal mentation. Some of the labels he used for these phenomena were reverie [sic], sublimatory reformulation, selective inattention, and unformulated experience. Nevertheless, these observations were never consolidated into a unifying metaconstruct considered in relation to the functioning of the self. A more consistent application of field theory would indicate that what is not included in self-reflexive thought is neither necessarily excluded from adaptive interactions with environing circumstances nor unconnected to the personified self. In section III, reformulations are proposed for an integrative description of how nonverbal mental processes coordinate with the personified self for productive participation in social situations.

III. The Interpersonal Self Updated

In modifying Sullivan's own paradigm for personality, I have tried to be mindful that conceptual constructs, at best, are somewhat arbitrary ideas imposed upon the study of living human beings. Theoretical constructs are justifiable only insofar as they provide clarity and convenience for potential users. Toward this objective I suggest reexamination of particular features of two Sullivanian concepts, namely the personified self and the rest of the personality. The first of the two, personified self, refers to self knowledge that is readily available to awareness because its referents have positive or at least minimally tolerable emotional connotations. By contrast, the rest of the personality refers to modes of functioning that are barred from consciousness because their significance is emotionally unbearable.

Simple logic suggests that these categories do not exhaust all possibilities. Conceivably, for instance, psychological activities may exist that are not readily accessible to awareness but not because of any emotionally intolerable significance. In fact, we perform many essential functions more or less without clear awareness of what we are doing either because they were learned without benefit of syntaxic verbalization or because they no longer require conscious attention (e.g., certain grooming skills). They are discussed later in this paper under the designation of intuitive orientations and are mentioned here in connection with an outline of the remainder of this paper, as the only major innovation to be considered. Discussion is organized, first, around the personified self, then intuitive orientations, followed by the self-system and by concluding observations.

Revisions are proposed for all three of these major constructs pertaining to the self, with field theory as a principal consideration for the revisions. Better known currently through the formulations of social constructionism, the field theory idea is earning increasing currency in philosophy and the social sciences. The fact that this principle has provided a reference frame for Interpersonal theory from the start has much to do with its continued viability. It should occasion little surprise, however, if the accumulating experience of the past fifty years suggests some changes.

Personified Self

A good place to start is with the personified self as a synthesis of self-reflexive experience gradually emerging from the second year of life onward, with the learning of language. It is an integration of accepted "good-me" memories with tolerable, if anxiety-tainted, "bad-me" interactions, from the time of birth. Unbearable "not-me" experiences are excluded from the personified self. Shaped out of efforts toward emotional security from the beginnings of life, self-personifications develop through interactions with the defining reactions of significant others.

Since reflected appraisals are the stuff of self-esteem, and since secure positive self-regard contributes a comfortable sense of psychological well-being, concern with approval and disapproval can be expected to affect personality throughout life. In that sense, we are all narcissistic. What tends to be called narcissism is only an unduly intense preoccupation with the adequacy of the self-personification. It affects those who have been insufficiently confirmed.

No compelling need exists for radical alterations in Sullivan's general delineation of the personified self. It has the virtue of being framed along lines that lend themselves readily to clinical and research exploration. What may be useful, however, is to amplify the concept, giving more explicit attention to how people actively participate in the construction of their own identities.

The Interpersonal explanation of self-personifications is that children begin to acquire them even before they become able to use consensual language. They start to learn what is "good-me," "bad-me," or "not-me" through the favorable or unfavorable quality and the intensity of the responses of caretakers with whom they interact. Sullivan regards that tripartite set of characterizations as "rather inevitable" in "this or any culture" (1953:161). And he adds that "Good-me as it ultimately develops is the ordinary topic of discussion about 'I' " (1953:162).

In short, self-personifications are defined through social transactions in which the child seeks to "integrate situations" (i.e., to satisfy its needs) with various family members. Obviously implied is that not everything the child wants to do is "good." Put another way, matters of goodness tend to be closely linked to the question of intention, although other considerations may also affect evaluations. Sullivan was very skeptical about "The illusion of choice . . . entabled with dogmatic assertions of freedom of will" (1940:192). Authorities who share this position with him are likely to rely less on punishment as the principal mode of control, although some limit-setting is unavoidable. Thus, having repudiated the freedom-of-the-will doctrine, Sullivan does discuss intentionality from another reference frame. He states that "Decision and choice are functions of the memory and prospective reverie . . . which often eventuates in foresight. They are, however, interpersonal processes; they do not occur in the vacuum of an isolated individuality, and they correspondingly include the function of the self-system" (1940:193–194).

That statement clearly recognizes that the wellsprings of intentionality cannot be neatly ascribed entirely to the reflective personified self (a matter to be pursued in considering other components of the total personality). Also recognized is the importance of looking at choices as adequately understandable only within the contexts to which they are addressed. Undoubtedly it is useful to characterize personalities by abstracting regularities from accumulated observations. At the same time, human activities do not repeat themselves in purely mechanical ways, so that it is equally pertinent to track shifts in those regularities, especially if change is what is sought, as in psychotherapy. Then it becomes important to be mindful that personality shows only a "relatively enduring pattern," and only insofar as it is linked to "recurrent interpersonal situations" (Sullivan 1953:111). That is, because our actions are in the service of purpose, we both seek and respond to alterations in the state of affairs.

It follows, by implication at least, that the self can best be understood through statements that take account of the interplay between self and others in contexts relevant to personal intentions, that is, to struggles with one's own good-me, bad-me, and not-me. This suggests narrative as a way of organizing descriptions. As Bruner tells the story, it falls into a distinctly Interpersonal form. "The child learns to play a part in everyday family 'drama' before there is even any telling or justifying. What is permissible and what is not, what leads to what outcomes, these are first learned in action" (1990:85). We have already considered the subjective consequences of that drama and how, with the emergence of language skills, family imperatives are reflected in the personified self. Nowhere are these self-personifications more actively developed than in explaining triumphs and transgressions to parents and other elders. Here the greatest reward lies in casting one's actions as "an extension of the canonical transformed by mitigating circumstances" (1990:87).

Exactly because it relates the protagonist to his or her world, narrative appears to have been serving as a universal human mode for organizing emotionally meaningful cognitions. Although appreciation of this fact by theorists is relatively recent, it is becoming quite widely accepted. Marshack, the anthropologist, suggests that the key characteristics of stories is that they are communications about a happening over a span of time, one that has a beginning, and a change leading to a result or solution, always told from the perspective of a person or thing. In fact, he insists that "every process recognized and used in human culture becomes a story, and every story is an event which includes characters (whether spirit, god, hero, person, 'mana,' or in modern terms, element, particle, force, or law) who change or do things in time" (1972:283).

Certainly within psychoanalysis, the dream offers a spontaneous human expression of the predisposition to organize experience into stories (Jones 1979). Psychoanalytic treatment itself has traditionally emphasized the life history, and now more than ever, especially among those who view change as achieved via re-creation of the life narrative (e.g., Spence 1984). Rather than add many other available examples of current interest in the story form, I think it may suffice to indicate such attention is spurred by recognition that narrative provides a cognitive frame that helps the human mind to pull together experience better in relation to situational contexts and across time. Current neurological evidence indicates that conscious memory itself, the source for data constituting the personified self, is organized in terms of situational cues. Moreover, our awareness must continue to be reorganized in response to altered life circumstances in order to retain utility. As a neuropsychologist puts it, "Our memories are organized when we are fully awake, they must be or our responses would not be appropriate to the given circumstances" (Rosenfield 1988:184). That is, the focus of our conscious awareness alters as our contexts do. Thus, for instance, unused learning recedes from recall. In short, our subjective lives are not separated from the world but, willy-nilly, attuned to its fluctuations.

If we reconsider self-personifications, it becomes increasingly evident that self-personifications presented *in vacuo,* as a list of attributes or an unchanging cameo, leave out a great deal. The chances are that the most richly informative accounts of oneself can be elicited through stories of transactions in the world of people and events. Through such experiences personifications emerge in childhood and continue to be redefined afterward. Therefore, when the analyst's attention is confined largely to stories of early life and to family relationships, the resulting portrait of the personified self is placed into too small a conceptual frame. Change is not confined to early years, or to the mother–child dyad, or even to the family of orientation. Although normally with maturity there also comes increasing ability to sustain one's own independence in assessing messages from others, influences from emotionally meaningful encounters in all kinds of situations continue to affect self-personifications over the life span (see, e.g., Sorensen, Weinert, and Sherrod 1986).

At the same time, with increasing maturity also comes greater exposure to multiple, often conflicting criteria for right conduct, especially in our own pluralistic society. Clashing value systems of fellow workers versus family, of marketplace versus religion, and religion versus science, etc., cannot always be readily reconciled. Some find sanctuary in reference groups outside the mainstream, but choose as we will, concern with the canonical is inescapable. Bruner argues that not only autobiography but also all narratives revolve around efforts to *"find an intentional state that mitigates or at least makes comprehensible a deviation from a canonical cultural pattern"* (1990:49–50; italics are the author's).

Whether or not this proposition holds universally is beyond the scope of our concern here, but it does seem to hold for the kinds of threats to self-personifications that are of particular interest to psychotherapists. That is, this conclusion from nonclinical data coincides very closely with Interpersonal treatment observations that each of us needs to feel a sense of connection with a personally valued reference group, however apart that group may be from mainstream conventions. One major function of self-personifications, then, is to actively reconcile private motives and actions with prescribed conduct. Not only in autobiographical accounts but even in the most casual exchanges, all of us develop an elaborate repertoire of cultural devices to obscure and deceive, toward that self-enhancing end, including "propitiation," "verbalisms," and "as if performances" (Sullivan 1953:200, 208–211).

Beyond that, when events lead us radically outside the socially prescribed, they impel far more drastic efforts than mere verbalisms to render deviations comprehensible. Extreme deviations call for more fundamentally reconstructed self-personifying narratives. For instance, the Nazi genocide campaign led to a flood of autobiographical reports by survivors, both published and unpublished. DesPres quotes an inhabitant of the Warsaw ghetto who wrote of "a flame imprisoned in my bones, burning within me, screaming: Record!" Struck by the abundance of records by Holocaust survivors, DesPres concludes that "When men and women are forced to endure terrible things at the hands of others—whenever, that is, extremity involves moral issues—the need to remember becomes a general response" (1976:30–31). But more than a memory, it is a reaffirmation of self. Whenever death occurs, tombstones, newspaper notices, and mourning help to reconfirm the roles and motives of survivors, as well as of the departed.

Less extreme, but also a profound rending of social ties, is divorce. Here again, it is observed that "For months after the end of the marriage, the events leading to its breakdown are likely to occupy the thoughts of the separated husband and wife. . . . They develop an *account,* a history of the marital failure, a story of what their spouse did and what they did and what happened in consequence." As the underlying need is perceived by Weiss, who studied these accounts, it is "to understand the experience in terms of identifiable issues and eventually . . . as past, over and external to the individual's present self" (1975:14–15). Another noteworthy study concerns adoptees who, in adulthood, sought information about their previously unknown natural parents. The motivation for the quest proved to be to maintain "the ability to give an intelligent account and hence to be seen as accountable" (Haimes 1987:366).

In short, the autobiographical story is a spontaneous and universal way of ordering personal experience. It connects the protagonists with their circumstances in ways reflecting the quality of relationships with significant others. What emerges is seldom an accurate portrait of the narrator's personality but rather a subjective view—a self-personification. In that sense, such accounts provide particularly informative sources for understanding the individual's personified self. A reasonably useful grasp of anyone's self-personifications calls for systematic sampling of tales located over a variety of times and places in the narrator's recalled history. Preferably these tales are collected from a range of emotional states, all experienced by the same informant, as in long-term treatment (see, e.g., Sullivan 1954:168–172). The result is not an image of a single self but a gallery of selves with some family resemblances, selves that vary with the settings.

Even so, such self-reflexive accounts remain limited in several respects. For one thing, although they deal with personal history, these descriptions no longer faithfully reflect past self-personifications, since they are inevitably revised from present perspectives. For another thing, autobiographical anecdote "renders the exceptional comprehensible and keeps the uncanny at bay," as Bruner recently put it (1990:52). His choice of the term *uncanny* here is essentially identical with Interpersonal usage (Sullivan 1953:10). It refers to the overwhelming threat to self-esteem aroused by recognition of breaking a taboo, of venturing into the gravely uncanonical. Once the unspeakable has been committed, then the person is subject to profound self-loathing and revulsion that is psychotic in intensity. But, instead, most of us are able automatically to marshall self-system security operations that consign such knowledge to the "not-me" and the obscurity of the rest of the personality.

If terms like *personified self, self-system* and *the rest of the personality* slip into decontextualized usage, they are in danger of becoming reified into "structures" or ideas of that sort. So it remains essential to keep in mind that narrators are presenting their self-personifications under particular circumstances that affect how boundaries are drawn between the acceptable and the taboo. Thus a theft or a sexual act that is perverse in one context can become amusing in another. Undoubtedly some aspects of our personality repertoires can remain fixedly as personified self or the rest of the personality for most or all of our lives. Flexibility will vary according to the nature of the biological endowment, the socialization experiences, and the subsequent course of those lives. At the same time, if people were not endowed with some capacity for flexibility, then the very processes of psychotherapy would be impossible.

To change the focus of the personified self from the original Sullivanian description in terms of mental contents to a process orientation in the form of autobiographical narrative is to use a perspective more in harmony with field theory and with the requirements of treatment. Narrative encourages greater information about specific transactions between self and others. It offers clues to the conscious guidelines followed by the storyteller in actual transactions with others. Moreover, the anecdotal contexts facilitate the possibility for the listener to introduce precise inquiry. These advantages help to locate lacunae in the tale and thereby to identify the narrator's blind spots, major sources of inept and nonintegrated social encounters. To identify and mend these scotomas through insight is a central objective of psychoanalytic treatment.

No implication is made here that the difficulty caused by unawareness is that the "not-me" fails to be expressed behaviorally. It is, rather, that when they do occur, these expressions are more likely to lead to trouble and will be inaccessible to the potential benefits of self-reflexive reassessment and amelioration. These liabilities undoubtedly lay behind Sullivan's assertion that "One achieves mental health to the extent that one becomes aware of one's interpersonal relations" (1940:207).

Intuitive Orientations

If Sullivan's dictum about awareness has the appeal of simplicity, unfortunately it also fails to take account of important psychological phenomena that did come to Sullivan's attention in other connections. Possibly it unwittingly carried over a dichotomy built into Freud's metapsychology. Here I refer to a conception of unconscious mental processes as barred from awareness and even from real-world influences by censorship, in contrast to the realm of the conscious and preconscious, as knowable and readily accessible thinking. Still a third kind of experience, with no orthodox equivalent, remains to be considered as part of the updated Interpersonal functioning self. It is a type of psychological activity also outside awareness, but not for reasons of censorship or isolated from everyday influences.

This third kind of functioning is usually motivated by the same intentions as conscious actions of the personified self are and undertaken in close coordination with personified interactions. In the Interpersonal literature references are sometimes made to particular varieties of these phenomena, using such terms as *selective inattention, reverie,* or *sublimatory reformulations,* terms to be further explained shortly. Processes of this sort are learned without having required formulation into *syntaxic* (or consensual verbal) discourse. In that sense, they can be described as "unformulated experience" (Sullivan 1940:185; also Stern 1983) and belong to "a vast bunch of abilities which do not manifest as such if the contents of consciousness are involved" (Sullivan 1964:210).

Such activities occur at referential levels that Sullivan called "prototaxic" and "parataxic" and quite different from "syntaxic" speech. As types of cognitive–emotional processes that children use before syntaxic communication, they are very loosely reminiscent of what Freud called primary process. Actually their cognitive aspects much more closely resemble Piaget's formulations of "sensory–motor" (the *prototaxic*), and the autistic preoperational (the *parataxic*) levels of thinking. As understood in Interpersonal theory, all three of these levels of mentation, including *syntaxic* (consensual) verbalization, normally continue throughout life and may simultaneously affect any given interaction. Variants on the preverbal type of functioning that deserve at least brief mention here are what I call "enactions." They are skills that required conscious verbal effort while they were being learned but that no longer involve self-reflexive attention and that are even impeded by self-conscious attention. Many essential and characteristic personal ways of behaving belong here, such as the masculinity or femininity of one's gestures, how one knots a tie or makes a bow, the ability to type, athletic skills, and so forth.

In any case, so many vital functions are performed outside awareness for reasons other than censorship that they are integral to the maintenance of our socially distinctive selves. Therefore, it is useful to designate them collectively as *intuitive orientations,* a label introduced earlier in this paper. With the inclusion of that construct it is proposed that the updated Interpersonal self can be described in terms of five aspects. They include (1) the *personified self,* or ipsative information that is self-reflexively available and (2) *knowable intuitive orientations* that operate without verbalization, although they are not blocked from awareness by censorship. Then (3) *the rest of the personality* is an awkward and ambiguous term that can now be understood as *censored intuitive orientations* because although they are enacted on occasion, awareness of them is blocked by censorship. Next are the vital functions of (4) the *self-system,* a collective designation for security operations to censor awareness of matters threatening to self-esteem, that is, to self-personifications. Finally, there are (5) *situations* or the specific Interpersonal contexts that affect how the four preceding aspects of self are expressed and that are themselves affected by that interaction.

The implication here is that it is not adequately meaningful to look at the self as a dynamic construct apart from the settings in which it participates. Interplay with situations must be considered for an Interpersonal understanding of the self. But the same holds for each other aspect noted. All five of them refer to psychological phenomena whose continual mutual interplay requires shifts in how the boundaries between them are understood from one circumstance to the next. Examples have already been noted of how what is admissible into the personified self at one time may be consigned to censored intuitive orientations at another and of how personified skills may become enactions of the knowable intuitive orientations in due course. The ensuing discussion further illustrates how conceptual boundaries between aspects of the functioning self can change and flow so that distinctions between self and personality are essentially arbitrary and justifiable only in terms of theoretical convenience.

As fruitful a point of departure as any for that purpose may be some further consideration of intuitive orientations of both varieties. Nothing is particularly new about recognizing that some mental processes are censored and concealed owing to strong defensive motivations nor even in the fact that some uncensored psychological processes occur only at the margins of focal awareness. But it is another matter for analysts to give adequate attention to the possibility that relatively undefended preverbal processes may be our most characteristic form of mentation for carrying out most of the business of living.

What is especially noteworthy here is that when knowable intuitive orientations are compared with those functioning defensively (i.e., censored intuitive orientations), the possibility arises that, at least in some instances, freedom from defensiveness is situationally variable. If so, out-of-awareness may not at all mean "out-of-touch" with changing circumstances or rigid automaticity. Of particular interest are distinct anticipations of such possibilities to be found in Interpersonal literature and in observations currently emerging in cognitive psychological research (e.g., Singer and Kolligian 1987; Lazarus 1991a, 1991b).

Given the experimental and, indeed, the clinical evidence, then knowable intuitive orientations might best be considered as submerged extensions of the personified self. Or, to be more precise, perhaps the state of affairs is best stated the other way around: *the personified self is an extension into awareness of one's intuitive orientations in living.* From this perspective, our work as analysts can be understood in broader terms. Perhaps more often than we think about, we work with individuals whose knowable intuitive orientations are inadequate for coping with unanticipated life circumstances. In such cases, the analyst's skill at identifying unverbalized mental processes and bringing them to self-reflexive attention is of no less benefit. In fact, that may be much of the actual task with some instances of "analytically suitable patients" or with people who "only need some help in growing up." Possibly a more precise distinction between varieties of difficulties at the nonverbal level can make for more appropriate treatment efforts.

But such speculations are best undertaken after closer inspection of the observable manifestations of the phenomena under discussion. For that purpose we might review some clinical descriptions already identified in the Interpersonal literature. Among the varieties of intuitive orientations referred to as separate and particular covert processes by Sullivan, for instance, are what he called *sublimatory reformulations* (e.g., 1956:14–18), sundry forms of *reverie* (e.g., 1940:37 n.; 1956:21–24 and 315–316); *integrating tendencies* (e.g., 1956:6–8), *selective inattention* (e.g., 1956:38–76), and *substitutive processes,* more particularly *obsessionalism* (e.g., 1940:112–119; 1956:14–18).

Sublimatory reformulations or, as they are more generally known, *sublimations,* were originally described by Freud, although from rather different premises. As understood Interpersonally, this process is understood as the substitution of one interaction pattern for another, when the new alternative avoids disapproval and even earns favorable recognition from significant others. What qualifies it as an intuitive orientation is that the substitution is accomplished outside awareness. The particular substitution may prove adaptive throughout life, as when the need for special attention motivates an individual to become an outstandingly careful and conscientious worker. Or it may prove effective only for a time. For instance, feelings of rivalry with fellow students may be directed toward rewarded competitive effectiveness in high school athletics but become disruptive to relations with co-workers in adulthood. In the case of the popular student athlete, what once was personified self or knowable intuitive orientation becomes a censored intuitive orientation when life situations change the consequences of competitiveness.

Reverie, also called "prospective reverie," "constructive reverie," and "brown study" in various of Sullivan's writings, encompasses an especially wide range of intuitive psychological performances. Described in the dictionary as a state of dream, meditation, or fanciful musing, the Interpersonal discussions further indicate that in the reverie state one is temporarily out of touch with immediate surroundings and also with syntaxic levels of thought, so that the experience itself is not recoverable in words. But the meditator was often distinctly aware of some besetting problem in the real world immediately before that reverie and may even be able to state a workable solution upon returning to full awareness.

What is suggested by these observations is that the referential complexity of intuitive orientations can range through a series of preverbal gradations, finally to function at a level communicable to the personified self. Occurrences of that sort clearly indicate that knowable intuitive orientations cannot be assumed to be apart from experiences of the real world. On the contrary, in well-functioning personalities they share motivations of the personified self and contribute significantly to the maintenance of self-esteem. But, depending on a variety of circumstances, reverie may express only "not-me" censored intuitive orientations.

An instance of the knowable sort of reverie process in a well-functioning personality is nicely illustrated in recollections of J-H. Poincaré, the distinguished French mathematician (1924/1970) about any instance of his own sudden inspiration:

> it is possible, and of a certainty it is only fruitful, if it is on the one hand preceded and on the other hand followed by a period of conscious work. These sudden inspirations (and the examples already cited sufficiently prove this) never happen except after some days of voluntary effort which has appeared absolutely fruitless and whence nothing good seems to have come. . . . These efforts then have not been as sterile as one thinks, they have set agoing the unconscious machine and without them it would not have moved and would have produced nothing.

It is hardly necessary to travel so far afield as mathematics for examples of how reverie can contribute to conscious functioning and self-awareness. An ever-expanding accumulation of papers on countertransference reactions attests to how reveries evoked by the analyst's participation in the treatment situation yield clues to the ungraspable complexities of the therapeutic relationship. This literature includes the collection edited by Epstein and Feiner (1979), and writings by Tauber and Green (1959), Levenson (1991), Wolstein (1975, 1981), and Stern (1983, 1989, 1990), among others.

All these papers depart from the classical assumption that unconscious phenomena are essentially confined to the intrapsychic sphere, an assumption that led to Freud's original view of countertransference as basically a neurotic replication of the analyst's own early childhood traumata. From that perspective, countertransference was a confusing or even dangerous interruption of the unfolding of the patient's purely intrapsychic conflicts. Instead, the premise shared by the cited papers is that the analyst's preverbal subjective experiences during a treatment session are responsive to presyntaxic levels of interactions with the patient. From this newer perspective, countertransference is understood as an unavoidable kind of participation in the treatment relationship and potentially a very valuable information source, if the analyst is observant not only of the patients' activities but also of their interplay with his or her own subjective and overt participation.

In other words, countertransference reactions are intuitive orientations that can profitably serve as inadvertent guides for the analyst's functioning in the treatment dyad. And with equal inevitability, intuitive orientations stir in all of us in every situation. A special advantage of the treatment process is that it can be focused to bring these cues to the self-reflexive level of awareness for advertent understanding as an important added resource toward unraveling our difficulties. In clinical practice, then, it is at least tacitly recognized not only that preverbal cognitive/emotional processes influence transactions but also that they are sensitive to the circumambient circumstances in ways that involve more than mere replications of earlier experiences.

When this now reiterated observation is placed in the context of the entire preceding discussion, the emerging picture is of the Interpersonal self as in dynamic and at least tolerably harmonious balance, during states of psychological well-being. That is, its component aspects—knowable intuitive orientations and the personified self are in fluid mutual exchange, so that what belongs to each mode of mentation can shift to the other in shared responsiveness to situations, their integration motivated toward fulfillment of overarching intentions. Less obviously, perhaps, this is also true of censored intuitive orientations whose contribution is to conceal what must be concealed to reconcile personified self-evaluations with canonical imperatives.

If the alleged synchronism between so many complex components of the Interpersonal self arouses skepticism, perhaps the simplest explanation for suggesting it is that most people are apparently able to manage their lives at least tolerably well, at least most of the time. Nor is there any lack of evidence, thus far, of the success of human beings as a species, however dubious the future may seem. Thus, any skepticism may be due more to limitations in the constructs than in the remarkable repertoire of human capacities they are designed to describe. Admittedly, however, the synchronism becomes more understandable through consideration of one last set of functions deducible from observation of social interactions. And that is the self-system.

Self-System

The self-system was Sullivan's central explanatory device to account for most repetitive problems in living, including difficulties impeding the clinical interview. He described the self-system as "a vast system of processes, states of alertness, symbols and signs of warning" to protect the sense of well-being tied to self-esteem (1954:96). As he employed the construct, its essential function is as an automatic and dissociated censor. "The interviewee's self-system is at all times, but in varying degrees, in opposition to achieving the purpose of the interview" (1954:131). Interviewers also struggle with these self-same limitations to their own awareness (1954:97). During any interview (or other social interaction) self-system operations can be inferred by noting precisely when any of a variety of behaviors is manifested by either participant.

Among the more common indicators of self-system activity are abrupt shifts in the focus of discussion, rambling and irrelevant asides, difficulty in immediate recall of a question or comment, somatic signs of discomfort, and so forth. What these sundry manifestations have in common is that they are security operations to remove sources of anxiety by obstructing awareness and thereby the possibility of profiting from experience. They expurgate the personified self. Principal self-system devices include the conscious pretense of a false self ("as if" behavior), inadvertent me–you pattens at the parataxic level (as in transference reactions), substitutive processes (devices to redirect awareness), and paranoid transformations that automatically ascribe difficulties to hostile agencies (see Sullivan 1953:346ff.).

But this view of the self-system accounts for only two of the alternative modes of functioning available to the personality—a knowable conscious sphere of syntaxic functioning, the personified self, and an unknowable range of censored intuitive orientations (the rest of the personality). It neglects to account for those undefensive psychological performances harmonious with the personified self, the knowable intuitive orientations. When this oversight is recognized it becomes apparent that a construct somewhat more intricate than a simple "yes–no" censor is required to account for the observable psychological repertoires of human beings. The gatekeeping task for engaging situations would seem to involve allocating mental activities to any of at least three alternatives: (1) yes—for matters suited to the conscious attention of the personified self; (2) yes—for matters attuned to knowable intuitive orientations; and (3) yes—for matters requiring defenses against intolerable anxiety.

This newer understanding does not require replacement of the familiar term, *self-system.* The same label can refer to a more complexly conceived set of functions that includes security operations but refers more broadly to the nonreflective assessment of the immediate situation, particularly with reference to oneself and to the sort of participation best suited to one's concerns under the circumstances. Integral to this assessment also are allocation and coordination of psychological functions so that, when matters go well, the contribution of the personified self is integrated smoothly with intuitive orientations. Such assessment must obviously involve a wider scope of feelings and other influences than merely anxiety. It includes a varied range of preverbal cognitions, motivations, and emotions. Nor does assessment end with a single initial appraisal. Reassessments continuously keep pace with the flow of experience in relation to contextual changes.

In short, most adult interactions involve shifting combinations of processes for each of them—a mix of self-reflective awareness with knowable and censored intuitive orientations. To put it metaphorically, the self-system operates more like an anonymous traffic policeman, or perhaps orchestra conductor, than as an agency that merely obstructs and censors. In that orchestration, the very category in which any specific mental process is employed will vary in terms of its contribution under the ongoing circumstances. Specific processes in our cognitive/emotional repertoire serve as tools, like musical instruments whose very coloration and role fluctuate back and forth, from silence to background accompaniment, to carrying the theme, in response to demands of the scoring and interpretation.

Thus Sullivan was particularly interested in "selective inattention" as a self-system defense for reducing anxiety through ignoring overwhelming stresses. At the same time he noted that in other contexts selective inattention can achieve a desirable economy of effort when it dispenses with conscious attention under conditions where thought is unnecessary to bring about favorable results (1953:233). In effect, then, selective inattention can be employed to avert a threat by shunting it into the limbo of censored intuitive orientations. Or, in other cases, selective inattention may serve as a knowable intuitive orientation that conveniently protects against irrelevant distractions for better concentration on a task, or it may even be evoked consciously by the personified self for that same purpose. Lest this discussion be perceived as merely a classificatory exercise with a glossary of neologisms, some judicious selectivity here can preserve the central focus. The point is to emphasize the intention to preserve a fluidity built into the conceptualizations that is in keeping with living psychological processes and thereby avoid reifying constructs or decontextualizations. Unless confined to a very fixed and limited range of situations, relatedness requires fluidity.

If the well-functioning personality exhibits what Goldstein calls a "self-actualizing" organismic wholeness, with flexibility of boundaries between component processes in an orchestration facilitated by self-system assessments, an understanding of that wholeness requires attention to one more essential aspect. Here I refer to the behavioral side of human functioning, a matter typically neglected in orthodox analytic writing as almost unworthy of attention. One way in which behavior is treated as part of personality in the Interpersonal literature is through Sullivan's conception of "integrating tendencies" as activities "operating unconsciously or externally to awareness" (1956:9). In the updated terminology of this paper, integrating tendencies are intuitive orientations expressed directly in the form of behavior that has achieved automaticity, like finding one's way home, or the muscular coordinations involved in spoken or written speech. I prefer the term *enactions* to supplant *integrating tendencies* for a variety of reasons, including that it sounds more like what it means.

Examples of enaction are so rife as to overwhelm efforts at exhaustive listing because they constitute the most familiar routines of everyday life—how we dress and button our clothes, tie our shoes, perform urination and defecation, and when we grow up, how we wash a baby or change a spark plug, type a message, and so forth. All these tasks demand a complexity of coordinations that strikes us anew when called upon to instruct our small children. But once learned, thinking about them can interfere with smooth performance. Sports skills as complex as archery, occupational skills like those of the surgeon, are best accomplished in this intuitive fashion (e.g., Herrigel 1953/1989; Tauber and Green 1959).

Enactions are more than one-way processes, and if self-reflexive learning can become an intuitive performance, reverse functions also occur. In the development of children, enactive performances precede verbalizations, and enactive communications are used by mothers to guide movements their babies are striving to master (see, e.g., Trad 1991). Throughout life, enactive experience provides information for self-system reappraisal in so simple a matter as throwing a ball, when the consequences inform estimates that guide the next throw. Empirical study of such interplay led Hever and Sanders to a "growing awareness that the human mind may like dichotomies but that nature does not, and in particular not a dichotomy between clearly separated input and output processes . . . cognition and action" (1987:ix). Enactions contribute to the foresight required for self-system functioning.

This updated formulation of the Interpersonal self is completed at this point, at least in general outline. Its divergences from the original version are shaped primarily by an effort toward greater implementation of the constructionist guidelines that informed Interpersonal theory from the outset. More specifically, the variety of constructionism applied here is rooted in contemporary social science as well as in clinical considerations.

What emerges is a personified self still described in terms of self-reflexive knowledge and skills, still motivated by feelings and needs of which the most compelling are for human relationships that nurture self-esteem. Self-personifications are thus understood to be organized around situations in which essential abilities to learn and to function are greatly affected by the quality of approval and disapproval accorded by significant others. But of overarching importance to the maintenance of the personified self is a self-system whose unaware assessments serve continually to reorganize the personified self and to coordinate it with other personality resources drawn from a wide repertoire of socially acquired intuitive orientations (both knowable and censored) sensed as appropriate for coping with the ongoing situation.

This conceptualization rests on the premise that matters of considerable complexity can be handled almost instantaneously through nonsyntaxic and automatic processes collectively called the self-system and intuitive orientations. Moreover, as understood here, these intuitive processes diverge from metapsychological views of the unconscious in several ways. For one thing, unconsciousness is no longer understood as confined essentially to the primitive and regressed. If certain preverbal patterns are inaccessible and deeply entrenched, many others remain educable and significantly contributory to mature functioning. For another thing, what is out of awareness is no longer seen as insulated from "material realities" of everyday life but, on the contrary, as inevitably sensitive to those circumstances. Because knowledge is recognized as related to social experience, sophisticated (if bizarre) fantasy lives are not attributed to very young children nor are all intuitive orientations of adults assumed to be basically infantile.

Insofar as the Interpersonal perspective demands that its formulations be consistent with social science evidence as well as with clinical observation, it is appropriate to consult the research literature on what has been said. Findings consistent with these assertions are indeed available, at least in part. Some of it has been cited here and there in the preceding pages. While an exhaustive review would be out of place here, at least two efforts by others can be cited. The first, by Singer and Kolligian (1987), reports on unconscious "schemas" or ways of organizing experience about self and others. Such schemas (1) are found to occur and to "operate automatically" in a fashion generally consistent with such generic analytic ideas as transference (p. 558), but also (2) "small situational changes were capable of producing related changes in the ways individuals process information about others" (p. 559), indicating that unawareness does not necessarily preclude sensitivity to current experience.

More recently available, too, is Lazarus' (1991b) extensive review of experimental studies of person–situation interactions, with particular attention to what he calls "appraisal," understood in ways germane to the self-system construct. He defines appraisal as "a continuing evaluation of the significance of what is happening for one's personal well-being" (p. 144), including construals outside awareness. Among his conclusions are that (1) most appraisals by adults involve a mixture of automatic as well as conscious processes (p. 155), that (2) automatic processing "can involve complex, abstract and symbolic significances that through experience can be condensed into instant meanings" (p. 155), and also that (3) what is unconscious is not necessarily merely automatic and reiterative (p. 153).

If research of this sort points in the same direction as the Interpersonal self described here does, it should be noted, too, that the Interpersonal self also continues to be in accord with some of Freud's discoveries. Both analytic schools see all of us as largely unknown to ourselves but still hold out the hope that self-knowledge can be increased with sufficient well-directed effort. Still another of Freud's opinions is sustained, if on a different basis than what he proposed. It is that what we know is filtered through prior beliefs and values we bring to our perceptions. Yet Interpersonalists do not trace the sources of these reference frames to universal biological determinants. Rather we see biology as guided into varied cultural perspectives invented by ourselves.

In at least one important respect, however, the Interpersonal position diverges most sharply from Classical metapsychology. It is the realization that if we human beings are largely unknown to ourselves, we are not unknowing about our relation to the world immediately around us. What is "unconscious" is not buried in some cellar insulated from "reality." Rather, at all times *our unconscious as well as our conscious selves are intuitively and sensitively attuned to our situations.* Nor could we afford to have it otherwise if we are to survive biologically. Wordsworth expresses this when he says we live:

> Not in Utopia—subterranean fields—
> Or some secreted island, Heaven knows where!
> But in the very world, which is the world
> Of all of us—the place where, in the end
> We find our happiness or not at all!

Neither what we know within awareness nor intuitively is separable from the contexts of our daily lives, past, present, and anticipated.

References

Bruner, J. 1990. *Acts of Meaning.* Cambridge, Mass.: Harvard University Press.
Carson, R.C. 1969. *Interaction Concepts of Personality.* Chicago: Aldine.

Cushman, P. 1990. Why the self is empty: Toward a historically situated psychology. *American Psychologist* 46(5):599–611.

Cushman, P. 1991. Ideology obscured: Political uses of the self. In Daniel Stern's infant. *American Psychologist* 46:206–19.

Dean, A., A.M. Kraft and B. Pepper, eds. 1976. *The Social Setting of Mental Health.* New York: Basic Books.

DesPres, T. 1976. *The Survivor: An Anatomy of Life in the Death Camps.* New York: Oxford University Press.

Epstein, L. and A.H. Feiner, eds. 1979. *Countertransference: The Therapist's Contribution to the Therapeutic Situation.* Northvale, N.J.: Jason Aronson.

Grey, A. ed. 1969. *Class and Personality in Society.* New York: Atherton Press.

——. 1973. Oedipus in Hindu dreams in Gandhi's life, and in Erickson's concepts. *Contemporary Psychoanalysis* 9:327–55.

——. 1975a. A myth of heroes, patients, and human growth. *The Academy* 19:13–17.

——. 1975b. Modern alienation and the good old days. *American Journal of Psychoanalysis* 25:123–33.

Haimes, E. 1987. "Now I know who I really am." Identity change and redefinitions in adoption. In T. Honess and K. Yardley, eds., *Self and Identity: Perspectives Across the Lifespan.* London: Routledge and Kegan Paul.

Herrigel, E. 1953/1989. *Zen in the Art of Archery.* New York: Vintage Books.

Hever, H. and A.F. Sanders eds. 1987. *Perspectives on Perception and Action.* Hillsdale, N.J.: Lawrence Erlbaum Associates.

Jones, R.M. 1979. Freudian and Post-Freudian theories of dreams. In B. Wolman, ed., *Handbook of Dreams: Research, Theories and Applications.* New York: Van Nostrand, Reinhold.

Lazarus, R. 1991a. Cognition and motivation in emotion. *American Psychologist* 46:352–67.

——. 1991b. *Emotion and Adaptation.* New York: Oxford University Press.

Lerner, R.M. 1990. Changing organism—context relations as the basic process of development: a developmental contextual perspective. *Developmental Psychology* 27:27–32.

Levenson, E. 1991. *The Purloined Self: Interpersonal Perspectives in Psychoanalysis.* New York: Contemporary Psychoanalysis Books.

Marshack, A. 1972. *The Roots of Civilization.* New York: McGraw-Hill.

Perry, H.S. 1982. *Psychiatrist of America: The Life of Harry Stack Sullivan.* Cambridge, Mass.: Harvard University.

Poincare, J-H. 1924/1970. Mathematical creation. In P.E. Vernon, ed., *Creativity: Selected Readings.* Baltimore, Md.: Penguin Books.

Rosenfield, I. 1988. *The Invention of Memory: A New View of the Brain.* New York: Basic Books.

Schachtel, E. 1959. *Metamorphosis: On the Development of Affect, Perception, Attention, and Memory.* New York: Basic Books.

Schachter, S. and J.S. Singer. 1962. Cognitive, social, and physiological determinants of emotional state. Psychological Review 69:379–99.

Segall, M.H. 1986 Psychology in global perspective. In M.R. Rosenweig and L.W. Porter, eds., *Annual Review of Psychology*. Palo Alto, Calif.: Annual Reviews, Inc.

Singer, J.L. 1978. The constructive potential of imagery and fantasy processes: Implications for child development, psychotherapy, and personal growth. In E.G. Witenberg, ed., *Interpersonal Psychoanalysis: New Directions*. New York: Gardner Press.

Singer, J.L. and J.K. Kolligian. 1987. Personality: Developments in the study of private experience. In M.R. Rosenzweig and L.W. Porter, eds., *Annual Review of Psychology*. Palo Alto, Calif.: Annual Reviews, Inc.

Sorenson, A.B., F.E. Weinert and L.R. Sherrod, eds. 1986. *Human Development and the Life Course: Multidisciplinary Perspectives*. Hillsdale, N.J.: Lawrence Erlbaum Associates.

Spence, D. 1984. *Narrative Truth and Historical Truth: Meaning and Interpretation in Psychoanalysis*. New York: Norton.

Stern, D.B. 1983. Unformulated experience: From familiar chaos to creative disorder. *Contemporary Psychoanalysis* 19:71–99.

Sullivan, H.S. 1940. *Conceptions of Modern Psychiatry*. New York: Norton.

——. 1953. *The Interpersonal Theory of Psychiatry*. New York: Norton.

——. 1954. *The Psychiatric Interview*. New York: Norton.

——. 1956. *Clinical Studies in Psychiatry*. New York: Norton.

——. 1964. *The Fusion of Psychiatry and Social Science*. New York: Norton.

——. 1972. *Personal Psychopathology: Early Formulations*. New York: Norton.

Thompson, C.M. 1964. *Interpersonal Psychoanalysis: The Selected Papers of Clara M. Thompson*. M.R. Green, ed. New York: Basic Books.

Tauber, E.S. and M.R. Green. 1959. *Prelogical Experience*. New York: Basic Books.

Trad, P.V. 1990. *Infant Previewing: Predicting and Sharing Interpersonal Outcome*. New York: Springer-Verlag.

——. 1991. Previewing: A developmental phenomenon and a therapeutic strategy. *Psychoanalytic Psychology* 8:283–304.

Weiss, R.S. 1975. *Mental Separation*. New York: Basic Books.

Wolstein, B., ed. 1988. *Essential Papers on Countertransference*. New York: New York University Press.

7

The Daseinsanalytic–Phenomenological Approach to Narcissism

Gian Condrau

"Ewig jung ist nur die Sonne, sie allein ist ewig schön" (Only the Sun is forever young, it alone is forever beautiful)—this is how the Swiss novelist and poet Conrad Ferdinand Meyer (1825–1898) described the narcissistically attuned relationship to the world in a poem, although discussion of narcissism did not dominate the professional world and public opinion in his time as it does at present. With these verses, the poet simultaneously expresses the desire and dismissal of narcissism of modern man, for who would not want to remain young and beautiful forever, radiant as the sun—but alas, *only* the sun itself enjoys the privilege of being young and beautiful forever. From the Roman poet Ovid's Narcissus who scorned nymph Echo's love and fell in love with the reflection of his own image, consumed by his unrequited longing, to the modern *homo faber* who conquers, processes, and changes the world, who falls in love with his own creation and consequently admires himself, there is but a small step in the history of mankind. The mirror wherein human beings see themselves reflects not humanity's beauty but the power

they have acquired, which raises them to the level of lords and masters of the world. Whether this was intended by the history of creation is more than questionable in this era of general world destruction. Equally open to question is whether beauty is not a part of power, and in what ways youth, beauty, and power represent the trinity of the highest bliss. For who is happier than a person in love?

My purpose cannot be to reduce the theory of narcissism to a totally unspecific statement, leveling all human behavior. On the other hand, I do not intend simply to criticize the psychoanalytic term *narcissism*—which would be impossible for the simple reason that several terms exist. As is well known, Freud (1914) presented the first bases for later debates in his treatise *Zur Einführung des Narzissmus,* and this later led to the situation where the development of the psychoanalytic theory of narcissism not only reflects a part of the history of psychoanalysis but also has become its authentic, internal "apple of discord."

If we take a look at the personality traits of the narcissistic person, as indicated by Kohut (1978) and Kernberg (1981), it is difficult to arrive at a holistic, clinical picture for the purposes of symptomatically delimiting a specific and distinct neurosis. If in his works Kohut concentrated on patients whose self-love, self-respect, and self-assurance proved to be weak and continuously in danger of disintegrating, the question is whether this is specific to the narcissistically attuned person or at least characteristic in a very special manner. For have we not encountered the same, or similar, circumstances with hysterical patients? Are they not extraordinarily touchy; dependent on immediate, interpersonal sympathy; and incapable of relating? And does all this not apply to all other forms of mental illness? If we go one step further, we will have to admit—although we may classify ourselves as more or less healthy—that the narcissistic mood is in no way unknown to us, on condition, of course, that we have enough insight into our own behavior and are ready to admit it.

Not by chance, two conclusions result from this, which I shall state before going into the discussion of narcissism as such: on the one hand the statement, proven time and again, that a theory of neurosis with a fixed, nosologic systematization is questionable, and second, that in all neuroses, moods and types of behavior are to be found that are also typical of the "healthy" person. Therefore, if we cannot deal with neurotic diseases in the same way as with somatically different disturbances—such as liver or kidney ailments—but as restrictions of human freedom wherein certain aspects of relating are more or less in the foreground, we must, however, remember that for the term *neurosis,* the *degree* of the restriction of freedom is decisive. For this reason, some authors differentiate a good or sound narcissism from the pathologic one. Healthy narcissism encompasses everything required for developing an authentic Being-oneself: to remember one's own authenticity, trusting and being rooted in one's authenticity, knowing one's own limitations and possibilities, and accepting both one as well as the other. Such Being-oneself does not need to constantly set itself off from the "They-self" [*Man-selbst*], nor does it need to consistently rely on outside (intervening) support by ideal human beings, ideas, or absolutes, which have to be so absolute and ideal because this makes their support appear reliable and safe enough. The authentic Being-oneself understood in this manner corresponds to the mood of a good self-worth, satisfied with itself, but not complacent, reliable, and self-asserting. Only this type of Being-oneself allows one to experience some other person as another self and thus experience the great variety and wealth of life in the world. In the pathological variant of narcissism, however, the They-self dominates, and the evolution toward the authentic self has not yet taken place.

And here we are in the middle of Heidegger's classification of language and the existential condition of Dasein as authentic being and inauthentic being, as explained in *Being and Time* (Heidegger 1927). The Daseinsanalyst Alois Hicklin (1984) tries to build a bridge between the self of psychoanalysis and Heidegger's "Self," or rather, from the narcissistically attuned Being-oneself to the They-self. "In anxiety, Dasein's concern is for Being-its-Self," says Heidegger, or "What man owes his Dasein is Being-himself. Conscience calls to itself," and even more clearly: "Conscience summons Dasein's Self from its lostness to the 'They' " (p. 319). At this point, however, the question arises whether Heidegger's "Self" is identical with, or only comparable to, Kohut's "Self" and that of psychoanalysis. After closer scrutiny, the answer is negative. For it has to be remembered that the psychology of psychoanalytic orientation is worlds apart from that of ontologic phenomenology. This is why Hicklin pointed out that the fundamentally different philosophical approaches "had to be set aside on purpose, at least initially." But unfortunately, this does not work. Without doubt, Heidegger's philosophy also provides a basis for Daseinsanalytic anthropology, but a comparison with a psychoanalytic interpretation, and consequently a bridging of the gap, is possible only if these very principles are included. The question of "Being-oneself" therefore has to be asked and clarified. For the purposes of Daseinsanalysis, the human being has to learn—and this is one of the objectives of analysis—to accept the possibilities of existing as his or her own and to live them out responsibly. In this, he or she moves from fallenness to They, which was designated as the everyday type of Being, in other words, to move from one's inauthentic existence to one's authentic potentiality-for-Being and thus unite with one's most authentic Being-himself or Being-herself. Thus, the "They" is mediocrity, unauthenticity, and leveling, that which we know under the term *the public.* Being-oneself, however, is everything consistently enduring as itself through all possible human behavior, so that humanity can time and again find itself as the same. This Being-oneself temporalizes in bringing to a head the possibilities of human existence. But Heidegger always refers to the decisive aspect: "The characteristic of man is that as a thinking being, open to Being, he is confronted by Being, he is related to Being, and consequently corresponds to it. Actually, man is inherently this reference of correspondence, and he is nothing else" (1957:18).

Psychology, on the other hand, speaks of a totally different Being-oneself. In psychology, it derives from humanity's determination as a subject, although it may not be understood specifically as a theme. As a subject, humanity is an isolated ego that correspondingly faces the givens of the world as objects. Thus relying on oneself alone, one becomes the authoritative subject for all that is.

Hubris and Presumption, Fallenness for Entities (Things That Are), Oblivion of Being, and Blindness to the Essence Are the Core Contents of Narcissistic Mood and Narcissistic Behavior

In hubris and presumption (arrogance), humanity experiences itself as the *subject of need* (Holzhey-Kunz 1988), for whom fellow human beings and things are nothing but objects for satisfying one's own needs, to which one is entitled. Being-with is reduced to the nature of matter (things) in its ontic delivery, or, to put it more bluntly: the "other person" is turned into a consumer good, an article of merchandise. In other words: the other person is not left and seen in his or her authenticity. The ek-static relationship to them is lost. As long as the other person or thing is useful to the narcissistically attuned person, raises one from the general, flatters one, confirms one in one's Being-as-is—however questionable that may be—offers one power and honor, the fellow person is in demand. It is the pedestal on which the statue rests in its glory. In antiquity, hubris was seen as overweening, "sacrilegious" pride, as self-glorification.

Although we do not talk of "sacrilegious" pride in narcissism, it certainly does have its share of arrogance. We experience this in a particularly impressive manner in the therapeutic analysis of narcissistic personalities. These patients frequently look for only the best and best known analysts above any reproach—probably for reasons of self-confirmation; they adore them, considering them as their idols up to the point in time when they tumble them from their pedestals owing to a (possibly insignificant) frustrating experience. These patients apparently seem to accept only a spoiling, intervening care, even though they emphatically deny this when it is pointed out to them. Their self-worth needs confirmation by the other person. If confirmation is not obvious, this often leads to senseless arguments in analysis, all the way to open discord. In therapeutic practice, the so-called know-all-transference is well known. It is found among patients who serve their own psychologic knowledge to the therapist at every opportunity, calling attention to possible omissions or erroneous interpretations, who prove how well read they are and try to get the analyst involved in rational discussions.

Others, on the other hand, give in much too quickly. They attribute negative meaning to every observation of the analyst, however value free its intention. They suffer, not so much a delusion of grandeur (megalomania), but rather a delusion of insignificance—with the closeness, even identity, of the two becoming evident. In the delusion of insignificance, in continuous, tiresome self-accusation, the narcissistically attuned persons declares their exceptional, aloof, position—the same as in megalomania—fed by the need for recognition and love. Of course, this applies not only to the narcissistic patient but equally to narcissistically unsatisfied therapists. The profession of analyst is frustrating enough, but if therapists have not learned to live without the admiration and loving affection of their patients, they should refrain from working in this field—for their own benefit and that of their patients.

These are very extreme statements, of course. But in a more mitigated form they are probably very common. If we remember how many analysands judge their fellow persons, in what—often hair-raising—manner even didactic analysands in an institutional situation, such as a clinic, a school, or institution, observe each other with envy, grudges, and jealousy, it will scarcely surprise anyone if psychologists and psychiatrists are sometimes blamed for not having made much more progress in their own process of maturing than the patients entrusted to their care. The "idle talk of analysis" mentioned in the discussion of hysteria also belongs to the area of narcissism. Whether such idle talk takes place on the street, in the subway, in a coffee shop, or in a pseudoscientific work makes no difference for diagnosis. The unqualified denunciation is still the same. Envy and jealousy have to do with *ownership*. The hybrid narcissist envies the others their material and spiritual property, begrudging the other person's freedom and leisure. In short: the narcissist is intolerance incarnate.

From the envy and resentment on which it is based, it is a short way to incrimination, to feelings of hatred and revenge, and ultimately to narcissistically motivated aggression. "What I don't have, you are not to have either!" Not by accident do we speak of the envy of the have-nots and their understandable motivation to commit violent acts, as if the envious person could commandeer the other person's property simply by the use of force. Unemployed youngsters will, of course, have our empathy if the sight of a jeweler's shop windows galls them and kindles their anger about the injustice of the world. But this type of ire can evidently not be interpreted from the angle of a narcissistically attuned person but may rather be seen as an adequate reaction, although aggressive acts, such as breaking shop windows, do not cure the social injustice, and therefore have to be seen as simple acting-out. It is different in the case of aggressiveness fed by envy and jealousy, which cannot bear the envied person to be freer and happier, where the resentment is rooted, not in social, and objectifiable, injustice, but simply in the narcissistic incapacity to shape one's life properly on one's own.

In a similar way as envy, *jealousy* is also a typical mood of the narcissist wherein the ability to relate to fellow human beings can be substantially impaired. The same as with envy, we may also have to differentiate a "mild," even healthy, jealousy that can be beneficial for creativity, from the profound, destructive, pathological form. Besides, both phenomena, envy as well as jealousy, have a common root in narcissistic frustration over an apparent, or real, deficit, be it in material value, or in the love and affection of a person. But the difference is that envy usually applies to a relationship of two people, whereas jealousy usually has to do with the relationship of three people (triangular relationship). This is why the term *narcissistic triad disturbance* is used.

The wish to be loved, respected, and honored for one's own self is, in all certainty, not to be seen as diseased. The need to be able to face oneself and one's fellow human beings without shame, to be independent and able (eager) to make decisions, must not be mistaken for narcissism. It is rather common that a person who, thanks to knowledge and ability, is performing better than permitted by the *"égalité de la bourgeoisie"* (equality of the bourgeoisie) is descried as a narcissist. But if we admitted that, the term *narcissism* would be so inflated that it would no longer make sense. If "narcissism" is to be nothing but self-assertion and Being-free—phenomena lifting the individual in his or her individuality from anonymous generality—then we do not need this term. This is why in my opinion it is obsolete to talk of "healthy" narcissism. If we are to be autonomous and free, Being and appearances must match. Where this is not the case, we speak of a narcissistically attuned world relationship.

The mythological Narcissus of the Roman poet Ovid recognized, not his Being, but merely his reflection, his appearance. The essence of narcissism—this is what this story tells us, and this is what we experience in daily encounters with narcissists, inside and outside the analytic situation—is the negation of what is truly showing, and instead the chasing after an illusion that can never be reached. The narcissist is striving for wholeness, oneness, perfection (Kastrinidis 1988). Wholeness and oneness can do without the "other"; whosoever is "whole" and "one" within oneself does not need an opposite, a complement, a Being-with. The same applies to perfection. Perfect persons have achieved everything that can be achieved; nothing remains open to them. "Self-love" is sufficient to them, they need no other love. The "other person" merely serves as a confirmation of themselves, as a "projection," as a mirrored image, and they will be needed only as long as this function is fulfilled. This is why the narcissist has only two ways for dealing with fellow human beings: either as a means of self-aggrandizement (idols) or of debasement. In the first case, the other person serves the so-called megaloself, in the second, the feeling of inferiority that overcomes the narcissist with equal strength whenever the sorely needed value support by the environment fails. The narcissistic collapse leads to depression and aggressiveness, as already indicated, whereby the former—unlike other types of depression—is characterized by the absence of guilt feelings. If narcissistic collapse does not come about, the patient has the choice of leading a life characterized by chaotic moods and extreme modes of behavior that often give the impression of almost psychotic states. This is where the transitions occur from the so-called "narcissistic neurosis" to "borderline disorders." This is not the place to discuss the latter, because, to my thinking, they still represent a diagnosis of discomfiture with negative prognosis, in spite of the attempts made to characterize their uniqueness by differential diagnosis.

Coming back to the narcissistically attuned relationship to the world, I have to state that—in a similar way as with the hysterical patient—the ontic fulfillment of several existentials is particularly disturbed. On the one hand, the narcissist's relationship to time and space, but above all in the range of Being-with, and lastly, of bodyhood and mortality, is severely impaired. The narcissistically attuned reference to the world does not admit any limitations in the ideal of perfection. Space and time are contained in the Here and Now. The narcissist does not know any future. "For the narcissist, the future is now" (Holzhey-Kunz 1988:190). The ideal of never-fading youth does not admit aging; any discomfort must be eliminated at once, any indisposition, any symptom of disease must be healed right away. Narcissists cannot wait; they are unaware of the meaning of leisure, they do not linger with their fellow beings and things of this world. As mentioned above, the others are merely there to serve them.

Consequently, Being-with in the narcissistic relatedness to the world is marked by continuous insecurity about who is the First, the Best, the Most Beautiful—in the certainty that the one who is asking is all that, of course. The bodily states of narcissists are endangered by hypochondria and psychosomatic illnesses; mortality is simply negated. With their perfection and lack of future, the narcissists are potentially "immortal." They are unaware of Seneca's *cotidie mori,* nor of a "Being-towards-death" in Heidegger's sense.

Now, what is the *outlook for treatment* of narcissistically attuned patients? What is the primary source of their need of therapy? Are they not the most unsuitable patients conceivable for an analytic type of treatment, which presupposes the ability to relate and tolerance of frustration?

Without any doubt, narcissists are difficult clients. The stress of suffering in itself is not always sufficient to motivate them to go into analysis. It is possible to avoid it in many ways. They make arrangements to live with suffering and to neutralize and immunize the therapist. Now, what is the specific stress of suffering of narcissistically disturbed patients? If they claim to be in harmony with themselves, to have reached the ideal of perfection, there is no reason why they should ask for help. They do not suffer from their own imperfection, much less from their ideas of grandeur. Suffering occurs only when they encounter resistance in their relationships, when they feel that they are not respected and loved in keeping with their own self-evaluation, when the "grandiose self" collapses. And even then, the stress of suffering is not the consequence of insight into their own inappropriate behavior. Blaming others is the only explanation for their suffering accepted by narcissists. With patients suffering from anxiety neurosis, it is possible to talk about their anxiety; with depressive and obsessive-compulsive patients it is possible to speak about fears, doubts, compulsions, and guilt; but it is impossible to discuss narcissism with narcissists. This is why narcissistically attuned patients have to debase the therapist, too, unless the latter agrees with them one hundred percent. The narcissistic touchiness, conjured up time and again, is not only a symptom of the patients but is also a weapon they will apply at least tentatively to increase their self-worth by putting down the therapist; this is probably the most characteristic element of narcissistic behavior in therapy.

And yet, Kohut calls for the therapist's *empathy* in treating narcissistically disturbed persons. According to Kohut, continuous, lingering attention and empathy by the analyst are required, besides correct interpretation, to reach the self-defects of the analysand. This is why the function of analyst can never be taken over by a computer, however sophisticated its programming. Kohut further states that human beings cannot survive in an environment that does not react to them with empathy, just as they cannot survive physically in an environment without oxygen. He criticizes the stiffness, artificiality, and buttoned-up reserve, the lack of emotional spontaneity, and the grossly frustrating atmosphere reigning in many analysis rooms where the neutrality of analysts and their reflecting attitude—on the grounds that transference should not be influenced—are equal to emotional coldness. From the Daseinsanalytic standpoint, Kohut justifiably criticizes an often rather frosty climate of many orthodox analysts who sometimes demand standards of frustration tolerance from their analysands that might occasionally overtax the self-worth of "healthy" human beings. This is where the mirroring attitude of the analyst, which is certainly based on a valuable therapeutic principle, is carried *ad absurdum.*

Equally *ad absurdum* is another attitude, which holds that the poor, suffering patients have to be smothered with a specially considerate, pampering, and overindulging type of love, since therapy should provide what they missed in life so far. "This is where adequate love, that is, a balanced ratio of intervening and anticipatory care, is equalled to spoiling" (Hicklin 1984:111). By understanding terms such as *empathy* and *love* ambiguously instead of unambiguously, relationship phenomena cannot be defined more clearly.

The therapist must not be blinded by feelings of sympathy, for this means compassion, pity, agreement, and unanimity. On the other hand, apathy will not help the patient either, nor will insensitivity, callousness, indifference, and dispassionateness. Sympathy, or empathy, all too easily entices analysts into offering "intervening care," also when this is contraindicated; apathy, on the other hand, leaves patients totally to their own devices. This must be borne in mind also in cases where the demarcation line between apathetic comportment and "anticipatory care" seems blurred. Especially with the narcissistically attuned patient, the analyst will have to bear this demarcation line in mind, and the analysand will have to recognize it. That this is not an easy task is evidenced by daily practice dealing with narcissists. But empathy on the part of therapists is possible only if they have managed, in the course of their own didactic analysis, to reduce touchiness and frustration intolerance to a "reasonable" level. That this can never be achieved completely will not require substantiation. A person who is totally free of mortification would be a robot, not a human being any more. Consequently, it is not a matter of whether therapists are also touchy (able to feel mortified), but rather how they cope with their touchiness. This is what defines their self-worth, their authenticity, their self-assurance—which must not be mistaken for narcissism.

If up to now the emphasis was on the difficulties encountered in the analysis of narcissistically disturbed patients, we must not forget, however, that a narcissistically attuned relationship to the world has equally positive, inherent features that can be utilized therapeutically. For on principle, narcissism—as practically no other psychopathologically describable syndrome—contains the impetus to the quest for becoming oneself, to coming to terms with one's own identify, to the search for meaning of one's very own Dasein.

References

Freud, S. 1914. On narcissism: An introduction. *Standard Edition* 10:62–102. London: Hogarth Press, 1957.

Heidegger, M. 1957. *Identität und differenz.* Pfullingen: Neske.

——. (1927) 1962. *Being and Time.* London: SCM Press.

Hicklin, A. 1984. Daseinsanalyse und narzissmustheorie. *Daseinsanalyse* 1:81–131.

Holzhey-Kunz, A. 1988. On the meaning of desire: Psychotherapy for freedom. *The Humanistic Psychologist* 1:186–202.

Kastrinidis, P. 1988. The phenomenology of narcissistic neurosis: Psychotherapy for freedom. *The Humanistic Psychologist* 1:168–85.

Kernberg, O.F. 1981. *Objektbeziehungen und praxis der psychoanalyse.* Stuttgart: Klett-Cotta.

Kohut, H. 1978. *The Restoration of the Self.* New York: International Universities Press.

PART III

Clinical Narcissism

8

The Concept of Narcissistic Interactions

Leston Havens

What does it mean to approach the theme of narcissism from an Interpersonal perspective? One could say that no other way to approach it is available. The self looking at itself, evaluating itself, the self's investing or overinvesting in itself—all these depend upon the self's taking itself as an object, which already suggests the interpersonal. The same thing can be said in traditional Freudian terms. Granted that the idea of primary narcissism postulates a world without other, a world before other, the more serviceable secondary narcissism not only speaks about the other, especially the frustrating other, but then treats the self as precisely another and less frustrating other, to which the libido can retreat. This is the same taking oneself as an object. In Kohutian Self psychology, too, the whole structure hypothesized for the birth and development of self and for the development of that disorder of self called narcissism is interpersonal—so much so that those students of the psychoanalytic schools, Greenberg and Mitchell (1983), place Kohut among the relational as opposed to the drive theorists.

Self psychology has certainly illuminated narcissistic phenomena, but it has also added to the confusion. The confusion has been deepened by linking the term *narcissism* with any disorder of the self. Since distortions of the self are omni-present in the psychiatric taxonomy, suddenly narcissism appears everywhere. (Similar unsettlings have attended most psychopathologic innovations, as with the discovery of latent homosexuality.) For example, the prominence of self-depreciation in depression renders depression a state of narcissistic depletion. I make this criticism despite my conviction that delineations of the state of the self are every bit as important as Kohut believed. Nevertheless, we need a clearer (and more limited) idea of what we mean by narcissism.

My candidate for the definition of narcissism is this: being in love with one's perfect image (as opposed to depression, which is being in hate with one's imperfect image). This is not the same as being in love with one's image of perfection, which may be only a loving attitude toward the ideal. Narcissism involves a love affair with an image of oneself, to the point of not admitting any other possibilities. (It is, therefore, a very sharp restriction on the possibilities of self-reflection, a particular kind of self disorder.) It stands in contrast to those aspects of healthiness called accepting one's shortcomings, being open to and sober about their rediscovery, what has been described as "a shy acceptance of having been at once entrusted and exposed to this singular existence of our own" (Craig 1988:181).

Taking up the challenge of an Interpersonal approach to narcissism requires, therefore, that we define both narcissism and what we mean by the interpersonal as something, it is hoped, both less general and more provocative than the first-mentioned concepts. We might mean, for example, something very dear to Sullivan's heart: the idea that no one-person observations exist, that all statements about narcissists are really statements about the narcissists and observers of narcissists. This is not just a bland commonplace, because Sullivan's claim has a double edge. It pointed to both the epistemology of our clinical hunches (how we know what we think we know) and something even more unsettling: perhaps we observers of the narcissist were contributing to the narcissism, even, lo and behold, sometimes bringing it about! And if this idea seems too repugnant, we can entertain a related one, also dear to the Sullivanian heart. Perhaps we are not actively contributing to the patient's narcissism; perhaps we are only failing to respond helpfully to it (now we move closer to Kohut). We may be unwittingly continuing the narcissism by continuing the social response or field or earlier game that society and the narcissist had set in motion. Of course, this is a large part of the Sullivanian psychotherapeutics: let us not play those games.

Here is an Interpersonal approach to narcissism distinguishable from much of the Object Relations part of psychoanalysis and even from Kohut's late development of Self psychology. I want to examine first its implications for the recognition of narcissism.

I begin with two postulates. Human beings need both to express themselves and to get along with others. The needs are, however, in tension with one another, not only because I may offend the others, but more fundamentally because I can never know what the fate of my expressions will be. To some measure, we live always alone, while we hunger not to be alone. And this statement is just as true in reverse. We often hunger to be alone, all the while finding ourselves in society, at least the society in our heads.

Narcissism has to do with the way we conceive of ourselves and how we react to the way others conceive of us. Narcissistic sensitivity is said to mean a touchiness about how others conceive of us. I mention this double relationship because it reflects the two postulates I stated. Because I need others, I must be sensitive to the way they see me. What is the clinically acceptable measure of that sensitivity? Similarly, I must respect my own wishes and ambitions, if I am not to neglect them. When does this so-called self-respect go over into narcissistic entitlement? In practice we let the patients tell us; we often work from their complaints. This may, however, mislead us. Overentitled people do not, as a rule, feel overentitled; they are more likely to feel they do not get as much as they deserve. On the other hand, underentitled people often feel they are getting more than they deserve, so that they may feel narcissistic for making any demands at all. The judgment of the degree of one's sensitivity to others may be similarly flawed. Many people judged insensitive by others do not feel that way about themselves; they may, for example, be very sensitive about just that judgment. On the other hand, truly sensitive people, in my experience, often feel they should be even more sensitive than they are and therefore term themselves by that high standard, insensitive.

How are we to tell? I contend that it is very difficult and that efforts to make an absolute judgment, that is a judgment not, for example, contingent on the observer's own attitude and the observed's hypothesis about it, commonly mislead us. Once I heard a leading student of narcissism say, "Normally people feel complete on their own." I found this puzzling. This same student of narcissism had often asserted the importance of transitional objects in normal, adult life, those objects that are both our own and not our own. I suspect too that "normal" narcissism is frequently a product of stable sources of support, so that the feeling of being complete, "on one's own," conceals deep-running dependencies. In any case, it seems to me very difficult to know and that any diagnosis of narcissism not based on detailed knowledge of the individual's social history and contemporary context must be incomplete. As a result, I propose that we first try to describe narcissistic *interactions* and postpone judgments about one another, as separate selves, for later, perhaps much later.

The concept of narcissistic interactions reflects the Interpersonal stance I am taking. It comes down to a single claim: most human beings are very sensitive both to others' and to their own opinions of themselves: they are deeply reactive and interactive. (In one sense we can say they are very narcissistic.) Therefore, any claims about human beings (for example, that this one is pathologically narcissistic) must respond to the counterclaim: how do you know the appearance of narcissism is not a result of the observer's or someone else's interaction with the patient? Perhaps the patient is only narcissistic with you. Or perhaps the patient's narcissism is being fed, reinforced, or even created by someone pumping the patient up. Surely this is a hypothesis that cannot be simply dismissed.

For example, in the course of the more than thirty years of study of matrimony that a long practice of psychotherapy provides (and in the course of watching one's friends get married and remarried), instances of what I call matrimonial narcissism appear. A quite humble, down-to-earth acquaintance of mine became in the course of his second marriage remarkably full of himself. This self-confidence, which went over into self-adulation, seemed related to a striking difference between his two wives. Specifically, the second wife took him a great deal more seriously than the first, or more accurately she gave that impression. Furthermore, this same woman's first husband remarried a woman who took him not so seriously at all. The result was a quite dramatic humanization of the first husband attested to across a broad front. The word *modest* was even used about the man once consistently described as arrogant and overbearing.

Very similar are those group *folie á deux, trois,* etc., in which charismatic individuals find their perfect image supported by an adoring cult. This serves not only their narcissism but the followers' too, as their imperfections are erased in the identification with the leader.

I have seen examples I thought related to psychoanalysis. Some patients, particularly after what are called "successful" analyses, become remarkably full of themselves. They may have felt "cured" or in some way drawn above the common clay. Sometimes, too, I suspect they feel elected to a very special and superior club, which can be heady stuff indeed. Patient and analyst may have entered into a quite unconscious pact to buck one another up. If the analysis has been a training analysis and the club an analytic institute, you then have one of the various graduation phenomena that have been widely remarked on and may take years for recovery. Harvard graduation seems to carry much the same risk.

It is wonderful how awareness of these phenomena can co-exist, even happily, with their continuance. I suspect the two are carried in such different parts of the mind they affect each other very little.

To all those who feel narcissism is an easy diagnosis to make, I refer these obvious claims on human nature. For those more serious students of diagnosis, for whom a great number of personal traits and historical events are required, again I ask that they look carefully to the situations of their patients' lives. Even to those students of narcissism who let diagnosis rest on the course of treatment, that is, on the events of treatment as they unfold in a relationship gradually developed and neutrally allowed to reveal itself, there are such common abuses as the one just mentioned.

It helps me in any of these calculations to imagine what a nonnarcissistic relationship would be like, that is, to start from an idea of health, rather than the other way round. Many advantages reside in this, not the least of which is providing goals for the work, benchmarks of progress, guides to the success of the second purpose of this paper, not recognition now, but therapy of narcissistic interactions. I once told a story about hearing Desmond Tutu speak (Havens 1989). By coincidence this occurred soon after a friend, learned in quotation, placed a new one at the top of his stationery: "Angels can fly because they take themselves lightly." This was amusing, but I had not thought it might be true until I heard Desmond Tutu. At one point, he said something like this: "My wife had said, we must go back to South Africa immediately. I asked her why. She said 'Since you have been in the United States, they have made you a bishop and now you have won this Nobel thing. Every time I wake up in the morning, I feel like I have been sleeping with the Pope.' " Surely Tutu is a man entitled to take himself seriously, much more so than you or I. But apparently, he does not. He recounts his wife's little joke on him with every sense of putting himself in perspective. Or we might have anticipated that he would err in an opposite way, of putting himself not up but down. In the Harvard church where he spoke, he was attended by Secret Service men. Was he not afraid of death or depressed by the little progress up to then made on his great cause of apartheid? It did not appear so.

He took himself lightly, neither weighted up nor weighted down, while he took his great task very seriously indeed. He seemed to have a nonnarcissistic relationship with himself. In psychoanalytic terms, we can say he had shifted his narcissism to his ego ideal, the structure that Freud (1921) claimed to be the heir of primitive narcissism. Freud contended we should move from "I am great" to "There is a greatness I aspire to." So here we have a series of tests for narcissists and nonnarcissists. Phenomenologically, do they feel pulled up or down? Socially, is there evidence of work toward an ideal apart from themselves, in which we can suspect the location of their narcissistic libido? Developmentally, have they grown just that way? Narcissistic interactions may be partly defined, too—do we weigh the other down, fostering either grandiosity or depression?

So far I have discussed the recognition of narcissism and narcissistic interactions. I have been particularly alert to what we can call tertiary narcissism, narcissism that results from such interactions. This already points toward treatment. How do we recognize and create nonnarcissistic interactions? The least we can do is not reinforce narcissistic interactions by our example. The touchstone that Desmond Tutu provides also suggests a developmental task for the treatment. How do we discover and embrace the patient's ideals? There is a more familiar way to state this, very dear to Freud's heart. The drive gains its "character" (we can say nowadays, the form of its self) from the sublimatory transformations it undergoes. In different words, psychotherapy can afford neither to legislate morality nor to be without ideals, however much those ideals will be a celebration of diversity. We do not attach ourselves to the world only because of our attachment to objects. Ideals carry us still further into the world for the simple reason they involve changing that world.

In making a transition from the discussion of recognizing narcissism to its treatment, let me suggest how the development of technology (including psychotherapy) may have fostered narcissism. Narcissus himself was frustrated by seeing himself only in a pool of water; when he tried to grasp that beautiful image, it dissolved. The modern narcissus is luckier; mirrors and photographs provide a permanent image one can saturate one's self in.

Homer had to hear his words in the shifting responses of an audience. Now authors can literally hold themselves. This is as great a source of joy to authors as still pictures are, I understand, to movie stars. We will be less disdainful of these moments remembering the historic place they may hold. Jaynes (1976) has hypothesized a step in psychological development from what he calls the bicameral mind dominated by gods and obediences to gods toward something like self-possession. Perhaps self-possession can emerge only through the concrete meeting with parts of the self provided by mirrors and artifacts; perhaps a period of infatuation with the self is necessary to stabilize the self. Something similar is suggested by Kohut's concept of a mutually idealizing phase between parent and child as necessary on the way to a coherent self.

But earlier I was myself disdainful of analogous graduation phenomena with all their potential for pumping people full of themselves. (In the old jargon I could have written: their libido was drawn out of the world and back into themselves.) This returns us almost to where we began. When is narcissism pathological? For example, á la Tutu, must all that narcissistic libido be pumped into the ego ideal?

These issues are important for the psychotherapy of narcissism (and have been partly engaged in the exchanges between Kernberg and the Self psychologists). I suggested elsewhere (Havens 1989) that sometimes we need to help patients find ideals. The implication was: a flourishing ego ideal is our birthright. I have just suggested that nonnarcissitic interactions can be weighed by their very lightness; neither party gets weighed down by self-importance or self-depreciation. But the merest glance at the clinical scene reveals case after case where people "lose themselves" in the adulation of others, often joyfully, often sorrowfully. How is that different from Tutu's giving himself to apartheid?

Here parts of the Buddhist critique of Western ideas of the self seem to me useful (Epstein 1988). Contemplation of the self, it is claimed, reveals a self both there and not there, supremely transient, shifting, ineluctable, like the stream of consciousness William James described. We cannot find ourselves the way we find our wallet. Even those seeming reflections of self, in mirrors and books, are only images and artifacts thrown off by a fleeting and fleeing agency. Any effort to anchor the self in such products weighs the self down, ultimately traps and kills the self, we are told.

In fact we do not find the self. What we find are fleeting images (sometimes a face in the mirror), memories, intentions, convictions. They comprise a self most firmly, as in narcissism, when all have collected around a simple view of myself, for example, that I am marvelous or beautiful. This pre-ego ideal stage Freud (1921) called infantile narcissism. Both Freud, and more explicitly, Kohut argue it is a necessary stage on the path of development. The claim is, if it has been missed, it must be substituted for. Now the possible place of both narcissistic and nonnarcissistic interactions in psychotherapy appears.

In his review of the psychoanalytic and Buddhist conceptions of the self Engler (1983) trenchantly suggests: you have to be someone before you can be no one. A certain amount of what many would call pathological narcissism is necessary before one can achieve perspective on oneself, before one realizes that the fixed view of self is a delusion, that we are at bottom many and changing things, there and not there. In achieving the first stage, either in the family or in psychotherapy, narcissistic interactions seem necessary. Surely this is the center of Kohut's claim. But in transcending the developmental narcissism, I suggest, nonnarcissistic interactions are equally necessary.

I will not dwell on the creation of coherent self through what I call narcissistic interactions; I cannot add much to Kohut's descriptions of these last, especially his mirroring and idealizing interactions. I do want to say more about nonnarcissistic interactions. Here I must address a variety of problems: How is ego ideal nurtured? How is mature ego ideal separated from cult adorations? If narcissistic interactions can develop a healthy narcissism (and also overcarry), how, in detail, do nonnarcissistic interactions transcend narcissism?

Ego ideal is approached through the future. This can also be true of the study of drives and wishes: What do we want? But the analytic study of wishes has tended pastward, to the earliest wishes and the structure of repetitive wishes, as sometimes revealed in dreams. Such is appropriate to the analytic interest in timeless instincts that are postulated to root the human enterprise independent of past, present, or future. As soon, however, as analysis turns its attention to the transformations of instincts, especially to sublimations and idealizations, it turns treatment toward the future: What can we become, what is it our ideal to become?

Ego ideal changes the question, "What do you want" into "What do you want to be?" This emergence of being out of wanting has deep connections with the meaning of self, which I cannot address here (Havens 1986). Suffice it to repeat that the emergence of ideal has at least one path through narcissism ("I am great") on its way to ego ideal ("There is a greatness I aspire to"), in accord with Freud's formula. The question "What do you want to be?" straddles the two answers, as well as acknowledges the patient's right to such aspirations.

How is mature ego ideal separated from cult adorations? I think the answer lies within the developmental formula. Cult adorations, hero worship, whether the hero is another or oneself, barely escape primitive narcissism. It is little more than "I am great"; "I am great because he calls me so"; or "He is great and I partake of his greatness." In different words, self-love is not lost to the ego ideal; it is still largely merged with it. Graduates enamored of their graduation merge self with institution. The clergy know this phenomenon even more intimately than we do. I am told it is a terrible problem, this merging of self with church and god. There is an old story of two clergymen mistakenly asked to officiate at the same funeral. The second arrived late, interrupting with "No, no, *I* am the resurrection and the life."

And how are nonnarcissistic interactions clinically effected? Here there is much to be said for the old anonymity, neutrality, abstinence: keeping one's self free of the work. There are, however, extraordinary limits on this selflessness; it is frequently broken into as we meet or part, when you see my house or office, in the very way I withdraw myself. It seems to me, therefore, a nonnarcissistic relation cannot simply be based on the classical rules. A more nearly complete answer must lie, I suggest, in the nature of self presented.

I return to the perhaps enigmatic words cited earlier, "A shy acceptance of having been at once entrusted and exposed to this singular existence of our own" (Craig 1988:181). I have implied they characterize a nonnarcissistic relation to the self. What do the words mean? First, a shy acceptance: it is as if the self contemplating itself peeps out from behind a veil. Intimations of coyness aside, I read this as bespeaking an adventitious relation to oneself: the self I am has arisen from another, much larger source, has come to me largely accidentally; I only a little make or even shape it; like the throws of genetic dice with which I began, my life events assemble around me. On the one hand, like and unlike Margaret Fuller's full-throated acceptance of the universe, I must accept this self. On the other, it is a partly unknown gift plumped down before me; I unwrap it carefully. As I live it, I find elements of which I should be very shy, angers, destructiveness, mistakes made and remade: I cannot disavow them; many I will make still again. But how do I seize all this with enthusiasm?

Much the same mood is created by the words "at once entrusted and exposed." This is mine to keep, but it can be like keeping a bomb. Again the theme is of mine and not mine, both inside and outside. But a fresh note is sounded by *entrusted,* the note of responsibility. The acceptance cannot be so shy after all: this is mine to keep, protect, have and hold, control, too. And it may be *all* I have! Entrusted. This does not mean I can trust myself. I long ago learned I cannot do that, so I formed a cabinet, ran things by the secretary of the treasury and the secretary of defense; only then is there reason for some trust. No, it is entrusted *to* me, not because I can be trusted but because I know I cannot be, and have taken other precautions. The trust is not *in* me. I am entrusted with it.

What of the final words, "This singular existence of our own"? *Singular* seems to me very apt. The word means individual, unique, distinguished, exceptional, but also strange, odd, even whimsical; one could almost say absurd. It is a lesson of psychotherapeutic experience that in fact the most commonplace-seeming existence turns out to have all those qualities. One would not guess it from experience of oneself; one is too close to know. But a long experience of others' joy and suffering, above all the experience of trying to understand joy and suffering, pushes forward the conviction of human singularity. And it is not the person who is singular but the existence, "of our own." Any pride or shame we take in that existence must be tempered, even largely eliminated, by the fact that this existence of mine is not owned the way the land is owned, with boundaries, titles, the whole endlessly complicated body of rules, documents, and disputes. I am at a loss even to state where my existence ends and yours begins. We go on existing in the minds of others, often more potently than we have in our own lives. Moreover, I can be walking around, buying and selling, with no discernible existence of my own: I am simply the instrument of another. Existence is a psychological state; if it has a physical analogue it must be to the metabolic and respiratory processes by which minute substances and gases are moved across cell membranes.

My ideals are part of my existence; they may be, however, peripheral to that existence: that to which my existence hearkens. Similarly, what gifts or talents I have may be equally peripherally mine: their working seems to come out of the blue, largely unbidden, something given *to* my existence. I may identify with them, but this is an imposition of mine that must always seem at least partly an impostership.

I believe from these attitudes toward our existence a nonnarcissistic relationship springs. Our ability to assume such attitudes toward ourselves prepares others to be seen in these ways and to see themselves. Because psychotherapy is primarily a reflective process, that is, one in which memories, ideas, perceptions, moods are presented and in part reflected back or seen in the reflections the mind gives any idea or mood as it glances off our own interests, prohibitions and ideals (much in the way we see ourselves in the varying triptych of a tailor's mirrors), no meeting passes without opportunities to show or not to show what I have called nonnarcissistic attitudes.

References

Craig, E., ed. 1988. Psychotherapy for freedom. *Humanistic Psychologist* 16:178–87.

Engler, J. 1983. Vicissitudes of the self according to psychoanalysis and Buddhism: A spectrum model of object relations development. *Psychoanalysis and Contemporary Thought* 6:29–72.

Epstein, M. 1988. The deconstruction of the self: Ego and "egolessness" in Buddhist insight meditation. *Journal of Transpersonal Psychology* 20:61–69.

Freud, S. 1921. Group psychology and the analysis of the ego. *Standard Edition* 18. London: Hogarth Press.

Greenberg, J. and S. Mitchell. 1983. *Object Relations in Psychoanalytic Theory.* Cambridge, Mass.: Harvard University Press.

Havens, L. 1986. A theoretical basis for the concepts of self and authentic self. *Journal of the American Psychoanalytic Association* 34:363–78.

——. 1989. *A Safe Place.* Cambridge, Mass.: Harvard University Press.

Jaynes, J. 1976. *The Origin of Consciousness in the Breakdown of the Bicameral Mind.* Boston: Houghton Mifflin.

9

Love and Sexuality in Narcissistic Personalities: A Clinical Report

John L. Schimel

The term *narcissism* derives from the Greek, *Narkissos,* "the son of a river god who conceived a passion for the reflections of himself which he saw in a fountain." Primary narcissism, in Classical psychoanalysis, is the original psychic energy embodied or invested in the ego. Secondary narcissism is the psychic energy, once attached to external objects, now withdrawn from those objects and reinvested in the ego. Freud considered melancholia and paranoia to be examples of narcissistic neuroses, and because these patients fail to develop a transference neurosis they are thus not amenable to psychoanalysis.

A narcissistic personality disorder has been considered to have a number of the following characteristics:

> (a) a longstanding pattern of grandiose self-importance; (b) fantasies of unlimited sex, power, brilliance, or beauty; (c) an exhibitionistic need for attention and admiration; (d) either cool indifference or feelings of rage, humiliation, or emptiness as a response to criticism, indifference, or defeat; and (e) various in-

> terpersonal disturbances such as feeling entitled to special favors, taking advantage of others, and inability to empathize with feelings of others. (DSM III)

Sullivan (1940) noted that Freud's concept of secondary narcissism is one of "retreat from object-love, so that one is compelled to seek pleasure in one's own attributes, fantasies and so forth (pp. 62–63)." He condemned this notion of narcissism and noted that Freud formulated modifications and presumably came to regret its usage.

Freud (1914), in his treatise on narcissism, had declared that "It is easy to observe that libidinal object-cathexis does not raise self-regard. The effect of dependence on the loved object is to lower that feeling: a person in love is humble." He allowed the possibility of "a real happy love," noting that: "Loving in itself . . . lowers self-regard; whereas being loved, having one's love returned and possessing the loved object raises it once more."

Holt (1989) notes that Freud's theory is one of a closed system of energetics: if there is a limited supply of libido and if a large part is committed to a love object, it must follow that less is left over for the self, an economics of scarcity. Holt surmises that Freud's position would include the odd contention that "schizophrenics have a great deal of self-esteem." Freud's basic assumptions derived "from biological propositions" (pp. 58–60).

Fromm (1939, 1947, 1956) writes that "The selfish [narcissistic] person is interested only in himself, wants everything for himself, feels no pleasure in giving, but only in taking. The world outside is looked at only from the standpoint of what he can get out of it: he lacks interest in the needs of others, and respect for their dignity and integrity. He can see nothing but himself; he judges everyone and everything from its usefulness to him; he is basically unable to love" (1947:135). The assumption that "concern for others and concern for one's self are unavoidable alternatives" would follow if selfishness and self-love were identical.

Fromm (1956) points out that this assumption is a fallacy: "*Selfishness and self-love, far from being identical, are actually opposites.* The selfish person does not love himself too much but too little; in fact, he hates himself. This lack . . . leaves him empty and frustrated . . . actually he only makes an unsuccessful attempt to cover up and compensate for his failure to care for his real self . . . *selfish persons are incapable of loving others, but they are not capable of loving themselves either*" (1958:60–61).

Fromm (1956) quotes Meister Eckhart on this topic: "If you love yourself, you love everyone else as you do yourself. As long as you love another person less than you love yourself, you will not succeed in loving yourself, but if you love all alike, including yourself, you will love them as one person and that person is both God and man. Thus, he is a righteous person, who, loving himself, loves all equally" (p. 204).

Silverberg (1952) notes an important distinction between Freud's and Sullivan's theories of human development and of the origins of narcissism. Sullivan suggested that human development is essentially a social product. The essential nuclear factor in human psychology, for Sullivan, is self-esteem. Freud, on the other hand, considered the central factor to reside in the need to restore psychophysiological homeostasis. He regarded libidinal impulses as arising within the individual without reference to external relationships. And this would be true whether self-esteem is based on the opinions of others regarding oneself or whether it is based on effective aggression (Silverberg's term), the ability to achieve regardless of obstacles. Libidinal impulses, of course, necessarily involve other human beings and their behavior. Sullivan, too, postulated libidinal factors, drives for satisfaction and security, as indispensable, also in relation to other human beings. Freud, in his later work, also postulated ego factors as important in motivation but still subordinate to libido. All psychic energy, for Freud, still resided in the libido.

Shapiro (1989) notes that families of patients who manifest pathological narcissism show evidence of assumptions that equate separation–individuation with loss and abandonment. These assumptions activate family regression in which differentiation between family members is compromised and defenses of splitting, denial, and projective identification are seen. The individuating and separating adolescent activates a level of primitive splitting in the parents and projection of badness or devaluation into the adolescent.

Many of the foregoing considerations may be seen in the history and treatment behavior of two narcissistic personalities, Abel and Bea. The clinical evidence also illustrates how each of these two contrasting views, Freudian and Sullivanian, initially can be found plausible.

Clinical Examples

Patient No. 1: Abel

Abel's presenting complaints included debilitating anxiety, temper outbursts, and marital difficulties. He was a tall, physically well-developed, fifty-year-old white male professional. He had had two previous experiences with psychotherapy and spoke disparagingly of both his therapists and his therapy. He expressed antipathy toward and disparagement of his wife, one of his daughters (he favored the other), his business associates, and his parents, particularly the mother.

In the treatment situation he was alternately ingratiating and disparaging. His speech was pressured and rambling, with digression from one subject to another in rapid succession. In time, after being encouraged to speak more slowly and coherently, he revealed that, as instructed in previous therapeutic encounters, he was trying to "free associate" by telling every thought that entered his mind. The result was one of incoherence, although basically he was trying to please the analyst. He was, in fact, fearful, anticipating that the analyst would be critical and punitive. He revealed a number of remarks by previous therapists to him that could be construed as hostile and demeaning.

In professional encounters he was often explosively angered and attacked both superiors and subordinates, rarely expressing anything about their performances, personality, or integrity that was not pejorative.

It became obvious that he was afraid of his wife and daughters, and indeed, they often assaulted him verbally and, on occasion, physically.

His wife exhibited many characteristics that also warranted a diagnosis of narcissistic personality.

Both his parents had also engaged in explosive rages toward each other and toward the patient as a child and adolescent. Denigration of others was routinely engaged in. The patient and his sister exhibited hostile and demeaning behavior toward each other; this persisted well into their adult lives. The patient was contemptuous of his mother and, particularly, of his father. The father repeatedly insisted that he loved the mother, although the patient would not believe that this was so, as the mother certainly did not deserve to be loved.

An acrimonious divorce ensued between the patient and his wife, with many furious disputes about the terms of the divorce. Considerable relief seemed to result, nevertheless, for both parties, punctuated by quarrels about the children, the disposition of property, etc.

A subsequent relationship developed between the patient and a woman who was better integrated than his wife. This relationship, although frequently harmonious, was marred by the fiancée's fear of the patient. Her fear of the patient was augmented by his caustic remarks, his derogation of her friends and business associates. He was explosive in his rages at what he perceived to be her poor judgment at times, particularly if her remarks could be construed as derogatory toward his children or himself. Themes of dominance/submission appeared regularly, often alternating rapidly, in encounters with others.

He reported early homoerotic experiences with other, usually older, boys, always accompanied by feelings of guilt and self-loathing. In subsequent heterosexual relationships, he exhibited patterns of dominance/submission vis-á-vis the female. He was given to pornographic films, particularly those that exhibited beatings and other forms of abusive behavior, especially those where women played both roles. With his fiancée he preferred their watching such films together as well as opportunities to act them out more or less gently with her, using a whip and chains. When she protested, mildly as it were, he felt denied and was angered.

The theme of dominance and submission was replayed in many aspects of their relationship. His fiancée, in fact, expressed her concerns that he was hypercritical, domineering, easily angered, and abusive. She declared that the struggle between them was a source of concern to her and a threat to the possible continuity of their relationship.

This brief description, I believe, indicates in this patient many of the facets described above as secondary narcissism, as exemplified in the contributions of Sullivan, Fromm, Holt, and others. Much evidence indicated that this man was motivated, not by self-love, but if anything, by self-loathing. His relations with others were exploitative and self-serving. He was quite oblivious of the feelings and wishes of others, nor did he show any evidence that he cared. His parents showed similar characteristics, and their lack of concern for others showed in their behavior toward the patient and his sibling. As noted, the patient exhibited toward me an attitude of fearful and almost subservient respect, alternating with sly innuendos about my mode of dress, my memory for details, my errors, my fees, and occasions necessitating a change of a scheduled appointment.

Patient No. 2: Bea

Bea is a thirty-year-old, unmarried, attractive white female whose presenting complaints included depression, agitation, uncomfortable tension, shaking episodes, and numerous somatic complaints, including nausea and vomiting in the morning, fear of fainting in confined places like restaurants and theatres, epigastric pain, and dizziness. She had had an operation for a ruptured appendix. Induction of anesthesia was not smooth and was accompanied by terror, which may have served as a prototype for subsequent symptoms. Repeated medical examinations revealed no significant abnormalities.

Her parents had been strict and hypercritical in her childhood and adolescence. Her first experience with having a boyfriend occasioned harsh denunciations of the boyfriend, with references to possible sexual misconduct by the patient. She was subsequently secretive about relations with boys and furtive in regard to dating. Her fear of her parents continued into adult life although she visited them frequently and remained involved in family affairs.

Bea's course in therapy was stormy. She was at once ingratiating and highly critical. She denounced her previous therapist while conceding that he was "a very nice, thoughtful, gentle and helpful person." Bea interrupted therapy in a rage on several occasions. On one occasion, she subsequently wrote a letter accusing me of saying things that made "little sense," hearing "illogical drivel from someone intelligent enough to know better." In closing, Bea noted in her letter, "I think you know things are good for me now. Work is better than it ever has been. I'm more at ease with people . . . and I feel more self-confident. I don't have words to express how grateful I am to you for helping me. . . . The world has never felt so firm beneath my feet. . . . You seem to be a truly kind, sensitive, warm, fun-loving and funny person." Bea had also stormed out of her internist's office when he was late for her appointment with her. Her anger toward her employers was marked.

She had had a brief affair with a married man. When he was derelict in his attention to her, she would call him in the middle of the night and remain silent when he answered the phone.

She had had a long-standing live-in relationship with a man who did not "earn enough, was not interesting enough, didn't dress well enough." All of these matters were reviewed with girlfriends who presumably sympathized and had their own horror stories regarding relations with men. Sex with her lover was infrequent, "unimaginative and unsatisfying."

Bea subsequently had another affair with a married man whom she idealized. She prepared for their rendezvous with meticulous care. She gave considerable thought to picking out the most enticing perfume and donned a seductive negligee. Her description of her costume was reminiscent of an Arabian night's fantasy. She wondered if anal intercourse could entice him and expressed her willingness to do "anything" that would please him. The sexual experience was enjoyable but not accompanied by orgasm. When her lover asked her what he could do to enhance her pleasure, she could not bring herself to tell him, but responded, "Everything pleases me."

When Bea's lover, complaining of pressures of his business affairs, called her infrequently, she became embittered and scornful, while recounting the delightful times they had when he was available. She was filled with fantasies of revenge, such as telling his wife of their affair. She, like Abel, fits the description of secondary narcissism as described in the contributions of Sullivan, Fromm, Holt, and others. There was evidence that this woman was motivated, not by self-love but, if anything, by self-loathing. Her relations with others were exploitative and self-serving. She was impervious to the feelings and wishes of others, nor was there much evidence that she cared. She was vindictive when disappointed. Her parents showed similar characteristics, and their punitive attitudes were expressed toward the patient from an early age. Her attitude toward her parents was distrustful, demanding, alternating with a fearful submissiveness.

Similarly, with present and past therapists, the patient exhibited an attitude of fearful and subservient respect, alternating with angry denunciations of their ineptness and failures.

Clinical Reflections

On reflection, I realized that a number of my patients had fit the foregoing descriptions and a number of questions immediately came to mind. Why had the patterns described not come into sharper focus? Why had the obnoxious aspects of these patients not proven more troublesome to me and resulted in more reactive negative countertransferential responses to the obnoxious behaviors vis-à-vis myself?

A partial explanation may be in my concern with the genuine suffering these people experienced. Abel's assaults on the therapist were basically perceived as an expression of his basic pathology and analyzed as such. Bea's intemperate attacks were accompanied by such pain and confusion and self-recrimination that compassion rather than counteraggression was experienced. I suppose that my own interminable analysis and long experience with conducting psychotherapy may inure me to much of the trials and tribulations endured in the practice of psychotherapy with such patients. Indeed, many of Abel's attacks were couched in such elegant and reasonable language that they appeared comical to me. In fact, both patients showed such marked improvement, in spite of their ongoing dissatisfactions, that much compensating gratification resulted for all concerned. Withal, a genuine liking for these patients developed. It is perhaps not too much to suggest that a task shared and well enough accomplished can cover a multitude of sins and that a state that can be called "love" developed during these treatment situations.

A number of therapeutic goals and caveats flow from the foregoing observed phenomena. Since these patients have heavily rationalized their difficulties in living, it is imperative to elicit detailed descriptions of their interactions with others to obviate the endless recitals of wrongs they have suffered at the hands of those with whom they interact. They have to be, in other words, trained to report in a manner recommended by Sullivan (1954) so that one hears an approximation, at least, of "He said . . . and then I said," in reporting encounters. One encounters remarkable amnesias in these and some other patients. They may report, with some passion, the terrible thing someone said or did to them but are unable to recall what transpired prior to the reported transgression. When more facts about such encounters are elicited, the patient's passive-aggressive behaviors may be open to scrutiny. An early history may usually be obtained of similar behavior by the patient's parents, not only resulting in reaction formation in the patient but also serving as a model for acceptable adult behavior.

Bergler (1949) early described such habitual behaviors and referred to such people as "injustice collectors." They are, indeed, avid in their collection of and recital of alleged injustices. Bergler suggested further that people whose psychosocial level of development was arrested at an early stage often found mates fixated at the same level and manifested similar behaviors. This seemed true of Abel's wife and possibly of his subsequent fiancée. Perhaps the most difficult task for such patients is the acceptance of their own intolerant attitude toward others and, importantly, toward themselves. When these matters are clarified and accepted, one may then catch glimmers of more tolerant and compassionate feelings in these people, with a resultant diminution of anxiety and somatic complaints.

The therapeutic task is difficult, time consuming, and, at times, wearing for the therapist. There can be gratification for both patient and therapist as the patient's living becomes more rewarding.

The analysis of the transference must be a delicate matter. Early in treatment it tends to be experienced by the patient as criticism and as an expression of hostility on the part of the therapist. It can be a useful strategy to make transference interpretations in a light or even humorous manner. The sting will, nevertheless, be there for the patient. Such responses by the patient are, of course, part of the patient's psychopathology. The task, then, is to help the patients integrate their transference reactions into the broader scheme of reactions to a variety of other, early and late, experiences with other people, as previously elucidated in the course of therapy. The transference interpretation is, perhaps, best made after considerable areas of the patient's interpersonal difficulties have been clarified and agreed upon by patient and therapist.

I believe that the caveat for therapists is to be aware of their impatience with the tediousness and repetitive use by the patient of rationalism, denial, and counterprojective techniques. It can be frustrating, and I believe that some of the hostile remarks by previous therapists, as reported to me by these patients, may have actually occurred. These patients tend to be stubborn, negativistic, argumentative, unreasonable, and, at times, downright insulting. The task for therapists is to maintain their cool, regard the phenomena as symptomatic and keep in mind the therapeutic goal.

Many aspects of the patient's psychology can be seen in sexual appetites and practices. Qualities of submission and dominance loom large in their sexual behaviors. Bea revealed that extreme behavioral submissiveness was her clue to successful sexual experiences. She believed this and acted it out despite repeated disappointment in her sexual encounters. The practice of sexual "perversions" by Abel confirmed for him notions of prowess and dominance. The practices also assured him of the validity of grandiose notions of being able to do anything and still be approved. Any, even minor, reluctance on his partner's part resulted in rage, accompanied by feelings of guilt and apprehension. Both Bea and Abel acted out, copycat fashion, a variety of aspects of stereotypical sexual behaviors they had read about or seen in books or films, regarded then by them as ideal sexual behaviors.

Both of the patients described here can be regarded as successful vocationally and intellectually. They maintained numerous ongoing relationships that, unfortunately, helped them maintain the illusion that they were competent in interpersonal contexts. I have reason to believe that less competent individuals, with similar developmental arrests, can be seen among the homeless and the more seriously disturbed treated in clinics and hospitals. In extreme cases one can see similar phenomena in those diagnosed as schizophrenic.

References

American Psychiatric Association. 1980. *Diagnostic and Statistical Manual of Mental Disorders, 3d ed. (DSM III).* Washington, D.C.: American Psychiatric Association.

Bergler, E. 1949. *The Basic Neuroses.* New York: Grune & Stratton.

Freud, S. 1914. On narcissism: An introduction. *Standard Edition* 14:67–102. London: Hogarth Press, 1957.

Fromm, E. 1939. Selfishness and self-love. *Psychiatry* 2:507–24.

——. 1947. *Man for Himself.* New York: Holt, Rinehart, and Winston.

——. 1956. *The Art of Loving.* New York: Harper & Brothers.

Holt, R.R. 1989. *Freud Reappraised.* New York: Guilford Press.

Shapiro, R.L. 1989. The family in the adolescent individuation process. In A.S. Silver, ed., *Psychosis and Psychoanalysis,* pp. 371–94. New York: International Universities Press.

Silverberg, W.V. 1952. *Childhood Experience and Personal Destiny.* New York: Springer.

Sullivan, H.S. 1940. *Conceptions of Modern Psychiatry.* Washington, D.C.: The W.A. White Psychiatric Foundation.

——. 1954. *The Psychiatric Interview.* New York: Norton.

10

An Interpersonal Approach to Idealization in the Narcissistic Personality

Dale H. Ortmeyer

As concepts, neither idealization nor narcissism originated in the pragmatic Interpersonal frame of psychoanalytic theory and therapy. Why, then, disembed these concepts from their Freudian theory of origin? Why view them within an Interpersonal perspective? Would it not be better to have theories as distinct as possible from each other, thereby enforcing a "purely" pluralistic point of view regarding psychoanalytic knowledge and treatment? An examination of this issue will serve as a conceptual point of departure for review of the role that idealization plays in the psychological functioning of the narcissistic personality. I also briefly present clinical material that illustrates the Interpersonal play of idealization in psychoanalytic treatment.

Pluralism offers more than one kind of reality, metapsychology, theory, and set of techniques. It poses a unique challenge: to develop different theoretical formulations and clinical procedures that may be complementary but are utilized differently. Schorske (1979) maintains that pluralism will be fundamental to psychoanalytic knowledge for the remainder of this century.

I agree. A purity of theories may have heuristic advantage and aid clarity of thought. Such abstraction, however, has in it the danger of losing the complex frame of reference of the person. Pluralism can allow the portrayal, as best we can, of our way of treating, and it permits the recognition of limitations of usefulness. Thereby, we can choose the most suitable reference frame for entering into a shared and informed communication with patients about our therapeutic procedure as the patients unfold their stories. It is pragmatic, far from an ideal. Pluralism need not be elegant in its differentiation of theories.

Sandra Scarr (1985), attuned to the postmodern constructivist movement, says that scientific knowledge is an interpretation by the human mind. The realities of the body and mind are representations, and meanings are derived from language, history, and culture. From that position, theories about idealization and narcissism are "representations of reality" that reflect the assumptions and interests of the theorist. This view is compatible with the pluralistic position. Like pluralism, it frees us to see the limited usefulness of theories, limited by the sociocultural time and space in which they occur and by the limitations of the author of the theory. This postmodern view, as Barrett (1988) states, says that knowing and awareness are always limited by nonrational processes of desire and sensuality. Our reasoning, awareness in process, is dialectic. Awareness is eminently worthy of pursuit but always limited by ourselves and by the milieu in which we live. Issues of idealization and narcissism must surely fall in this postmodern era.

But how do we keep on the cutting edge of discovery and creativity when we pursue idealization and narcissism? We do it by deconstructing as well as constructing meanings for these processes. Deconstruction examines the way language creates meaning outside awareness and can be complementary to constructivism and pluralism. Earlier, it was an approach to literary interpretation (see Bloom 1986; Atlas 1988). Psychoanalytic work centers on meanings as the patients tells their stories. Language is still the major medium of involvement and communication in psychoanalysis, with due respect for the nonverbal. The patient's reconstructed memories, present and past, can never, however, be a full reconstruction of the original experiences, nor is that a current work goal in psychoanalysis. The patient, as narrator, describes moments of experience in detail, and the analyst helps organize and reveal meanings in the narrated experience other than those in which the patient is encapsulated. The "analytic work" thereby reframes patients' understanding of their reality by deconstructing their meanings for their experience. We need such a deconstructive approach to question beliefs and convictions regarding idealization and narcissism and their influence in our work.

In this paper I discuss idealization in the narcissistic personality. How do we view idealization? It surely cannot be pragmatic or realistic. It cannot be an accounting, past and present, of what actually occurs in the patient's life. It is an abstraction, often outside the awareness of the person, that serves as a powerful motivating, guiding force in the patient's life, toward neurotic and self-destructive ends or positive life goals. Witness, for example, Pines' (1989) portrayal of Freud's relations with men, both his real relationships and his use of male idealizations, in the pursuit of both self-destructive and positive life goals. Freud had several intimate–competitive relationships with men, e.g., his nephew John Braun, V. Adler, Fliess. They were peer relationships although it is apparent in historical hindsight that Freud played out various transference idealizations with them, e.g., Fliess in the role of mentor. Particularly salient in his life goals were the motivating idealizations of Hannibal, Joseph, Moses, Cromwell, Bonaparte, Garibaldi, Bismarck, and Woodrow Wilson. They no doubt served to perpetuate his grandiosity and defensive idealizations. As well, however, they serve as constructive motivating forces in his productive efforts. Both positive and negative sides of idealization are there in abundance in the life of Freud.

The conceptual intertwining of idealization with narcissism, based upon clinical experience, goes back to 1914. Freud (1914), at that time, was trying to understand both conceptually, and clinically, utilizing his psychoanalytic approach with severely disturbed patients. Today, we would label such patients narcissistic, borderline, and schizophrenic. Jung and Bleuler, working together at the Burgholzli Hospital in Zurich, had by 1907 (Ellenberger 1970) offered an approach to treating schizophrenic patients by the psychoanalytic method. Bleuler first and Jung not far behind became fascinated with Freud's psychoanalytic treatment. Bleuler quickly became disillusioned, but Jung worked for several years in the adapting of psychoanalysis to working with hospitalized, schizophrenic patients. Jung perceived, in the severely disturbed, issues of aggression, retreat from reality through grandiosity and idealization, and fragmentation of thinking.

As an interesting aside, one of the reasons Jung severed his ties with Freud, in 1912, was Freud's overly strict insistence on psychosexual issues and the oedipal dynamics as the content that needed to be interpreted in the transference and dream analysis. Such interpretive work did not help the severely disturbed. Abraham, in Berlin, was trying to use psychoanalytic treatment with psychotic patients. He, like Jung, struggled with the fragmentation of thinking and the intensity of aggression in his patients. In 1921, he invited Melanie Klein to come to Berlin, from her work with Sandor Ferenczi in Budapest, to see if her work with young children would evidence fantasy and dream content similar to that he found in psychotic adults. He contributed the negative oral stage to Freud's theory of psychosexual development. This time of exciting discovery was motivated by the hope that psychoanalytic treatment would cure severe emotional disturbances. Also, Freud could not explain the terrible unleashing of violence and aggression in World War I by libido theory. He sought to expand his own views of aggression and clinical work with severely disturbed patients.

Returning to the central theme, in his view of psychosexual development, Freud (1914, 1920) posited that primary narcissism is the libidinal cathexis to the body. It is prior to the oedipal phase, before there is cathexis to external objects. During the oedipal stage, much of libido is transformed into object-seeking. Part of the libidinal energy, however, attaches to the ego in the form of idealization of one's sexual body and in the form of the ego ideal. Idealization, for Freud, was essentially defensive in that it was a fixation in the pre-oedipal stage, i.e., a regression, a retreat from reality and socialization.

Freud's use of idealization was very narrow, referring today to what we might describe as a delusional fixation on one's own body. If too much libido remains fixated to the body, there could not be the libidinized mental representation of imago wishes for intimacy and involvement that would allow for socialization to develop and for a transference neurosis to occur in treatment.

The concept of relationship and the use of countertransference in treatment were not part of Freud's approach. The ego ideal was a different kind of idealization, a more mature kind. It was part of the superego, having to do with one's morality and conscience. Milrod (1988) maintains that the ego ideal is that part of the superego that has a "direction giving function," following Jacobsen's (1964) view of the ego ideal. The idea of the ego ideal had to do with the internalizing of parental values, including the disciplined control and sublimination of libidinal impulses.

Several analysts have built on Freud's ideas and changed or expanded his view of idealization. I will discuss M. Klein's, Kohut's, Kernberg's, and Sullivan's views of idealization. The discussion is based, in part, on a previous paper (Ortmeyer 1987). Questions to be posed are: (1) Is idealization to be seen as healthy or pathological or both? (2) Is idealization archetypal, i.e., universal, including a possible genetic linkage? (3) Is it most usefully viewed as embedded in the specificity of an individual's experience?

Melanie Klein followed closely in the footsteps of Freud and worked with Ferenczi in Budapest, then with Abraham in Berlin, and finally with Jones in London. She lived much beyond the death of Freud (1960 vs. 1939). Klein (1975) saw idealization as an early and primitive defense aimed at unlimited gratification, i.e., greed. Its function is to defend against envy. Envy is the wish to destroy what the other person has that one does not have, and, for Klein, envy stems from the aggressive instinct via the process of projective identification. Idealization, for Klein, was a defense against instinctual aggression rather than Freud's libidinal fixation. Like libidinal fixation, it is not object-seeking, and it occurs in the first six months of the paranoid–schizoid position of the infant's normal stage of development. It is universal.

Coming to today's views, Kernberg (1975) maintains that idealization is a process that occurs differently in different diagnostic groups and normal persons. Expanding on Klein's ideas, he takes issue with her and says idealization is pathological when it occurs; it is not part of a normal stage of development. It is a projection of a loving, giving experience as a defense against ambivalence and the negative array of experience. Infatuation occurs in normal people. In the neurotic, idealization is projecting a loving, giving parental image on the analyst as a defense against ambivalence and guilt over hating the analyst.

In the borderline personality, Kernberg says idealization is a defensive protection against a sadistic, paranoid projection onto the analyst. In the narcissist, idealization is a projection of the grandiose self, and patients essentially talk to themselves. The adult patient's demand of the analyst is: "I am perfect, and you are part of me." Idealization is pathological for Kernberg because the ideal self and ideal object are fused with the real self. Following Klein, Kernberg says the "idealizing transference" is a defense against envy, the wish to devalue and destroy or possess the analyst. Kernberg maintains that his concept of the "idealizing transference" is different from Kohut's notion of the "mirroring transference," since his concept is pathological and not, as Kohut maintains, a therapeutic remobilizing of the grandiose self in a regression to an early normal level of development.

Kohut (1977, 1984), in his expansion of Freud's ideas, sees narcissism and idealization as interpersonal. He says that normal development goes through two early stages to which the patient needs to regress in the analytic transference. The earliest stage, the mirroring transference, is the mother admiring the grandiose self of the infant. The adult patient's demand of the analyst at this level of regression is "I am perfect and you admire me." The second stage of normal development, the idealizing transference, is the infant self fusing with the idealized imago, usually the father. The adult patient's demand of the analyst at this secondary level of regression is "You are perfect, and I am part of you." Kohut believes that strong values and ideals in the adult follow from an early healthy infant self fusing with the idealized father. Ambition and assertiveness in the adult follow from an early healthy infant grandiose self mirrored and admired by the mother. The transitions, or transmutations, are internalized from a failure of the mother or father to fulfill completely these needs of the infant.

Kernberg has the analyst remaining in a neutral, objective role, interpreting the defensive idealization and encountering and experiencing over time the patient's envy, rage, and devaluation of the analyst. Kohut has the analyst empathically promoting a facilitating environment in which the patient can regress. The patient will experience health and gratification in the idealization process, and interpretation will occur when the analyst has not calibrated correctly the facilitating environment. Mitchell (1988) essentially follows the Self psychologist's conceptual view of the three kinds of transference of the narcissistic personality: "I am all important and you must agree with me," "we are equally important," "you are all important and must rescue me." He places idealization under the clinical heading of illusion and maintains that three major transferential illusions of the narcissist are found in treatment: grandiosity, mutual admiration, and idealization. He suggests that the analyst playfully participate in the patient's idealization of him and at the same time lightly puzzle about it with the patient.

In both Kernberg's and Kohut's formulations of the inner interpersonal (or intrapersonal) struggle, someone is perfect, i.e., an ideal, and the other person does not exist. These formulations are clear. What is not so clear, however, is how patients mature or "get over" these interpersonal struggles once they become central to the analyst–patient relationship. Sullivan was very concerned with calibrating the optimal analytic distance with patients and with working with patients' distortions of their relationships with significant others. Is it the extra analytic interpersonal field or the analytic dyad that the analyst focuses upon in order to bring distortions into awareness? This is an area of disagreement between Interpersonal and Object Relations views of treatment. The Interpersonal clinician focuses on the former and also on areas of health that are not in the awareness of the patient, consistently bringing them to the attention of the patient (Singer 1965; Szalita 1958). Such interpretive work is valuable in strengthening the patient's self-esteem.

Sullivan (1965), impressed more by Adolph Meyer's ideas on development than by Freud's, discusses idealization as both a healthy and a pathological phenomenon. For Sullivan, healthy idealizing is characteristic of the juvenile era, roughly ages four to eight, when children have a need for interpersonal relationships with their own age group outside the family. This is an important time for the development of consensual validation. Sullivan (1965) speaks of the healthy integration of the personality in that developmental era: "the character factor that is potent in preservation of the personality in the face of great handicaps. I refer here to the idealization of the self as the person shall presently come to be" (p. 156). Sullivan goes on to say it is a powerful tendency system that wraps and protects the personality in an implicit assurance of ultimate worthy achievement against the warp of current disappointments and misfortunes. Sullivan here recognizes the positive value of idealizing as a teleological motivator to sustain one in the face of immediate frustrations. An example would be the acute frustration and embarrassment of juveniles in their bumbling social skills, ameliorated by the hope that they are learning and that, in time, social relations will be easier. Sullivan, thus, does not stress the oedipal family drama or infantile defensiveness in his account of idealization but anchors it in peer group socialization. Although Sullivan did not refer to Adler, his ideas on idealization were not unlike Adler's (cf. Ellenberger 1970) emphasis, several decades earlier, on the importance of peer relatedness for personality development. In fact, a major reason for Adler's break with Freud in 1911 was his focus on peer imagos vs. Freud's focus on oedipal parental imagos.

Idealization can be a healthy process, says Sullivan, which helps one through major life transitions at any point in adolescent and adult life. We err if we limit ourselves to the story of infancy or of the family drama. Sullivan was one of the first analysts to note and attempt to correct that misconception that Mitchell (1984) discusses as the "developmental tilt." Our great concern with beginnings, i.e., infancy, as the necessary key to unlock all understanding of later developmental progression and pathology is an unfortunate heritage from Freud's deterministic causal thinking and traumatic view of neurosis.

Sullivan's view of pathological idealization processes refers to the obsessional or paranoid process in which the personifications of self or others are rendered perfect and then projected onto significant others. Sullivan (1965:202) states "In idealizing, one projects upon another personality a body of desirable characteristics that exist within the self as a stereotype." He discusses the importance of reducing the patient's idealization of the therapist at any time that it occurs in the therapeutic process.

What is the essential difference between healthy and pathological idealization? Healthy idealization appears to be defined by its flexibility, openness to selective attention, and its lack of projection, which thereby reduces distortion in the interpersonal field, an issue that Cooper (1986) discusses. In the therapeutic situation, therefore, we interpret or act in such a way as to reduce idealization as it enters the selective attention of the therapist. The distinction between realistic appraisal of experience and projection is crucial. In the Interpersonal approach, unlike Freud's approach or that of Object Relations or Self psychology, the idealized transference is brought to the patient's awareness as soon as the analyst guesses its presence, and consensual validation is sought through a detailed inquiry. Such hypotheses of an idealizing transference always need to be validated with data from the patients' relatedness with significant others in their life.

It is most important to differentiate "ideal" from "real" in reference to concepts of "self" and "other." To understand this complexity requires a background rationale. Interpersonalists differ from Self psychologists and Object Relations analysts in their conceptions of "self" and of "other." Interpersonal theorists, coming from the tradition of Sullivan's open-ended, pragmatic, and operational theorizing, use the concepts of the "significant other" and "reflected appraisals" with reference to the "other" and to the "self." This develops into a complex inner map of Interpersonal representations.

The Freudian approach is primarily concerned with the parent imagos as they are projected onto the analyst. The English school of Object Relations has evolved from Klein's (1946–1963) concern with projected parental "objects," to Fairbairn's (1952) radical removal of inner object and self representations in normal development, to Winnicott's (1971) envelope of self–other representations as indivisible gestalts as far as the mother–infant representation is concerned, to Khan's (1983) unfolding of "hidden selves" in treatment. Object Relations theorists have moved from object relations to self-object to self-relations, but only Khan posits many selves. Kohut and his followers in Self psychology developed Winnicott's ideas to the point where Atwood and Stolorow (cf. Stepansky and Goldberg 1984) write of the intersubjective self–object field. As noted previously, Kohut posits two "other" transferential imagos, the mirroring transference and the idealizing transference. Mitchell (1988) refers to three transferential imagos: the projected grandiose other, the projected self–other mutual admiration society, and the projected idealizing other. This conception is built upon Kohut's (1984) delineations of the three transferential imagos of the mirroring transference, the twinship transference, and the idealizing transference. Only the Interpersonalists clearly entertain the concepts of *many* self and other representations, which may be hidden or apparent.

It is my conviction, based upon my understanding of Interpersonal principles and my clinical experience, that in each instance with each patient, an inquiry is required to find each particular "self and other" and their connection with prior development. The prior development can involve peers, parents, mentors, and extended family members and be placed anywhere along the developmental benchmarks, i.e., from early infancy through here-and-now experience. This complexity needs to be recognized when one attempts to understand any dream symbol or motif or any aspect of transference. An inquiry is essential for a shared dialogue and eventual consensus. This demands an open mind on the part of the analyst and of the patient to recognize the many self and other representations possible within the totality of the patient's life experience.

In this complex field of representations, the need exists to differentiate the "ideal" from "real" in regard to "self" and to "other." Granted, overlap always occurs, never exclusivity. However, a significant difference is evident here. The real self–other comes from lived experience with others. It is best revealed through a consistent inquiry intended to arrive at a gestalt of the patient's life experience. Data may come from many sources: recall, dreams, associations, and reports from significant others about the patient's life. On the other hand, the idealized selves and others are much more hidden, repressed, and therefore more likely to be projected onto the analyst or onto significant others in the patient's life. Their sources may be movies, television, advertising, passive observations, or lived experience with real people. For example, a major idealized other for Jung was his namesake grandparent Carl Jung. And as previously mentioned, Freud had several idealized others, from Moses to Garibaldi. The idealized self and other are often fused with each other in inner representations and need to be differentiated. They, not unlike Freud's "wish," are typically repressed and are most readily discerned through dreams, transference, and fantasy material.

A clinical example follows that illustrates the bringing to awareness of idealization when it is expressed in significant relationships, including the analytic dyad.

> This patient was presented in a previous paper (Ortmeyer 1987): a fifty-five-year-old, successful financial officer for a public corporation. He was initially quite guarded and had spells of depression. In the first few sessions of treatment, he said he had come to the analyst because he had been highly recommended by his good friend, a therapist colleague of the analyst. He was very observant about the analyst's home and office. He would critique any perceived fault in the office, e.g., a sticky door, and then sit back and ask for comments. The analyst was direct and forthright in recognizing the validity of these critiques and shared with the patient his own thoughts about the issue. The analyst asked him if his thoughts met the patient's approval. The patient grinned but said nothing about it. So the analyst and patient were aware that the patient was interviewing the analyst and his thinking ability before committing himself to treatment. He gave his implicit and tentative stamp of approval to what he heard, because he had moved from a guarded, critical position to one of revealing himself in a detailed, prepared explanation of circumscribed problems he was having at work. The analyst's reaction was to feel good about the work, suggestive of a countertransference reaction to the patient's idealizing transference.
>
> In talking about his work, the patient said he was very good at it. He wanted, however, too much approval and admiration from his boss, and he knew that his wish was not appropriate. The analyst questioned what he meant about appropriate. His boss, he said, was considerate of him in his gruff way and complimented him, so he could see he already had his boss's approval, yet he kept seeking it. He should be able to take or leave his boss. He choked up and had tears in his eyes. The analyst agreed with what he had said, then asked him what he cried about. The patient haltingly said that he always had felt that his father should know best. The analyst asked what he meant. He said he had spoken to his father a couple of days before and had been telling him he had a problem at work. He described to his father what he had described to the analyst. His father's advice was to get another job where he felt more comfortable. He either would make it or not; above all, he should not worry about it. The analyst said it sounded as though his father lectured him in a moralistic manner and that his father had not understood the self-change he sought. He again choked up.

> The analyst asked him to tell about his father. He said his father was a retired executive of a corporation in another state, a respected authority in the town where he had always lived. His father saw no reason why the patient should have left home. The patient was the oldest child and, in his father's eyes, should have followed in his father's footsteps. The analyst felt an urge to compliment this man on his independence and ambition, refrained from doing so, and asked him how, from his current perspective, he saw his father when he was growing up. He said his father was always right, knew he was right, and had definite views on everything. His father never wanted to live in the larger world and was still very critical of his son for doing so. His mother obeyed his father and never questioned his authority.
>
> How about you, the analyst asked? The patient lapsed into silence, his face flushed, tears came to his eyes, and he appeared ready to get up and bolt from the room. The analyst insisted that he talk out his feelings. The patient haltingly said that he had never questioned his father's authority and believed him to be right. His father would get angry if his point of view were doubted.
>
> The session was near its end. The analyst summed up what had been said. He pointed out that the patient's father did not seem curious about the complexity of people and the world; he tried to protect the patient from the world rather than help him understand it. His father is idealistic, and the patient, in turn, colludes in the idealization of his father. The patient, the analyst suggested, participated in this by his difficulty in not accepting the limitations of his father, himself, or his boss. He wants his boss to be an ideal to him and to have his boss view him in an all-approving manner, even though he knows better intellectually. The analyst guessed that he might be asking the same of the analyst. His choking and crying was mourning the loss of this ideal.
>
> Through this summation, the patient watched the analyst very closely, with a serious deadpan expression on his face. As the analyst became silent, the patient started laughing, slapped his leg, and wagged his finger at the analyst as the session ended. In subsequent sessions, the patient has worked with his impatience, his need to be in control, and his high expectations of himself and of others, including the analyst. The analyst has no illusion that the idealization issue is resolved.

In this clinical example, the analyst interpreted the patient's idealization in the first few sessions, as it came up in relation to significant others, his boss, and his father. The transference interpretation of idealization was referred to only in passing. This kept the frame of the patient's projected idealization in his current interpersonal field. A summary at the end of a session highlighted the mutual collusion between his father and himself to idealize paternal authority and its implications for his difficulties.

References

Atlas, J. 1988. The case of Paul DeMan. *New York Times Sunday Magazine,* August 28, 1988.

Barrett, B. 1988. Why is psychoanalysis so controversial? Notes from left field. *Psychoanalytic Psychology* 5:223–39.

Bloom, H. 1986. Freud: The greatest American writer. *New York Times Book Review,* March 23, 1986, pp. 25–27.

Cooper, A. 1986. Resolution of the transference from an interpersonal perspective. Presented at the 5th Annual Meeting of Division 39, American Psychological Association, Ixtapa, Mexico.

Ellenberger, H. 1970. *The Discovery of the Unconscious.* New York: Basic Books.

Fairbairn, W.R.D. 1952. *An Object-Relations Theory of the Personality.* New York: Basic Books.

Freud, S. 1914. On narcissism: An introduction. *Standard Edition* 14:67–102.

——. 1920. Group psychology and the analysis of the ego. *Standard Edition* 18:69–143.

Jacobsen, E. 1964. *The Self and the Object World.* New York: International Universities Press.

Kernberg, O. 1975. *Borderline Conditions and Pathological Narcissism.* New York: Jason Aronson.

Khan, M.M.R. 1983. *Hidden Selves.* New York: International Universities Press.

Klein, M. 1975. *Envy and Gratitude and Other Works (1946–1963).* New York: Delta.

Kohut, H. 1977. *The Restoration of the Self.* New York: International Universities Press.

——. 1984. *How Does Analysis Cure?* A. Goldberg and P. Stepansky, eds., Chicago: University of Chicago Press.

Milrod, D. 1988. The ego ideal. Presented at the 24th Annual Convention of Psychoanalytic Psychotherapists, New York.

Mitchell, S. 1984. Object relations and the developmental tilt. *Contemporary Psychoanalysis* 20:473–99.

——. 1988. *Relational Concepts in Psychoanalysis.* Cambridge, Mass.: Harvard University Press.

Ortmeyer, D.H. 1987. Idealization in the transference and countertransference. *Contemporary Psychoanalysis* 23:221–29.

Pines, M. 1989. On history and psychoanalysis. *Psychoanalytic Psychology* 6:121–35.

Scarr, S. 1985. Constructing psychology. *American Psychologist,* 40:499–512.

Schorske, C. 1979. *Fin de Siecle Vienna.* New York: Knopf.

Singer, E. 1965. *Key Concepts in Psychotherapy*. New York: Random House.
Stepansky, P.E. and A. Goldberg. 1984. *Kohut's Legacy: Contributions to Self-Psychology*. Hillsdale, N.J.: Analytic Press.
Sullivan, H.S. 1965. *Personal Psychopathology*. New York: Norton.
Szalita, A. 1958. Regression and perception in psychotic states. *Psychiatry* 21:53–63.
Winnicott, D.W. 1971. *Playing and Reality*. New York: Penguin Books.

11

Patterns of Narcissism in Japan

Mikihachiro Tatara

Research on narcissism and narcissistic personality disorder in Japan is being spurred somewhat through the influence of Kernberg's work and Kohut's work (Ito 1982; Maruta 1982). DSM III also influenced Japanese psychiatrists, psychoanalysts, and psychologists. Several attempts have been made to describe and understand clinical material from the point of view of narcissistic personality disorder (Kondo and Mizuno 1985; Hashinoto 1987; Kondo and Muroya 1988). However, the fact is that at present, few original research papers on narcissism have been published in Japan. Understanding narcissism as referring to insecure self-esteem, I would like to describe clinical groups of psychoneuroses and approach their psychology and psychopathology in terms of the development of the self-image through interpersonal relationships in Japan.

Typical Clinical Problems in Japan

One of the most frequent and idiosyncratic psychoneurotic problems in Japan has been *taijin kyofu sho,* anthropophobia. It is so common that it is said to be a reflection and shadow of the Japanese mind; *taijin kyofu sho* is characterized by fear of eye contact with other people and fear of being watched. When patients make eye contact, they feel that they are doing something wrong and harmful to others. Because of this fear, they cannot venture outside their homes and they withdraw from social-interpersonal relations. Many Japanese psychiatrists and psychologists have discussed this problem (Kora 1955; Yamashita 1968; Uchinuma 1977, 1983; Ogawa 1978; Satomura 1979; Fukui 1980; Ihida 1981; Kimura 1982; Kasahara 1972, 1988). I myself also have written of it elsewhere (Tatara 1981).

The following symptoms characterize *taijin kyofu sho:*

1. The most active symptoms appear among friend and acquaintances.
2. Patients feel guilty about whatever they are doing, fearing that they are injuring others they encounter.
3. This symptom appears mostly after the onset of puberty and till the end of adolescence. Among college students, this is the most common psychoneurotic symptom. More than one third of the population of students is said to have some minor form of *taijin kyofu sho.*
4. In severe cases of borderline or schizophrenia, *taijin kyofu sho* continues and is hard to relieve until the basic psychopathology is resolved.
5. In severe psychopathological cases, *taijin kyofu sho* is accompanied by other kinds of symptoms.

Other Newly Developed Psychoneurotic Problems

In the past two decades, two clinical symptom groups seem to be increasing. The first group is *school phobia* or *school refusal* among elementary school and high school students, and the second group is the *student apathy syndrome* among college students. These two clinical groups seem idiosyncratic to Japanese culture, because even though many Japanese psychiatrists and psychologists devote a great deal of attention and research effort as well as many papers and books to the topic, I have found very few clinical reports dealing with these problems outside Japan.

School Phobia or School Avoidance

The first report on school phobia was published by Sato (1959). Since then it has received increasingly greater attention among researchers. Sumi (1962), Takagi (1963), and myself (Tatara 1964) are the first group who did these researches. In the past two decades, the incidence of the problem has increased explosively, and accordingly, research on this problem has also increased (for research reviews, see Takagi 1984; Tatara 1981).

Students who suffer from this problem have psychosomatic reactions, such as morning fever, stomach ache, nausea, and *sukumi* (body stiffness) in response to psychological pressure to attend school. They seem eager to go but cannot. They fear school, but when school hours are over, they resume normal life and function as other children do at home. They repeat this behavior pattern everyday. Sufferers gradually become withdrawn totally and stay at home. As symptoms become worse, they do not even talk with family members. They stay alone in the dark and show something like schizophrenic behavior, though no obvious sign of schizophrenia is evident. They watch television and play with personal computer games. They read weekly magazines and listen to music. They reverse sleep habits, waking at night and sleeping in the daytime. Parental advice is rejected, and they are resistant to outside help. Sometimes, they become violent toward family members, particularly toward mothers when forced to attend school or compelled to receive professional advice.

In sum, leading characteristics of school phobia as follows:

1. The problem begins to appear in prepubescent children, continuing through puberty and the preadolescent level. Put in terms of school age it extends from elementary school to high school age, although it may also affect college students.
2. They usually have the *sukumi* symptom, i.e., body stiffness caused by psychological conflict about whether or not to attend school. The outcome is that they become immobilized.
3. When at school, their achievement is high. They are considered to be good boys and girls. They are self-conscious about achievement and are competitive with classmates, though they do not show aggression and competitiveness overtly.
4. Symptomatology is usually triggered by a small incident that injures self-esteem. Typical precipitating incidents may be forgetting homework,

leading to punishment by the teacher, or failure to perform as expected by themselves at physical education lessons or music class.

5. They externalize injuries to self-esteem, attributing them to poor leadership by the teacher, roughness of classmates, and so on. Usually, parents accept and agree with such rationalizations.

Student Apathy Syndrome

Student apathy syndrome occurs among college students. It is the lack of motivation to study or pursue a career. Those students who suffer from this problem find it difficult to attend class, to take courses and tests, and to write reports that are integral to the college life of students. However, they are eager to concentrate on hobbies, such as playing music, operating personal computers, or taking a part-time job. Because they retreat and avoid the college campus, they are called retreat psychoneurotics (Kasahara 1988).

In the past decade, these students have gradually increased in number, up to 1 or 2 percent of the total population of college students. It is difficult to discern them by their outward social behavior because they seem like ordinary students and show no pathological signs in their interpersonal relations with others on the college campus, though their contact with fellow students is minimal.

The following are characteristics of this problem:

1. Superficially they appear to be students living an ordinary school life. However, they do not take courses or attend classes. They have minimal contact with classmates. They have few friends at the college where they registered.
2. They do not show specific psychoneurotic symptoms but continue this pattern of life. They do not give up student status to take jobs outside the college. It seems important for them to be students.
3. After several years of college life, they leave school without any degree or achievement. Afterward, they maintain a marginal way of life with parental financial support.

Now I would like to propose some hypotheses about these problems, which seem idiosyncratic to Japanese culture. The issues are considered from the point of view of development of self-image and the pathology of narcissism.

Hypothetical Interpretations

taijin kyofu sho

As I mentioned before, *taijin kyofu sho* is so common that clinicians meet this problem often. Some psychological characteristics of the syndrome are the following:

1. They seem very self-conscious about their status in interpersonal relationships, particularly within their social circles, such as with school classmates, friends, and neighbors. They feel that they have to be perceived as unique, prominent, and visible. These concerns for high regard are not manifested outside the circle of friends and very close family relationships. Because symptoms tend to be confined within their social circle, the syndrome suggests a label of the "doughnut phenomenon" (Tatara 1981; see figure 11.1).
2. Presenting themselves as prominent reflects needs to preserve grandiose self-images as the most successful and capable people in the world. This grandiosity is fostered by their mothers who, during their childhoods, acted as auxiliary egos for them. The mother–child relationship is very close and sometimes seems symbiotic (Takahashi 1980).

FIGURE 11.1 *Interpersonal sphere in which the symptom appears.*

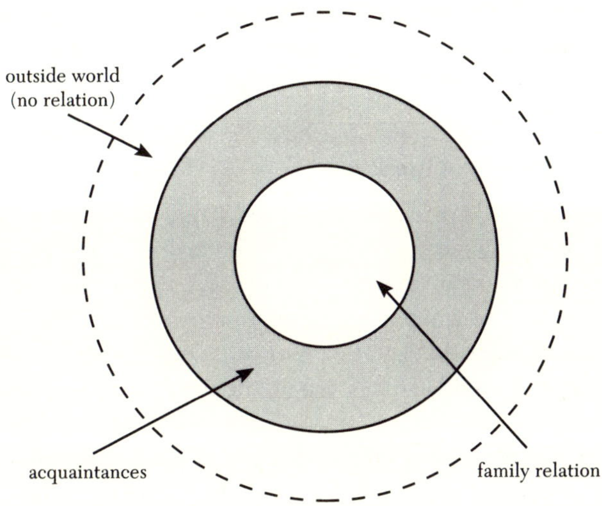

3. Without exception, the mother whose child is suffering from this problem has difficulty in her marital relationship, though, for financial and traditional reasons, which emphasize woman's place in the home and divorce as the fault of women, she does not want to leave the marriage. She suppresses her frustration, using her child as her own extended ego. She helps and controls the child for her own satisfaction, to prove that she is not a failure but a successful mother. She gears her child toward what she wants even though she realizes that she is assuming social responsibilities for the child that her husband cannot and would not take.
4. Until her child reaches puberty, the mother can meet the child's needs and can use the child as an extension of her own ego. However, when children reach puberty they must carry out their own tasks by themselves, particularly in school situations. At this point, they are limited by their own realistic abilities, which have been underdeveloped, owing to their mother's protectiveness. They become self-conscious about the gap between their needs to be prominent and visible and their shadowy existence in reality. Then they have to face the conflict of inability to earn the prominence and visibility that they have come to require.
5. This conflict seems to result in the symptom of "not-to-be-seen" though there is desperate need "to-be-seen." It is the dilemma of image beset by limitations that realistically cannot meet requirements for outstanding accomplishment.

Thus far I have described the interpersonal and psychological functioning underlying *taijin kyofu sho.* The two other syndromes mentioned above are similar with respect to interpersonal and psychological functioning.

School Phobia and School Avoidance

As I mentioned above, the school phobia and school avoidance syndrome is prevalent all over Japan among elementary and high school students at present. This became so common within two decades that it is one of the main topics in the fields of education, psychology, and psychiatry. Many factors of social and educational pathology affect this pathological phenomenon. However, in this paper I would like to focus on the psychopathology of the individual patient.

In terms of interpersonal relations and psychological functioning this syndrome is quite similar to the previously mentioned *taijin kyofu sho.* The psychological characteristics are as follows:

1. At the outset, children in this grouping show anxiety upon separating from their mothers when they begin to attend kindergarten. This separation anxiety continues into elementary school. Usually, it simply reflects lack of social skills for meeting others in social and interpersonal situations.
2. During their prepubescent phase, these children become more self-conscious about how to integrate inner needs with their own realistic limitations in meeting those needs. They become very sensitive to the imbalance between needs and abilities.
3. The inner self-image is usually grandiose and omnipotent. It is fostered by the mother's own problems, as I mentioned above when I discussed *taijin kyofu sho.*
4. The children introject the mother's ideal image of her children being the best and brightest, resulting in a self-image that is grandiose and omnipotent. When these children meet difficulty in fulfilling mother's expectations, their frustrations turn against the mother, blaming her for the failure. Then they reproach her with: "Give my life back to me, mom!"
5. The mother usually becomes a target of the child's anger when frustration becomes panic and bursts into violence and resistance against parental advice. However, outside the home, such a child will be very quiet and behave nicely. Consequently nobody outside the family realizes what is going on in the home situation.
6. The mother usually becomes depressed by these narcissistic injuries to her self-image and rejects the child in return. The patient becomes autistic, withdrawing from reality and hiding at home. The father of the family is ineffectual and unable to be helpful in this situation.

These two syndromes, *taijin kyofu sho* and *school avoidance,* both involve interpersonal malfunctioning in response to narcissistic wounds. The symptom syndromes serve as defenses against injury to grandiose self-images. That also is the case in the third type of difficulty, the *student apathy syndrome.*

Student Apathy

The student apathy syndrome has also been increasing in the last decade. Students manifesting this difficulty are not dropouts but are caught in a social limbo. Since the university system in Japan is different from those in the United States or Europe, it is best to explain the situation. First of all, entrance into college or university is no easy matter, particularly in the case of national universities. A principal obstacle is the entrance examination with a pass/fail rate of 1:5 or more. When students fail the examination, they have to wait for another year to try again. It is hardly rare to find students who have tried several times. They spend several years at preparatory schools (*Juku*) as *Ronin* (candidates) to enter the particular university they want.

However, once admitted to the university, it is not terribly difficult to go through to graduation, aided by the tutoring system, which helps them to get through the final examination.

It is also true that when students cannot pass semester finals, this stirs up personal problems. Kasahara (1988), a leading psychiatrist and researcher on this problem, called students caught in these dilemmas retreat psychoneurotics. The following are the characteristics of such students:

1. They look like ordinary students. Interpersonally and behaviorally, they do not show any sign of psychopathology. The only problem for them is that they cannot concentrate on their study in class at the university.
2. They appear to be interested in preparing their course work carefully outside the classroom. However, they cannot concentrate or focus on their studies.
3. They engage eagerly in side interests such as part-time jobs and playing music, computer games, and so on, which are not part of their university studies.
4. They suffer from identity confusion or diffusion, as described by Erikson (1968), unable to decide which area represents their real interests. They fear that if they commit themselves in a specific area, they must lose other possible opportunities. Therefore, they suspend their decisions.
5. Behind this undecidedness lurk grandiose self-images of being able to do whatever they select if they concentrate. Their excuse for not accomplishing anything is that they simply do not spend enough time and energy on the job. In this way they prolong their student role as long as they can, until expelled from the university.
6. At that point, they have not accomplished anything. They have no choice but to do manual labor or equivalent work. They look like cases of avoidant personality disorder, in the DSM III classification, in their efforts to escape from facing themselves. In this sense, they not only retreat from reality and interpersonal relations but they also retreat from themselves, as described by Fromm (1941).

Culturally Bound Psychoneurosis and Its Mechanisms

Though *taijin kyofu sho* has been considered as a neurosis peculiar to Japanese culture for a long time, these clinical groups of school phobia or school avoidance and student apathy syndrome are recent phenomena in Japan. Moreover, the number of patients in these categories is currently increasing rapidly all over Japan.

I would like to propose a formulation addressed to the interpersonal pattern underlying these symptoms. In the first place, I would like to describe the interpersonal structure of *nikoh–kankei,* I–I (subjective–subjective) relationship in contrast to the western individualistic I–you (subjective–objective) relationship. Second, I would like to describe and analyze the psychological structure in terms of a vulnerable, grandiose self-image and difficulty in facing interpersonal and social realities. This self-image is related to the shame experience described by Benedict (1946). Third, I would like to examine three ways of handling situations, that is, explosive aggression, avoidant-withdrawal and indifferent-apathetic reactions. Clearly, these psychological tendencies are closely related to the psychology of narcissism in Japan.

Nikoh–Kankei, I–I (Subjective–Subjective) Relationships

Arimasa Mori, a Japanese philosopher who lived in France for thirty years and died in Paris in 1968, analyzed the language structure of Japanese as contrasted with Indo-European languages, particularly French and English (Mori 1970, 1976). He found Japanese speech to be different from French or English. Although sentence structure may be the same, other features are quite dissimilar. Customarily the word *you* is employed in directly addressing the other in English, whatever the accompanying nuances. However, in Japan, when people speak, the quality of the interpersonal situation (whether it is intimate or formal) and interpersonal structure (i.e., whether the person is older or younger or whether higher or lower in social status than you) are fundamental considerations. Without them, there is no proper social conversation.

Moreover, when people speak, they have to choose language variously, even when the content is identical. This interpersonal speech situation includes my assessment of what I (speaker) think the person addressed thinks of me. *Nikoh–kankei* means that the subject speaks to the reflected subject, that is, I speak to myself reflected in you. In this sense, this interpersonal relation becomes an I–I relationship. Figure 11.2 illustrates this dynamic interpersonal speech situation.

This interpersonal situation is dynamically changed according to the person to whom one speaks. The speaker always has to perceive and grasp the

FIGURE 11.2 *Contrasting interpersonal situations.*

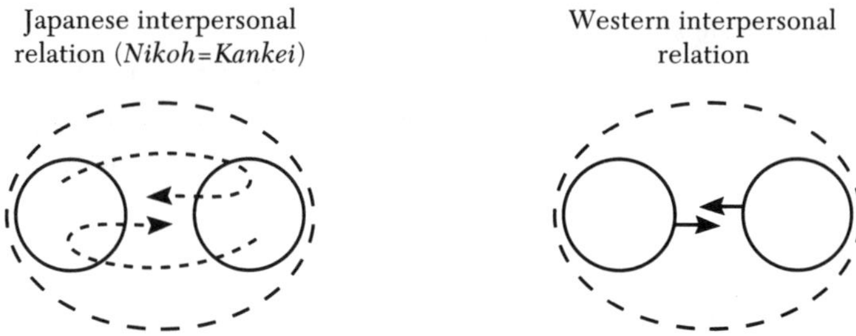

dynamic quality of the interpersonal relation. Otherwise, the speaker fails to communicate with the other person. As the number of speakers increases in the speech situation, this relationship becomes more complex. It is energy consuming.

The speaker always has to be mindful of the structure and the nuances of the interpersonal situation. The speaker is always required to be field dependent in Japan in contrast to a field-independent orientation in Western culture. These language conventions grow out of fundamental aspects of Japanese culture. People emphasize the beauty of this way of speaking, this emphasis not on "what to say," but on "how to say." In Japanese schools there are *hanashi kata kyoshitu,* "how to speak classes," which contrast with content-oriented debate classes in the United States.

The above-mentioned interpersonal structuring is the background of the symptom. Now, I would like to describe the development of the self-image and the particular focus it puts on the development of a narcissistic image. We might begin with studies such as those by Caudill (1959, 1969) and Vogel (1963), who observed and described mother–child relationships in Japan. Since those researches were conducted, many changes have occurred both inside and outside the Japanese family. For example, there are more divorce cases, more two-generation families than three-generation families, more housewives getting jobs outside the home, and so on. Despite these changes in family life, the basic pattern of the parent–child relationship has not changed much. Instead, a basic narcissistic pattern in the family relations, which heretofore was hidden by culturally bound passive–aggressive patterns of behavior, now becomes more visible (Roland 1988).

It seems to me that a key word for understanding development of the self-image and interpersonal relationships in Japan is *tutumu. Tutumu* is an ordinary Japanese word, meaning to cover and wrap, but typically wrapping is overdone, beyond what is necessary for protection of the object. That is, *tutumu* is the practice of always wrapping things as if they were Christmas presents or birthday presents in the United States. *Tutumu* seems to be ritualistically important, though it is the everyday pattern of social behavior in Japan (Nukada 1977; Lee 1989).

Tutumu is prevalent in Japanese culture not only in the field of merchandise wrapping but also in family relationships and other social relationships. I would like to focus on family relations in terms of the *tutumu* metaphor. Adults in the family, particularly mothers, hold children as protectively and ritualistically as they wrap things. They also use *tutumu* to cover and (with) hold their feelings and thoughts. This withholding is different from suppression or repression in the psychoanalytic sense. It is more like keeping things or thoughts inside oneself tenderly. "Tenderly" and "graciously" are the keys to handling anything lest you crush what is inside, whether it is things, ideas, or feelings. In interpersonal relationships, people have to express ideas, thoughts, or needs tenderly and covertly, not directly and aggressively, lest confrontation crush the ideas, feelings, or thoughts.

Modes of expression that are abrupt, direct, or assertive are antithetical to *tutumu* as a means of exploiting or taking advantage of people. Such exploitation is usually successful up to the extent that people can tolerate it. If it goes beyond people's tolerance, they fall into panic and behave destructively, losing touch with realistic considerations.

This *tutumu* also prevails in parent–child relationships and family relationships. The child is usually treated as a treasure and wrapped tenderly in the mother's arms. Symbolically speaking, the child is held in the mother's womb. The home also is the mother's womb. All people, whether they are adults or children, are protected and become children in the mother's womb. It seems that this relationship is basically a *tutumu* relationship.

As to the development of self-image, the child's feeling can be oceanic and its self-image omnipotent in this *tutumu* relationship. In the clinical setting, the clinician always has to face this omnipotence and quick regression to the preanaclitic level in the therapeutic relationship. When patients are frustrated with the therapist, they become angry covertly. They do not express their anger, and when it becomes intolerable they prefer to quit. Switching one's own therapist, one for the other, whether physical and mental, is a common phenomenon in Japan. It is the usual mode of expression of anger.

If there is no way to avoid or withdraw from the situation, people easily fall into panic and become destructive. In panic states, they become destructive toward themselves. *Shinjuh* (family suicide) and *kamikaze* suicide can be understood in this context. In the clinical groups, such as school phobia or school avoidance, this parent-child *tutumu* relationship often develops to the extreme form of violence toward parents.

The child's oceanic feeling and omnipotent self-image has to face reality for the first time in the child's life when the child starts to attend kindergarten. The child has to emerge from the mother's womb to another womb, the kindergarten teacher's. However, for certain children, this transition is difficult and they cannot separate from the mother. This is the first sign of school phobia and school avoidance. These children usually show strong *hito mishiri* (stranger anxiety) as described by Spitz (1956), which is, however, prolonged to the kindergarten level. This anxiety continues further until the later ages of prepuberty and adolescence. This anxiety also seems to be the basis of *taijin kyofu sho.*

Difficulty in this transition from mother's womb to teacher's womb becomes an important step of the symptom formation. Usually little effort is made to strengthen the child's ability to cope, that is, to strengthen the ego or to increase the ability for a realistic self. Instead people wrap up the child gently to avoid difficulties. Accordingly, the basic psychological structure and the basic pattern of interpersonal relations is unchanged. As a result, such children receive injuries to their omnipotent and narcissistic self-images many times over, in the course of their lives.

As I mentioned earlier, it is very difficult to acquire the basic *nikoh–kankei* interpersonal orientation and also to maintain an omnipotent self-image. That becomes very complex and energy-consuming psychological work. On the one hand, it demands keeping an omnipotent and narcissistic self-image. On the other, one must develop the social skill to deal with dynamic hierarchical orders in interpersonal social situations. These two processes are mutually conflictual.

As contrasted with *taijin kyofu sho* and school phobia or school avoidance, the student apathy syndrome has its own special psychological make-up. There seems to be a lack of self-consciousness. Those manifesting student apathy appear not to be afraid and not to care about what other people think of them. They show indifference toward others, outside their own circle, but interest in people within their group. They live essentially normal-appearing lives without any particular pathological signs except for this selectivity in human relations. They do not show their narcissistic injuries, which are deeply repressed. There is a diffusion in time perspectives, as Erikson pointed out. Patients seem like children who are waiting forever for the day when their omnipotent and narcissistic needs will come true. However, since they have not tried to study or acquire professional skill, they have little chance for getting jobs comparable to those of college graduates.

Psychoanalyst T. Doi (1970) proposed the concept of *amae* to interpret Japanese culture and interpersonal relations. *Amae* might be understood as the qualification of passive mother–child dependency longings through traditional Japanese etiquette. It is an interesting idea and important for the field of psychoanalysis and psychotherapy in Japan, though it is still controversial because of its vagueness (Takotomo 1989). *Amae* is a pervasive phenomenon in Japanese interpersonal relationships. Unfulfilled *amae* becomes the source of psychopathology (Roland 1982–1983, 1988; Tatara 1982).

It seems that *amae* is a reaction against frustration of omnipotent and narcissistic needs. The need for *amae* expresses a wish to regress to a prenatal state in the mother's womb to recover an omnipotent self-image. If Doi's view of *amae* is correct and can serve as a key for interpreting Japanese culture and interpersonal relations, it suggests a strong regressive force in Japanese national character. In that case it becomes important to recognize the narcissistic insecurities behind this psychopathology.

References

Benedict, R. 1946. *The Chrysanthemum and the Sword.* New York: Houghton and Mifflin.

Caudill, W. 1959. The cultural context of Japanese personality. In M. Kopler, ed., *Culture and mental health.* New York: Macmillan.

——. 1969. Maternal care and infant behavior in Japan and America. *Psychiatry* 32.

Doi, T. 1970. *Anatomy of Dependency.* Tokyo: Kodansha International.

Erikson, E.H. 1968. *Identity, Youth, and Crisis.* New York: Norton.

Fromm. E. 1941. *Escape from Freedom.* New York: Norton.

Fukui, Y. 1980. Taijin Kyofu and adolescent initiation. *Ehime Daigaki Research Studies* 26:77–90.

Hashimoto, M. 1987. Borderline personality disorder and narcissistic personality disorder. *Japanese Journal of Psychiatric Treatment* 2:327.

Ihida, M. eds. 1981. *Taijin Kyofu.* Tokyo: Igaku Shoin.

Ito, K. 1982. Studies of narcissism: From the genetic and structural point of view. *Japanese Journal of Psychoanalysis* 26.

Kasahara, Y., ed. 1972. *Seishi Kyofu and Taishu Kyofu.* Tokyo: Igaku Shoin.

——. 1988. *Retreat Neurosis.* Tokyo: Kodansha Shinsho.
Kimura, S. 1982. *Taijin Kyofu in Japanese.* Tokyo: Keiso Shobo.
Kondo, M. and N. Mizuno. 1985. Clinical considerations of narcissistic personality disorder. *Japanese Journal of Clinical Psychopathology* 6:151.
Kondo, M. and T. Muroya. 1988. Hypochondriasis and psychotherapy: From the viewpoint of narcissistic personality disorder. *Japanese Journal of Psychiatry* 30:131.
Kora, T. 1955. Taijin Kyofu Sho and historical–social environment of Japan. *Kyushu Neuro-psychiatry* 9:3.
Lee, O. 1989. *Furoshiki Culture and Post-modernism.* Tokyo: Chuo Koronsha.
Maruta, T. 1982. Narcissistic personality: Theoretical comparison of Kernberg and Kohut. *Japanese Journal of Psychoanalysis* 26:30.
Mori, A. 1970. *On Being and Thought.* Tokyo: Kodansha.
——. 1976. *Thought on How We Live.* Tokyo: Kodansha.
Nukada, I. 1977. *Tutumi.* Tokyo: Hosei University.
Ogawa, K., ed. 1978. *Taijin Kyofu Sho.* Tokyo: Shibundo.
Roland, A. 1982–1983. The therapeutic relationship and resistance-analysis in Japan, India and America: A cross-cultural psychoanalytic perspective. *Hiroshima Forum for Psychology* 9:35–39.
——. 1988. *In Search of Self in India and Japan.* Princeton, N.J.: Princeton University Press.
Sato, S. 1959. Clinical studies on school phobia. *Okayama Child Guidance Research Bulletin.*
Satomura, J. 1979. Comparative studies on Taijin Kyofu Sho between Germany and Japan. *Clinical Psychiatry* 8(1):329–37; 8(2):1343–50.
Spitz, R. 1956. *The First Year of Life.* New York: International University Press.
Sumi, T. 1962. On school phobia. *Research Studies of Japan National Institute of Mental Health.*
Takagi, R. 1963. Mental mechanism of school phobia and its prevention. *Acta Paedopsychiatrica* 30:135–40.
——. 1984. School refusal children and present social situation in Japan. *Japanese Journal of Child Psychiatry* 25:63–77.
Takahashi, K. 1980. Adolescent symbiotic psychopathology: A cultural comparison of American and Japanese patterns and resolutions. *Bulletin of the Menninger Clinic,* vol. 44, no. 3.
Takotomo, Y. 1989. *Critique of Amae Theory of Dr. Doi Shoso.* Tokyo: Iwanami Shoten.
Tatara, M. 1964. Clinical studies on school phobia. *Japanese Journal of Child Psychiatry* 4.
——. 1981. Taijin Kyofu Sho: Anthrophobia and Japanese culture. *Hiroshima Forum for Psychology* 8.
——. 1982. Psychoanalytic psychotherapy in Japan: The issue of dependency pattern and resolution of psychopathology. *Journal of American Academy of Psychoanalysis* 10:225–39.

Uchinuma, Y. 1977. *Anthropology of Taijin Kyofu Sho.* Tokyo: Koubundo.

——. 1983. *Psychopathology of Taijin Kyofu Sho.* Tokyo: Kinokuniya.

Vogel, E. 1963. The salary man and his family in a Tokyo suburb. In *Japan's New Middle Class.* Berkeley, Calif.: University of California.

Yamashita, K. 1968. Psychological mechanisms and therapeutic approaches. *Japanese Journal of Psychiatry* 10:554–57.

PART IV

The Therapeutic Relationship

12

Narcissism and Obsessionalism: An Interpersonal Psychoanalytic Approach

Leon Salzman

The prevailing tendency to label and identify psychopathological disorders according to a cluster of described behaviors belies an understanding of etiological factors and overlooks dynamic issues involved in the behavior. This tendency follows the medical model of identifying diseases where there is a clear and often single cause. Behavioral theorists have been trying to get away from this model, particularly when they view psychological problems as defenses against anxiety that develop in an interpersonal context. We can then identify maladaptive behavior as symptoms of disordered living. Approaching behavior from this perspective we would be inclined to speak of reactive or adaptive types, in which the total personality seems to be directed toward fulfilling some goal in an effort to achieve and sustain some viable mode of living. Particular and well-identified behavioral tactics and techniques are available that are universally used in this endeavor.

Sometimes one type of defense may be more in evidence than another, and in certain individuals the tactic may be prominent and compulsively utilized so that it is inappropriate and unconstructive. It may be the major tactic in all of a person's interactions, presenting a consistent and durable style to which we can assign a label identifying it as a personality type. However, in most instances, mixture of various defenses exists, and the personality configuration does not produce malfunctioning; we tend to see such individuals as well adjusted.

The present diagnostic manual (DSM III) with its diagnostic criteria for the range of personality disorders, catalogues behavior and conveys the impression that we have identified a specific disease. What has been done, however, is to describe a cluster of behaviors that is the result of overpowering defense tactics, viewed from a particular perspective. The same cluster of behaviors, if described from a different orientation, could elicit the label of a different personality disorder. This is especially true in the labels of borderline, narcissistic personality, and the obsessive-compulsive personality. An examination of the descriptive characterization of these personalities reveals a remarkably similar set of behavioral manifestations, with emphasis on differing aspects of the behavior.

The essential feature of the narcissist is the pervasive pattern of grandiosity and hypersensitivity to criticism and the focus on the person's own needs, desires, and feelings of entitlement. This overwhelming focus produces the range of behavior that accompanies the person's living, such as self-centeredness and demands for immediate satisfaction. In their grandiose sense of self-importance, such people may exaggerate their skills, talents, and entitlements. They may tend to exploit others and be unable to visualize the rights of others. They demand exclusive recognition and acknowledgment of their interests. This constellation of features clearly relates to persons whose focus is on their own needs; when this behavior becomes extreme, it can be called a disorder.

Similarly, obsessional persons are focused on satisfying their own needs by maintaining control of themselves and the outside world through behavior that produces a grandiose view of themselves. The drive for perfection, coupled with the intellectual emphasis on knowing everything in order to be certain and to guarantee control over events, invariably develops a grandiosity that leads to contempt and derision of others. The obsessional person's demand for certainty and guarantees requires a procrastinating indecisiveness that prevents closure. Commitments must be avoided so as to maintain control, and indecisiveness avoids making mistakes by postponing action. This is all designed to give obsessional persons the illusion of control, thereby enhancing their grandiose view of themselves. The restriction of affects and an overly conscientious scrupulosity leads to a rigid preoccupation with rules and precise patterns of behavior. This is often the background for distressing obsessive or compulsive behavior that overshadows their characterological traits and becomes the focus of therapeutic efforts. However, the egocentric focus and the demand for acknowledgment of their high ethical and moral principles signals the grandiose elements in the disorder despite loud and insistent claims of only wanting to be simply human.

In the narcissist the emphasis is on the individual's grandiose uniqueness and privilege, which stem from the excessive need for recognition and love. In the obsessive person, the grandiosity is an attempt to demonstrate power and control in order to feel safe and secure in a dangerous and hostile world. Whatever the source or background for the behavior of these two personality types, the behavior that alienates and destroys interpersonal relationships and intimacy must be dealt with in therapy. Tactics in the psychoanalytic therapy of these two personalities may be very similar but must take into account the idiosyncratic elements in the dynamics of these states, as well as the individual's current life experiences.

Once the labels are put aside and we look at the predominant issues and difficulties in the individual's living, we must consider how to deal with these matters, especially the grandiosity, which is a major factor in both narcissism and obsessionalism. We need to distinguish the manner in which patients attempt to achieve and utilize grandiosity in their living. Certainly family history and genetic background are involved in the choice of defensive style. In the therapeutic process it is necessary to deal with the behavior, no matter what its source, once we have dealt with the biological or biochemical matters that may be involved.

Treatment

Grandiosity as a Narcissistic Feature

The major task for the analyst dealing with narcissistic disorders is to convey insight into the patient's egocentric focus, which is bolstered by the grandiose and privileged sense of need and entitlement. The process is invariably hampered by transference and countertransference phenomena, which result from unrealistic expectations of therapy and of the analyst, and from resentment and hostility when these demands are denied, and also by the analyst's reactions to all of this. As with all neurotic difficulties, the therapeutic work is in the identification, clarification, and, whenever possible, in the transferential amplification of the patient's dynamics. Inevitably, too, there must be a prolonged period of working through of new insights with the goal of changing behavior.

Premature exploration of the patient's early experiences will only complicate the therapy, for it will consist largely of a profusion of complaints about parental failures to love or nurture the patient adequately, which will justify present-day demands for special consideration. While much of the patient's recall of early life events may be accurate, much is also exaggerated. Efforts to explain or explore the reality of these recollections too early on in the treatment will lead the patient to assume that the analyst is insufficiently allied to the patient's grievances. A primary requirement at the outset of therapy is to develop a feeling of alliance and sensitivity to the patient's expressed complaints even while we are aware of their excessiveness. Knowledge and understanding of the narcissist's neurotic structure should enable therapists to be patient in their desires to interpret prematurely the significance of the patient's reports, for this would alienate the patient and terminate the treatment. This is especially relevant in dealing with narcissistic disorders, since the grandiosity that the patient brings to therapy leads to expectations of privileged and supportive responses.

Failures in interpersonal relationships are often the basis for bringing patients into therapy. Blame, for narcissists, always lies with others who, out of envy, fail to acknowledge their specialness. Their flawed capacity to get recognition in their job or relations with others leaves them unhappy and uncertain in spite of their grandiose assumptions.

The grandiose elements in narcissists' behavior are often obvious to the analyst, though the patients view them as justified and reasonable. Therefore many of the early interactions in the therapeutic sessions may be involved with exploring reactions of the patients with the aim of clarifying how their behavior looks to other persons. Since the narcissists have great difficulty in putting themselves in the other person's place (which we call lack of empathy), we must accept the difficult task of focusing repeatedly on this issue in order to convey some insight about it. In doing this we take into account their sensitivity to criticism and move cautiously to convey this understanding.

Grandiosity and Paranoid Trends

The exaggerated self-referential tendencies of narcissists readily translate into paranoid distortion when their expectations are thwarted. In the absence of a clear instance of its occurrence, as during a therapeutic session, one must be very careful in exposing this dynamic lest the analyst be viewed as a derogating conspirator in the guise of a helper. This is expectable given the contradiction between patients' grandiosity and their inordinate need for approbation from others. The analyst is idealized as a true believer in the patients' virtue; any deviation of this role is viewed as disloyalty. This dynamic is reminiscent of the earliest mother–child relationship, which is a model for narcissists' expectations as adults.

This brings us to the etiological dilemma of the relationship of narcissism to what has been described as the primary narcissism of infants who, in their omnipotent splendor are, in fact, the center of the world for their parents. This concept of primary narcissism has been challenged by many who do not view child development in libido therapy terms and do not consider infants as living in a world in which they are the central powerful and omnipotent figure. Rather, they see infants as being helpless and totally dependent upon the good will and the tolerance of adults. In this context, the notion of primary narcissism is perceived not only as fallacious but also as misleading in terms of understanding the development of narcissism. It is important to recognize that the concept of primary narcissism is contrary to the obvious extreme dependency of infants since grandiosity carries the notion of total independence. Narcissists, while grandiose, are paradoxically extremely dependent upon the approval of others for validation of their specialness.

In the treatment process, the assumption of a notion of primary narcissism diverts one from insight into that defensive development of patients' ego-focused behavior. The actual source is their overpowering need, grown out of early failures, to receive recognition for skills and emotional support. An understanding of this will enable patients to see the defensive dynamics of their behavior, rather than support their complaints against the maternal figures who did not continue to make them the center of attention as in infancy.

It is not surprising that these "superior," grandiose individuals have great difficulty in enjoying their lives and activities. They need constant reassurance from others with whom they fail to empathize or whose needs they fail to recognize. Relationships are short-lived except with those more needy than themselves, for whom they have little regard and often contempt. Thus, the approval of those with whom they are integrated is deprecated. This incapacity for true enjoyment allows analysis to move actively to an exploration of the interpersonal difficulties of narcissists.

Relations are shallow and superficial and generally exploit the other party, who will then, after a while, terminate the relationship. Narcissists cannot understand what is happening, for they see themselves as being so desirable that everyone should be flattered and overjoyed to have them as friends. Narcissists feel they have a right to control and exploit intimacy. With their pseudo-modest tactics and charm, they completely distort situations. Paradoxically, narcissists see the refusal of their excessive demands as selfish and charge others with lack of consideration. Narcissistic individuals will then interpret the rupture as due to their partner's neurosis. Only in the most detailed and careful exposition of the nature of such relationships can one hope to help patients to accept the provocative role of their grandiose behavior in the crisis that developed. As such patients are required to become more and more aware of their egocentric demands and injustices to others, they will become more and more hostile to the analyst.

Subtle and, at times, obvious derogation of the analyst will occur, as well as threats to discontinue the therapy. Self-destructive activities may increase to prove that the treatment is damaging. These activities should not provoke countermeasures, which would only serve to validate their complaints. The provocations can be relentless and be directed as personal attacks. Skillful analysts recognize and divert these attacks by interpreting them as transferential and by helping patients see that these are aspects of their narcissistic behavior.

Transference

The focus of therapy in treating narcissists, as I have suggested, must be on exposing the grandiosity that is the main support of their neurotic structure. Their grandiosity is supported by the affirmation and validation of others, who are required to acknowledge their privileged entitlements. This exalted view cannot be sustained merely by inner feelings or justifications and, in fact, is extremely fragile, for it is not based on real achievements. Therefore the patients are dependent on interpersonal relationships to maintain their grandiose self-image. What has brought the patients into treatment has been a failure in some area of their functioning and difficulty in achieving desired goals. In spite of their charm, narcissists may be lonely and isolated and overwhelmed with anger, resentment, or envy.

An admission of need or request for help is painful and humiliating for narcissists since they need to appear independent and invincible. Therefore, narcissists enter therapy appearing aloof and superior, yet also relating to the analyst as a child in need of a supporting parent. In the transference both sides of this dilemma are played out in the patients' reaction to the therapist, depending on the issues involved at the time. The therapist may, at times, accept these contradictory roles, and when the relationship with the patients is strong enough to sustain an attack on their grandiosity, the transference distortions must be presented to them. In most cases this will be readily accepted; however, patients will insist that they need the support and cannot abandon their demands. The task of the analyst will be to enable the patients to develop sufficient self-esteem through a recognition of true but undeveloped capabilities to enable them to function without this childish requirement. Then we may expect some reduction of grandiosity and the growth of true self-esteem.

In the treatment of the narcissistic personality the resolution of the infantile transference takes on great significance, for the neurotic and defensive structures are closely related to the infantile demands that characterize the earliest periods of development. For other personality configurations like the obsessive personality, transference issues are different, for the patients deal with their analysts more in paternal than in maternal terms. Here, grandiosity is based more on the adult intellectual requirements for perfectionistic performances and the ability to be independent and in control, and not on a constant need for affirmation of love and acceptance from others. The narcissist demands love while the obsessional patient demands respect. This distinction between the narcissistic personality disorder and the obsessive-compulsive disorder is highlighted in the following description of two patients.

Patient A: Narcissism

The patient is a forty-year-old mathematician who came for therapy because of problems in his second marriage. He was arrogant, reckless, and markedly egocentric and felt exempt from conventional requirements of dress and behavior. He considered traffic or parking limitations as personal inconveniences that he need not obey. He refused to pay tolls on unsupervised roads and claimed privileges beyond his legitimate rights. In pursuit of approbation, and to enhance his image as an exceptional husband, he gave his wife extravagant gifts and excessive attention when it suited his plans. His grandiosity resulted in stock manipulations that produced serious financial losses.

His grandiose view of his intellect required that he avoid situations where he might be challenged. He avoided dealing with peers and maintained his illusions in secret fantasies, which he shared only with his wife, who quietly suffered his pretentious attitudes in order to avoid arguments. No obsessive or compulsive rituals were present in his living. Though depressive reactions occurred periodically when his grandiosity was pierced, patient A recovered quickly with a fresh grandiose scheme and failed to acknowledge his prior losses. He could not learn from experience, and by the time he came for marital counseling his financial and marital affairs were in total disorder.

In treatment, a persistent emphasis on the deficiency and arrogance of others was difficult to dislodge. Only in the clearest and most immediate crises could he agree that *his* arrogance, grandiosity, and irresponsibility were the basis for the disaster. Joint sessions were mutual attack sessions that were extremely difficult to manage since his wife was as severe a narcissist as he. A description of her behavior and dynamics would be similar to her husband's, except in minor details. This was her third marriage; each one was characterized by extravagant demands for acknowledgment and acceptance of her requirements. Treatment ended when she took steps to separate and began divorce proceedings.

Patient B: Obsessionalism

Patient B contrasts sharply with Patient A. His behavior was marked by multiple compulsive rituals. He constantly checked everywhere to make sure that he had not dropped anything, and he had chronic concerns about disease, germs, and other noxious agents. He is a thirty-five-year-old insurance agent who has been very successful professionally. His intense workaholic and perfectionistic drives have supported a grandiose assessment of his talents and skills, which stands in contrast to his underlying doubts. These are covered over and unrecognized in his secret evaluation of himself. While his compulsions are not entirely incapacitating, his marital situation has deteriorated because of his distressing social behavior, which embarrasses his wife and children. Acknowledging the excesses in his behavior has not diminished his grandiose orientation and demands for approbation and reinforcement of his more positive behavior. He has great difficulty accepting his deficiencies and blames all his problems on his wife, who also has emotional problems. Therapy is more productive than that with patient A since patient B will examine his own role in the difficulties in his living, for he cannot avoid recognizing the excesses in his compulsive rituals. His grandiose self-perceptions are slowly giving way to a recognition of his being human and fallible. Unlike the narcissistic patient A, he does not view such scrutiny as an attack or criticism.

While grandiosity approaches delusional qualities for both patient A and patient B, their responses to therapy are different. Each patient clings to his expanded view with a tenacity proportionate to the underlying low esteem. It becomes clearer, as therapy proceeds, that in the narcissist, grandiosity is a primary, essential defense. In the obsessive-compulsive patient, grandiosity is secondary to the perfectionistic, overly intellectualized need to know everything and feel superior to everyone else. As patient B's obsessive-compulsive patterns decrease with his recognition that he does not need to be in control of all his living, his grandiosity slowly decreases or disappears. As his concerns about losing control diminish, his needs for a grandiose view of himself decrease.

Countertransference

The narcissists' needs to be seen as unique and privileged persons with entitlements tend to raise many countertransference problems in the therapy. The appeal for special privilege cannot be peremptorily denied until the patients can recognize and identify their requirements as grandiose. Unreasonable requests are viewed as reasonable and justified in light of the traumas of early experience. Therefore narcissists will react to any rejection of their demands with feelings of being wronged, and they will try to provoke the analyst's guilt and compliance. The narcissist's capacity to control a situation by accusation and producing guilty feelings in others has been successful enough to reinforce this tactic. The analyst must be tuned to this issue in order not to fall prey to the maneuver.

This type of patient has an uncommon ability to deal with others in a manner both flattering and contemptuous whenever demands are fulfilled or denied. The analyst must be aware of this tendency and not deal with either of these responses as if they represent valid feelings. The analyst must be prepared to deal with flattery, whether in the form of words or gifts, with an understanding that it represents a transferential view of the therapist as a maternal figure who can fulfill the patients' demands. The analyst must view the situation with a clear distinction between the patients' realistic demands and their grandiose expectations and help them to differentiate the two. In this way, the analyst will avoid being the denying mother and represent instead the concerned parent who helps the maturing child distinguish between these kinds of demands. This is difficult to accomplish, and one cannot expect that one or two such confrontations will result in a revised attitude. It will need to be done over and over again, and each time analysts will need to display their objectivity and avoid any resemblance to the idealized perfect parent or the exaggerated denying parent. An accumulation of such occasions will ultimately support therapists' efforts to demonstrate the splitting tactics of narcissists. This tactic is also demonstrated in the patients' tendency to praise and exaggerate therapists' skill and understanding while, at the same time, condemning and accusing them of incompetence and prejudice. This capacity for splitting characterizes this behavior.

Narcissists have great difficulty in expressing any tender feelings since this is seen as weak and dangerous. They are therefore more often apt to be critical and condescending. True feelings are either denied or distorted. In the therapeutic process it is crucial that patients be encouraged to discover and acknowledge feelings of warmth and affection for the therapist as well as for others in their life.

Similarities Between the Obsessive-compulsive Disorder and Narcissism

The presence of obsessional features in predominantly narcissistic personalities is very common. The compulsive nature of their demands and an insistence on perfectionistic performance (along with a distrust of the ability of others to perform adequately) define their interpersonal behavior. The narcissists' indecisiveness and demand for reassurance is a part of both personality types, though we see the great influence of rituals and obsessive ruminations more in the obsessive-compulsive disorder. The description of the borderline personality, which features a decreased capacity to manage one's affairs and an impulsiveness that can result in self-destructive activity, shares diagnostic elements of these two diagnostic types.

A close examination of the DSM, which attempts to define these activities in separate diagnostic categories, suggests that it overlooks the similarities in the underlying dynamic features of these two psychopathological categories. Both narcissists and obsessionals are similarly characterized by:

1. An unusual degree of self-reference
2. Contradiction between a grandiose self and inordinate needs for admiration from others
3. Little empathy for others
4. Minimal capacity for enjoyment other than acknowledgment from others
5. Envy of others while deprecating those from whom they expect nothing
7. Relations with others that are often exploitative
8. A sense that they have a right to control and possess others, without feeling guilt

9. An ability to be charming and engaging in their constant effort to get admiration from others

Similarities in Therapeutic Approach to Narcissism and Obsessionalism

Given the dynamic similarities of narcissism and obsessionalism, it follows that the therapeutic approaches to both conditions are similar. One must, however, take into consideration individual expression of tactics for dealing with anxiety, insecurity, and fear of rejection. The therapy of both narcissism and obsessionalism requires the following.

1. Discovery and elucidation of the basis for feelings of insecurity, which require absolutes to guarantee one's existence before any action is attempted. This calls for the examination of each symptom and defensive tactic to show how it ties into an overriding need to control or to be superior. Rituals, phobias, and personality traits are explored in terms of their roles in giving the patient illusory feelings of absolute control.
2. Demonstration by repeated interpretation and encouragement to action that such guarantees are not needed, and instead, interfere with living. This involves motivating the person to attempt novel and unfamiliar patterns of behavior through active assistance in stimulating new adventures. This process may help patients attempt counterphobic activity and overcome conditioned avoidance reactions to unexplored areas of functioning.
3. Recognition that the foregoing is possible only when patients can accept some anxiety as part of living. They must acknowledge the universality of anxiety as a companion to all human endeavors. This means abandoning attempts at perfection and accepting limited goals, utilizing the most creative resources available. Patients must learn to accept their human limitations.

In this process the anxiety may be so severe that antianxiety drugs should be used to enable patients to attempt changes in their lives. The analyst must maintain the anxiety at a level that will facilitate learning rather than impede it. The therapeutic focus must be on feelings rather than cognitive exchanges, which is facilitated by a confronting, here-and-now approach to the role of defenses. Before patients will relinquish their extensive defense system they must allow themselves to experience and accept failure, some loss of pride and prestige, and possible humiliation.

Further Treatment Issues

As just noted, the major treatment considerations in the psychoanalytic therapy of narcissism are very similar to the essential factors involved in the treatment of the obsessional patient (Salzman 1980). These are as follows.

1. Focus on the patients' insistent need to deny dependency and emphasize their ability to manage.
2. Emphasize the resistances, without mentioning their dynamic significance.
3. Emphasize the countertransference because of the patient's tendency to deflate and degrade the therapist. I emphasize the issue of feelings of powerlessness and defensive needs to control.
4. Focus on the patient's ability to switch from admiration to condemnation of the analyst. I often see underlying feelings of threat and danger in expressions of positive feelings.

The capacity of obsessional patients to develop relationships is very limited by their needs and distrust. What Object-Relations theories emphasize in terms of narcissism I see mainly as evidence of the obsessional patient's need to control. Object Relations and Interpersonal-Relations theory seem surprisingly similar in their treatment techniques.

Narcissistic patients come to therapy because of failures in their performances, especially in the area of interpersonal relations. Their inability to enter into loving relations with commitment and equality leads to destroyed relations with the same and the opposite sex. Unless there are continual assurances that come from recent relations, narcissists are lonely and dissatisfied. Intimacy is almost unknown to narcissistic people, since their concern is centered around the issue of their significance and approbation. Although they may achieve this for a while, sooner rather than later, their relationships are disrupted by their demands, which are egocentric and viewed by others as exploitative.

This is especially noticeable in relations with the opposite sex. At the outset, narcissists will put on a grand campaign to captivate and seduce their partner. Charm, attentiveness, and other forms of attraction to the partner may be displayed. However, once the goal is achieved, a sharp change in behavior will occur that reflects their narcissistic demands. At first this may be confusing to the partner, but a succession of such events will dramatize the egocentricities of the narcissists, and the relationship will fall apart, but not before many attempts on the part of the narcissists to revitalize their position by renewed efforts.

The main complaint of narcissists who come for treatment will be their distress over failing to develop a sustained intimacy. Narcissistic patients will appear to be asking for help, but one must be clear that this appeal is superficial and will be overshadowed in the therapeutic process by their grandiosity and arrogance in deriding the therapist and the therapeutic process.

At the outset the therapist must take, not a moralistic attitude, but rather one of concern and empathy with the continuing interpersonal problems of the patient. One must be sympathetic and an objective observer before *one is able to highlight patients' roles in their failures.* The patients will initially represent all their difficulties as instances of the other person's selfishness, and represent themselves as the victims.

In short, the analysis of narcissism and obsessionalism requires that the analyst be sensitive, but confronting; patient, though active; in control while being attacked. And the analyst must utilize countertransference reactions to clarify the patient's behavior, rather than to defend and counterattack.

Reference

Salzman, L. 1980. T*reatment of the Obsessional Personality.* New York: Jason Aronson.

13

The Relation of Monologue And Dialogue to Narcissistic States and Its Implications for Psychoanalytic Therapy

Arthur H. Feiner

> Mirror, mirror on the wall
> Who is the fairest of them all?
> (Maybe it's you, oh beautiful queen, but
> Madam why do you think you need to ask?)

I

This essay is an attempt to examine the meaning of dialogue and monologue in psychoanalytic therapy. My belief is that the terms have become cliches. "Dialogue" seems to refer most often to sequential speech utterances between two people, and "monologue" commonly refers to speech engaged in by one person. I believe a discussion and clarification would be helpful to psychoanalysts.

Drawing on the concepts of M. Bakhtin (1981), philosopher and semiotician, in this paper I present two uses of the term *dialogue.* First it is viewed as part of a historical, developmental process underlying the origins of all communication and personality development. In the second and more conventional sense of the term, *dialogue* refers to the quality of orientation of conversation by one person in relation to another. This suggests openness, a readiness for accessibility, and a potential for intimacy. The reason I emphasize the two ways the notion of dialogue is used is to help clarify those typical situations in which a monologic mode takes place in the disguise of conventionally attributed dialogue.

The primary meaning of dialogue (derived from the writings of Mikhail Bakhtin and his circle) implies a fundamental interpersonal basis for the formation of the self. The secondary use of the term is in sharp contrast to monologue, which is cast as a later mode, and defense against contact and penetrability, a guardian of the necessity for transcendence. This is particularly true for the narcissistic states. In sum, dialogue as process refers to the formation of personality and the organization of thinking; dialogue as stage refers to a way of relatedness. This paper focuses on the latter.

I believe people establish and continue relationships in more or less monologic or dialogic modes and express themselves accordingly. They do this especially in psychoanalytic treatment, more often than not, reflecting a monologic style. Although this is not so for every moment of every analytic session, and though it may seem self-evident, I believe the thrust of any psychoanalytic therapy must be dialogic to be transformative. In this sense the dialogic mode suggests contact and intimacy.

Let us start with an example. A patient, a thirty-five-year-old married psychologist starts a session quite assertively with the following:

"You owe me five minutes; we started late last time." (I say that he is correct, and we arrange for him to arrive five minutes earlier at the next session. After we complete the arrangements)

I SAY *(wryly):* "What do you think you owe me?" (And I wonder why this pops into my head. Do I want him to say, "my life?")

HE RESPONDS: "I owe you for this month's sessions that we have had thus far."

There is some talk about the obviousness of his response and that I have never asked about it before and most probably would not. Could there be something else I might have in mind? (I am searching. I am really in the dark about my impulse. And I trust the dialogic mode will clarify it for me.)

HE SAYS: "Well I do wish I could feel more thoughtful about changing. And I thank you for your patience with me."

I SAY *(gently):* "Look I ask what you owe me and you respond with what you'd like to feel, and what you desire. Both are valid thoughts, but neither answers the question about what you think you owe me."

HE SAYS: "Well I didn't understand the question. I don't know what you mean."

I SAY: "Then wouldn't that have been an appropriate response? After all that's what's in your mind. You could say, I owe you nothing, or whatever do you mean. Wouldn't that have been appropriate?"

(This patient functions with two thematic aspects to his ideology: All are charlatans! You must rely on yourself [which came from his father]; and "Gotcha!", meaning "I've caught you in an error," which derives from his mother. Both of these necessitate his knowing something before he inquires, explores, checks, experiments.)

HE SAYS:"I just got anxious and I killed the idea that I did not know what you were getting at." (I ask what he thinks the anxiety is about. He doesn't know.)

I SAY: "Do you think that the idea of not understanding or not knowing is being different, different from what you assume is expected?" (I want to get to that ideological theme.)

HE SAYS: "Well if you don't know you don't know and that's who you are."

I ASK: "Well is who you are so distressing that you can't be who you are; let me know who you are? In this case not knowing what I have in mind is who you are."

HE SAYS: "I have a hard time with that, so I fill in what I think you want."

I SAY: "Well but that's not who you are—what *you* think, or what *you* feel. It's what you guess *I* think. It seems that it makes an interchange difficult."

HE SAYS: "I do it with colleagues, with my mother, my patients, my wife. I get blank. And then I fill in. It's why my supervisor says I may not have the stuff" (to be a therapist).

I SAY: "Maybe she's not seeing the stuff you have because you keep it out as though it were forbidden to bring it in. In this case the right stuff is who you are. And who you are in this context is a man who doesn't know what the other fellow is asking about."

HE SAYS: "I'm not allowed to not know for some reason. It isn't that I'm dumb or supposed to have the answers, but that I think if I don't know I may fall apart. I get anxious. Why did you phrase it the way you did? Why did you say, 'What do you owe me?' "

(The leap from the idea of anxiety to my motivation was noted by me silently; he can't tolerate not knowing.)

I SAY: "Well I don't know, but let's look together. What's the key word? What? Do? You? Owe? Me? What do you think?"

HE SAYS: "I think it must be 'owe.' It's the only thing that's new or different from the usual."

I SAY: "Well maybe I wanted to get something going together. You and me don't do that. But the word *owe* has a relationship embedded in it, don't you think?"

HE SAYS: "You mean I run from that?"

I SAY: "Well, I really didn't have the idea in mind when I asked the question. But I think you do run from that, and we have to find out why it's necessary to be not present."

HE SAYS: "Jesus, I do it everywhere."

The patient went on to associations about parental lies and deceptions, which he had described many times in the past, particularly in relation to not being permitted to not know, and that all people are charlatans, so one has to be cautious. The relationship between the two themes was not made.

My purpose here is to illustrate the registering by me of monologue following some anxiety over an implicit demand for a connection and anxiety in response to not knowing. I cannot account for a conscious decision to ask my question the way I did. I do not rule out that I felt a countertransference expectation of gratitude (even warranted) that the patient picked up and that was not being met. The fact is I saw the moment as a reenactment of the patient's symptomatology. My immediate goal—consciously—was to encourage some form of dialogue, some genuine interaction, that would be useful. He is forbidden to "not know." Why this is problematic for him and what the patient experiences by my engaging him this way remains to be explored, but it is a fundamental part of analysis.

To do this, I believe, the dynamic lawfulness of the two modes of communication and relatedness needs to be grasped. This essay is an attempt to explore this issue and relate these modes to narcissistic ways of living. If the mirror in the title epigraph were Freud's "mirror," that is, any analyst-in-action, and if the queen were that analyst's patient, it might have behaved the way I have indicated. The content of a reflected appraisal (Sullivan 1940) is not at issue here, but its compulsory quality is. One could ask, at some point, why the epigraphic queen needs to be reassured about her beauty, which is a crucial element in her structure. I think this would be arrived at somewhat later in the scenario. At the moment of interaction I would be interested in the queen's ideology, simply stated, with a minimum of defensiveness on her part.

Two characteristics, among others, are essential to being human. These are self-consciousness and speech. Speech (in this paper) refers to the spoken word or gesture, as signifier. This is necessary for psychoanalysis since the act of communicating, that is, the act of symbolizing, brings the sense of self, the sense of "I" with all its assumptions, into reality. In psychoanalysis this is a shared social reality. It makes the "I" and its experiences real in a world with others who are real or imagined. It is necessary for human existence. For change to take place in psychoanalysis, therefore, there has to be an exchange of speech (or its substitute). This would be an exchange between two who consider that what each other has to say is valuable and translatable, and each is willing to be influenced by the mutual experience.

It so happens that we may be aware of, or at least sense, the unavoidable experiential changes actually caused by our speech with each other. Sullivan (1950) wrote, for example, that "All you have to do is say, 'And why did you do that?' and [a person] rattles like a machine gun . . . [to demonstrate] how . . . easily he deceives himself into feeling that he knows what he is doing" (p. 206). Some find it extremely difficult to speak spontaneously simply because they see the process as speaking about thoughts instead of communicating thoughts (or feelings) directly, or of being "in" the feeling. In their intimidation, their felt experience of a lack of safety, it is as though they assume a priori they will be misunderstood or perhaps hurt in some way if they are understood, as though the ultimate goal in life is to feel comfortable or to live risk free. Furthermore, its articulation and imagery transform an idea or a thought about a perception, or a feeling that is experienced internally, because of the verbal symbolization.

Some find it much too painful to observe these transformations that come about via communicating, and so the changes, which are necessary and inevitable for there to be any apparent contact with others, any intimacy or union (Feiner 1991b), are simply intolerable. Some find the exposure equally distressing because one is then on the spot or will come to be known. Despite all the propaganda and political editorializing about uniqueness and individuality, the point is that to be different, to be separate and differentiated, may be a basic threat. To avoid these dangers some attempt to communicate using monologue, that is, to maintain a connection. And their attempts at union seem to be in contradiction. (In this case the monologism is the significance of the communication.)

Resistance to therapy or change is essentially a function of monologistic speech since this mode supports one's investment in the survival value of the status quo. It offers the poor, temporary comfort of transcendence and imperviousness. By transcendence I mean the assumed necessity to overcome, surpass, or not be subjected to those ordinary forces to which all are subject. It is a felt necessity for superlatives or specialness, without which one's worth is in danger or one is vulnerable to eventual disorganization. In its extreme it is manifested in a need to be special and not have to be subject to the laws of nature or the social surround. In interpersonal relationships I see it as a necessity to avoid the influence of and the demands of mutuality, the inherent requirements of union (Feiner 1991b). In a word, the analyst is of no, or minimal, value with regard to change.

If it is necessary for the status quo to remain the status quo, nothing can take place since one cannot afford genuine dialogue or therapeutic exchange. In therapy, therefore, an essential issue is to facilitate a dialogic mode or at least provide the conditions for a dialogue to come about and exist. The importance of this is that dialogue not only offers the possibility of the idea of plausibility, and this notion's influencing one's perspective, and new alternatives or self-reflective ideas involving accountability and responsibility, but, ultimately, also presents the possibility of choice. With the act of choosing made possible in this way, prior mystifications, reifications, and any or all other inauthentic necessities can be abated (Buber 1955; Feiner 1970).

The unraveling, deciphering, and translating the messages revealed in the patient's utterances permit the analyst to help the shift of a monologic expression to a dialogic one (Feiner 1988). I am not referring to the resolution of varied defenses that ward off painful ideas or feelings, like negation, avoidance, evasion, or even conscious resistance, such as reluctance. *Monologue,* as I use the term, is stylistic, and while encompassing these to be sure, it also favors the absence of interpenetration in ordinary exchanges. Thus at any moment the therapist's task is to have the mutual messages pass through each other. This "passing through" is critical since a monologic stance implies that ideas simply bounce off a person, which is the very opposite of passing through. Passing through transforms a solipsistic mode and its impenetrability and consequent isolation to one of genuine interchange. But when it does not happen, the analyst has the task of finding out why it does not happen and what would be useful to make it so for both participants.

In psychoanalytic training institutes it is commonplace that supervisors of candidates-in-training tend to complain that some students repeat over and over again what the students had worked on with their first supervisors. In training committees it is often noted that advanced students are retaught inefficiently and endlessly the same lessons struggled with years before. One explanation might be that some students learn only to get past the supervisor. This represents a kind of impenetrability that surely inhibits the candidate's growth. It is like a fourth grader motivated to learn long division only to pass a test and needing to learn it again in the sixth, seventh, and eighth grades so as to curry favor, warding off disapproval. As such it is a pseudolearning, similar to the imperviousness of a patient who complains that despite her "experiences" nothing sticks inside, with the consequent feeling of emptiness. Nothing sticks because, to learn, one must admit not knowing and take pleasure in the learning process. But this pleasure must be an expression of passion for the process primarily (Feiner 1991a).

We know that any patient's interaction with the analyst reveals the troubled, repetitive, contradictory nature of the patient's life, often lived with an assumption of minimal personal responsibility and with little or no hopefulness for change. This is life lived without sensitivity to the contexts in which one finds oneself—internal as well as external. It is a life denying, avoiding, or in some way defending against influence, a life of merry-go-round monologue. In essence, time is stopped. In some, since the worst is thought of oneself, often experienced and expressed as an emptiness—an antiself—the worst is thought of others. Relationships are reduced, better, minimized, to their use value. The psychoanalyst is only a "doctor," the patient is only a "case." Analytic orderliness or routine is advised, the patient believes simplistically, because the doctor needs money. In fact any person, except as object for exploitation or avoidance, is feared and/or ignored. All are charlatans, and one had best avoid showing how one is ignorant or wrong, all the imperfections that open one to someone else's saying, "Gotcha!"

Life remains an aggregate of discrete events, and instead of enriching interchange, one experiences chatter. No matter how many others are involved with one—family, friends, or events—concerts, operas, theatre, films, meetings, books read, games played, or travels—nothing accumulates inside. Nothing sticks. One feels eternally, hopelessly empty. There is no safety in contact.

To counteract this profound, grim view of oneself, when it is ultimately realized in consciousness, one comes to therapy to be "relieved," "gratified," "repaired," "to be filled up," to be provided with rules, methods, "tricks," steps. One believes naively that in the common garden variety of ordinary exchanges with the therapist one will change, and similarly, of course, therapists hope their patients will "get something out of it," i.e., "the analytic exchange will provide understanding," or the patient will "get in touch with his real feelings," or the patient will "get to know who she is." Psychoanalysts also use other similar phrases, all of which are the counterpart of patients' monologic expectations. If patients vocalize (or express themselves nonverbally) in monologue, the goal of which is to make their monologic way of life more satisfying, only gradually do they permit themselves to be influenced by the inquiries of the therapist, whose assumptions are entirely different.

In response to this therapists attempt to speak dialogically, and if frustrated, spend their time trying to comprehend why so that they can. This attempt to achieve what the analyst originally set out to do is the heart of the therapy. Therefore, in psychoanalytic therapy we have two people with entirely different assumptions and goals, engaging in speech or its substitutes and calling it by different names. Their only shared given is an assumed benignity (although even this, in some cases, may be doubtful). The quality of the presence of the patient and the therapist in response to that is the prime issue.

It cannot be genuine dialogue when a patient responds angrily to five seconds of silence with the idea that she has been ignored, derived as her interpretation or translation is, from an assumption of anticipated dismissal, nonrelevance, trashing, or abandonment. I discuss this patient in detail later in this essay. In the context of an analytic setting, where, after years of analytic interaction, the patient knows, or at least is familiar with the possibility that the analyst will take a moment to formulate a serious inquiry—an inquiry whose purpose is the expansion of the patient's consciousness—it cannot be. If it has been anticipated or experienced that the analyst will possibly ask why do you think you are telling me this today, or what does this mean to you, or how do you think I am to hear this, or how do you feel telling me this, the actual preliminary silence could be experienced—in the present—as characteristic routine, even useful. But the patient's inability to discriminate her experience of the analyst's assumed intentionality from the actual five-second, silent behavior provides the ground for the immediate flare of accumulated past hurts. In essence at that moment it becomes a real repetition for the patient of prior, infinite, quotidian, mundane experiences in her history that inhibits the dialogic movement. The differentiatedness of the analyst is simply not entertained, and consequently no dialogic choreography is possible, let alone imminent. There is only a bare stage, with no dancers, no audience, and it will remain so unless the analyst accomplishes the necessary shift. I think the transferential issue is self-evident.

Here is an another example:

> A patient reports that he bickered with his wife over the intended meaning of a comment he had made during a long-distance telephone conversation with a friend whom the wife was visiting. "My wife had just left so I said, 'Oh, I missed her.' " The friend, who had been di-

vorced recently, heard the comment as a statement of tender feeling—about the patient longing for his wife. The patient stated, "True, I did miss her, but I didn't mean that then. On the phone I just meant I missed contacting her before she went out." We fought over that. She asked, "Why did I need to correct her friend's impression?"

To me, the patient is reporting monologue. I could ask what he thinks makes it necessary to invest all that energy in the correction. If he engages this idea, something new might happen. Second, I might assume the patient is denying tender feelings, but it seems evident he does not do that. He insists he knows how he felt, and the friend, and the wife, who enjoyed the idea that her husband missed her, were simply wrong about the meaning of his remark. What is the significance of their being wrong?

I tell him he is literally correct and I ask him about his difficulty in entertaining plausibility. Does he object to that? Why does he think that is a problem? I raise some questions about his history. Was he misunderstood? Did someone, in the past, tell him how to feel or how to think? Did he have to insist on the reality, the literalness of his feelings? And if so, why did he think he had to do that? Were the words of someone important painfully untrustworthy? Unfortunately the patient refuses to consider any of these questions. He adds he simply wants to know that he is listened to, heard correctly, and that he is taken seriously. He says emphatically that he only has this trouble with his wife. I say he may be having it with me. I say he might ask what that means to him? He says he wants to be certain he has been heard, that's all! He softens a bit, and we ultimately discover there was a lot of miscommunication with his father, mother, brother, and sister. I say that if it were true that he was not heard in the past he must have felt absent and that he had no impact. Or others were occupying his mind. Now, currently, in an odd way, he seems to keep on repeating the effect of his assumed absence by insisting on the intended literal meaning of his words. He is intrigued by this idea. I continue. What stops him from pushing the experience to another level, one where he and his wife can be enriched in their intimacy by his knowing, as in this example, that she knows that he knows she knows how he feels? How about his being known by his words or by inferred feelings? Won't that be acknowledgment?

These are entirely new ideas for him. In this conversation he uses the word *I* in its full implications as a subject for the first time.

Here is another example:

A patient starts off a session pleasantly and says seriously, "I appreciate you and your help," and in the very next sentence says in a depressed, dejected tone, "Next week I'll probably want to commit suicide." I can tell from the tone of voice, the head held down, the hands held open, suggesting supplication, that this is not meant as irony. There is no humor here. She wants to lean on me.

I ask myself why the sudden dramatic shift from one sentence to the next, from affirmation to dysphoria. Is there something somewhere in the admission of helpfulness or tenderness that lowers her esteem? Is admitting getting analytic help from me a source of difficulty? Is it being seen or found? If there is ambivalence in her relatedness, about what is she ambivalent? Will I turn on her, hold her in contempt, abandon her? Am I to be her new savior? I think by including me she is made to feel too vulnerable, too open to potential victimization. I can hurt or abandon her unpredictably. She must move deeper, therefore, into a monologic mode that restores the power to exclude.

Fulfillment in dialogue is a contact characterized by inclusion, by penetrability. That puts me in a position to ask more about her or to fail her. By her exclusion of me I am rendered helpless. She can tolerate me one way only, by her being in abject dependence. I now must wonder about being included. So she ends up exactly in the place she was when she started in treatment—repeating the painful symptom that brought her, her lonesomeness. That is the tedious but poignant way of life this woman lives.

So far I have discussed the need for dialogue in psychoanalysis and its relation to monologue, its antithesis. I wish now to illustrate some aspects of narcissistic consciousness about which I will make some comments. Here is a clinical vignette to introduce the discussion.

A thirty-five-year-old male patient, an investment banker, with intellectual and athletic gifts, starts a session with the following:

I had a dream about Shirley and Diane. Shirley was around with all this delicious food. Diane was also there but in her usual nondescript way. Then I was at a resort skiing, and my buddy Frank was also there. He's a real charmer and Diane apparently was seeing him. That is, she sneaked away to have a date with him.

The patient goes on:

I was sleeping with Shirley that night. You know she's a real nurturing person. Quite upbeat, lots of friends and funny. She wants me to go to Aspen with her. I do on one hand but I don't. Lovemaking is very easy with her and I care for her a great deal. But then I step away and I say

> she just doesn't have those physical characteristics of Diane. Those big tits, and nice, small butt and all that. I rely on those physical characteristics. I never realized how important it was to me before, and I can't get away from thinking of all the other guys, all those other good-looking guys who are now doing it to Diane. It makes me feel that they are better than I am. I can't be alone without thinking about Diane and those tits—what she has, and the time when I had it. Or, what she has, and now other guys have it. When I think of her as a person I see her as quite distant and aloof. She's not angry, but she always seemed to have a blank expression on her face. I did care for her in the beginning, but it turned into a lot of competition with other guys. Competition with them for me to get her. And of course I've lost her. The other night I was playing chess with Shirley and she was beating me and I had this very serious look on my face. She said don't be so serious, it's only fun. I told her that the look of this pained expression on my face is what I have when my esteem is down. What's the right thing for me to do? What am I supposed to learn? With Shirley it comes from the heart for me. She really cares for me. And it is quite easy with her, but she doesn't have what I want.

Note that for such a person sexual excitement often comes about as the result of the stirring of unconscious competitive envy and greed or a felt need to take possession of and own the parts of the other. This is usually the result of having been related to that way and developing an attitude that inhibits a whole view of the other person as well as oneself and limits perception to those parts, those aspects (real or imagined) that bear on the irrational necessities, and of course, the fears of the perceiver. One looks for something the other possesses rather than interact with the other person, making contact and experiencing feeling. This is determined by what one thinks one needs to get or of what one is afraid. All this, of course, has been learned in early family experience. These are usually interrelated, as this patient describes, but may not be.

He continues:

> I remember my father—he was always interested in the trophies I brought home. He would say he wished his mind was in my body, referring to my athletic ability. My mother was always a blank. I never had a warm conversation with her. It was very important to bring a trophy home to father. All show. When I wasn't doing very well in baseball during one season, he didn't even want to talk to me. Then, when I would see him with one of his buddies he seemed to be embarrassed.

> When we won the state championship he introduced me to all his friends. My son the champ. When I got my own apartment he told the landlord I was a ballplayer. Like I was a star or something. I remember going to a prom with a small-breasted girl. He said, "Why her? She isn't sexy, why would I want to go with her?"

Ultimately, with people like this, there is a tendency to devalue and spoil that which is envied or desired. At first there may be an llusion of beauty, of grandeur, even glory, particularly in that which is sought after. It can be food, wealth, or power, or rewards due to competitive attempts at prevailing. Sometimes it follows a definition of worth set in the past by a parental figure. Such enthusiasm for any desired object, sexual or otherwise, may be experienced mistakenly as a state of falling in love (Kernberg 1976). But authentic loving as a way of relating, as a kind of experience involving thoughts, feelings, and action, is wanting. Intimacy, therefore, becomes a never achievable end-product, not an interacting style.

The term *narcissism* is used in three ways: (1) to communicate states of selfishness, omnipotence, arrogance, self-centeredness, or some defensively inordinate concern with one's own person; (2) to refer to early self-worth, value, integration or well-being; and (3) in a way referring to trauma, usually called a "blow" or an "insult," invariably serving the purpose of explaining sudden dramatic losses of esteem and implying why a person is rageful, depressed, or anxious.[1] All this, I believe, derives from or follows Freud's split of the term into its primary and secondary manifestations (Freud 1914). I think this was his attempt to give his idea of self-interest and its quantitative facets some scientific aura.

I think we have not improved very much on Freud's notions. Because we think of Freud's tying his concept to libido theory in that Freud sees narcissistic persons as those who invest themselves with all their libidinal energy, we forget that Freud actually did comment that owing to a refusal to enter into a loving relationship, Narcissus fell for his own image and died—which is what the myth is about (see Freud 1910:100, 1917:139).

Freud seems to have been very much aware that in its early stages the infant is a locus of realistic dependent necessities. The infant exists at the will of others and its well-being or integration as a viable creature—sensed or not—is entirely dependent on others' largess. Later, when a precipitate self is actually crystallized and is articulated, the human being's concerns about self may or may not be to the detriment of relations with communal members. For example, Freud (1910) wrote, that young boys, like Narcissus, may seek out in other males some equivalence of the reflections they have received from their mothers. And later, in 1933, he commented that narcissism is "only an extreme exaggeration of a normal state of affairs" (Freud 1933: 102–3). I do not see how we have added much to these simple, pedestrian facts. The therapeutic technique, about which vast changes have developed, is another matter (Kohut 1971).

The anticipated narcissistic achievement, like the original myth, is the image fulfilled, the image affirmed, or the image sustained. And in the context of a person's life the functional significance of this is what contributes to meaning. The psychoanalytic inquiry ascertains where the image or self-definition comes from, the purpose it originally served as well as its current function, and how it is maintained. Like all symptomology, behavior, or language, little is known without contextual meaning. There is no etched rule that behavior must mean one and only one thing to a person or the same to many. It is polysemous. Without our understanding the dynamic, contextual significance of so-called self-love, its potential pathology cannot be understood (Spiegel 1985).

Freud (1914) described in great detail that state he called primary narcissism. This refers to the beginning of development as an attachmentless existence. Freud asks, therefore, what makes it necessary at all for mental life to pass beyond the limits of primary narcissism and to attach libido to objects (p. 85)? Freud said, referring to Heinrich Heine's (1982) "Songs of Creation," that one must love so as not to fall ill and that when we do fall ill, in consequence of frustration, we are unable to love. Freud quotes Heine, who in his poetry, has God claim the reason He had the urge to create was His own illness. That is, He believed that "burned through my soul like a thrusting blade [was] a sickness as surely the basic ground/on which creative drive had depended,/creating, I could be healed and mended,/creating I could be well and sound" (Heine 1982).

Perhaps the so-called narcissistic injury is related to this. If one is offended this way, it may make the possibility of loving another doubtful. One is confronted then with terrifying isolation. Thus the potential for catastrophic illness may be enhanced.

I believe Freud's concept of primary narcissism to be biologically untenable in the sense that he seems to see it as a pathological state. It is possible that what he meant to convey was that attachmentlessness is pathological if it continues after its original appropriate context. I see this as Freud's intention when he wrote of the necessity for beginning "to love in order not to fall ill." Furthermore, whether attachmentlessness accurately describes the actual infant state is no longer moot (see Stern 1985).

One thing is certain. Regardless of orientation, most analysts do consider narcissism a dynamic part of a state of distancing and nonmutuality, whether in actuality or in the organization of one's self-definition, and view it as something to be repaired. In a word, it is seen as a problem. Its repair resides in its opposite. Carefully spelled out by psychoanalyst or poet, repair results from a way of relating openly and positively to others in the world around. It is the act of loving that prevents illness, according to Heine and Freud, and cures illness, according to Fromm (1947) and Kernberg (1976).

But what is an act of loving? Many acts are called love, and these acts and/or feeling states are used by various people to mask aspects of relatedness that are not necessarily acts of loving. The behavior may be concerned with self-enhancement, expansion, the avoidance of depression and/or anxiety, or rage. In fact, these acts may be entirely self-serving and monologic. I would include here the fantasy that one needs to feel, or possess, to be more nearly complete so that the other is often experienced as a missing, suppressed, or denied part of oneself—sometimes thought of as "masculine" or "feminine" in analytic discourse. One variation of this theme occurs when the incomplete-now-complete person is seen as exactly the same as the beloved. This overall, generalized, iconographic fantasy leads to a kind of idealization of the partner and to his or her alleged perfection or presence. Two can come to believe and feel that they are actually, or should be, one. This is one + one = one, with no interactive influence.

In another way, people do respect differences and recognize the frailties and imperfections of the other. If loving is genuine and authentic, these become irrelevant, so that their transcendence is included in a loving relationship. It is not so much that an act of love disregards the blemishes of the beloved but that love is viable despite the imperfections, and the differentiatedness is lauded and celebrated. In Sonnet 116 Shakespeare states: "Love is not love which alters when it alteration finds . . . [it] looks on tempest and is never shaken." Far from idealization, this suggests actual acts in an attempt to achieve a certain kind of intimate contact, and it is in stark contrast to the self-serving nature of a monologic way. In this kind of structure, within the mutuality, individuals are enhanced. This is one + one = three. Each retains individuality, and a new organization comes into being as a result of the interaction.

When a new thought does run through patients in analysis, when the tears flow, a deep need is being satisfied as though a deep wound is starting to heal. Then the patients come out of an isolated position to something else. And we know then that the patients may be enriched since they have become influenced by something that is really important to them, and they experience an alteration in consciousness, however small. This, I think, is what Freud may have intended when he commented that only love will cure the illness of the earlier state.

Buber (1957) addresses human existence as "a setting at a distance," and an "entering into relation." He makes the point that one can enter into an authentic relation only with a being who has been set at a distance. More precisely, this optimum distance and differentiatedness evidences an authentic independence of the other—and entering into a relation, a preferred, chosen contradiction. These two "movements," as Buber calls them, have been described by psychoanalysts using the terms *separation* and *connection* (Fromm 1947; Feiner 1983). From an Interpersonal point of view, neither can be split from the other, despite their inherent contradiction. But this is a contradiction that exists in communal unity. This contradictory unity is contrasted to those familiar contradictions that exist in adversarial antagonisms or disunities. For example, we see this kind of contradiction in the relationships of individuals to families, or to groups, as well as in one's relationship to another. In other words, a group could not exist without individual members, and yet individual members develop their individuality by being members of a group. The failure to deal with the tensions created by these inbuilt contradictions, for example, by following dichotomous principles like either/or, or all/none, leads to negativism, antagonistic disruption, and disjunction. Separateness in its most extreme form leads to a state of isolation, and in a similar way, connection, without the affirmation of a kind of difference and individuation, results in a state of utter conformity, idealization, merger, or fusion. Freedom and integrity, perceived only as an absence of restraint, lead to isolation and rebellious antagonism. On the other hand, aspirations of freedom experienced as an awareness and willingness to realize necessities within a communal unity can enhance one's existence.

Buber (1957) puts the mechanistic split this way: "the two movements can also contend with one another, each seeing in the other the obstacle to its own realization. And finally, in movements and forms of grace, unity can arise from the extreme tension of the contraction, as the overcoming of it which is granted only now and in this way" (p. 100). Monologic modes of relating imply the defensiveness of states of narcissism, which itself is a defensive outgrowth of the two "movements" gone awry, contending with each other.

In the next section I return to the concept of a developmental process in dialogue.

II

We come into consciousness speaking a language permeated with many, many voices (Bakhtin 1981). In this historical sense we speak a social, never a private, language, for we are derived from a variety of social dialects—parental, familial, class, caste, religious, racial, communal, and national. We mature in consciousness by taking on more and more voices, blending them with our own. We are influenced by them and they in turn are influenced by us. We accumulate them from total social experiences, considering them externally authoritative. They are more than an aggregate since each voice influences the expression of the form and content of the other. Through our interpersonal learning, we fix them internally and make them part of our structure, and consequently, define ourselves accordingly. This is, in essence, an ongoing interpersonal process. In this sense, our basic individuality can never be a private, purely autonomous, individuality (Sullivan 1950). In a word, the self-identifying, self-experiencing phrase, "I am a man who . . ." did not come from the thin air. There is an "I am a man who ..." interpersonally derived and interpersonally enacted.

Even though we are tempted to deafen ourselves to other voices so as to master what we may experience as the chaotic and the ununderstandable and to try to dominate the world around, there is a social centrifugal force that pushes us outward. We live in a world that invites action, influence, and relationships. At the same time a personal, centripetal force preserves us from memorial fluidity (Bakhtin 1981:271–72). In this way we realize a self that has some kind of coherence—a form of internal unity—with more or less reliable boundary lines. It is a patterned unity that does justice to openness, to variety, to creativity, to experiment, or as Fromm (1947) called it, generativity. Like any other living organism, we simply cannot develop in isolation. It is a biological platitude, but there must be exchanges of some sort—food or tissue—some kind of taking in of what is necessary for life for growth to take place and for survival, whether protozoan or human.

What we do develop that is special for human beings is an expanding "I," and it is this "I" that is referred to in concepts of individuality. This result of the given matter, and of its historical, dialectical, environmental exchange, is the newness, the new property that comes into being and makes human beings human. And this "I," an outgrowth of the previous dynamic states of existence, is what interacts with others in the present (Sullivan 1950). This "I" is what embodies all facets of "self-experiencing," what Bakhtin calls interior speech (Volosinov 1973; Emerson 1986; Morson 1986; Stewart 1986). In our human dimensions of adaptation we actually develop inconsistently or unevenly, depending on our particular life's experiences, but these inconsistencies, or unevennesses, are held together in a consistent, patterned integration. One might say that this integration is entirely personal, but even that, the way it is shaped and textured, that is, what is important to a person and what is not, is influenced by the outside world.

When we talk of autonomy we seem to be referring to that part of an interpersonal interaction of which, at the outset, the person is entirely responsible and about which the person is thoroughly voluntaristic. But what the person brings to the interaction comes from infinite interactions in places in his or her history, and that, I believe, is the reworking of the many voices with which he or she has come in contact since birth. This is the internalization of the interpersonal (Sullivan 1940). Although he writes about language and the voice of the novel, I believe this is what Bakhtin (1981) implies by his notion of a dialogical imagination. Now in this section I relate this to the issue of narcissism.

So as not to fall victim to aimlessness, facelessness, meaninglessness, and irrelevance, we try to find, to identify with, and live by, our fantasies, our sense of our own true selves. But in so doing we sometimes may move too far in one direction, trying to impose our own brand of organizing monologic unity of life around us.

Monologic thinking insists on a single consciousness. This is a consciousness that views everything in an alleged unity, a totalistic spirit or history. It is false because its idea of oneness and consistency is only apparent. The fact is that it actually abstracts its sense of unity, excluding various possibilities, appealing to varied superimposed assumptions. Only from a position within this closed off, amputated system can everything be seen as one. Instead of genuine unity there is an insistence on unanimity.

On the other hand, a dialogic mode encourages a larger expanding and more inclusive unity. This would be unity in diversity, and it occurs through a comprehension of and regard for opposites and contradictions, but not adversarial, in antagonism. In dialogue the unity of a relationship is evidenced by the fact that any view of the world is linked with a specific position. Any particular view of an individual personality exists in a unified community (Bakhtin 1984).

In a monologic view, truth and reality become abstract and impersonal. The patient's words are merely the carrier of ideas, assumptions that are reflective of the inner structure of the personality. Little room is available for expansion. In such a world a new idea cannot be acknowledged on its own terms. Too little safety exists for diversion. An idea will either be affirmed or repudiated. Only one principle is recognized in monologism—and in psychoanalytic theory; it is based on the patient's belief in one's own inevitable inadequacy, nonrelevance, unseemliness, and unsafety. Without a genuine interaction between the consciousnesses of the patient and of the analyst, dialogue is veritably impossible or, at best, didactic. Thus there cannot be influence or any genuine interpenetration of points of view. Either the patient or the analyst knows all the answers. Nothing is present to wonder about or to be discovered. Either the patients know and insist that they teach the analyst, or the analyst knows and in turn is supposed to teach the patients (see Emerson 1985). (In the therapies where this prevails it may be therapeutic and "corrective," but indeed it is not analytic.) No room is available for play (Ehrenberg 1990; Feiner 1990), nor does any pleasure reside in the excitement of error (Feiner 1991b). Buber (1955) remarks that when genuine dialogue exists—spoken or silent—each of the participants has the other in mind, and each is faced with the prospect of establishing a mutual relation. In monologue disguised as dialogue, two or more people speak with each other in sequential ways and imagine or fantasize that they have been in contact with each other, even to the point of "having escaped the torment of being thrown back on their own resources" (Buber 1955:19). But it is monologue.

The narcissistic way, like the monologic mode, is a suppression of, and/or an avoidance of the multiplicity of human influences. It is an attempt at transcending them or offsetting them with some single, unique principle or voice—one's own. Actually it is a poor attempt at an escape from the real biological, interpersonal quality of life at its best. In narcissistic states, therefore, attempts at a so-called individuality result in a false one, with an independence that is much more apparent than real.

Thus one of the key issues in the narcissistic personality structure is one's desire to remain impervious, that is, impervious to outside necessities—influences of any sort—whether they have to do with information in terms of facts or concepts; or the emotionality, desires, or needs of another; or even responsibility toward a mutually loving object. It really is, in the long run, an avoidance of the smell of mortality. The idea of necessities affects the way we perceive others, their behavior, their bearing, their physiognomic characteristics, their experience of their movements, their voices, their ways of speaking, and their silences (Schachtel 1959). Of course, one can also be impervious or deaf to one's own experience.

Here is an example:

> A young analyst-in-training meets a well-known, international statesman. As they exchange differences of opinion about the geopolitics of the statesman's country, the young man's mind goes blank. He feels embarrassed. Later in session, he sees this as proof of his inadequacy. Instead of examining his anxiety derived from his definition of himself, and despite no evidence whatsoever, the young man explains, "Oh I could see he was in a hurry to leave and he just couldn't continue our conversation." The necessity to avoid looking at his apparent tension was ignored. Even a query about his experience and telling his analyst about it is challenged as irrelevant. A patient whose integration is based on maintaining a narcissistic consciousness cannot permit the validity of an analyst's inquiry. He is too intimidated to reveal and articulate something he thinks of as a weakness.

This kind of consciousness is based further on the tendency toward transcendence, that search for some sense of absolute, personal autonomy and independence from the natural laws of causality. Absolute free will is assumed to reside somewhere exclusively within the transcendent personality. Solipsistically, the external world exists by virtue of one's own thought or feeling. Hence transcendence is also characterized by an assumed sense of invulnerability. Falsely, there seem to be no external forces that could do damage or injury, so that one grants oneself God-like qualities in power or assumes their exhibition is necessary for safety or even survival. The shock of recognition of reality can push one into profound depression or even paranoia. It is this that is referred to as the narcissistic blow.

While these persons regard themselves above causality and beyond the influence of history, they are in actuality reactive slaves to all external stimuli, since they make no rational connection between the stimuli and themselves. They are unable to experience themselves in cooperative social endeavors, seeing each event discretely, and they dread loss of independence. They see no pattern to their way of living, to their interpersonal transactions, no recurrences, and they never feel they are, or could be, a force altering their own history—or that of others. Therefore they are unable to profit from experience (Robbins 1956).

The Greeks called all this *pleonexia*—a label for this way of relating to others in one's surround. It refers to the character, but most of all to the behavior of one who claims more than one's share. It is expressed in selfishness, greediness, imperiousness, arrogance, and imperviousness. Being above the ordinary, narcissistic persons simply refuse coaching, or advice, or even admitting its value. Their smugness implies a supposed fullness and completeness (Zaphiropoulos 1989). They do not listen.

Often the process of panic is the result of having to face the need to engage external necessities. One pales at the idea of behavior that would violate one's transcendent world outlook and one's necessity to initiate some elements of a new consciousness or a new existence. One's feeling is terror in the face of having to risk change and be accountable for error. Therefore, one tries to be impervious to any kind of influence that would have the effect of external, internal, or contextual change. Since imperviousness is such a necessity for narcissistic personalities, they can engage only in monologic posturing, denying, refusing, or warding off influence. As they were made to feel nonrelevant in the past, so are others nonrelevant now.

In essence, one is never aware of the other as someone who is absolutely not oneself. Conversation is characterized "by the need neither to communicate . . . nor to influence . . . nor to come into connection with someone, but . . . by the desire to have one's self-reliance confirmed . . . or to have it strengthened . . . [or to] regard[s] himself as absolute and legitimate and the other as relativized and questionable" (Buber 1955:19–20).

Here is a patient, a professional woman in her late forties, desperately dealing with failed transcendence and imperviousness. She starts off the session as follows:

> I have so much to talk about I don't know where to start. Of course I had this dream and I don't know what it means. The dream was I wrote a note to you, and you wrote to me. It came out that you were my therapist. There was nothing shameful about sending notes, but there was a quality of affection in the notes to each other. So it was a good feeling dream. In another section of the dream I was telling my brother to tell my mother angry things. She was walking way ahead of me. This scene had to do with her not walking with me, but walking someplace else.
>
> Last night I was thinking of the progress I've made and I thought I'm not as angry as I used to be. I don't jump to interpretations as readily. It's

> not so automatic anymore. There's a noticeable difference. This morning I thought seriously of being a borderline. I thought that really was my diagnosis. If you had that in your mind about me there's nothing I could do that would be a disappointment. You wouldn't expect so much. It made me feel better to think that way. It made me feel better about my lack of progress. It's not clear whether I can change. Can I change?

I said something like you know you just told me you have changed. Did I not hear that accurately? She continues:

> But I still have so many problems. I drink alone at night. I drink a lot of wine. I think I'm an alcoholic.
>
> I never thought I'd turn out to be like my father. I really understand him, his primitiveness, his wanting to withdraw. I realize I have the same tendency. To you it's probably all obvious. But the realization came about when I noticed I came back from the Hamptons earlier than I needed to. I just couldn't stand the anxiety in the social situation. The tension in meeting attractive men and the sleeping arrangements of the group, sleeping in a sort of open place. I just have to withdraw. I get disappointed and depressed and anxious. Someone who likes me said, "Ann just disappears. Why does she do that?" It all seems so overwhelming. [Tears] But if I can't change what's the big deal? Well I want to stop, I want to stop withdrawing today. I'm wasting my life. I'm wasting my time. Like you were telling me about that last week when I thought you didn't understand. I really believed you were literally yelling at me. I heard you yelling and I know you weren't. You must have felt frustrated.

As gently as I can, I say something like: "I sure did feel frustrated was I walking too far ahead of her?" I did not remember, at this moment, what my internal thought processes had been, but I must have felt something reciprocal to what the patient goes on to describe.

> SHE CONTINUES: "I was anxious and depressed on top of that. I wish I could feel one thing and be consistent. I'm like the animal that chews off its foot to get away."
>
> I THEN SAY: "Are you saying that you feel trapped by me and other people? That social business with the beach group, and here with me must be pretty threatening for you to do something that's so self-hurtful or contradictory—leave when you don't want to; hear me yelling when I'm not."

> When I admit her impact on me (simply put that I am not impervious), which she anticipates as being deleterious, she communicates her imperviousness, her necessity to avoid any influence that she feels has her trapped, so she becomes self-hurtful. First I communicate that I have been subject to her system and still survive. Then she begins to deal with her own sense of her victimization.

Nothing indicates that workaday analysts are not subject to the same monologic, stylistic devices, as their patients are. In fact the vast literature on countertransference could be recast in this light and consequently understood this way. Furthermore, the details of the ramifications of interactive monologism between analyst and patient are an area of interest that has yet to be explored. But I leave all this for another occasion.

I believe that life is lived in longing. Northrop Frye puts it this way:

> Civilization is not merely an imitation of nature, but the process of making a total human form out of nature, and it is impelled by the force that we have . . . called desire. . . . Desire is . . . not a simple response to need, for an animal may find food without planting a garden to get it, nor is it a simple response to want, or desire *for* something in particular. It is neither limited to nor satisfied by objects, but it is the energy that leads human society to develop its own form. Desire in this sense is the social aspect of what we met on the literal level as emotion, an impulse toward expression that would have remained amorphic if the poem had not liberated it by providing the form of its expression. (1957)

Yet, longing leaves us vulnerable in that the perpetual experience of frustration leads to a feeling of engulfing anger, and little choice remains except for self-protective gestures. A patient once told me that on his vacation to Firenze he had been so angry, "So wacked out with Susan, that I missed the Bruneleschi Dome. Oh, we walked up there, we looked around, but I missed it. I didn't see it. I was all anger, all rage. I was all into myself, not with her, and certainly not with that architectural miracle." Self-protection leads only to more frustration—a circularity in which we start somewhere, start flailing, and end up exactly in the same place. Authentic self-nurture must, of course, take place via others, other places. If the therapeutic action is restorative or reparative, a variety of choices comes into being. If it is useful in this way, we do not feel dismissed, and we move to authentic self-nurture, leaving behind our self-aggrandizement, which was protective.

Of course, this wiping out of someone via monologue can be done through inauthentic communication. It is not so much an ignoring as a dismissal of differentiatedness and separateness, the very viable experience of the other, of his or her right to exist as a differentiated person, with ownership of his or her own thoughts, feelings, ideas, beliefs, values. It is what was done to us in the past, facilitating our antiself image (Feiner 1991a).

> A patient complains to her husband that a circuit breaker trips whenever she uses her hair dryer. Facing a wall and talking to no one, he responds with, "What's she doing now?" She rages. He rages back. There is mutual vituperative name-calling. Later, with me, she wonders why she rages and what had she done wrong, and why is she so helpless and vulnerable? She focuses on the word *doing.* "How could I be so dumb?" she asks, floundering with her feeling of having been victimized once again. She is so stupid, she says, and he is so crazy. I focus on the word *she,* which I believe impersonalized or dismissed her. When she grasps what I'm saying to her, her rage subsides. She remains angry. But not at herself, at her husband's inauthenticity, his objectifying her (Feiner 1970), and she goes on to talk about her mother's characterizations of her, i.e., "It's a good thing she's pretty," or, "All she's good for is to find someone to marry her."

It is characteristic of narcissistic patients that they have difficulty, if not inability, acknowledging the therapist or any other as autonomous. The idea that the patient may have heard inaccurately or attributed something to an analyst can rarely be entertained. It is as though the other is a mere fingernail extension of one's self. Analysts have interpreted this kind of assignment to the other as part of narcissistic transferential processes. They refer to the patients' needs for fusion or for merging. Analysts see the patients responding to their own internalized image of what the therapist ought to be for their own well being. This is of limited use unless we inquire about the necessity for this, that is, the key difficulty in differentiatedness or in separateness. It makes little difference whether the relationship is blissful or adversarial, or whether it is positive and affectionate, or hateful, angrily anticipatory of hurtfulness. Furthermore, on hearing the words "I can't avoid it," we are reminded that these patients' basic assumption is the unchangeable nature of their inadequacy, which can only support their feeling of helplessness.

The dismissal of differentiatedness involves reifications of all kinds—double binding, attributions, mystifications, stereotyping, intrusions, and invasions, and time binding. Conversations that include these mechanisms really trash the other's otherness. Consequently, regardless of how these conversations, as sequential exchanges, may appear to a third party, they are essentially monologic and cannot be construed as genuinely dialogic (Feiner 1970). If others are perceived as things for use, rather than persons in their own right, they are related to as commodities, not as viable others whose differentiatedness is to be respected. Monologue is always available in the narcissistic mode regardless of its disguise. People are talked to, at, for, on, or about, but not with. To talk with another person, of course, is a dialogic engagement.

Narcisstic persons come to believe that only in their monologic stance is some sense of their original self affirmed. In their anxiety about the influence of others they believe that their identity or consciousness will be lost if they were to accept and admit that influence (Feiner 1979).

Actually one's consciousness as the creator of oneself cannot be lost or absent in a dialogic view of the world. The very opposite is true. One's consciousness and existence is present in every situation, but the function and forms of its activities are different than in monologue. What happens in dialogue is that the "I" consciousness does not transform others into manipulated things, nor is it manipulated in turn. The dialogic "I" in therapy thinks, not in assertion, but in integral points of view. Sullivan (1956) defines collaboration similarly.

> Now I regard cooperation as a rather juvenile way of working with others because it pays—as against collaboration, where there is a strong interest in mutual achievement in the other person's achieving as well as in one's own (p. 98).

To understand another person at any given moment, therefore, is to come to terms with the boundary lines between one's own and another's language and presence. That is, there must be translation, which is what Interpersonal psychoanalytic interpretation is all about (Feiner 1988).

III

We know that children and other family members sometimes sacrifice their own sanity and/or their safety for the sake of their individual parents or the couple, or the intactness of their parents' relationship, which is a realistic dependent necessity for young people (Feiner and Levenson 1968). Searles (1979) sees patients not merely as exploited victims but rather as persons who have been thwarted in their capacity for the development of mature responsibility and responsiveness because of the abusive, inauthentic handling by their parents. Thus they do not develop the ability to engage in authentic, loving relationships. They maintain only themselves and their survival, hoping to enhance others and thereby provide themselves with a model for identification and further maturation. This is, of course, in contradistinction to any kind of dialogic orientation. What the analyst presents that is new in this regard is that the patients are provided, not with the avoidance of mutual interdependency, but rather with its acceptance, analysis, and the opportunity to experience more mature ways of relating and connection than were possible before (Searles 1979). Thus the analyst enters another's system, which is designed to function monologically, and in so doing begins to encourage the conditions for dialogical movement to take place.

Here is an example. The context for the session I will describe is as follows:

> A patient in her thirties, who has had a childhood highlighted by verbal and physical abuse from an older sister, a mother, and a violent father, has lived an adult life devoid of close relationships. While intellectually astute she has never found in her varied employment a position that is satisfying. She says she longs for approval from others and a loving relationship with the opposite sex. But her recurrent rageful responses in the face of disappointment and/or her imagined disapproval, criticism, humiliation, and possible abandonment keep getting her into trouble. She wakes up often feeling angry, not knowing why. In the early stages of therapy she was prone toward suicidal thoughts, threatening the therapist with her intentions to end "the torture of her wretched existence." She presented herself stiffly, with a sort of waxiness that seemed to communicate her anticipation of hurt. She dressed in a bland way and gave the appearance of someone walking on thin ice.
>
> After several years of therapy she improved considerably. She no longer had the suicidal thoughts, and she joined a church where she responded enthusiastically to the humanistic sermons of the pastor but still found herself painfully yearning for a person with whom she might have a loving relationship and still presented herself in the old manner. One day she found herself unable to deal effectively with the several subordinate employees in the financial institution where she was an executive. Because of her reactive arrogance, top management suggested that she either step aside from her responsibilities or resign from her extremely well-paid administrative position.
>
> She arrived at her session on time (for the first time in a month) one morning and stated immediately, "Have you seen such and such (the name of a film)? It's a good one." I then spent about five seconds trying to phrase a query that probably would not be experienced as critical. She immediately responded in a rage, "I do not like being ignored!" A flurry of furious, hateful, hurtful, insulting remarks followed

fast, ending with the phrase "I do not understand how you could possibly have a practice. You are evidently incompetent, useless, and nothing more than a cold, thoughtless phony!" This barrage took about ten minutes. When her harangue subsided she said, "Well don't you have anything to say?" By this time I had recovered from her onslaught. My own irritation and slowly rising, cynical anger, about what I thought of at the moment as "this ungrateful bitch" had dissipated completely. I began thinking several associative possibilities as to what might be going on. I said something to the effect that, indeed, I was appreciative of her suggestion and that I knew I had no intention of ignoring her even though she might plausibly perceive my silence that way. She protested angrily, "No, no, you did ignore me and that's that! Why did you do so? I should have expected nothing more from you." She then said imperiously, "I don't even know why I am so angry, but that is the way I feel." It was evident to me that her monologic posture was being maintained. What would she have lost if she gave it up? Integrity? Honesty? Would it have been a capitulation? An injustice?

Now my thoughts were something like this: (1) She is bringing me a gift—her recommendation for an experience that she thinks I might enjoy. And she surmises, probably correctly, that I would enjoy it, so it is in the nature of a gift. (2) I have been in her mind, and there was probably some gratification and ambivalent fantasy connected with that. That I have been in her mind this way indicates a readiness for a dialogic position. My presence has had an influence on her. (3) This is probably the arrogant, overbearing way she treats most people: her subordinates at her former job, her ex-boyfriend who had lapsed in some attention owing to his son's birthday, and many other associates and friends, when she feels threatened. (4) I think this was probably the way she had been treated as a child. What she has described in an overall generalized way as abuse, insults, dismissiveness, denigration, and/or anger from siblings and parents is more likely akin to this kind of interaction. She might have brought something home to her mother or perhaps her older sister, something out of her own experience, and endeavored to make a positive connection. She would be abused, rejected, ignored, suppressed, or denied. This is a reenactment of the cat bringing the master a mouse. Her appearance tells me she is the mouse. Her gesture and voice indicate she is also the cat.

I believed my options were to pick up the dread about the giving of a gift or to make some hypothetical assumption implying some understanding about her family experience and inquiring about that. Since I thought she would be too sensitized and raw and, in her state of fury, reject the possibility that she was intending anything positive (so as to maintain some sense of dignity and self-esteem), I chose the latter issue about her history. I made some tentative, cautious statement about her own experience in similar situations when she was a child or as an adolescent and was about to initiate an inquiry, hoping to move to the positive nature of her gesture.

I was dead wrong. My incorrect option, perhaps, indicated I was not ready to enter her system. In simple language, I should have gone with the affective flow (Feiner 1991a). My comment evoked nothing less than a cold, aloof remark to the effect that I was now lecturing her, telling her it was all her problem, and as an analyst I was absolutely of no use, and therefore, she had better leave. Whereupon she stood up and left.

By this time I was so bound by what I thought was the impossibility of maintaining any kind of dialogue with this angry, brittle woman that I looked at her and said nothing. I began to think that I simply should have affirmed her positive gesture. I wondered what had inhibited me. I love gifts. I enjoy the inquiry about them. If this were a genuine one I should have had no trouble with it. Was there a string attached? I had no idea.

At the next session she started the discourse with a question, "Have I changed?" I took this to be an attempt on her part to begin a conversation, to initiate a rapprochement. She insisted I respond, yes or no. I answered in what I thought was a truthful way. I said, "Yes and no." She was intrigued with my answer, wanted me to explain it, and despite her request that we not renew the interaction of the previous session, she wondered out loud why that painful hour had taken place. I got an idea. I said that the "offering" may have been the key—not necessarily that it was positive. I introduced the possibility that change is very threatening, despite her desire for it. Then I said something like it looked as though she tried something new in bringing a gift to me, only to experience it, in the midst of her enormous dread, as rejectable or dismissible. Consequently it had to become a painful repetition of old dangers and hurts. Now she agreed and told me about some horrendous incident with her sister. Then she made one more comment—it was about her pastor who had sermonized that loving was a better way of living and that acts of generosity are fulfilling. I did not articulate at this time the full implications of this association for our relationship (placating or otherwise) other than to remark that it seemed like confirmation of her trying to change in this regard with me, and I was sorry she had not been fulfilled. Whether this was reform or transformation, I noted to myself, remained to be determined (see Feiner 1991b).

IV

M. Bakhtin (1986), a philosopher of language and linguistics, points out that speakers shape their utterance, not only according to the content of discourse (whom or what they are talking about) or the immediate addressee (to whom they are speaking), but also according to the particular image in which they model their belief of being understood. This is a belief that is the a priori of all communication. Psychoanalysts express it in different words, but here are Bakhtin's words:

> in addition to the immediate addressee the author of the utterance, with a greater or lesser awareness, presupposes a higher superaddressee, responsive understanding is presumed, either in some metaphysical distance or in distant historical time. In various ages and with various understandings of the world, this superaddressee and his ideally true responsive understanding assume various ideological expressions (Bakhtin 1986:xviii).

Bakhtin's notion of dialogue underlies his approach to a wide range of issues in esthetics, philosophy, and psychology. It provides the foundation for his account of human consciousness. (Bakhtin relies on the dialogic notion of inner speech in order to account for the social, semiotically mediated nature of psychological processes in the individual.)

To Bakhtin, contacts in dialogue are not those of an isolated, ahistorical individual; they are the reflections of ideological perspectives or belief systems. These can adequately be understood only in terms of a specific sociohistorical setting.

Bakhtin writes that however monologic an utterance may be (for example, a scientific or philosophical treatise), it cannot avoid being, in some measure, a response to what has already been said about the topic or the issue, even though this responsiveness may not have assumed a clear-cut external expression. Its dialogic quality will be manifested even in the overtones of style or in the nuances of composition. Any utterance is filled with dialogic implications, and these must be taken into account in order to understand fully the style and meaning of the utterance. Thus Bakhtin sees dialogism as the very essence of inner speech as well as of outer production. For the analyst, Bakhtin's comprehensive theory of dialogic history suggests that when we hear the patient speak we are listening to the person's mother, father, aunt, uncle, or siblings but that these voices have been metabolized in terms of the patient's experienced adaptation and organized into a viable whole (see Sullivan 1940). There is an analytic truth to this, and it is the underpinning of the need for analytic inquiry into experience and its meaningfulness (Sullivan 1956).

If this concept of dialogue, which is entirely historical, is taken ahistorically, it implies that nothing exists but dialogue. However, I believe Bakhtin is referring to an entire overarching, dialogic process of development, not to a stage of relatedness at any one moment. It is true that mind develops out of interpersonal, social formations (Wertsch 1985), and in this sense there really can be no language or speech that is not dialogic, but at the stage where psychoanalysis makes contact with patients the monologic quality of defensiveness must be respected and the operations that go into it, along with its necessities, scrutinized. True, analysts inquire into transference and the history that explains it with a serious regard for the self-evident quality of dialogic influence. But their presentation of their own new influence needs to be seen as struggling with the patient's monologic necessities, whose intention is to preserve a hard-won status quo.

Bakhtin (1984) identifies negation as one of the only two possibilities available within a monologic world view. He comments: "A thought is either confirmed or negated."

> Ultimately *monologism* denies that there exists outside of it another consciousness, with the same rights, and capable of responding on equal footing, another and equal *I (thou)*. For a monologic outlook (in its extreme or pure form) the *other* remains entirely and only an *object* of consciousness, and cannot constitute another consciousness. No response capable of altering everything in the world of my consciousness is expected of this other. The monologue is accomplished and deaf to the other's response; it does not await it and does not grant it any *decisive* force, monologue makes do without the other; that is why to some extent it objectivizes reality. Monologue pretends to be the last word. (Bakhtin 1984, quoted by Todorov 1984:107; italics in the original)

To Bakhtin, ideological creation is not within us but between us. He (1986) states:

> The idea *lives* not in one's isolated individual consciousness—if it remains there it degenerates and dies. An idea begins to live, i.e., to take shape, to develop, to find and renew its verbal expression, and to give birth to new ideas only when it enters into genuine dialogical relationships with other ideas, the ideas of *others*. (pp. 87–88)

Therefore, thoughts uttered in words or their equivalent signs can become real thoughts for another person as well as thoughts for oneself. The other person, however, is not only the immediate other. The word moves the thought forward in search of responsive understanding. To Bakhtin, being heard as such is already a dialogic relation. From the point of view of this essay, it only indicates a potential for a dialogic relation. In psychoanalytic therapy that remains to be seen, for valid reciprocity is necessary. It cannot be taken for granted, relying as it does on the analyst's inquiry and engagement, whether the analyst goes where the patient is, not where the analyst assumes the patient is, or should be (Feiner 1991a).

According to the linguist Yakubinskii (one of Bakhtin's colleagues—as reported by Wertsch 1985) the criterion that distinguishes monologic from dialogic forms of speech is obviously not the number of individuals involved; it is always assumed that a speaker or writer addresses a listener or reader. What distinguishes the two speech forms is the degree to which both parties participate in the concrete setting to create a shared text.

Yakubinskii points out that dialogue is a genetically prior, "natural" form of verbal interaction, whereas monologue is a later, "artificial" form. The analyst might see it as defensive, once having recognized the developmental aspect of the dialogic.

Here is an excerpt of a patient's monologue changing rapidly into dialogue. She is single and in her late thirties (*Pt* = patient, *AF* = the author):

PT: I'm depressed today. I missed the session last time because I didn't want to be in conflict with the therapy. I have such a defect. I am hopeless. I guess I always was this way. Yes, it was always this way.

AF (I think: No matter what I say, it will be "in conflict." She does not want to be adversarial today. I venture the following): I don't think it could have been all bad, as bad as it was and is.

PT: I am so damaged, I cannot even articulate it. What went wrong? Other people don't respond the way I do. I am so different.

AF: Maybe you lack the words to express the feelings you have. It's rough without words.

PT: It is no wonder I can't articulate it. It's like Sanskrit. It's outside my knowledge. I'm not even conscious of any meaning. You know when I was one and a half years old I would wake up screaming and crying sometimes. We had moved a few times and I was frightened. I remember being terribly frightened but my mother hit me to stop me. Do you think I could have started it all there (tears)? No, no, no, that's not what you do to children. Now I don't know how to respond to you. To this, I mean in my adult life, today.

AF: Are you saying you think you don't have a language? Didn't develop one? Blame yourself? But you are sad, aren't you? Sad over what was and what might have been? And you missed a session because you wanted to keep it positive in here?

PT: You know something, it's true I'm sad, but somehow I'm feeling a little better.

I did go with the flow and the result was positive (Havens 1974; Feiner 1991a).

Usually people tell the story of their lives when asked in terms of what they think are the important events and big decisions. The really important events are not the great ones but the infinitely numerous and apparently inconsequential ordinary ones that, taken all together and accumulated, are far more effective and significant (Morson 1988). Trivia are as important as crises. For the analyst this follows Freud's point that all experience is symptomatic. But it is symptomatic of what? In essence we keep on repeating to ourselves the traumatic theory of neurosis when we relate history in terms of large, cataclysmic events. When analysts ask and listens to how patients dealt with small, typical, ordinary occurrences, those things that are barely noticed, we can get an image of how the persons experience their passions, in essence live their life. And the living of their life in action tells us how the persons have forged an ideology, how they have expressed it, how they have been influenced by it in turn, and what the forging meant, for the ideological assumptions explain their presence before us.

The fact is that selfhood is not discovered, it is made. What if no secret central core of a self exists? And the so-called self-system, what is that but a reaction, that is: "An organization of experience for avoiding increasing degrees of anxiety which are connected with the educative process" (Sullivan 1953; 166). What if there are only organizing principles and that when we ferret, uncover, reveal, expose, articulate, or interpret ultimately through our inquiry, we discover, not a core self like some little homunculus sitting on haunches behind behavior symptoms or character traits, but a set of principles that I like to call an ideology. Is it possible the self, the premier analytic concept (of our time), is nothing more than our latter-day, reified transformation of the nineteenth century's machine spinning our wheels? I believe that self we call self, that individuality we call uniqueness, can be revealed only through infinite acts of socialization.

We regard choices—shaped by the climate of our minds—as including those principles by which we are guided and which themselves were shaped by the countless small decisions and ordinary moments that we have experienced, particularly at the hands of parents and intimate others. And these principles, conscious or not, are what guide us. What is it that we experience in early growth? Is it the getting or the not getting? Is it what is present in an interaction or the absence of something? Or is it more than that—that is, each and both?

What was present for the patient in my last example, when she was hit for being afraid (as she recalls)? What was absent? And the patient whose father reveled in his son's trophies, and the breasts of the youth's girlfriends, what was absent? What was present for him with a mother who was flat and cold? What was absent? These are the infinite, minuscule, day-to-day experiences that facilitate our taking on ideological principles with which to order our lives. And in their repetition, their patterning (dare I say laying down of neuronal tracts?), they shape what a psychoanalyst calls experience. As Spiegel puts it for narcissism:

> It is precisely the looking for grand meaning, looking for the great, the poetic, the utterly romantic, or the special event that reveals a narcissistic orientation and the disappointment or defeat of which inevitably leads to depression. Furthermore these excessive standards usually have been imposed from without by some formidable evasive, apparently "loving" parent and accepted by the patient placating over the impotence of his anger. (Spiegel 1970:73)

Looking for the grand moment, the great passion, the superlative gesture, regarding the ordinary as uninteresting and unreal, fosters negligence and dismissiveness. In this way the prosaic and the people involved in the banal or mundane have no claim on us, and we are not touched by the values inherent in those situations in which we find ourselves. In so doing we are less moved—and we lose the opportunities to be enriched in feeling and value (Morson 1988).

It is out of the quality of routine ordinary human activities that the human spirit and its moral courage are born. Such courage not only is the province of the so-called independent and the intellectually privileged but also is available to all through the nature of dialogic relatedness, interpenetration, connectedness, commitment, and the quality of relationships developed in interactions.

Evil usually results from something very simple like irresponsibility, unaccountability, or negligence, sort of looking the other way. It happens, not because we become part of a grand design, or even give in to banal desires, but because we do not pay attention, we simply do not evaluate and exert the energy to make corrections (Morson 1988). We then become part of a grand, evil movement as an end-product.

We see, in essence, what we have learned to see, what we desire to see, what we demand to see, what we need to see. Translations and interpretations of events are human inventions, and these, together with what and how we choose to see (and hear), shape our responses and thus the very fabric of our lives. It is this way for the psychoanalyst as well as for the patient.

Too often we simply do not hear each other, or we break into the other's speech with self-serving monologic chatter. This is what provokes anger, boredom, or apathy. Human life exists not only through contact but also because of it. Authentic dialogue, genuine interchange that is mutually enhancing, is the ideal contact, with its contents determined by our self-defined functions.

The narcissistic way, from this point of view is the impoverishment of living. Buber comments that when "the word comes to us the answer proceeds from us." Only when that occurs can there be fulfillment. This comes from a relation between persons characterized by inclusion (Buber 1955). In this sense we cannot do better than baboons. In fact we would be served superbly if we did as well. How it comes about that one person is good for another, what magic lies in interpenetration, and what principles are at work in the analyst's facilitation of growth in both patient and therapist remain to be spelled out thoroughly.

My essential point in this essay is that the narcissistic aspects of our own personalities, narcissistic gestures, and their monologic ways of relating, to which we are all heirs, fix us like photographic plates despite our intentions. They represent our ideologies, which ossify how we see, how we experience life—in a word, how we live. To change this, to move a patient from a monologic style to a dialogic one requires our understanding of the dynamics of each mode, going with the affective flow, and that means our efforts at translation. It is our task and our responsibility.

Persons suffused with general anxiety have a double-edged problem that is in constant flux. On the one hand, if faced with a task that brings them into the public eye, they must guard against the debilitating aspect of their tension—their assumption of a loss of prestige—with an appropriate defense. On the other, they have to function as best they can. Yet these two external demands are in opposition since the energy involved is split. This split is experienced by these persons in mind and body, so that one preoccupation is to try to feel "safe." They must avoid the disdain and denigration they believe others will have for them because of their being anxious, since being anxious and feeling vulnerable may mean being weak and helpless. If there is this kind of split, a momentary transient success in the task, or feeling calm and relieved, can be exaggerated and aggrandized. With a reduction of anxiety one is suddenly extremely cool, contented, or on top of things. The phrase "manic defense" does not quite capture the investment the person puts in the illusory belief in quasi-integration. In the same vein, since one cannot maintain this position owing to the unpredictability and uncontrolability of others, one is completely lost when the pendulum swings in the opposite direction. Then one is totally "unsafe" and approaches the nadir of worthlessness and wretchedness.

Two questions immediately emerge from this prevailing dichotomy. The first is how can a person best function under these conditions? The second is how did the split occur, and how can it best get resolved and the patient reintegrated?

In practical terms, the obvious way to function under the conditions of anxiousness is total immersion in action, somewhat akin to jumping into a swimming pool, despite one's fear of water, and swimming to the other end. Despite one's subjective state the task requirements then hierarchically dominate consciousness. The best one can do, therefore, is go with the fright, to let it be—like Manolete, the classic bullfighter who engaged the bull week after week despite his extreme fear.

The resolution of the split is another matter and requires further discussion. For one thing the original source of tension and insecurity lies outside oneself. Parental figures, who themselves were supposed to be the providers of basic security, and who were expected to help build an inner reservoir of esteem, were also the prime instigators of tension and danger. What they presented in their dismissiveness, disapproval, and criticalness was the absence of the needed reservoir of safety and good feeling (Sullivan 1940). Over time, this internalized store of well-being and esteem is supposed to be available to be drawn upon. Since no one is immune from threat, this is necessary to avoid the sense of imminent dissembling. With inner esteem as anlage the person expects and desires a reflected response that further contributes to the reservoir. All this follows the concept of dialogue as presented here.

The natural tendency of any organism is to integrate itself, and this will push it to seek out whatever is necessary to accomplish it (Goldstein 1940).

What is needed then is to reestablish, better, recreate what was missing in the past, that is, what was originally absent. This is the trustableness that might have been inculcated by the parents and can be discovered in the present in a momentary, dialogic relationship. If not successful the person will go elsewhere, until he or she finds, the way a newborn whale finds a succoring nipple, what is needed. And that will be something that reenacts transformationally what happened early in life except now there will be a different outcome. What was absent because of what was present will now be present because of what is absent. Thus the self-abusive, self-critical force that is carried around internally like an undrained cyst will be absent because of its being replaced. In essence the persons have to find, in or out of therapy, dialogic moments in which they come to know that it is permissible for them to be who and what they are (Ehrenberg 1974; Havens 1974; Feiner 1990). After several experiences like this they can draw on memory when necessary. But this can happen only through repeated dialogic experiences, which by nature are horizontally composed of momentary, conversationally defined equals.[2] This is in sharp contrast to the supportive aspect of vertical, monologic modes, which may be comforting but fail to change the inner structure of the person. In this mode the source for repair remains outside the patient in the superior position of the one who teaches, guides, coaches, supports.

One patient illustrates it this way:

> You said something last time that was like a bolt of lightning. It went right into my head. I couldn't stop thinking about it. You were so right, and the funny thing is I knew it all the time. In fact I've heard it from you before lots of times, but this time it went into me. Would you say I was ready for it? I know that's the commonplace idea. The psychologist and social workers who work for me say that all the time. Oh, he was ready to hear it finally. You know what I think? I think that's bullshit. I heard it, and the reason I heard it, was sort of magic. What makes someone ready? No, it's something else. Look what you said was no big deal, it's really old hat. You've said the same thing, a hundred times before. Okay maybe not in the same words, but this time somehow it was different. Here's what you said this time. You said my head is full of "shoulds" and "oughts" and that these are laws or rules like a religious code. I should do this and I should do that. Like jogging the other day when I have free time, and you said somehow I've got the shoulds connected in my mind with musts. Like the French, *il faut que.* It's necessary, One must do this or do that. The musts are my behavior. You said it's okay to have a religion and I could keep the "shoulds" if I want to, but I didn't have to keep them tied to the "musts"

> with the authority outside me. Well I sort of knew that but it sounded fresh and then at the end of the session that thing happened. Since I was dressed in a suit you asked was I going to the gym? And I said no, not today. I had to meet with some committee about the school. But I said I have an exercise machine and I'll get to it today or tomorrow and anyway I know I should do it 52 times a year and I reassured you that if I missed this week and next it would all come out right eventually and I'd do it 52 times a year or at least get around to that. I said yeah it's really pretty funny. And you laughed and you said you were really chuckling not laughing at me and that's when it happened. You said that I shouldn't be offended if you chuckled because it was also with sadness for me like it was old Polish–Jewish irony. And then I left. Now before I got down your driveway I thought my head would split open. But it wasn't really painful. It was just a bolt of lightning or a rush of fresh air. You were in there. Somehow with that remark you were in my head and I said to myself, that's right I don't have to tie the shoulds to the musts. You went in there and you were somehow you were all part of it. You had the same craziness inside me only you didn't stay with it. You felt it and you got beyond it and if you were in there and got beyond it I could do it too. Like it was okay to be this way. And I don't have to cover it or if I do I don't have to worry about the cover. That is I don't have to be split. I could get into it and go beyond it. And so I did. For the first time I did. It was as if I came out into light. There was nothing really new in it, just if you got inside me and experienced the system and you didn't succumb to it, I could probably do the same thing. But it couldn't happen unless you had gotten inside. It isn't insight but the system that has to change. I had all the insight that's why I was complaining. It's like being tense and your wife says why don't you relax. Big deal. Or my wife with all her phobias, so I tell her not be afraid of driving and so what? She knows that but in her system she's got to be afraid of driving and whether her doctor says so in fancy words or I say so in anger or irritability she's got to be the way she is. She's got to be afraid and we are all saying now don't be afraid. It can't work. It's the system that has to change. A whole philosophy. And you can't do that unless someone gets inside you and is victimized by it just the way you are and can still live that way or give it up and let go of it. In that way you get the idea that you can change it or let go of it yourself.

Psychoanalysts have no difficulty with the concept of narcissism as a grandiose attempt to protect oneself from deep, cynical feelings that life is empty and that, underneath, one is worthless or irrelevant. Claims that a healthy adaptation and a gratifying, successful life are based to some degree on narcissism, however, lead one to come up with the idea that a healthy narcissism exists. Self-esteem and omnipotence are much too developmentally advanced experiences to be part of infant life. Therefore, if narcissism is defined as self-love. and an ultimate investment in only an image at that, it should be recognized that it is far beyond the capacity of an infant. To juxtapose narcissism on the one hand as a failed attempt at the self-healing of a profound wound that originated in childhood and to claim at the same time that there is such a thing as healthy narcissism—a label used for ordinary self-esteem and serious, respectable concerns for one's own integration and relatedness to others—seem to be a contradiction in terms (Bonime 1989).

When does normal narcissism become abnormal narcissism? How much normal narcissism is abnormal? These kinds of semantically absurd questions seem to me to reveal a weakness in our theory and make for difficulties in organizing a viable therapeutic approach. It can only lead to confusion and ultimately to linguistic pyrotechnics. With this in mind, rethinking our use of our abstract terminology might be useful (Bonime 1989).

Clearly, however, a dialogic mode is in contradiction to narcissism. Its vigorous establishment reflects a viable aim in psychoanalytic therapy as well as a way of life. People continue to grow like "novelistic images continue to grow and develop even after the moment of their creation; they are capable of being creatively transformed in different eras, far distant from the day and hour of their original birth" (Bakhtin 1981:422). And that is our goal in psychoanalysis.

Notes

1. As we were taught in the original fairy tale referred to in my epigraph, when the mirror answers, "Snow White," the Queen becomes murderous.

2. I am indebted to Dr. L. Levy of the Westchester County Medical Center, New York Medical College, for the insights in this discussion.

References

Bakhtin, M. 1981. *The Dialogic Imagination,* M. Holquist, ed. Austin: University of Texas Press.

——. 1984. *Problems of Dostoevsky's Poetics,* C. Emerson, ed. Minneapolis: University of Minnesota Press.

——. 1986. *Speech Genres and Other Late Essays,* C. Emerson and M. Holquist, eds. Austin: University of Texas Press.

Bonime, W. 1989. *Collaborative Psychoanalysis.* Cranbury, N.J.: Fairleigh Dickinson University Press.

Buber, M. 1955. *Between Man and Man.* Boston: Beacon Press.

——. 1957. The William Allanson White lectures. *Psychiatry* 20:97–120.

Ehrenberg, D. 1974. The intimate edge in therapeutic relatedness. *Contemporary Psychoanalysis* 10:423–37.

——. 1990. Playfulness and the psychoanalytic relationship. *Contemporary Psychoanalysis* 26:24–95.

Emerson, C. 1985. The Tolstoy connection in Bakhtin. *PMLA* 100:68–80.

——. 1986. Our word and inner speech. In G.S. Morson, ed., *Bakhtin: Essays and Dialogues on His Work,* pp. 21–40, Chicago: University of Chicago Press.

Feiner, A. 1970. Toward an understanding of the experience of inauthenticity. *Contemporary Psychoanalysis* 7:64–83.

——. 1979. Countertransference and the anxiety of influence. In: *Countertransference,* L. Epstein and A.H. Feiner, eds., pp. 105–28. New York: Jason Aronson.

——. 1983. On the facilitation of the therapeutic symbiosis. *Contemporary Psychoanalysis* 19:673–89.

——. 1988. Countertransference and misreading. *Contemporary Psychoanalysis* 24:612–49.

——. 1990. Playfulness and the interpersonal ideology. *Contemporary Psychoanalysis* 26:75–107.

——. 1991a. The analyst's participation in the patient's transference. *Contemporary Psychoanalysis* 27:208–46.

——. 1991b. The thrill of error: Image and appearance, articulation, union. *Contemporary Psychoanalysis* 27:624–53.

Feiner, A. and E. Levenson. 1968. The compassionate sacrifice. *The Psychoanalytic Review* 55:552–73.

Freud, S. 1910. Leonardo Da Vinci and a memory of his childhood. *Standard Edition* 11:63–137. London: Hogarth.

——. 1914. On narcissism: An introduction. *Standard Edition* 14:73–102. London: Hogarth Press, 1963.

——. 1917. On transformation of instinct as exemplified in anal erotism. *Standard Edition* 17:127–33. London: Hogarth Press.

——. 1933. New introductory lectures. *Standard Edition* 21:7–182. London: Hogarth Press.

Fromm, E. 1947. *Man for Himself.* New York: Holt, Rinehart, and Winston.

Frye, N. 1957. *Anatomy of Criticism.* Princeton, N.J.: Princeton University Press.

Goldstein, K. 1940. *Human Nature in the Light of Psychopathology.* New York: Schocken Books.

Havens, L. 1974. The existential use of the self. *The American Journal of Psychiatry* 131:1–10.

Heine, H. 1982. *The Complete Poems of Heinrich Heine,* tr. by H. Draper. New York: Suhrkamp/Insel.

Kernberg, O. 1976. *Object Relations Theory and Clinical Psychoanalysis.* New York: Jason Aronson.

Kohut, M. 1971. *The Analysis of Self.* New York: International Universities Press.

Morson, G.S. 1986. Dialogue, monologue and the social. In G.S. Morson, ed., *Bakhtin: Essays and Dialogue on His Work,* pp. 87–88. Chicago: University of Chicago Press.

——. 1988. Prosaics: An approach to the humanities. *The American Scholar* 57: 515–28.

Robbins, B. 1956. Schizophrenic consciousness and practice. *Psychotherapy* 1:195–208.

Schachtel, E. 1959. *Metamorphosis.* New York: Basic Books.

Searles, H. 1979. Concerning therapeutic symbiosis. In *Countertransference and Related Subjects,* pp. 172–91. New York: International Universities Press.

Spiegel, R. 1970. Discussion of *Depression in Adolescence* by M. Symonds. *Science and Psychoanalysis* 17:71–74.

——.1985. Review of *Narcissus and Oedipus* by Virginia Hamilton. *The Journal of the American Academy of Psychoanalysis* 13:269–72.

Stern, D. 1985. *The Interpersonal World of the Infant.* New York: Basic Books.

Stewart, S. 1986. Shouts in the street. In G.S. Morson, ed., *Bakhtin: Essays and Dialogues on His Work,* pp. 41–57. Chicago: University of Chicago Press.

Sullivan, H.S. 1940. *Conceptions of Modern Psychiatry.* Washington, D.C.: The W.A. White Psychiatric Foundation.

——. 1950. The illusion of personal individuality. *Psychiatry* 13:317–32. Also in: *The Fusion of Psychiatry and Social Science.* New York: Norton.

——. 1953. *The Interpersonal Theory of Psychiatry.* New York: Norton.

——. 1956. *Clinical Studies in Psychiatry.* New York: Norton.

Todorov, T. 1984. *Mikhail Bakhtin: The Dialogical Principle,* tr. W. Godzich. Minneapolis: University of Minnesota Press.

Volosinov, V. 1973. *Marxism and the Philosophy of Language.* New York: Seminar Press.

Wertsch, J.V. 1985. *Vygotsky and the Social Formation of Mind.* Cambridge, Mass.: Harvard University Press.

Zaphiropoulos, M. 1989. Personal communication.

14

The Ubiquity and Relativity of Narcissism: Therapeutic Implications

Irwin Hirsch

Life is simplest and the world most easily negotiable when ambiguity is at a minimum. Even the Talmudist who spends his life in the study of the most complicated and unanswerable questions does so with an absolute belief in God and in his own calling as a scholar. The psychoanalyst too is plagued with the profoundly difficult task of understanding human functioning in general, making sense out of particular individuals and providing an interaction that will lead to change of enduring personal characteristics. In confrontation with such responsibilities where certainty about what one is doing is not generally achievable, many different solutions are available. One way to accommodate is to adopt a dogma, to proceed as if the very clarity and definite knowledge that is absent is indeed present (Becker 1983). Most individuals in the psychoanalytic profession, however, are personally beyond such a rigid solution. Nonetheless, it is not uncommon for a point of view to be arrived at, which are modifications of dogma. These are usually sophisticated and intelligent enough to escape detection as overly fixed and satisfy the desire for a reasonable amount of certainty. One example of this is to view psychoanalysis as a science as opposed to a hermeneutic enterprise (Holt 1976). Actually, operating in this field is impossible without guiding theoretical ideas, and by definition, each of us is limited to some degree by our articulated or unarticulated positions. Another solution to this problem is to be aware of our theoretical positions as ways in which we make sense out of unknowable psychoanalytic data and to view these, not as truths, but as our own personal structuring points. The work of Levenson (1972), Spence (1982), and Schafer (1983) have aided the analytic community to think in more modest terms about some widely accepted formulations. It is now, for example, considered less radical to suggest a wider variety of ways to conceptualize psychoanalytic data, and the profession seems to be moving toward a greater pluralism (Cooper 1987).

One of the bastions of psychoanalytic absolutism has been the notion of diagnosis and the type of treatment, analytic or otherwise, that corresponds to a particular diagnosis. Though this is not universally accepted, the adaptation of the medical model to analytic work is still pervasive, and diagnostic considerations are the focal point for a considerable body of psychoanalytic literature. The aim of using diagnostic categories is usually a worthy one since it allows a constellation of characteristics to be identified and provides a shorthand way of letting others know one's observations and one's experiences in treatment. The risk is, of course, that the categories and models of treatment get reified and uniqueness and nuance are overlooked. The psychotherapist's response may be to the group norm or diagnosis and not to the unique individual. One can work with diagnostic categories without these categories becoming viewed as absolute, fixed entities, if indeed, the diagnosis is not viewed as such, but instead, as a personal characteristic of the patient. It can be used descriptively, more as an adjective than as a noun. I do not intend here to discuss the general question of diagnosis per se but will restrict my remarks to the key characteristic of narcissism.

Narcissism is pivotal because essential distinctions about personal development are often dependent upon whether the patient is deemed "narcissistic" or at a higher level of psychological integration. Historically, patients have been divided into analyzable vs. unanalyzable, based, to a degree, on the extent of narcissistic involvement. Those individuals who were perceived as essentially narcissistic were considered too immature or developmentally arrested to benefit from psychoanalysis. Psychoanalytic technique was thought to be too austere and depriving as well as too verbal for the more contact-hungry narcissistic patient. Further, it was believed that such individuals could not form a transference to the analyst since they were not sufficiently personally related to do so. Narcissism was and still is a broad category and could range from those who function well in life to blatant schizophrenia. It often seemed that anyone toward whom the analyst could not relate was deemed narcissistic and unanalyzable. Until recently the solution was simple; well-functioning to schizophrenic patients diagnosed as narcissistic were not seen by most analysts in analytic treatment, or if they were, were not diagnosed as such. They were relegated to supportive or other nonanalytic forms of therapy, and the population of patients was divided into neurotics who were analyzable and narcissists who were not. The efforts of American analysts (e.g., Sullivan 1953; Fromm-Reichmann 1959; Searles 1965) and British analysts (e.g., Balint 1968) to adapt psychoanalytic treatment to these categories of patients were largely ignored by the American mainstream analytic community.

Precipitated by the work of Kohut (1971), a representative of the American psychoanalytic majority of Classical analysts, narcissism began to become of great interest to many American analysts in the 1970s. Kohut and those influenced by him became a breakaway school of their own (Self psychology) and have been very prolific in communicating their analytic perspective. At least initially, one of the characteristics of their viewpoint was to dichotomize all analytic work into a neurotic–narcissistic (nonpsychotic) division. They proposed traditional, Classical analytic procedure as the appropriate treatment for the first category and a much modified and really quite different analytic stance for the narcissistic category of patient. Without going into considerable detail and therefore not doing justice to their method, the Self psychologists tried to provide sufficient analytic gratification for a population who would not remain in treatment if subject to the silent and depriving atmosphere of the standard American Classical technique. Their aim was to help strengthen the patients' "lack of self" or thwarted development by being available as a selfobject. This object sufficiently admires and is offered for identification in order to encourage arrested development to complete its natural evolution. The analyst tries to assist the patients in their defensive grandiosity and omnipotence, both as a way to maintain them in therapy and to keep their tenuous sense of self afloat long enough for them to get back on their natural (prewired) developmental course. After sufficient strengthening, the analyst might then be in a position to conduct a traditional, Classical, drive-defense conflict analysis. Some Classical analysts have been critical of

Kohut's methods as simply another version of supportive therapy and of their reported results as nothing more than transference cures (Rothstein 1980).

Kohut's point of view is actually in considerable harmony with that of the British Object Relations school (e.g., Winnicott 1965; Guntrip 1968), who up until the 1970s had very little influence upon American psychoanalysis. The interest stimulated by Kohut led to a strong surge of interest in the British Object Relations school and their own literature in psychoanalytic work with severely disturbed patients. Though British school patients were not specifically called narcissistic, those described in the literature often possess qualities associated with some of the less well-functioning narcissistic patients described by Self psychologists. Also, although the terminology used to describe the patient population is different, the British analysts have also been inclined to divide the patient population into two broad categories and provide considerable gratification to those who are not seen as neurotic and treated by traditional, Classical methodology. The term *developmental arrest* (see Stolorow and Lachmann 1980) came to characterize the broad narcissistic population, and it appeared as if two distinct modes of treatment, according to diagnosis, were solidified. Matters became somewhat complicated when Kohut (1984) in his later work moved toward a broadening of the way he worked with narcissistic patients to include all (except psychotic) patients. That is, the line of development he originally viewed as present only in narcissistic patients had become, in his eyes, the basis of all psychopathology, narcissistic or otherwise. Once again, close examination of the major British Object Relations theorists leads to a similar conclusion; that is, what was originally viewed as diagnosis and treatment for a specific segment of patients was both the way of understanding and treating virtually all patients. As Greenberg and Mitchell (1983) have discussed, new theories of human development and of therapy are advanced by initially introducing the concepts through an atypical population.

It could be said that what had begun as a firmly prodiagnostic orientation developed into a more unified way of viewing people in treatment. Both Self psychology and the British Object Relations school began to view narcissism for one and regressed positions for the other, as present to some degree in all people and the locus of psychopathology in general. The patients used as case examples for each group were sometimes well functioning and sometimes not, but their narcissistic (Self psychology) or schizoid (British school) characteristics were always the focal point of the analysis. This nondichotomous method of analytic treatment made diagnosis in its medical sense relatively useless. There is, however, some profound irony here. Despite Kohut's advance and numerous case examples from both schools, the thrust of the literature in the field lags behind and still speaks of two different lines of development and treatment—neurotic on the one hand and development arrest on the other. Further, even within these two schools, the literature stills pays lip service to diagnosis and prescribed treatment.

Similarities between Self psychology and Object Relations (as exemplified by Winnicott and Guntrip) theories of development and of therapy are numerous. Both view psychopathology, narcissistic or otherwise, as a function of developmental deficiencies—essentially, a deficiency disease. Both view the role of the analyst as one who compensates for these deficiencies by providing nutrients that were absent in the analysand's early years. The self-object and the "holding environment" or "good enough mother" are designed to upgrade the patient's feeling of narcissistic adequacy or strength. The therapist-provided ingredients of unconditional positive regard, admiration, and encouragement of identification are designed both to strengthen the analysand's sense of self and facilitate a new beginning of natural growth of the self. The analyst assesses what the patient needs and objectively tries to provide it, within the confines of a professional relationship. The role of the patient can be described as somewhat passive and receptive. The analyst is the good parent who, in a sense, rescues the patient and reawakens the dormant growth potential. Like the Classical analyst who adopts a blank screen position, this model calls for objectivity and the analyst's sober judgment of what the patient needs before providing it. The analyst operates from outside the patient–therapist system and if functioning effectively, does not become caught up in the system, as say, in the participant observation model (Hirsch 1987). Essentially, the analyst decides in advance what is the *best* relationship to provide for the patient and believes that this can be done without repeating with the patient some of the "bad" early experiences. Fairbairn (see Greenberg and Mitchell 1983), by the way, is an exception to this point of view. The Self psychology model and the normative Object Relations model thus adhere to diagnostic thinking. A clear method of treatment is prescribed according to the assessment of the problem. Judged from case examples provided by Kohut, Winnicott, and Guntrip, the problem is inevitably related to deficiency. The model is a reparative one and the role of the analyst is clear; within the confines of the therapy relationship the analyst must be a better parent than the originals. The two models do differ in a variety of ways that are not being addressed here, but their fundamental theories of therapy are concordant.

Perhaps the school of thought that least emphasizes diagnosis and clear prescriptions of therapy is the Interpersonal school. Sullivan's famous statement, "We are all more simply human than otherwise," captures much about an analytic perspective that is nondichotomous in its views of human development and treatment of problems in living. Though Sullivan did speak of entities and some Interpersonalists still do, only minimal literature exists about specific diagnostic lines, and it is the exception when distinctions are drawn based upon quantity of narcissism. Searles (1965, 1979), perhaps more clearly than anyone in the literature, has drawn similarities between psychotic and neurotic development and functioning and has advocated that modes of treatment not be divided along diagnostic lines. He believes that all people possess similar personal qualities to varying degrees and that narcissism and regressive qualities are quite present in the best functioning individuals. For the prototypical Interpersonal analyst, psychoanalysis is not a clearly specified technique, prearranged according to the diagnosis of the patient. It can be called more an approach than a technique, and the aim is to help the analysands see themselves and others as clearly as possible. Inquiry is geared toward that aim and is altered, not on the basis of diagnosis, but on the basis of the unique dyadic relationships that develop between each patient–analyst pair (see Wolstein 1974). Though Sullivan himself viewed the analyst as an expert, the trend in the contemporary literature, highlighted by Levenson (1972, 1983), views the analyst as anything but objective. Participant observation or "observing participation" has come to mean that the analyst naturally becomes enmeshed in the patient's system and repeats with the patient the early "bad" integrations. Active inquiry and focus on the transference–countertransference interaction help both parties see this repetition and are an aid in working toward forging new interpersonal and intrapsychic configurations.

Individual psychopathology, narcissistic or otherwise, is learned adaptive integrations of early interpersonal experience and is imminently visible in the transference as well as in the examination of the patients' extratransference relationships. What is inside the patient is visible in interaction with others, and the world is arranged to coordinate with and repeat familiar interpersonal configurations. Individuals are viewed as architects of their own current world, and the patient is seen as active more than passive. Notions of "will" and existential thinking are strongly reflected. Examination of past and present configurations and drawing parallels between them help provide the analysand with the clarity necessary to function with less confusion or mystification (Levenson 1983). Considerable effort is directed toward assisting the patient to see how past difficulties are perpetuated. Some Interpersonal analysts will work largely within the transference to reach these aims, and others will focus on relationships outside the transference. Those who work more within the transference are less divergent with mainstream psychoanalysis. Gill (1983, 1984), for example, has recently gone a considerable way to integrate the Interpersonal school with the rest of the American psychoanalytic tradition, using the analysis of transference as the bridging link. Though the focus on transference divides Interpersonal analysts from one another, virtually all agree that analytic treatment ought to be based on unique dyadic interactions and not on fixed techniques of treatment for clear diagnostic categories of patients.

Another distinguishing characteristic in Interpersonal thinking is that it is a two-person and not a one-person psychology. Sullivan's (1953) conception of participant observation in contrast with the blank-screen model of psychoanalysis is probably his most powerful contribution to psychoanalytic therapy. More recent literature (e.g., Greenberg and Mitchell 1983) has successfully flushed out and articulated some profound differences in philosophy that draw distinctions between the Interpersonal model and those models that view the analyst as operating from outside the system. The participant observer is no longer the expert that Sullivan originally posited. The analyst is an unwitting player in the analysand's field. Starting out as an observer, the analyst becomes drawn in as a participant. Once in the system, examination of countertransference leads to clarification and a potential modification of the patient's repetitive patterns. In the two-person psychology model the analyst always speaks from his or her own perspective. This also contrasts with the Self psychologists' emphasis on the empathic position where the analysts disregard their own perception and speak from an assessment of what is the patient's point of view. In this latter model the patient is viewed as too fragile to hear the other and the analysts subserve otherness in favor of efforts toward pure empathy. In the two-person psychology, the object of study is not the patient alone but the patient in interaction with the analyst or with others. This contrasts with a purely intrapsychic orientation, as well as with a pure empathic orientation, where the effort is to isolate the unconscious of the patient as a pure source of data, free of both the analyst's participation and point of view. These references should be examined for a thorough discussion of this important issue, but for the purpose here, note that objectivity and absolute certainty are never possible as long as the observer is part of what is observed. It can never even be known whether or not empathic attunement reflects the psyche of the patient or whether analysts are really reading themselves. From this two-person perspective it becomes difficult to talk of the patient in total separateness from the participating analyst. The analyst engages both as a trained professional and as a unique individual with his or her personal countertransference as well as countertransference evoked by any given patient. From this philosophical position it is hard to think of knowing the patient with certainty, or of distinct entities such as the patient's pure narcissism. It is equally incongruous to speak of prescribed methods of treatment for objectively determined clinical entities. If anything could be diagnosed it would be the relationship and not the analysand in vacuo. Much of the lack of acceptance of the Interpersonal point of view from within the psychoanalytic community can be attributed to anxiety provoked by the inherent relativism and lack of clear structure.

Whatever one's perspective, the treatment of patients with strong narcissistic characteristics is difficult (see Bromberg 1983) and maybe more difficult when the analyst does not choose to adopt a prearranged method of treatment. Though a standard technical procedure may reduce anxiety, it can lead, as noted earlier, to excessive stricture and blurring of life's relativities. A two-person psychology (Bromberg 1989; Ghent 1989; Aron 1990), by definition, makes the analyst a *real* object and not simply a pure transference or fantasy object. From standard Classical technique as well as with Kohut's and most British school writers' technique, the analyst is outside the system and is not a real object. The focus is upon the empathy that the patient *needs* from the objective analyst. Kohut's selfobject is not a real object; it is preordained that the analyst provide empathy, mirroring and identification to the patient in order to stimulate the latter's growth. Though some disagree, I think that this is similarly true for the supplier of the "holding environment" or "the good enough mother." Empathy is part of a technique that the analyst gives to the patient, whether or not the analyst actually feels this empathy (Blechner 1988; Levenson 1989). In contrast, in the Interpersonal approach, growth occurs in dyadic interchange and struggle, with the analyst as a real object. The analyst as second party has an actual effect on the patient with whom he or she participates. As noted earlier, the analyst becomes enmeshed in the analysand's world and uses the observing function to work out of it. Though the analytic aim is for the analysand to be able to fully utilize all potentials, he or she is always viewed in the interaction with either real or past objects that have been internalized, real current individuals in the analysand's life or the coparticipant analyst's. The analyst does not know in advance what will be done with the patient (Greenberg 1981). The analyst tries to clarify the quality of the relationship that has spontaneously evolved between a full participant and an observing participant. The patient fits neither the Classical model of the intrapsychic, self-stimulated unconscious fantasizer nor the Self psychologists' or Object Relations' baby in developmental arrest, in need of analytic nutrition (Mitchell 1988).

The pure quality of narcissism is most widely known (see Lasch 1979) to be characterized by vanity, exhibitionism, arrogance, grandiosity, and self-absorption. The other person tends to be used to make the narcissist feel good, and well-being depends upon receiving a continuously adequate quantity of positive regard. The other is not usually viewed as a whole person and is generally used as a supplier of nutrients—a selfobject, to use a technical term. The basis for this is an absence of a sense of inner strength or substance, an emptiness that leaves one vulnerable to annihilation. The narcissistic individual does not tend to feel a clear and meaningful sense of self at the center or core. How others view this individual is likely to be taken as a reading of the self. This is why the prototypical narcissist so desperately searches for positive regard. If such a person is not admired, the result may very well be flight or a deep depression based on confrontation with feelings of nothingness. This extreme or pure narcissist is also inclined to avoid feeling dependent at all costs. Dependency is often profound but is not consciously experienced as such, for the feeling is strongly feared. Other people are important for the provisions they supply and thus are fragmented as individuals. To be dependent or to feel conscious love for a whole other person is to risk annihilation. The devastating effects of dependency on others are often what has led to a narcissistic withdrawal in the first place.

Bach (1977) and others have written about the difficulty for an analyst, as well as for anyone else in the life of an extreme narcissist, to be subject to the stimulus deprivation of not being heard, experienced, or even registered as a fellow human being. In attempting to analyze individuals with strong narcissistic characteristics the analyst is often subject to feelings of utter uselessness. A common inclination for an analyst is to withdraw into personal narcissism as a way of self-nourishing. Another typical reaction is anger, and it is always a possibility that this can be used to retaliate for the patient's attack on the analyst's very relevance or significance. It is understandable why individuals with strong narcissistic traits have always caused a dilemma for psychoanalysts. As noted earlier, such patients were traditionally turned away because they were believed to be insufficiently capable of personal relatedness. A rejection of the patient's request for psychotherapy may be a form of retaliation (Hirsch 1984). Another legitimized form of countertransference acting-out may be efforts toward harsh confrontations with reality. Though the analyst may be right on target, the analytic response may be based more on anger than on the desire to clarify. The sensitive patient may decipher this and flee from the relationship. Bromberg (1983) and Mitchell (1986) both convey that no new techniques are required to deal with strong narcissistic characteristics, though they caution the analyst to be aware of the angry wish to aggressively strip away illusions.

Writers who reflect Interpersonal psychoanalytic thought have not readily addressed the problem of narcissism because of their general disinclination to think in terms of clear diagnostic entities. Though both Bromberg and Mitchell isolate narcissism as a category, inherent in their thinking is a nondichotomous outlook on personal characteristics. They are describing individuals with very dominant narcissistic characteristics, virtually, the ultimate narcissist. Nonetheless, they do not support a distinct or prescribed method of treatment, and they view narcissism primarily as a way of relating to others and on a continuum. Though both authors convey that there is no need for a new or different form of psychoanalysis for such individuals, they do believe that in such work it is crucial to stay very attuned to the analysand's desire for affirmation. Fromm (1964), one of the seminal thinkers of the Interpersonal school, wrote extensively about narcissism, not so much as an entity, but, again, as a way of relating to others. His thinking and his willingness to work with narcissistic individuals reflected a clear advance over categorical and diagnostic points of view. His psychoanalytic emphasis was on delineating narcissistic qualities as they appeared in relation to others and, sometimes, in the transference. He probably placed too much effort on confrontation and was inclined to disregard the patient's wish to be affirmed. It is likely that he fared best with highly functioning analysands who were able to achieve narcissistic supplies from other sources in their lives. He nonetheless provided a valuable early model for those inclined to think in terms of two-person psychology and to eschew a more technique-oriented model of psychoanalysis. In addition, he referred to narcissism as a part of most individuals in contrast to thinking in terms of clear entities. His point of view about the pervasiveness of narcissistic characteristics was advanced by Singer (1970). Fromm, Sullivan, and Singer set a tone for viewing characteristics like narcissism as elements on a continuum in virtually everyone.

Barnett (1971, 1983) has been instrumental in further expanding the discussion of narcissism in its pure form to a more pervasive, everyday characteristic found in all individuals. Barnett refers to narcissism as a part of almost all character pathology and an intricate element in the two broadest neurotic character types, the hysterical and the obsessive personality. He is not referring to distinct and clear diagnostic categories but is describing ways of being with others that reflect learned, internalized patterns of adaptation, that is, character styles. Narcissism here is somewhat different from that discussed by Bromberg (1983), who addressed narcissism from an Interpersonal perspective, as narcissism is defined closer to its more pure form. Barnett speaks of narcissism largely as self-absorption or personal inaccessibility. It is narcissism as a characteristic, not as a distinct and clear character type. Any way in which the person/patient self-protectively hides within himself or herself qualifies as a narcissistic characteristic. Characteristics such as grandiosity and extreme vanity are not necessarily present but are viewed as other (perhaps more extreme) versions of this central narcissistic characteristic of self-absorption. Barnett notes that all forms of narcissism are related to some sense of inner emptiness and impoverished self-esteem. Again, he is not absolute in his definition and therefore does not speak of a total internal vacuum. This may be the case with extreme forms of narcissism, but for him as well as most Interpersonalists, everything is on a continuum. Qualities often not considered part of a narcissistic constellation, such as obsessive rumination or preoccupation, depression, and the dramatic emotionality associated with hysterical qualities, are, for Barnett, examples of varying degrees of narcissistic unavailability. It is a way of defining most psychopathology according to the degree of relatedness of the individual in tandem with the effectiveness of functioning in other realms. That is, to cite common examples, if one is preoccupied with achievement and starkly lacking in concern for others or in intimate relatedness, that individual may function very effectively in work and marginally, at best, in love. Or if one is depressed as opposed to sad, therefore ruminative, dwelling on the past, feeling sorry for oneself, and exhibiting only minimal concern for those in one's life, that too could qualify as a strong narcissistic involvement. Again, if one is preoccupied with how one looks or on the impact that one makes and the desire for others to express strong interest in oneself, that individual may, nonetheless, function rather well in life. However, it is likely that the individual is impaired with respect to what is consistently available for others or to the extent that life is a roller coaster of affects.

From the perspective exemplified by Barnett's writing, narcissistic characteristics do not come from only one etiological source. From examination of the Self psychology and much of the Object Relations literature, it appears that narcissism, like all other serious problems in living, evolves from deprivation or deficiency. Barnett points out that since narcissism is an aspect of most psychopathology, the development of those characteristics is inherently multiply determined. Many individuals who possess strong narcissistic traits come from families in which one or another parent was overinvolved, in contrast to depriving. In a family constellation where a parent infantalizes, overprotects, or overly admires the child, there may readily develop an overblown sense of self-importance and grandiosity. This may not be fully tested in the world, and therefore, the substance of their inflated feelings does not go beyond the doorstep of the home. In such instances the analysand may lead a private life of grandiose self-indulgence but not fully venture out to risk this fragile armor with the outside world. In other cases, perhaps where the parent is more encouraging of separation, the specialness and grandiosity may help catapult the patient to remarkable success in life. This achievement may be in work and not in love but can conceivably be in both. The individual who was given an inflated sense of importance and not selfishly kept locked at home by the family may be quite adept at getting others to be sources of admiration. As many configurations are possible here as there are unique parent–child combinations. What is of significance is the expansion of the characteristic of narcissism outside the slim range of a particular etiology and a one-dimensional, diagnostic scheme. The notion of unique dyads between patient and analyst follows from the viewpoint that developmental lines are pluralistic and themselves products of unique interactions that do not follow prescribed patterns.

It follows that Barnett does not offer new and clear methods of therapy for what he describes but makes us more sensitive to the prevailing narcissistic features at the core of many problems in living. In a sense, narcissism for him is like schizoid phenomena are for the British Object Relations analyst. Individuals retreat, more or less, to protect themselves from their vulnerable core of insufficiency. This does not imply "arrested development" or a "lack of self" as it does in some other psychoanalytic models. From this perspective there is no such thing as nonself. The individual is always viewed as having a self that comes from both identification with significant others and whatever independent development may exist from there. At worst, the self is tenuous and not very separate from early internalizations, but it is never a nonself. Psychoanalytic treatment, therefore, can never be a "replacement therapy" (Hirsch 1983; Mitchell 1988) and is always an analysis of character. The Interpersonal model of analysis is less a developmental model than an enrichment model (see Levenson 1983). The analytic aim is more an enrichment of the present than a reparation of past insufficiencies. At the very beginning of the development of Interpersonal psychoanalysis, Thompson (1950) posited that the current problems of our patients have to do with how they relive and repeat their past deprivations, not the past deprivations themselves. The individual is seen as unconsciously but actively shaping his or her life to conform to the past. The analysand is not viewed as the passive victim of the past. In the analysis of character it is crucial for the analyst to address the analysand's withdrawal as it occurs in the here and now of the transference. The emphasis is more descriptive than interpretive. A central aim is to help patients be clear and to understand the "what" of their experience and not necessarily the "why" (Levenson 1983). Analysts use their own experience to help clarify to patients the esthetics of their interaction. By so doing, analysts provide the enrichment of clarity of the self as well as an experience that is not a repetition of past interpersonal integrations, i.e., a new experience (Gill 1982; Fiscalini 1988).

Bromberg (1983) expresses concern that extremely narcissistic patients are incapable of hearing and taking in the analyst and thus may not benefit from some of the verbal aspects of analytic work. Particularly, he fears that transference observations may be viewed as expressions of the analyst's narcissism and may lead to termination of treatment. He suggests a gradient between the use of the verbal and nonverbal, admiring function of the analyst. This is a complicated issue, since in normal analytic interchange, dependent on how the analyst feels about any particular patient, there is always some gradient from admiration to dislike that is communicated. Unclear to me is whether or not mirroring (admiration) can be provided if the analyst does not genuinely feel this toward the patient. That this can really be part of a technique is uncertain. To be sure, the patient is better off if the analyst can find something to spontaneously like or admire. Since the analyst's feelings are inevitably unconsciously communicated, I believe the best that can be done is to try to get to the bottom of the dislike for some patients so that such feelings are not acted out (Epstein and Feiner 1979). A development of affection toward, and an active interest in, the analysand may lead to feelings of intimacy that in turn supply the necessary quantity of empathy (Ehrenberg 1974; Hirsch 1983). It may be that patients of all sorts drop out of treatment more often when they sense a lack of being liked or respected. Of course, it is inherent in contemporary two-person analytic procedure to carefully investigate all facets of the analytic interaction. Certainly, individuals who are more paranoid or narcissistic are more sensitive to like and dislike, and it is crucial to help them convey these observations to the analyst.

Gill's (1982) reemphasis of the significance of working in the transference merits note here and is offered in some contrast to those who recommend avoidance of transference dialogue with narcissistic patients. I say transference "dialogue" to distinguish from transference interpretation. In fact, if Gill is any example, most transference dialogue refers to observations of the patient by the analyst or invitations by the analyst to the patient to make observations about the analyst's participation. In working with patients who are highly sensitive to the analyst's subtle attitudes, it is especially significant that they be encouraged to articulate their perceptions about the analyst's involvement. This not only helps alert the analyst to affect that is out of awareness but also may counter patients' tendency to act out their response to insufficient attunement and related injury and anger. If, for example, narcissistic patients do not feel admired or feel actively disliked and say nothing about it, they may very well be inclined to terminate the analysis. If, however, analysands are repeatedly encouraged to be vocal about such perceptions, reactions to the analyst become much more a part of the analytic data and are less likely to lead to the flight or stagnation that silence will often precipitate. My experience, therefore, is contrary to those who find more fragile or narcissistically vulnerable patients unwilling to work in the transference. Like Gill (1982) and Searles (1979), I find that when I do *not* work in the transference with such patients, they are more likely to terminate or to remain unchanged. In fact, in line with Searles (1979) and Fromm-Reichmann (1959), I believe that the more severely disturbed the patient the more crucial it is to emphasize transference experience.

Case Examples

Mr. L is an economics professor and business consultant in his late forties. He has never been married and was raised in a lower middle class, Italian section of Brooklyn. His early ambition, sparked by his mother's desires, was to be a priest, and he attended Catholic school through college and got as far as the first year of seminary. He has four sisters, all married and housewives with children, and though he is in contact with each of them, Mr. L is not close to any. Until his middle college years, he shared a bedroom with two of his sisters. Mr. L's father was a barber and earned a better than middle-class income, but the family never moved from the ghetto-like neighborhood where they still reside in a two-bedroom, tenement apartment. The patient has always suspected that his father was a small-time operative within the criminal world and that his income did not entirely come from his shop. His father was and is a "macho," gruff, highly critical, and sarcastic man whose greatest pleasure is making others the butt of his jokes and his scorn. He is even this way with his grandchildren. His attitude toward his only son was taunting and mocking. Though he sent him to strict Catholic schools, his father himself was not religious and belittled his son for being a serious student, religious, unathletic, and awkward with girls. The father was quite strong and athletic and never shared this with Mr. L, who clearly belonged to his mother, for whom he was the apple of her eye. The patient's father was and still is extremely dependent upon his wife but does everything possible to disguise this. Mr. L's mother was also not especially religious but desperately wanted her only son to become a priest. She doted over him in every way from buying all his clothes through college to supplying him with *Playboy* magazine to satisfy his unrequited adolescent lust. The patient, through college, was a good boy in every way. He entirely obeyed his mother, kept away from girls despite being preoccupied with them, and was an outstanding student.

During his first year of seminary Mr. L "cracked-up," could not think or learn anymore, and had to drop out of school. Though he had to couch this change as an illness, in retrospect, this saved his life, for it gave him an excuse to leave home, travel, and do a variety of things he had always felt too disloyal to do. For a couple of years he "recuperated" by traveling around the country and Europe, both living and working in some places and having sexual experiences for the first time. When he returned to New York he started graduate school in his favorite academic area in college (economics) and earned his doctorate. He got a good faculty position because of some early publications, and his specific interest within economics made him desirable as a consultant to investment companies. He therefore has always earned a good living, but since he received tenure, has stopped publishing and tends not to pursue more potentially lucrative consulting positions, preferring to stay with older ties. He still ruminates that his true calling was the priesthood and that he is a failure for not being able to stay in the seminary. This is so despite a very lukewarm religious involvement. When he began therapy he claimed that he had never recovered from his "emotional breakdown" in the seminary and that he should have become a priest. This clearly helps him maintain a strong tie to his family.

Mr. L has led an active romantic life and in recent years has had a number of one- to three-year relationships with women who are very nurturant and who prize him as a potential husband. He has not been able to bear the idea of marriage and family, viewing it as stultifying and deadening, and when it comes to that level of commitment, he has always fled. When he began analysis with me he referred to his women as "fungible." They are all interchangeable, and he could get on well with any of them for a period, but to make a longer commitment was to lose the one great pleasure in life, sex. His stated aim was to have as active a sex life as possible, and he knew from experience that as soon as any relationship became too serious his sexual desire markedly waned.

He began analysis with me roughly three years ago after having had two other "analysts" who had retired. He had seen one for thirteen years and the other for ten, each once per week. He referred to them as analysts because they were quiet and nondirective, but he actually did not know if they were trained as such. I checked and found out that they were not. He sought further psychotherapy because he could not stop ruminating about his being a failure for not becoming a priest and he could not throw his whole self into his work. He ostensibly wanted to write in areas in which he had unique and extensive knowledge and wished to expand his consulting work to make it more interesting but had done neither for quite some time. He had no overt wish to change his pattern with women, to marry, or to have children. He desired a string of affairs with attractive women for as long as his sexual interests remained at high pitch. He was discontent, however, with a paucity of close male friendships.

Work with Mr. L has been unstintingly punishing. He has strongly identified with his father's brutal mocking, and there has hardly been a session when he has not condemned psychoanalysis in general, my particular incompetence, my failure to be helpful, my platitudes, my personal bankruptcy, etc. He unceasingly describes not being helped in his previous twenty-three years with his two other therapists and asserts how absurd he was to stay with them for so long and now to continue with me. He claims that he knows of no other alternative to deal with his constant unhappiness about not choosing the one calling where he really could do some good in this world, the priesthood. It sounds by now like an absurd obsession, but he holds to it.

It is obvious that Mr. L is profoundly tied to his family of origin, has identified with his father's sadistic way of relating to others, and is inextricably bound by dependency and guilt to his mother. He gives himself fully to no other women and does not allow himself to enjoy the profession he chose for himself based on his own intrinsic interests. Everything is a compromise; he has some involvement in love, some in work, and some in his analysis but most repeatedly demeans and diminishes each of the spheres. Women are interchangeable, work of no real value, and his analyst essentially a fraud. As with each of his women and the old firms for whom he still consults, he is as markedly dependent upon me as he was toward his two previous therapists. Yet, on a conscious level, he experiences no personal tie, connection, or affection whatever. I, like his women, am fungible. He is aware that if he gives himself more emotionally in any context, he will be as controlled and dominated as he was by his mother. He fears he will lose himself and his identification with his pseudo-strong father. He turns weakness into strength and is always on the offensive with me. He criticizes me for such insights being worthless and for not leading to change. His ties are either guilt or dependency based, and he hates himself for his dependency and hates me for his being dependent upon me, though he does not acknowledge the dependency as personal.

Though Mr. L lacks the extreme vanity and exhibitionistic characteristics of the prototype of a pure narcissist, his degree of self-involvement and his difficulty in making positive personal ties point to a decided narcissistic investment. One of the ways in which I have differed from his two previous therapists is in my considerable focus on transference experience. He rarely was overtly critical toward his two other therapists. I believe that something in their relationship to him helped him separate somewhat from his family and to make ambivalent involvement in love and in work. The process was very slow, particularly because it was once a week and, in part, because of the lack of immediacy present in transference work. Though Mr. L, based on his object ties, could easily be called narcissistic, my method of engaging him bares no essential difference from that with other patients who have made stronger personal ties in life or are less self-absorbed. I make no special effort to bolster his fragile self-esteem or to provide the warm paternal engagement he so sorely lacked as a child. As much as this was the case with his father, he was *too* admired by his mother. Sometimes narcissism comes from parental overinvolvement, the communication to the child of being too special or precious. His mother's involvement, as selfish as it was, has led him to feel rather confident with women and to expect to be the object both of their attraction and their eternal love. He does not feel compelled to give much in return. Indeed, he has been very able to achieve this with women who tend to find him quite appealing. In fact, I find him quite interesting and appealing in many ways and, despite his obsessional qualities, am rarely bored. Mr. L is very sensitive to any moments of withdrawal and will often accurately point out when my attention is flagging. Nonetheless, despite his self-absorption and consistently punishing ways, my involvement is almost always at a high pitch. This response may reflect my own unwitting maternal gratification toward him.

Much of what I consciously attempt to do with the patient is to draw parallels with me to his current and past relationships with other people and with his work. I am inclined to do this more or less with most of my patients regardless of how much narcissism is apparent. Mr. L often does accuse me of trying to make myself too central and reminds me unendingly that I am not important, that he feels nothing toward me, and that I could die tomorrow without his shedding a tear. If this were not also true for many others in his life, his women usually included, it would be difficult to bear for he is very vocal about this. I convey to him that he fears my being too important and thereby dominating and castrating like his mother, and he agrees but says, "so what." I point out that he is dependent on me as he is on his women and colleagues and hates me for this, and to that he says, "so cure me of this; it's only been twenty-six years." When he softens up at moments and then soon attacks again I note the sequence and how similar he is to his father with respect to softening-up and loving, and he attacks even more, reminding me once again how pathetic I am to use a word like *love* to describe his feeling toward me, a fee-for-service employee.

Though Mr. L does not acknowledge it, in the three years there has been progress. On an external level, he has found new companies that utilize his rather unique strengths, and the work has been more exciting and lucrative. He is still not publishing but has given a few oral papers that were very well received. Parenthetically, he has always been a highly rated teacher and liked by students, though he tries everything possible to get out of working with them on doctoral theses. The patient has had two experiences with women that he acknowledges as love. He is currently in a total obsessive quandary about whether to marry a woman who is threatening to leave if he does not. He claims not to be able to tell whether or not he really loves somebody or whether it is dependency and fear of losing that person. Though I think this is so, he is indeed showing more loving interaction than he has in prior times. He has recently said that he wishes to have at least one child of his own and no longer expresses the wish to spend the rest of his life in pursuit of numerous sexual experiences. Sometimes he says that in wanting a child he has succumbed to my values and it is not truly his. He also conveys that sex is not so central to him because of his desire for other forms of love and that this is a tragic loss for lust rather than a gain for intimacy. It is indeed possible that the patient has identified with what he views as my tame, sober, and asexual family life and that the therapeutic "movement" is a function of these identifications. My faith in repeated transference invitations leads me to think that this mitigates against such strong transference cure and that he is actually shifting from his attachment to the past and from his protective, narcissistic self-absorption and selfishness, to a new, albeit still quite ambivalent, stronger degree of engagement. It seems likely that his external changes reflect internal movement as well.

M is nineteen years old and began analysis when he dropped out of college less than one year ago. He is an only child and lives with his mother, who is of the "New Age" and works in a bookstore specializing in holistic medicine and nutrition. She comes from a wealthy family and is supported by a trust fund and by alimony from her two former husbands, the first of whom is M's father. M's father is a New York City physician who himself has been in analysis for issues related to passivity and depression.

The patient's parents were divorced when he was ten, and his mother moved with him and her new husband to Vermont. They lived a sort of wealthy hippie life, and M went to a good but very unstructured middle and high school. He had very little contact with his father, who was thwarted by M's apparent minimal interest in his phone calls and visits. M simply says that his stepfather was okay and he liked his friends and just felt no real interest in his father and avoided him as much as possible. He viewed his father as being too "right wing," and by this he means in favor of more rules, expectancies, structure, and standards. It is likely that M's father did not pursue his rejecting son with special fervor and was all too easily defeated. M reports being happy in Vermont and in the unstructured school, where little was demanded and where his creativity was nourished. His one complaint was related to being shy with girls. They seemed to like him, but he was always very awkward. His mother and stepfather divorced toward the end of high school, and when he started college at a good midwestern school, they moved back to New York City. However, he immediately missed the relaxed and laissez-faire atmosphere of Vermont and had great difficulty with the academic demands of this university.

He hung around school and befriended the more radical, drug-oriented crowd, but when exams or papers were due, he retreated. He also developed a problem with his potency and could not perform fully with a young woman at school. He clearly was not meeting scholastic requirements and left school on leave of absence and began analysis at his father's urging soon afterward.

M recognizes that he is bright (his SAT scores were very high) and yet has little ambition to even read or follow politics, both of which had been of strong interest at other times. He spends much of his time in bed watching TV or movies, staying up to the early morning, and sleeping much of the day. He has had few personal contacts since most of his friends are from Vermont. He is worried that his impotence will always prevent him from having girlfriends, and now, even when he masturbates, he fails to achieve full erection. He always experiences some vague sense of depression and pessimism about his life. He feels pressured by his father to get a job and/or take courses in preparation for returning to school full time but has resisted this pressure and continues to try to avoid his father as much as possible. He went to a urologist to try to determine if his impotence was physical but failed to go back for the conclusive tests, thus resting with the vague idea that he has a physical disability. His mother has directly conveyed to him that she is lonely and likes having him around. He often watches TV in her bed, sometimes with her there also. On some occasions they will sleep together in the same bed. Mother does not encourage him to take courses or to work and has made it indirectly clear that she opposes his analytic work with me. M fairly often misses sessions because he is sleepy or has a cold or just does not feel like coming, and his mother will call for him at times and make excuses. On one rainy day she forbade him to come and called to tell me that he was sick.

M relates to me much the way he does to his father. He views me as trying to wrestle him out of a passive, unstressful life in bed with his mother and is disappointed that I lack the accepting manner of the faculty at his high school. He is very bright and can be articulate, but he is often quiet and ethereal. He has some remarkable gaps in everyday knowledge such as not clearly knowing the sequence of the names of the month of the year. When he first came he also did not brush his teeth or shower very often, not recognizing that this was unusual. When I expressed surprise he began to brush his teeth and bathe more regularly. He readily acknowledges that he is living in his own world much of the time and that he holds back from telling me much of what is on his mind. When M started treatment he smoked marijuana daily but has since reduced this considerably. Nonetheless, he has a tired, stoned, disinterested manner much of the time. Periodically he will seem excited by something we address, but more often than not this will be followed by a missed session. He is never overtly angry with me but does not consciously convey attachment or affection. When with me he states or otherwise conveys that he would rather be back in bed or in Vermont. He does not ever speak of missing any of his friends in Vermont but longs for the atmosphere of acceptance and no demands. He actively does not express in words affectionate feelings for his mother either.

Certainly M can be seen as having strong narcissistic characteristics. He is profoundly self-absorbed and unrelated and again, though not particularly vain nor exhibitionistic, does view himself as very much the center of the world. He too suffers from extreme maternal overinvolvement, albeit also of a selfish maternal position. He expects people to come to him and has never had to reach out. He has also been injured by a father who has not had enough to do with him and whose depression and withdrawal he is in identification with. His poor personal hygiene and lack of awareness of some everyday facts of life contribute to suggesting that he could, with continued withdrawal and loyalty to his mother's desires, become frankly schizophrenic. Indeed, I believe without successful intervention he could one day wind up hospitalized. The extreme degree of narcissistic pathology, however, does not lead me to distinct modifications from normal technique. Though M has a poorly defined autonomous self, I make no conscious attempt at mirroring or becoming a selfobject. I do find him quite interesting and with great potential, and perhaps this is the unconscious mirroring that I convey. Though he lacks a sturdy masculine identification I make no conscious effort to have him identify with me. If he does, as with brushing his teeth and bathing, I examine it with him rather than silently encourage treatment as an identification process (Singer 1965). I have dealt with transference material from the outset, conveying to him his apparent lack of interest in me, his view of me as "right wing" like his father, his desire to get me to rescue him from his mother as his father has never done, what he may be conveying to me by missing sessions, etc. I have not provided the mirroring, unchallenging atmosphere that other analysts might. His narcissism is transference material that I actively point out and do not willingly try to gratify. I also try to identify when I fall into trying to mobilize him like his father or when I am enjoying his engagement with me like his mother. At times I fit into both patterns of interaction and try to address how the patient pulls me in and repeats with me his maternal and paternal integrations. I convey in words that I see aspects of will and of choice in his narcissistic withdrawal.

Aside from a few behavioral changes, a stronger recognition of the incestuous relationship he shares with his mother, and other broadened awareness, there is no clear change in his basic pattern of living to this point. The analysis is still young, and I believe that active interest and inquiry into his way of engaging in the here and now as well as outside has allowed a relevant connection to begin developing. To view him as suffering from a deficiency disorder would run the risk of repeating maternal overindulgence. It seems more productive to me to see him as actively identifying with his passive, depressed father and as fulfilling his mother's incestuous wishes at the price of his own autonomy. My multiple roles within this system need not be restricted to gratifications or promotions of compensatory selfobject ties. I do not think that he must be treated as fragile, nor would it be useful to adopt a position that would, in effect, throw cold water in his face to arouse him from his mother's bed. Trying to stay between these two extremes is often difficult, and his transference perceptions are useful in keeping me balanced.

I have fundamentally attempted to convey three things. One, narcissism, rather than a specific diagnosis, is a characteristic on a continuum. Second, it is a rather ubiquitous characteristic, to some degree or another, in individuals who might normally not be thought of as such. Finally, despite considerable current literature devoted to changes in analytic technique to accommodate extremely narcissistic individuals, it is not usually necessary to veer from one's normal analytic procedure provided that one pays close attention to the immediacy of the transference. I therefore disagree with those who have found individuals with strong narcissistic characters to be unavailable for the verbal aspect of analytic work and for work in the transference and in need of special technical innovations.

In these two case examples both analysands can be seen as possessing considerable narcissistic involvement. They are markedly self-absorbed and, at best, strikingly ambivalent in their relationships, when they have relationships at all. They share a history of overinvolved mothers who both inflated their importance and interfered with their developing autonomy and inner strength. They view themselves as special geniuses and, paradoxically, as weak and insubstantial at the core. They both have fathers with whom they identify considerably and who receded in contrast to their wives, leaving their sons with identifications with weakness and unrelatedness. They are both terrified of manifest attachment, love, and dependency, yet are profoundly dependent. Though these two individuals do not share all the characteristics of the *pure* narcissist discussed as a prototype in the literature, they have a number of such characteristics. It is possible that one can categorize them as having developmental deficits, particularly M, but no such formulation is necessary in order to work with them in an analytic frame.

In my participant observer or observing participant model, my aim is to actively inquire and to express curiosity and interest about the world of the analysand. The inclination is more toward questions and observations than it is toward interpretation. The latter implies more "knowing" than is often the case. In this role of inquirer and observer, I gradually and unwittingly become enmeshed as the weak father, the sarcastic father, the overly interested mother, my special and precious relationship with them, etc. When I am aware of the nature of the interaction it is usually immediately addressed. There is no effort to protect or nourish these individuals or to serve them in some compensatory manner. I always invite their transference observations of me and do not hold back my own observations about their characteristics as they appear in the transference. I do not offer myself as an object for identification by virtue of inquiring into whatever effort I see on their part to identify with me. I do not believe that I "hold" these individuals in a selfobject transference or always try to see things from their perspective. My own perspective in this two-person psychology is often clearly differentiated from the analysand's perspective. I do not view myself as especially cautious, though my aim is not to strip them of all their narcissistic illusions. In essence, though Mr. L and Mr. M may possess more narcissistic characteristics than the norm, I view this quality on a continuum and as requiring no special technique to address.

Finally, it may be evident from the description of these two analysands that I am considerably interested in them and that my engagement with them possesses more vitality than might be so with some other patients. They did serve as subjects for this essay. It can be said that work has proceeded with some success because of my interest and that my analytic perspective has little to do with anything. In that case I would be little but a good enough mother or a selfobject, despite my best efforts otherwise. Perhaps all patients, narcissistic or otherwise, change for the better based on the transference cure of love and admiration. I raise this possibility to underscore that the nonverbally expressed interest and involvement with the patient is always an issue and difficult to factor out of one's theory of therapeutic action (Fiscalini 1988). It is, therefore, necessary to proceed as an analyst in a way that best suits each analyst's theory and person, with the humble recognition that one can never be certain what confluence of interactions leads to the effects of the analytic enterprise.

References

Aron, L. 1990. One-person and two-person psychologies and the method of psychoanalysis. *Psychoanalytic Psychology* 7:475–85.

Bach, S. 1977. On the narcissistic state of consciousness. *International Journal of Psychoanalysis* 58:209–33.

Balint, M. 1968. *The Basic Fault.* London: Tavistock.

Barnett, J. 1971. Narcissism and dependency in the obsessional-hysteric marriage. *Family Process* 10:75–83.

——. 1983. Narcissism and dependency in the organization of personality. Unpublished paper presented at The Manhattan Institute for Psychoanalysis, New York, N.Y.

Becker, E. 1983. *The Denial of Death.* New York: Free Press.

Blechner, M. 1988. Differentiating empathy from therapeutic action. *Contemporary Psychoanalysis* 24:301–10.

Bromberg, P. 1983. The mirror and the mask: On narcissism and psychoanalytic growth. *Contemporary Psychoanalysis* 19:359–87.

——. 1989. Interpersonal psychoanalysis and self psychology: A clinical comparison. In D. Dietrick and S. Dietrick, eds., *Self Psychology: Comparisons and Contrasts.* Hillsdale, N.J.: Analytic Press.

Cooper, A. 1987. Changes in psychoanalytic ideas: Transference interpretation. *Journal of the American Psychoanalytic Association* 35:78–98.

Ehrenberg, D. 1974. The intimate edge in therapeutic relatedness. *Contemporary Psychoanalysis* 10:423–37.

Epstein L. and A. Feiner, eds. 1979. *Countertransference.* New York: Jason Aronson.

Fiscalini, J. 1988. Curative experience in the psychoanalytic relationship. *Contemporary Psychoanalysis* 24:125–42.

Fromm, E. 1964. *The Heart of Man.* New York: Harper & Row.

Fromm-Reichmann, F. 1959. *Psychoanalysis and Psychotherapy: Selected Papers,* D. Bullard, ed. Chicago: University of Chicago Press.

Ghent, E. 1989. Credo: The dialectics of one-person and two-person psychologies. *Contemporary Psychoanalysis* 25:169–211.

Gill, M. 1982. *The Analysis of Transference,* vol. 1. New York: International University Press.

——. 1983. The interpersonal paradigm and the degree of the therapist's involvement. *Contemporary Psychoanalysis* 19:200–37.

——. 1984. Psychoanalysis and psychotherapy: A revision. *International Review of Psycho-Analysis* 11:161–79.

Greenberg J. 1981. Prescription or description: The therapeutic action of psychoanalysis. *Contemporary Psychoanalysis* 17:239–57.

Greenberg, J. and S. Mitchell. 1983. *Object Relations in Psychoanalytic Theory*. Cambridge, Mass.: Harvard University Press.

Guntrip, H. 1968. *Schizoid Phenomena, Object Relations and the Self.* New York: International Universities Press.

Hirsch, I. 1983. Analytic intimacy and the restoration of nurturance. *American Journal of Psychoanalysis* 43:324–43.

——. 1984. Toward a more subjective view of analyzability. *American Journal of Psychoanalysis* 44:169–82.

——. 1987. Varying modes of analytic participation. *Journal of the American Academy of Psychoanalysis* 15:205–22.

Holt, R. 1976. Drive or wish? A reconsideration of the psychoanalytic theory of motivation. In M. Gill and D. Holzman, eds., *Psychological Issues.* Monograph 35. New York: International Universities Press.

Kohut, H. 1971. *The Analysis of the Self.* New York: International Universities Press.

——. 1984. *How Does Analysis Cure?* Chicago: University of Chicago Press.

Lasch, C. 1979. *The Culture of Narcissism.* New York: Norton.

Levenson, E. 1972. *The Fallacy of Understanding.* New York: Basic Books.

——. 1983. *The Ambiguity of Change.* New York: Basic Books.

——. 1989. Whatever happened to the cat? Interpersonal perspectives on the self. *Contemporary Psychoanalysis* 25:537–53.

Mitchell, S. 1986. The wings of Icarus: Illusion and the problem of narcissism. *Contemporary Psychoanalysis* 22:107–32.

——. 1988. *Relational Concepts in Psychoanalysis.* Cambridge, Mass.: Harvard University Press.

Rothstein, A. 1980. *The Narcissistic Pursuit of Perfection.* New York: International Universities Press.

Schafer, R. 1983. *The Analytic Attitude.* New York: Basic Books.

Searles, H. 1965. *Collected Papers on Schizophrenia and Related Subjects.* New York: International Universities Press.

——. 1979. *Countertransference and Related Subjects.* New York: International Universities Press.

Singer, E. 1965. Identity vs. identification: A thorny psychological issue. *Review of Existential Psychological Psychoanalysis* 2:160–75.

——. 1970. *Key Concepts in Psychotherapy.* New York: Basic Books.

Spence, D. 1982. *Narrative Truth and Historical Truth.* New York: Norton.

Stolorow, R. and F. Lachmann. 1980. *Psychoanalysis of Developmental Arrests*. New York: International Universities Press.

Sullivan, H.S. 1953. *The Interpersonal Theory of Psychiatry.* New York: Norton.

Thompson, C. 1950. *Psychoanalysis: Evolution and Development.* New York: Hermitage House.

Winnicott, D. 1965. *The Maturational Process and the Facilitating Environment.* New York: International Universities Press.

Wolstein, B. 1974. "I" process and "me" patterns. *Contemporary Psychoanalysis* 11:146–60.

15

The Psychoanalysis of Narcissism: An Interpersonal View

John Fiscalini

Narcissism and the Analyst's Concept of Inquiry

Sorting out the developmental origins and psychological meaning of a person's narcissism is often a difficult clinical task.[1] Each of us at any given moment represents a complex and singular integral of our shamed, spoiled, special, and self-respecting selves.[2] These aspects of ourselves are often simultaneously operative in myriad ways in any given set of experiences or behaviors. Thus it is seldom manifestly clear whether any particular instance of clinical narcissism primarily expresses or reflects the symbolic replay of dissociated egocentric and "grandiose" childhood needs or the defensive, pathological play of characterological narcissism, and if the latter, whether its roots lie in being indulged, infantilized, shamed, or exploited.

Only through the analyst's metapsychological openness—in the freedom to consider alternative or previously unthought or unknown understandings of the patient's and his or her own narcissism, does the analyst allow for the furthest possible analytic reach into the meaning of the patient's narcissism. Only in the analyst's recognition that each patient's narcissism, repressed or defensive, is not only complexly patterned but also uniquely configured and experienced can the analyst envision or imagine the possibility of a truly co-participant inquiry into the singularity, the specific and unique meaning and experience, of the patient's narcissism.[3]

The analyst need not, and in truth cannot, decide or determine the meaning of the patient's narcissistic behavior or experience before inquiry into it. The analyst can only come to it during the inquiry, co-found with the patient. In the freedom or self-permission to understand patients in their developing clinical life, rather than "know" them beforehand, analysts permit themselves to inquire with the patient into the patient's experience, not merely to inquire of the patient about the analyst's view of the patient. Only in this way is the analyst truly open and receptive to the patient and able to avoid, or at least minimize, procrustean understanding and indoctrination of the patient.

Rather than apply preset and universalist metapsychological blueprints or schemata—an a priori "knowing"—of the patient's clinical narcissism, in the authoritarian manner of many contemporary theorists on narcissism (e.g., Kohut, Kernberg, Masterson), analysts may come to a more truly individual interpretive fit of their patients by openly exploring with them, in a conjoint manner, the particular meaning of their narcissism, as it emerges or evolves in the psychoanalytic inquiry.

The inevitable ambiguity and complexity of much of what we, as analysts, daily confront is a source of enlivening challenge and wonder. But it is also the source of accompanying confusion, fear, and apprehension. And all too often it is the impetus for a defensive flight from freedom of experience and thought into the reassuring dogma of prescriptive metapsychology and methodology. It is a clinical irony that if analysts "know" what they are looking for and how they should do it, they learn only what they already know and nothing more. The opportunity for creation or discovery is lost, even if security is gained. Paradoxically, only when analysts do not "know" what they are looking for are they open to newness, to the singularity of the other, and to a full and unmeasured knowledge of that other's narcissism. The analyst need not preconceive the patient or the clinical process; each patient and his or her narcissism will, if allowed, emerge, fully singular, from open and coparticipant inquiry. To impose a preset interpretive schema on patients not only constricts our clinical understanding of the patients, and their narcissism, but also inevitably distorts it.

Narcissistic countertransference may not only emerge from interactive tensions within the analytic inquiry but may also be encoded in the very concept of that inquiry. Of course, each specific treatment perspective carries its own particular countertransference potential or tendency. For example, Kernberg's (1975a) recommended technique tends to carry a strong potential for countertransferential shaming of the patient, and Kohut's (1971, 1984) technique, a seductive potential for countertransferential spoiling. But more broadly, one's very philosophy or concept of inquiry may itself have a countertransferential structure. All aspects of the patient–analyst relationship are profoundly affected by the analyst's basic orientation to inquiry. I mean here not simply the specific presented theory of treatment but also the fundamental attitude the analyst has of the patient qua patient.

If analysts arrogate to themselves a position of metapsychological or methodological privilege or supremacy—i.e., assume superordinate responsibility and authority for the inquiry—then the coinquiring patient perforce is reduced to an analytic child upon whom analysts inevitably impose their preferred metapsychology and methodology. And no matter how benign the analysts, or how accurate their theory-derived interpretive understanding, the patient is infantilized, cut off from full participation in shared inquiry. Narcissism is countertransferentially recreated and reenacted in the analysis—the patient is once again defined by another, told who he or she is by the analyst. And whether the patient is defined as unmirrored Kohutian innocente, enraged Kernbergian insatiate, or undifferentiated Mahlerian symbiote matters little. For overriding such differences lies the inescapable fact that these analysts have cast the patient in the narcissistic image of their own theory.

This is not to deny the obvious contributions of such theorists but rather to critique their tendency to present their theories and techniques as though they were *the* way to understand narcissism and to treat it, not simply as some possible ways. Though they differ markedly in their specific theories and treatment of narcissism, Kernberg and Kohut share a similar authoritarian, and ultimately narcissistic, analytic attitude in which they presume to "know" what their patient's narcissism means and how one should treat it. All is foreordained, whether the call is for empathic mirroring or confrontative interpretation. For *prescriptive analysts,* with their superordinate–subordinate model of inquiry, both interpretation and technique are preset and prefigured.

This form of inquiry—whether it be Neoclassical, Ego-analytic, Self-psychological, Object-Relational, or Interpersonal-Relational in its metapsychology—is inevitably narcissistic: self-centered in its foreclosure of full coinquiry, grandiose in its arrogation of procedural and interpretive privilege, and disrespectful of unique individuality in its authoritarian definition of the patient. Such institutionalized narcissistic attitudes, when analyzed, may be seen to be rooted in the analyst's own unresolved defensive omniscience, strivings for omnipotence, or narcissistic imperviousness and inaccessibility to others.

My call here is for analytic humility. I submit that it would be far more helpful to the patient, and far less narcissistic of the analyst, to realize that there are many possible ways to proceed in the therapeutic inquiry. Analysts need not maintain, for example, that they must, or should, always mirror or allow idealizing, that this is the analytic way to be. Rather, it could be a way, at different times, with different patients, and for different reasons. Similarly, analysts need not insist that idealizing is always defensive and that an underlying contemptuous hostility must be immediately interpreted. This, too, could be a plausible understanding and a way to proceed at certain times with certain patients. Analysts, in other words, may permit themselves to consider the full range of therapeutic possibilities and meanings that emerge spontaneously in the analytic interaction with the patient. More anxiety may reside in this because one must make clinical choices and bear personal responsibility for error, without the narcissistically protective cover of prescribed clinical dogma. And thus one must stand alone, in full face to his or her human imperfections. But, by the same measure, one provides oneself the possibility of standing in full face to one's patients, truly open to their narcissism.

Coparticipant inquiry is premised on recognizing and respecting fully the patient's psychic resources and capability for analytic copartnership. Unlike the infantilizing, parentified analyst of authoritarian inquiry, the coparticipant analyst does not, as it were, shrink the adult in the patient to an analytic child. Patients are recognized for who they actually are—both regressive child and progressive adult, immature and mature, fixated and fixing. The coparticipant model of inquiry presents a countertransference risk that the analyst may *adultify* patients, expect of them more than they can cope with psychologically. The coparticipatory analyst must, of course, be alert to this danger, but in contrast to the authoritarian model of inquiry with its inbuilt narcissism, narcissism is built not into the coparticipatory concept of inquiry, but only in its abuse.

In sum, analysts' view of their participatory role may carry the seeds of countertransferential narcissism and the possibility of recreating old traumas for the patient. When this view is, however, respectful of both the child and the adult within the patient, it may provide the opportunity to create something new.

On the Interpersonal Relations Approach to Narcissism: The Clinical Centrality of the Interpersonal Self

Beyond analysts' interpretive metapsychology and guiding concept of inquiry is the question of how they specifically work with clinical narcissism as it emerges in the analytic process. Do analysts, for example, work differently with clinical narcissism if it is seen as an aspect of early childhood "narcissism" or as substitutive defensive narcissism? And in what ways? What defines analysts' view of therapeutic action, and how does this affect their analytic activity? What defines analysts' way of approaching and working with "narcissistic" transference and resistance, and countertransference and counterresistance? And how do Interpersonal-Relations analysts answer such questions; how do they work with problems of narcissism? Do Interpersonal analysts view narcissism as requiring a special technique or the application of basic principles of Interpersonal analytic technique?

It is, strictly speaking, inaccurate to think of a single or unitary Interpersonal approach to narcissism. The Interpersonal-Relations approach, rather, defines a variety of approaches, all sharing in common certain therapeutic principles and clinical emphases. Premised upon basic psychoanalytic principles of inquiry, the clinical approach of those analysts who consider themselves Interpersonal Relationists is characterized by a unique gestalt or set of therapeutic features.

The complexity and diversity of Interpersonal practice and of Interpersonal-Relations approaches to the treatment of narcissism derive from and are marked by a traditional emphasis on the clinical principles of: (1) therapeutic flexibility, (2) methodological and metapsychological pluralism, (3) analytic pragmatism, and (4) the field concept of participant observation. These clinical ideas or emphases form the foundation for a school of thought and clinical approach that is rich and complex and in some ways difficult to define.

The growing metapsychological and methodological complexity and heterogeneity within contemporary schools of psychoanalysis have made their differentiation an increasingly more difficult task. Differences among the schools are becoming increasingly blurred. This difficulty has been compounded by the considerable crossover of ideas and practices among the various schools of thought. This is particularly true of the Interpersonal-Relations school, which has played such a central, although often unacknowledged, role in the historically fateful *interpersonal turn* in psychoanalysis.

The uniqueness of the Interpersonal-Relations school has, in a sense, been obscured by its very success.

Nevertheless, certain family resemblances among the practitioners of each of the various schools of psychoanalysis broadly differentiate these schools and their clinical approaches. Although many of the clinical emphases of the Interpersonal-Relations school have been incorporated into mainstream psychoanalysis or have strongly influenced it, and though Interpersonal psychoanalysis is neither uniform nor unitary in its therapeutic approaches and tenets—it is, in fact, more pluralistic than most schools and houses a considerable diversity of clinical conceptions and practices—there are, nonetheless, some broadly defining features that, taken as a whole, uniquely mark this school's psychoanalytic approach. In brief outline, these are: (1) a broadly relational metapsychology, (2) an interactive conception of the intrapsychic or "inner life," (3) a clinical focus on the interpersonal and intersubjective field in the analytic situation, (4) a pluralistic sensibility, (5) a pragmatic orientation and philosophy, and (6) an operationist methodology that endeavors to hold theoretical constructs close to empirical observation.

Historically, Interpersonal-Relations theory developed as a metapsychological alternative to libido theory, and as an interpersonal—or "two-body"—clinical alternative to the impersonal technique of Classical—or "one-body"—analytic inquiry, with its quasi-scientific strictures of neutrality, objectivity, anonymity, etc. The Cultural–Interpersonal, or neo-Freudian, school pioneered by Sullivan, Fromm, Thompson, Horney, and Fromm-Reichmann, among others, advanced the then radical and revolutionary notion that humanity's psychic ills, including its sexual difficulties, sprang from disordered interpersonal or relational experience, rather than vice versa. Humanity's psychic problems were seen as psychosocial, rather than psychosexual. Along with British Object Relations theory and American Ego psychology, the American school of Interpersonal Relations has shared a general focus on the study of adaptation, defense, resistance, the self, reality, and character analysis. Unlike Object Relations and Ego theory, however, the American school broke completely from its ties with Freudian drive metapsychology. And unlike its relational cousins, it no longer retains, either in spirit or in language, its ties with orthodox Freudian theory. Although Interpersonal theory began as a metapsychological alternative to Freud's bioinstinctivism, and in this has made an important contribution to the development of psychoanalysis, perhaps its more enduring and pervasive, though less clearly noticeable—because so much of it has been incorporated in mainstream analysis—legacy lies in its contributions to the practice of psychoanalysis and the theory of analytic technique. In fact, the influence of the Interpersonal school on psychoanalytic technique has been so broad and so deep that its very success, as previously noted, has tended to preclude a full appreciation of its contributions. Many commonly held modern themes of freer and more active Neoclassical technique find their roots in the clinical and therapeutic conceptions of contemporary Interpersonalists and their precursors. This has been particularly true in the treatment of the severely disturbed neurotic, or "narcissistic personality," as well as that of the so-called borderline and the psychotic patient.

Because of its open-endedness, pluralism, and flexibility in technique, Interpersonal psychoanalysis, perhaps more than any other analytic school, is represented by a diversity of clinical thought and practice among its adherents. Although no uniform or unitary theory of Interpersonal therapy exists, and though each Interpersonalist is highly individual in his or her clinical approach, most Interpersonalists may be seen to fit, if only approximately, into one of four categories: the *traditional Interpersonalists* or *classical Sullivanians,* those whose approach to treatment follows Sullivan's focus on the "detailed inquiry" and whose field focus is on the nature of how the interactive analytic dimension affects the patient's narrative report; the *radical preservationists,* those who, like Sullivan, focus clinically on the interpersonal self but have extended Sullivan's participant–observer model with a new emphasis on the here-and-now transference–countertransference interaction or transaction as co-created participation, and whose epistemology is more relativistic than that of classical Interpersonalism; the *radical empiricists* or *experientialists,* who, like the radical preservationists, focus on the intersubjectively co-created transference–countertransference phenomena but have expanded upon Sullivanian metapsychology, the dominant Interpersonal theory, with organismic, humanistic, and existential ideas and sensibilities, and who bring a clinical focus on immediate experience and on the intrapersonal—or what Wolstein (1983) calls the first personal and I have referred to as the personal self (Fiscalini 1990a, 1991a)—to the analytic situation; and the *eclectic synthecists,* or *relationists,* those Interpersonalists who have attempted to build theoretical and clinical bridges between Ego psychology, Object Relations theory, Self psychology, and traditional and modern Interpersonal theory, attempting to synthesize or integrate these cognate approaches (see, for example, the work of Mitchell 1988 and Greenberg and Mitchell 1983).

Despite their many differences, large and small, all Interpersonal analysts share, first, a common clinical emphasis on the interpersonal self and on the field properties of the analytic situation. This was originally framed in terms of Sullivan's concept of participant observation and has been expanded more recently in such ideas as Wolstein's (1959, 1977b) post-Sullivanian field concept of coparticipation or Levenson's (1972, 1981) notion of the transformable analyst. All Interpersonalists, though they apply the field principle in many different and individual ways, are alike in that they emphasize the transactive, interactive, and intersubjective nature of the analytic process. This conception of the analytic situation now informs mainstream psychoanalysis in many ways, and so it may seem to many as neither uniquely Interpersonal nor as radical a concept as it, in fact, was when first advanced.

The conception of the analytic process as a two-way field of participant or coparticipant observation has been elaborated, in contemporary Interpersonal psychoanalysis, into a clinical approach in which transference and countertransference phenomena are seen as co-created by patient and analyst. Modern Interpersonal analysts, particularly the radical preservationists and the radical empiricists, view the analytic situation as an interpersonal field in which transference is shaped partly by countertransference and revealed in it, and, reciprocally, countertransference is partly shaped by and revealed in the transference. In this Interpersonal view, patient and analyst are thus seen as constantly influencing one another. In other words, the various aspects of the transference–countertransference continuum are seen as mutually created by both analytic participants, rather than as exclusively endogenous phenomena. A major technical implication of this view is that

> understanding of the patient's personality inevitably involves an understanding of the analyst's personality. Countertransference analysis becomes an integral aspect of transference analysis. The interpersonal analyst focuses variably on both the patient's and his or her own experience of their analytic relatedness, *and invites the patient to do the same.* This forms the interpersonal path to the understanding of the patient's unconscious problems in living [including his or her narcissism]. . . . In the interpersonal view, each analytic dyad is seen as generating its own interpersonally unique transference–countertransference matrix. . . . From this point-of-view, a monadic, and non-interactive, approach to transference, even if relational in metapsychology, inevitably limits, and often distorts, the analyst's understanding of the patient and him- or herself. (Fiscalini 1990b: 10–11)

Analysts, in the Interpersonal analysis of narcissism, constantly monitor how they may be playing out, in countertransference reciprocity, the shaming, spoiling, or exploiting parent to the patient's narcissistic analytic transference child, or, conversely, the needful or demanding, self-centered countertransferential analytic child to the patient's harsh and unempathic, or infantilizing and exploitative, transference parent. The focus is, of course, on the interactional properties of the narcissistic transference–countertransference. The analyst does not simply focus on what the patient is trying, or seems to be trying, to do, but more importantly, on what interaction is being sought out, or replayed, and how that is related to the analyst's narcissistic tendencies, both as enactive and interactive countertransferential parent and countertransferential child. The conjoint analysis of countertransference is critical in working with narcissistic patients, particularly since the anxieties, conflicts, and defenses of these patients characteristically provoke powerful, and often disruptive or disjunctive, countertransference experiences and processes in the analytic interpersonal field.

Second, when compared with analysts of other contemporary analytic approaches, Interpersonal Relationists are, in general, characterized by a more active use of themselves in their treatment of narcissism. This is evidenced in: (1) the use of more directive and specific questioning, instead of an exclusive reliance on free-associational methodology; (2) a greater technical freedom to reveal one's own thoughts and feelings, and greater self-disclosure in general. Interpersonalists, in contrast to most other contemporary analysts, are generally less concerned with assuming an analytic stance of neutrality, particularly in terms of the principle of anonymity or the blank screen, or a notion of a value-free analyst (cf. Protter 1988), and Interpersonalists tend to make (3) more active therapeutic use of countertransference, including freer expressive use of such analytic experience.

A third feature of the Interpersonal approach to narcissism is its general deemphasis on regressive technique. Interpersonal-Relations analysts, by and large, eschew the concept of technically inducing a regression to a transference neurosis, whether this is seen in narcissistic or other (e.g., oedipal) terms. Most Interpersonalists believe that "regressive" aspects of the patient's narcissism will spontaneously emerge, even in an active and interactive analytic encounter. In my own clinical experience, I have found that patients' unconscious shamed selves, their persisting unmirrored or disapproved egocentric and naively "grandiose" childhood yearnings, emerge transactionally in the transference from the very beginning of treatment. And patients' transference resistances, the various aspects of their defensive substitutive narcissism and narcissistically distorted self-personifications—in other words, their spoiled and special (and implicit aspects of their shamed) selves, also appear from the very start of analysis.

A fourth general characteristics of the Interpersonal-Relations approach to treatment is its acceptance of the curative role of the "real relationship." Many Interpersonal analysts, implicitly or explicitly, assign an important therapeutic role to the analytic formation of new interpersonal experience, particularly in the psychoanalytic treatment of more severely disturbed, and less verbally accessible, patients, such as the more severely narcissistic or borderline person (Fiscalini 1988, 1991b).

All Interpersonalists are characterized, fifthly, by the importance they ascribe to the role of reality in the historical formation and analytic transformation of narcissism, or character in general. This emphasis on reality, for many Interpersonalists, is joined, however, with a perspectivistic emphasis and relativisitic epistemology (cf. Protter 1985)—a stance that dictates neither that the analyst's "truth" must rule, nor, as Kohut (1984) would have it, that the patient's subjective "truth" must rule.

Reflecting its characteristic pragmatism, pluralism, and perspectivism, the contemporary Interpersonal approach to narcissism is characterized, lastly, by therapeutic open-endedness and flexibility of method. Interpersonal analysts tend to adopt a methodological pluralism, deeply convinced that many ways are available to approach the analysis of narcissistic patients or processes, not just one right way.

Although Interpersonal Relationists are typified in their work with narcissism by the characteristics that I have just outlined, each Interpersonal analyst expresses these in uniquely individual ways in the clinical situation. Interpersonal analysts are highly individual, as diverse as they are similar. Also, no one single characteristic of this clinical gestalt, identified here as typically Interpersonal, can, by itself, unequivocally identify an analyst as such, for any such characteristic may typify an analyst of another school. As previously noted, the Interpersonal school has been highly influential in the broader field of analytic therapy, thus contributing to the use of its characteristic principles and methods in all of psychoanalysis. Moreover, other schools, themselves, have undergone similar, or cognate, developments in their clinical theories. Nevertheless, this brief outline of Interpersonal inquiry shows it to stand in sharp contrast to Neoclassical Freudian orthodox technique with its emphasis on the blank-screen analyst: the anonymous, silent, "neutral," and non-self-disclosing "opaque mirror" (cf. Menninger 1958; Greenson 1967; Brenner 1976). Although Neoclassical technique has, over the years, grown considerably freer, epistemologically more relativisitic and constructivist, and more "interpersonal" and "human" in technique, it nonetheless still represents a highly conservative, strongly prescriptive, and decidedly reserved analytic posture. This clinical approach stands in sharp contrast to the far more active, flexible, and field-oriented Interpersonal-Relations approach. Many Object Relations and Ego-psychological theorists advocate and practice freer, more liberal versions of orthodox analytic technique and are closer to the Interpersonal-Relations position, but for the most part, they, too, fall short of the more active analytic stance and radical field orientation that is advocated by the American school of Interpersonal psychoanalysis. This, I think, is particularly true for work with the narcissist.

Interpersonal psychoanalysis has, from its very beginnings, placed issues of narcissism, in both the broad and narrow sense, at the very heart of its therapeutic effort. The interpersonal self, or the psychic dimension of interpersonal security, has always been a central focus of Interpersonal therapeutic work. The analytic vicissitudes of the self-personification or self-representation (of both patient and analyst) have traditionally been located at the very center of Interpersonal inquiry, as has the analytic play of such central defensive narcissistic processes as grandiosity, idealization, devaluation, alienation, symbiotic dependency, and psychic inaccessibility.

Interpersonal-Relations theory is uniquely characterized by its conception of anxiety, or insecurity, as an inherently social or interpersonal process. And the therapeutic pursuit of its analytic course forms the backbone of Interpersonal psychoanalytic work. All Interpersonal analysts, however they may differ, are characterized by their common effort to sensitively monitor this field process, in its various forms, as it occurs, not only in the patient, but in themselves as well. In fact, Sullivan's *The Psychiatric Interview* (1954), the essential technical primer for all Interpersonal analysts, is, in many ways, a text on the sensitive analytic management and understanding of the patient's anxious self (i.e., his or her "narcissistic" vulnerabilities) and concomitant security operations.

In this focus on the interpersonal self, Interpersonalists find much in common with Kohutian Self psychology, which also focuses on the vicissitudes of the reflected, or interpersonal, self. The Self-psychological approach, however, focuses exclusively on psychic reality and on a Rogerianlike emphasis on the "empathic" or client-centered (Rogers 1951) tracking of subjectively structured experience. Interpersonalists, in contrast, are more inclusive in their detailed inquiry into the interplay of psychic and material "reality" and in their openness to interventions that challenge or question the psychic reality of the patient. Interpersonal analysts, like Self psychologists, recognize that narcissistic patients are limited in their ability to tolerate any challenge to their subjective perspective and defensive narcissism, and Interpersonalists recognize that psychoanalytic work with such patients requires patient and painstaking attention to their narcissistic anxieties. Interpersonal-Relations analysts are also mindful of these patients' analytic need for long periods of "empathic" siding with their narcissistic defenses. Interpersonalists differ from Self psychologists, however, in their conviction that active and timely confrontation and interpretation of patients' narcissistic perspectives is essential to analytic growth. Of course, such an active approach, to be successful, demands considerable analytic flexibility, openness, and resourcefulness on the part of the analyst.

Although Interpersonalists have not developed an extensive clinical literature explicitly on narcissism and its treatment, Interpersonal analysts, from the start, have always worked with problems of narcissism and with those patients who are among the most "narcissistically" disturbed. In fact, it was the early Interpersonalist Relationists—most notably Sullivan and Fromm-Reichmann—who first worked successfully with the so-called narcissistic neuroses that Freud deemed unanalyzable. Premised on a relational and self psychology, Interpersonal theory has never found it necessary either to develop techniques special to working with narcissism—since there are built into the very fabric of interpersonal work—nor to regard narcissistic patients as qualitatively different, essentially unlike other forms of neurosis or psychic disturbance. To the contrary, all patients are seen as having a narcissistic core. Though narcissistic dynamics may be predominant or more severe in some patients—those whom we tend to call narcissistic personality disorders—such dynamics are seen to characterize all patients to some degree or other. Thus, Interpersonalists have generally applied their basic principles of treatment (cf. Fromm-Reichmann 1950; Thompson 1950; Sullivan 1940, 1954; Singer 1965; Levenson 1972, 1981; Witenberg 1973; Held-Weiss 1984; and Wolstein 1959, 1977a, 1977b, 1985 for a representative sampling of some traditional, preservationist, and empiricist statements of Interpersonal psychoanalytic technique) to their work with narcissistic problems or personalities, adapting them, of course, to the therapeutic needs and dynamic configurations of these particular forms of psychic disturbance. Thus, in a sense, there is but one, though infinitely flexible and individually practiced, Interpersonal technique, which is variably applicable to all forms of psychic disorder, including narcissism.

Self-disorder, rather than drive disorder, has always been the chief therapeutic variable in Interpersonal psychoanalytic treatment. Interpersonalists, with the exception of Fromm (1964), have not traditionally thought in terms of a diagnostic category of narcissistic personality disorder, though they have worked extensively with both the milder and more severe forms of clinical narcissism. Thus, they have not sought to create a special literature on narcissism, as have Kohutian Self psychologists, or to write specifically about clinical work with so-called narcissistic personalities. Rather, Interpersonal-Relations analysts have addressed these clinical features in the context of other, more traditional, diagnoses.

Nevertheless, in recent years, under the impact of the growing psychoanalytic popularity of this rubric, some Interpersonal analysts have begun to write in the language of narcissism and to speak of narcissistic personalities. Largely in response to the diagnostic popularity of the concept of narcissistic personality within mainstream psychoanalysis, some Interpersonal writers have begun to detail their particular Interpersonal approaches to the treatment of such narcissistic dynamics as idealization (Field 1987; Ortmeyer 1987), grandiosity (Tenzer 1987), symbiosis (Feiner 1983), and entitlement (Blechner 1987; Grey 1987; Spiegel 1987). And some Interpersonal writers have attempted to integrate their Interpersonal therapeutic sensibilities with Object-Relational and Ego-psychological concepts in their understanding and treatment of narcissistic and borderline personalities and processes (see, for example, the work of Bromberg 1979, 1983; Epstein 1979, 1981; and Mitchell 1986, 1988).[4]

Traditional Freudian psychoanalysis—with its concept of the analyst as the neutral, ungratifying, impersonal interpretive surgeon—has premised its stringent and austere therapeutic procedure on the presumed treatment abilities and requirements of the so-called oedipal patient, a presumably healthier and developmentally more advanced patient than the narcissist or borderline character. These patients are seen as having a primary self-disorder, whereas the oedipal patient is seen as primarily drive disordered. Traditionally, "narcissistic" patients, with their self-problems, have been seen as requiring parametric or modified forms of psychoanalysis—not *real* psychoanalysis, but "psychotherapeutic" variants of the real thing. Thus, there is a two-tiered system: psychoanalysis for Oedipus; psychoanalytic psychotherapy for Narcissus. Analytic orthodoxy has thus divided psychic pathology into two types: self and drive. This bifurcation of patients into those with so-called developmentally arrested self-disorders and those with psychically conflicted drive problems is, however, a spurious dichotomy, one that springs from the theoretical need to graft a self psychology onto an outmoded libidinal metapsychology. Interpersonal theory, with its inbuilt self and relational metapsychology, does not require such a theoretically cumbersome and empirically inaccurate division.

Until recently, the orthodox Freudian clinical literature, with its focus on the clinical methods and problems of treating Oedipus, produced relatively few papers on the treatment of narcissistic personalities or problems. In the past two decades, however, a veritable explosion of articles on the treatment of narcissism has occurred, from a variety of contemporary post-Freudian perspectives. It has become a vast literature. Chessick (1977, 1985), Gedo (1981), Giovacchini (1979), Guntrip (1969, 1971), Horner (1979), Kernberg (1975a, 1975b), Kohut (1971, 1977, 1979, 1984), Kohut and Wolf (1978), Masterson (1981, 1988), Miller (1981), Modell (1975), and Rinsley (1982) represent but a few of the more widely known analysts associated with a broadly Ego-psychological/Object-Relational/Self-psychological postclassical study and treatment of clinical narcissism (cf. Chessick 1977, 1985; Giovacchini 1979; Hedges 1983; and Morrison 1986 for comparative summaries of some of these approaches). All these approaches, each in its own individual way, adopt and adapt basic Freudian treatment principles, a Mahlerian–Jacobsonian symbiosis-to-separation developmental theory (or something similar), and a broadening and general loosening of strict orthodox technique to accommodate the specific treatment needs and psychic vulnerabilities of "narcissistic" personalities.

A review of these various approaches extends beyond the intent of this essay. I shall briefly consider, however, the ideas and work of Kohut and Kernberg. These two theorists arguably have been the most, or certainly among the most, influential contemporary Freudian theorists on narcissism. Their different clinical perspectives and contrasting therapeutic sensibilities in many ways represent central controversies in the understanding and treatment of narcissistic personalities and problems. Moreover, both Kernberg and Kohut have clinical approaches to narcissism that are, in many ways, compatible with the Interpersonal approach. Kohut, in particular, shows an Interpersonal bent in his clinical conceptualizations, although his technical recommendations, like those of Kernberg, remain, for the most part, truer to the Neoclassical Freudian tradition.

Kohut's Contribution: The Interpersonal Self in Freudian Psychoanalysis

Kohut's major contribution to psychoanalysis lies in his having provided Freudian orthodoxy the theoretical means for working analytically with patients or aspects of personality previously thought unanalyzable. Traditionally, Freudian analysts had considered only patients who could form a stable oedipal "transference neurosis" as capable of being analytically engaged; all others were considered unanalyzable. And not infrequently, "narcissistic" patients with marked self-esteem vulnerability were misidentified as oedipal patients with unresolvable narcissistic resistances. Kohut, in his formulation of the "mirroring" and "idealizing" transferences, expanded Freudian metapsychology to include the interpersonal self, and thereby legitimized Neoclassical analytic work with problems of narcissism and the self. Kohut interpersonalized Freudian metapsychology but not its methodology. His achievement lay, not in a radical or revolutionary restructuring of psychoanalytic technique, but rather in a broadening of its interpretive range—in the theoretical delineation of what to mainstream psychoanalysis were new clinical phenomena, the narcissistic or selfobject transferences.

Kohut, in his formulation of the selfobject transferences, called orthodox attention to the inevitably interpersonal nature of all transferences. Selfobject relatedness, as conceptualized by Kohut, refers to that psychic dimension that Sullivan called the need for interpersonal security, or what I call the domain of the interpersonal self—the innate human need for interpersonal approval, validation, or esteem. Kohut's selfobject, essentially, is Sullivan's reflecting appraiser—the interpersonal arbiter of the representational, or reflected, self.[5] Thus, broadly conceived, selfobject transferences represent not a special kind of transference characteristic of only certain patients, as is often thought, but rather a central, interpersonal, dimension of all transference structures. Selfobject needs, in other words, form an integral interpsychic aspect of all transferences. These selfobject needs may, however, differ in their specific content and nature, ranging from archaic security requirements of a more primitive narcissistic nature to more mature forms of the need for interpersonal security. In other words, the selfobject, or interpersonal self, dimension of transference experience, like its other dimensions—those of the personal, relational, or physical selves—exists on a developmental continuum.

In his concepts of the "mirroring," "idealizing," and "twinning" transferences, the selfobject transferences as narrowly conceived, Kohut called orthodox attention to the frequently archaic nature of parataxic (i.e., transferential) interpersonal relationships. These primitive "selfobject" transferences represent the repetition of early narcissistic aspects of the "not-me" self-personification and are born in traumatic (anxious) interpersonal experiences of early (and often nonspecific) needs for relational intimacy, personal fulfillment, or physical satisfaction. In the analytic situation, these unrequited "narcissistic" needs are symbolized and enacted in transferential bids for analytic approval in primitive mirroring and idealizing terms. These narcissistic transference paradigms do not differ in outline, just in dynamic and developmental detail, from other more "mature" ones, such as, for example, the classical oedipal transference. Like any other transference paradigm, they reflect arrested and dissociated personal and interpersonal experience that clinically presents itself as an organized structure of unconscious need, anxiety, and defense.

Interpersonal psychoanalysis, from its very beginnings a theory of the self and its interpersonal (or object and selfobject) relations, found it unnecessary to "discover" the narcissistic transferences for the analytic study of self-problems. Traditionally viewing all neurosis as self-disorder, Interpersonal Relationists did not find it necessary to distinguish two discontinuous sets of clinical transferences: oedipal for drive disorder and "narcissistic" for self-disorder. And repudiating narrow orthodox definitions of the psychoanalytic situation, Interpersonal psychoanalysts have considered all neuroses—"narcissistic" or otherwise—as capable of being worked with analytically. Though in recent years, contemporary Self psychologists have broadened their understanding of self-disorder and have come to view all transferences as selfobject transferences, the spectrum of self psychopathology is generally viewed by Interpersonalists in broader, and more inclusive, terms than those of Self psychologists. In Interpersonal-Relations theory, self-disorder is not simply delimited, as it sometimes is by Self psychologists, to problems of archaic or defensive grandiosity or idealization, although these problems are considered important, ubiquitous, and of paramount significance for some patients.

Though Kohut's work on the self and narcissism was preceded, in far more radical ways, by that of the Interpersonalists, his influence on contemporary Freudian conceptions of self psychopathology has been pervasive. In contrast to the radical heterodoxy of the Interpersonal-Relations theorists,

Kohut's work, in both language and sensibility, was set firmly within the Freudian tradition. Thus, framed in this familiar idiom, Kohut's ideas on narcissism and the interpersonal self found a ready audience among contemporary mainstream analysts. Kohut's ideas, unlike those of the Interpersonal Relationists, were, in other words, politically (i.e., metapsychologically) acceptable, and they could be housed, even if uncomfortably, within contemporary Freudian thought and practice.

Kohut's contribution was not, however, simply a political one. Though he was neither the first nor the most searching analytic theorist of the interpersonal self, Kohut did make a significant contribution to the further understanding of this aspect of the human psyche. In his emphasis upon and attention to the "narcissistic" aspects of self-disorder, to the idealized and idealizing nature of the archaic interpersonal self, and to the role of empathy in its treatment, Kohut focused analytic attention on these central human problems and processes and expanded our understanding of the primitive aspects of that broad and vital dimension of human relatedness that Sullivan had called the pursuit of interpersonal security. Though Sullivan had extensively studied this psychic domain much earlier, Kohut helped to map its archaic features. He detailed the egocentric and grandiose nature of the early interpersonal self and catalogued some of its analytic vicissitudes in the selfobject transferences and countertransferences.

Though the interpersonal self, or selfobject relatedness, forms an integral aspect of all transference configurations, it is clinically most apparent in its more primitive forms. In fact, in the more primitive "narcissistic" selfobject transferences described by Kohut, this aspect of the transference dominates the clinical picture. Patients, in these instances, are so needful of approval, and in such developmentally archaic ways, that it both rules and defines their analytic participation. Kohut's contribution to psychoanalytic thought and practice rests upon his detailed study and delineation of these primitive transferences, aspects of which characterize all patients to some extent. In his studies of narcissism, Kohut broadened our analytic understanding of early problems in reflected interpersonal appraisals and of how they may cripple subsequent living among others. As a clinician, Kohut was keenly sensitive to the extreme self-esteem vulnerability—the marked sensitivity to psychic hurt—of his "narcissistic" patients, and he recognized that an empathic hearing of their characterological narcissism was crucial to the analysis of their repressed and injured interpersonal selves.

Kohut's and Kernberg's Clinical Approaches: An Interpersonal Appraisal

Kohut expanded the interpretive range of mainstream clinical psychoanalysis and broadened its concept of therapeutic action, but he did not seriously challenge or deviate from generally accepted principles and procedures of clinical analytic orthodoxy. He remained, in this sense, a Neoclassical Freudian. Nevertheless, Kohut's Self-psychological approach to narcissism carries a distinctive clinical stamp—an analytic stance or listening perspective that places a radical emphasis on analysts' adopting an "empathic" position, technically enjoining them to, at all times, stay with, or attempt to stay with, the patient's subjectivity (which for many Kohutians reduces to some variant of "idealizing," "mirroring," or "twinning" relatedness).

Kohut's major clinical concern and technical focus was to foster the full development, emergence, and eventual interpretive resolution—via analytic insight—of the narcissistic mirroring, twinning, and idealizing transferences. Kohut believed that vigorous or systematic interpretation of the clinically manifest defensive narcissism would interfere with or handicap the emergence of the patient's repressed childhood narcissism, the dissociated aspects, in other words, of the shamed, spoiled, and special child. Kohut's clinical focus was on patients' shame, loathing, and anxiety about their unconscious or preconscious childhood needs for mirroring and idealizing and on the ease with which, in his opinion, such dissociated transference wishes could be submerged or driven underground again, once emergent. Thus, naturally enough, his whole technique was centered around the importance of fostering the clinical emergence of these brittle, easily shamed and frightened off, transferences. Thus, Kohut technically cautioned against the interpretation of narcissistic defenses, advising the analyst to support, instead, the gradual emergence of the narcissistic transferences by the consistent maintenance of an "empathic" connection to the unconscious or dissociated mirroring and idealizing longings—the unmet and unresolved childhood egocentricity and naive grandiosity—embedded in or lying underneath the manifest clinical narcissism.

According to Kohut, the analyst, by empathically understanding and accepting the patient's buried "narcissistic" longings, promotes their full analytic emergence. To do otherwise, in Kohut's opinion, would be to truncate or twist the development of these transferences. The analyst, in this view, accepts the transferential mirroring, twinning, and idealizing longings of the patient until they are fully mobilized and ready for interpretation—ready, in other words, for optimal analytic disillusionment. The clinical task, as Kohut saw it, is to maintain the requisite empathic contact with the buried, unconscious "narcissistic" aspects of patients' early loving, depending, asserting, or individuating needs in order to facilitate their full emergence and their optimal disillusionment via interpretive insight, instead of being prematurely disillusioned or protractedly illusioned. The main effort is to avoid traumatizing the fragile persisting "narcissistic" longings. Kohut believed that any attention to the social or personal inappropriateness, i.e., immaturity or irrationality, of defensive narcissism or persisting childhood "narcissistic" longings, including any moralizing about them, would be therapeutically counterproductive. Thus, Kohut favored an analytic acceptance of the patient's pathological narcissistic defenses until such time as the underlying childhood narcissism can emerge fully, be interpreted, and eventually worked through. Presumably, the defenses, no longer necessary, would then wither away.

Kohut acknowledged the impossibility of the analyst's maintaining constant empathic contact with the patient's narcissism. Kohut maintained, in fact, that lapses in empathy actually provide the opportunity for psychic growth via what he referred to as transmuting internalizations. In this process, disruptions in empathy, once reestablished, are explained and interpreted in all their aspects, particularly their transference genetics. According to Kohut, when misempathy is rescued by resumed empathy and acknowledgment of the previous "empathic failure"—the lapse in empathic understanding of the narcissistic need—patients experience a resumption of the empathic analytic connection, and they are also able, when the lapse is psychically digestible (i.e., not too traumatizing), to take in the perspective of the analyst, and in this way gradually alter their narcissism. This process is thought to mimic the "normal" developmental process of optimal disillusionment. For Kohut, this process and that of interpretive insight form the two means by which analytic self-transformation is brought about.

The striking feature of this approach lies, of course, not in its innovative changes in psychoanalytic procedure, but in its listening perspective—in its openness to "narcissistic" themes, and in its prescriptive order that the analyst should strive, at all times, to see things from the patient's subjective or narcissistic perspective.

The Kohutian (and post-Kohutian) Self-psychological approach to the understanding and treatment of narcissism has gained wide popularity and has influenced the clinical approaches of many psychoanalytic practitioners. Its strong impact upon psychoanalytic thought and practice has, however, been primarily among mainstream analysts. Self psychology has had less impact on British Object-Relations and American Interpersonal-Relations theorists and practitioners who had already developed central notions of the interpersonal self and its treatment. The popularity of the Self-psychological approach, thus, springs most centrally from its impact on mainstream analytic consciousness—as noted previously, it brings the study of the interpersonal self within the purview of Freudian psychoanalysis.

The great popularity of Self psychology is also grounded in the allure of its reductive simplicity. Self psychology, particularly when understood in naive terms, seems to provide a simple diagnostic and therapeutic blueprint—all narcissistic patients suffer from one of two universal narcissistic structures, either a mirroring or idealizing transference (or some variant); this is what must be identified, and from this diagnostic formulation, all other understanding derives—very neat and simple, and as reductionistic as the orthodox application of the Oedipus template to all pathology and psychology. When understood in more sophisticated terms, however, the idealizing, mirroring, or twinning transferences can be seen to refer to highly complex sets of clinical phenomena whose treatment cannot be reduced to some simple formula or easy-to-use rulebook.

Just as Self-psychological metapsychology tends to be seen in highly simplistic ways, so, too, does Self psychology, particularly when applied in unsophisticated ways, tend to offer the illusory promise of a simple therapeutic manual. In such formulations, the analyst has a clearly defined and prescribed role and only one, and in a sense simple, job to do—empathize with the idealizing or mirroring transference. From this, all else flows and follows. This therapeutic perspective offers an illusory notion of a simple and uncomplicated analytic technique. But again, as with the metapsychology of narcissism, things are never so simple.

Self psychology, in its therapeutic outlook, also tends to hold out a seductive promise that psychological growth, the psychoanalytic process, and even life itself can, somehow, be painless. Self psychology is often clinically applied in ways that countertransferentially reinforce patients' narcissistic demands or transference fantasies of an interpersonal nirvana—a euphoric life without conflict, guilt, regret, loneliness, or loss. In sum, Kohutian Self psychology, as practiced by many of its adherents, tends to falsely promise a mythic analytic paradise—an anxiety-free therapy.

Self psychology holds a special attraction for many, particularly unsophisticated, therapists who unconsciously cling to the passive, narcissistic belief that their patients, and by implication they themselves, can be transformed by the symbiotic sensitivity and "empathy" of a perfect, all-loving other—and thus avoid the painful conflict, uncertainty, and effort that is, in fact, inevitable in psychic growth and self-transformation. Such passive expectations or hopes of a narcissistic cure find a theoretical rationale in Kohut's overly interpersonalized account of the human psyche. Like Sullivan, Kohut, in his focus on the interpersonal self, or selfobject relations, neglects the domain of the personal self, the psychic dimension of selfsubject relations—of, for example, will, intentionality, unique individuality, personal agency, responsibility, and self-generative activity. Kohut's Self psychology, in other words, is concerned with the reactive "me"—the individual as socially defined and determined by his or her interpersonal surround—rather than with the proactive "I," the individual as unique, generative, determining self. This one-sided, overly interpersonal emphasis on selfobject relations tends to countertransferentially abet patients' narcissistic denial of personal agency, defensive blaming of others, and neurotic demand for emotional reparation for losses and injuries suffered in childhood.

Though it is true that all patients were once the intended or inadvertent victim of others' anxiety or antipathy (and lack of empathy), it is also true that all patients are active participants in the neurotic perpetuation of their narcissistic ways. Kohut's clinical approach, with its overemphasis on the therapeutic role of the interpersonal selfother, fails to account sufficiently for the active and interactive role that each patient plays in his or her own interpersonal and personal development. Patients are not to blame for their narcissistic problems, but they are accountable for them. In the final analysis, each patient bears ultimate responsibility for his or her therapeutic self-transformation. Analytic change always begins and ends with the self.

Despite its important, and liberalizing, influence on mainstream psychoanalysis, the Kohutian Self-psychological approach has been severely criticized, on a number of grounds, by theorists representing a broad spectrum of analytic thought (see, for example, Rothstein 1980 and Eagle 1984 for a contemporary Freudian critique; Bollas 1986 for a British Object-Relations critique; and Wolstein 1987; Bromberg 1989; and Levenson 1989 for a critique from three different American Interpersonal-Relations perspectives). Orthodox critics, of course, accuse Self psychology of being insufficiently *analytic*, the standard criticism of any new approach that even hints at heterodoxy.

Among the many criticisms, both theoretical and clinical, that may be leveled at Self psychology (which cannot be reviewed in this brief critique), Kohut's treatment approach may be justly questioned about whether it is not, in fact, a solipsistic and narcissistic form of analysis that tends to infantilize the patient and encourage neurotic dependency (as well as neurotically stimulate false hopes of pain-free living) and thus promote incomplete or partial, as well as protracted or interminable, analyses.

In the therapeutic analysis of the patient's narcissistic defensive structure, the analyst must, at some point, initiate a judicious but honest and direct appraisal of its harmfulness to the patient and to others in his or her life. To wait for inadvertent lapses in "empathy" in order to empathically interpret them to the patient, as Kohut technically advises, is, at the very least, therapeutically inefficient. An even more serious problem with this approach is that it fails to address sufficiently patients' unconscious strivings to grow beyond the confines of their constrictive narcissism and to face their neurotic participation in their narcissistic difficulties. It is important, in other words, that analysts maintain empathy with their patients' personal, as well as interpersonal, selves—with the patients' needs to fulfill themselves, as well as with their need to avoid narcissistic anxiety. Kohut would argue, of course, that such active technical intervention would be countertherapeutic and would reflect a countertransferential "maturity morality." True, such an approach could reflect the operation of countertransference, but not necessarily or invariably so. Countertransference is not built into this approach. On the other hand, Kohut's approach could be justly accused of reflecting an institutionalized countertransferential "immaturity morality" in its failure to actively confront the patient's self-destructive narcissism.

The Self-psychological clinical approach is particularly subject to the countertransferential replay of early spoiling experiences. While Kohut is right to advise against premature interpretations and to caution against the assumption of a "maturity morality," his own approach, as just noted, encourages an "immaturity morality." In its "benevolent" authoritarianism and passive view of the patient, Kohut's clinical approach implicitly underestimates the patient's psychic resources and reserves. And in this, the Self-psychological clinical approach courts the danger of being an analytic approach that is superficially supportive, rather than penetrating and challenging (Fiscalini 1991b).

One of the more outspoken and vigorous of Kohut's critics is the contemporary American ego-analytic Object-Relationalist Kernberg (1975a), who sharply criticizes Kohut's understanding and treatment of narcissism.[6] Whereas Kohut focuses therapeutically on the developmentally arrested, or fixated, aspects of the patient's narcissism—that is, on persisting unconscious infantile and childhood needs for mirroring and idealizing relatedness, Kernberg focuses on pathological developments in narcissism—on the patient's unconscious or preconscious defensive uses of narcissistic processes. Kohut's and Kernberg's analytic stances stand in sharp contrast. Unlike Kohut, Kernberg aggressively confronts and systematically interprets, from early on in the analysis, the patient's characterological pathological narcissism, particularly the patient's unconscious rage, contempt, envy, and other actively hostile ways of devaluing the analyst. Kernberg is sharply critical of what he considers to be Kohut's countertransferential neglect of the negative aspects of the transference. Whereas Kohut prescribes empathic connectedness and tolerance of the patient's childhood and pathological narcissism and disadvises confrontation of the patient's defenses, Kernberg stresses the importance of their active confrontation and working through. Kernberg, unlike Kohut, also focuses on patients' secondary conflicts over their aggressive "badness"—their contempt, rage, envy, demandingness, etc. Kernberg maintains that an important focus of treatment should be narcissistic patients' guilt and fear that their hostile aggression will destroy the analyst, provoke the analyst's retaliation, or destroy their own ability to love or receive love, and thus destroy any opportunity for a good and loving relationship. Kohut is not unmindful of aggression but focuses instead on analyzing its anxious underpinnings—i.e., patients' unmet childhood mirroring and idealizing security requirements. Thus, in contrast to Kohut, Kernberg emphasizes patients' fear and guilt about their destructiveness. Kohut analytically focuses on the early "narcissistic" injuries—i.e., patients' vulnerabilities, and he adopts a gentle, serene, and accepting analytic attitude sensitive to the patients' shame, fear, and anxiety. Kernberg, on the other hand, focuses on patients' defensive narcissism and its destructive and negative impact on the patients and others in their lives. And analytically, Kernberg calls for an aggressive, challenging, and confronting approach to patients' defensive hatred, envy, and contempt. For Kohut, the narcissist is an injured and fallen angel who needs to be rescued and restored; for Kernberg, the narcissist is a pathological devil who must be redeemed and reformed.

Though both Kohut and Kernberg, as befits their orthodox backgrounds, emphasize the importance of interpretation and insight as curative factors, Kohut, unlike Kernberg, also placed an increasing, if somewhat ambivalent, emphasis on the curative action of transmuting internalizations, a process not accepted as primarily curative by Kernberg. Kohut, in other words, allows for the possibility of emotionally corrective experience, whereas Kernberg sees interpretation as the only analytically curative instrumentality. Although Kohut's ideas on therapeutic action have been considered heterodox, and even unanalytic, I think that they are not radical enough. The process of transmuting internalization forms an important, but delimited, aspect of a broader and more inclusive curative relational process that I call *living through* (Fiscalini 1988). I believe that the working through of all neurotically or narcissistically conflicted patterns of living inevitably involves their experiential living through in new and curatively reconstructive ways in the immediate personal relationship between the patient and analyst. The therapeutic action of psychoanalysis, in other words, is premised on the formation, not just formulation, of new experience. The living through process occurs inadvertently, in both dialectic (i.e., as an integral aspect of the interpretive process) and direct relational (i.e., as direct reconstructive relational experience) forms. This process, particularly in its direct form, is curatively pivotal in the analysis of core, preverbal "narcissistic" difficulties and deficits.

In my view, both patients' archaic "narcissism" and their defensive characterological narcissism must be experientially lived through in new and different ways with the analyst as a new interpersonal other (Fiscalini, 1991b). This process also works in reverse order as well; that is, the patient, too, may become a new interpersonal other for the analyst. What takes place relationally between the narcissistic patient and his or her analyst experientially informs both of them about their specific narcissistic difficulties and about new interpersonal and personal possibilities and ways of being, and this can directly effect changes in the patient's or analyst's narcissistic character structure. This complex relational process, which evolves from the personal being of both analyst and patient, is not to be confused with an attitudinized "empathy" for the patient's narcissistic problems or a technically planned Alexanderian-like "corrective emotional experience" of them. This concept of the relational and experiential underpinnings of therapeutic action contrasts sharply with the therapeutic view held by those adherents of Self psychology who have formed what might be termed a cult of empathy. While empathic relatedness obviously forms a crucial aspect of any therapeutic process, the view that some saint-like dispensing of empathy is curative, or even possible, is therapeutically misguided and misleading.

Although the therapeutic sensibilities of Kohut and Kernberg represent radically different analytic temperaments, divergent clinical emphases, and distinctly different metapsychologies, they do not represent fundamentally incompatible visions of narcissism and its treatment. In fact, when viewed from a broad Interpersonal perspective, Kohut's and Kernberg's views may be seen as complementary. Their differences, in many ways, are not as broad as some may insist, and, in fact, Kohut's and Kernberg's approaches to narcissism present some generally unrecognized similarities. Though it is commonly held that Kohut conceptualizes clinical narcissism as arrested development and that Kernberg sees it as pathological development, this is not entirely true. Each theorist, rather, *focuses* on one of these complementary aspects of the problem of narcissism but considers both.

This fact is partly obscured by the metapsychological and semantic complications and confusions inherent in both systems. For example, both Kohut and Kernberg use the same term, *grandiose self,* but each theorist, consistent with his particular theoretical commitments, uses it to refer to very different phenomena. Kernberg asserts that his concept of a "pathological grandiose self" is the same as Kohut's "grandiose self" and that they both refer to the same phenomena. This is questionable. These two concepts do not, in my reading of Kohut and Kernberg, refer to the same thing. Though it may be that some of what Kohut refers to as developmentally arrested longings for mirroring and idealizing experience—i.e., the "grandiose self"—is seen by Kernberg as pathological development, his concept of the "pathological grandiose self" seems to refer, instead, to what Kohut thinks of as manifest characterological or defensive (i.e., pathological) narcissism. And, conversely, Kohut's "grandiose self" seems to refer to the narcissistic aspects of what Kernberg refers to as the "infantile oral frustrations and conflicts" that underlie all defensive narcissistic pathology.[7] Thus each theorist uses the same term to refer to very different aspects of "narcissistic" experience and different terms to refer to the same aspect.

In interpersonal terms, both Kohut and Kernberg, in their studies of narcissism, are essentially talking about very early anxious interpersonal relationships in which the child's various strivings for relational intimacy, physical satisfaction, or psychic fulfillment are traumatically rejected, dismissed, or anxiously disapproved of or misapproved by significant others. In such pathological relatedness, the child's archaic or early security needs (which are developmentally immature and of a grandiose and idealizing nature) either go unmet or are mismet. Clinical narcissism results when there is severe, prolonged, or repetitive injury to early "narcissistic" needs for approval (self-esteem) and a consequent development of overt or covert self-protective substitutive defenses of a narcissistic character (e.g., pathological sense of entitlement, demandingness, devaluation, idealization, etc.).

Both Kohut and Kernberg have made important contributions to the analysis of the interpersonal self within Freudian psychoanalysis. And both approaches are in many ways compatible with Interpersonal formulations of narcissism and its treatment. Yet, from an Interpersonal-Relations viewpoint, Kohut and Kernberg may each be seen to present an incomplete and one-sided account of narcissism and its therapy. Each theorist focuses on an essential aspect of the narcissistic problem but tends to neglect, or at least deemphasize, those aspects that form the focus of the other's attention. Although these two approaches may be seen as complementary, any effort to synthesize or integrate them into a more nearly comprehensive system (and thus more nearly complete account of narcissism) would be an extremely difficult task, and, given their very different theoretical and clinical sensibilities and metapsychological commitments, an unlikely or impossible coupling.

A more thorough understanding and more nearly complete, well-rounded treatment of narcissism requires a more nearly comprehensive approach that flexibly considers both arrested (repressed) childhood narcissism (i.e., Kohut's emphasis) and pathological developments in it (i.e., Kernberg's emphasis) and their analytic interplay. Such an approach would correct for the potential therapeutic excesses implicit in Kohut's and Kernberg's one-sided approaches. It would, for example, mitigate against the infantilizing and spoiling potential and danger of analytic masochism implicit in Kohut's approach and the adultifying and shaming potential and hazard of analytic sadism implicit in Kernberg's approach.

I think that an Interpersonal-Relations approach to narcissism that incorporates a broad and open-ended diagnostic and etiologic schema based on Interpersonal principles and a pluralistic coparticipant clinical approach focused on an analytic inquiry into both the interpersonal and personal selves offers a flexible and comprehensive understanding of narcissism and its treatment. Such an approach offers a more inclusive model of narcissistic processes and problems than either Kohut's theory or Kernberg's. And it possesses a greater therapeutic elasticity, which flexibly and comprehensively attends to the vital narcissistic dimensions emphasized by both Kohut and Kernberg, in an integrated and balanced way (and in simpler, more understandable language). In my opinion, the Interpersonal perspective, in its pluralism, pragmatism, operational methodology, and therapeutic open-endedness, offers an approach to narcissism that avoids the metapsychological rigidities, conceptual flaws, one-sided clinical emphases, and inbuilt therapeutic excesses of contemporary Freudian perspectives, such as those of Kohut and Kernberg.

Interpersonal-Relations theory deals with both childhood "narcissism" and defensive narcissism. And the Interpersonal psychoanalytic approach presents a flexible blend of therapeutic holding and confrontation—of active work with defenses and respect for the patient's self-esteem vulnerability. This approach, like Kohut's, attends to the patient's subjective reality, and yet, as noted previously, it also emphasizes the importance of attending to other "realities."

Therapeutically, the Interpersonal coparticipant inquiry into narcissism (as into any other form of human psychic suffering) is a method that gains in richness, power, and flexibility what it may lose in the comfort and security of prescriptive certainty. Contemporary Interpersonal coparticipant inquiry represents the flexible application of Interpersonal principles to fit the patient's therapeutic need and the analyst's uniquely individual way of working. This form of analytic inquiry reflects the basic Interpersonal conviction that there is no one right way to understand and treat narcissism. Interpersonal inquiry is also a treatment approach that is particularly attuned to the interactive, or intersubjective, properties of the experiential analytic field, certainly more explicitly so than most post-Freudian approaches, including those of Kohut and Kernberg.

Interpersonal-Relations theory is deceptively simple in its language. Its essential sophistication is somewhat obscured by its operational emphasis on clarity of communication and its tradition of using down-to-earth language. The Interpersonal approach, with its repudiation of libido theory and with its inbuilt self psychology and theory of internalized interpersonal, or object relations, easily encompasses the clinical phenomena of narcissism without the complicated metapsychology required of most post-Freudian theories of narcissism. It avoids the twisted complexities of accommodating traditional drive theory to a newer relational model of self and other and is thus able to frame its understanding of narcissism in simple, clear, and therapeutically more fruitful terms.

Notes

1. This critique is part of a larger unpublished study of narcissism and its treatment. Other parts of this study are planned for future publication.

2. See the second essay in this volume, Interpersonal Relations and the Problem of Narcissism, for my definition and discussion of these aspects of interpersonal experience.

3. The coparticipant model of inquiry implicitly or explicitly informs the work of many contemporary Interpersonal analysts. This model is most most explicitly and extensively articulated in the writings of Wolstein, who coined the term. See Wolstein (1959, 1977a, b, 1983, 1985) for a further explication of this post-Sullivanian concept of inquiry in which analyst and patient are viewed as both participant observers and observed participants.

4. See Fiscalini (1993) for a comprehensive and detailed review and critique of various Interpersonal approaches to the understanding and treatment of narcissism.

5. Kohut's concept of the selfobject refers to a broad range of human experience. At times, it is used by various theorists, including Kohut himself, to refer to those aspects of the psyche that I refer to as the personal and relational selves (Fiscalini 1990a, 1991a). However, Kohut principally used this complex concept to refer to the domain of the interpersonal self—to that psychic dimension that Sullivan (1940, 1953) referred to as the need for interpersonal security.

6. A number of secondary sources discuss the so-called Kohut–Kernberg controversy For a representative sample, see Chessick (1977, 1985), Hedges (1983), Morrison (1986), Akhtar (1989), and Akhtar and Thomson (1982). However, I recommend that the reader directly review Kohut's and Kernberg's writings, especially Kohut (1971, 1972, 1977, 1984) and Kernberg (1975a). Also instructive are Ornstein's (1974) delineation of Kernberg's differences from Kohut, and Kernberg's (1975b) reply.

7. Kernberg correctly points out that narcissism is inextricably linked to object relations and criticizes Kohut for postulating a separate developmental line for narcissism. I think, however, that Kohut does not deny the link between narcissism and interpersonal relations. He is simply, from my reading, emphasizing the narcissistic, or security, dimension of object relations—i.e., the interpersonal, rather than the relational, self, and importantly, he studies its developmental path. Conflictual interpersonal, or object, relations always involve issues of self-esteem and vice-versa.

References

Akhtar, S. 1989. Kernberg and Kohut: A critical comparison. In D.W. Detrick and S.P. Detrick, eds. *Self Psychology: Comparisons and Contrasts.* Hillsdale, N.J.: Analytic Press.

Aktar, S. and J.A. Thomson. 1982. Overview: Narcissistic personality disorder. *American Journal of Psychiatry* 139:12–20.

Blechner, M.J. 1987. Entitlement and narcissism: Paradise sought. *Contemporary Psychoanalysis* 23:244–54.

Bollas, C. 1986. Who does self psychology cure? *Psychoanalytic Inquiry* 6:429–35.

Brenner, C. 1976. *Psychoanalytic Technique and Psychic Conflict.* New York: International Universities Press.

Bromberg, P.M. 1979. The use of detachment in narcissistic and borderline conditions. *Journal of the American Academy of Psychoanalysis* 7:593–600.

——. 1983. The mirror and the mask: On narcissism and psychoanalytic growth. *Contemporary Psychoanalysis* 19:359–87.

——. 1989. Interpersonal psychoanalysis and self psychology: A clinical comparison. In D.W. Detrick and S.P. Detrick, eds. *Self Psychology: Comparisons and Contrasts.* Hillsdale, N.J.: Analytic Press.

Chessick, R.D. 1977. *Intensive Psychotherapy of the Borderline Patient.* New York: Jason Aronson.

——. 1985. *Psychology of the Self and the Treatment of Narcissism.* New York: Jason Aronson.

Eagle, M. 1984. *Recent Developments in Psychoanalysis.* New York: McGraw-Hill.

Epstein, L. 1979. The use of countertransference data with borderline patients. *Contemporary Psychoanalysis* 15:248–75.

——. 1981. Countertransference and judgments of fitness for analysis. *Contemporary Psychoanalysis* 17:55–68.

Feiner, A.H. 1983. On the facilitation of the therapeutic symbiosis. *Contemporary Psychoanalysis* 19:673–89.

Field, H. 1987. Some idealizing transferential and countertransferential experiences. *Contemporary Psychoanalysis* 23:230–38.

Fiscalini, J. 1988. Curative experience in the analytic relationship. *Contemporary Psychoanalysis* 24:125–41.

——. 1990a. On self-actualization and the dynamism of the personal self. *Contemporary Psychoanalysis* 26:635–53.

——. 1990b. The uniquely interpersonal and the interpersonally unique. Panel presentation. Clinical symposium of the W.A. White Institute: *Interpersonal Frontiers in Psychoanalytic Practice.* Nov. 11, 1990.

——. 1991a. Expanding the interpersonal theory of self-threat. *Contemporary Psychoanalysis* 27:242–64.

——. 1991b. Working with narcissism. Unpublished paper.

——. 1993. Interpersonal conceptions of narcissism. In M. Lionells, J. Fiscalini, C. Mann, and D. B. Stern, eds. *Handbook of Interpersonal Psychoanalysis,* vol. 2. Hillsdale, N.J.: Analytic Press (in press).

Fromm, E. 1964. *The Heart of Man* New York: Harper & Row.

Fromm-Reichmann, F. 1950. *Principles of Intensive Psychotherapy.* Chicago: University of Chicago Press.

Gedo, J.E. 1981. *Advances in Clinical Psychoanalysis.* New York: International Universities Press.

Giovacchini, P.L. 1979. *Treatment of Primitive Mental States.* New York: Jason Aronson.

Greenson, R.R. 1967. *The Technique and Practice of Psychoanalysis.* vol. 1. New York: International Universities Press.

Grey, A.L. 1987. Entitlement: An interactional defense of self-esteem. *Contemporary Psychoanalysis* 23:255–63.

Greenberg, J. and S.A. Mitchell. 1983. *Object Relations in Psychoanalytic Theory.* Cambridge, Mass.: Harvard University Press.

Guntrip, H. 1969. *Schizoid Phenomena, Object Relations and the Self.* New York: International Universities Press.

——. 1971. *Psychoanalytic Theory, Therapy, and the Self.* New York: Basic Books.

Hedges, L.E. 1983. *Listening Perspectives in Psychotherapy.* Northvale, N.J.: Jason Aronson.

Held-Weiss, R. 1984. The interpersonal tradition and its development. *Contemporary Psychoanalysis* 20:344–36

Horner, A. 1979. *Object Relations and the Developing Ego in Therapy.* New York: Jason Aronson.

Kernberg, O. 1975a. *Borderline Conditions and Pathological Narcissism.* New York: Jason Aronson.

——. 1975b. Further contributions to the treatment of narcissistic personalities: A reply to the discussion by Paul H. Ornstein. *International Journal of Psychoanalysis* 56:245–47.

Kohut, H. 1971. *The Analysis of the Self.* New York: International Universities Press.

——. 1972. Thoughts on narcissism and narcissistic rage. *The Psychoanalytic Study of the Child* 27:360–99.

——. 1977. *The Restoration of the Self.* New York: International Universities Press.

——. 1979. The two analyses of Mr. Z. *International Journal of Psychoanalysis* 60:1–27.

——. 1984. *How Does Analysis Cure?* A. Goldberg and P.E. Stepansky, eds. Chicago: University of Chicago Press.

Kohut, H. and E.S. Wolf. 1978. The disorders of the self and their treatment: An outline. *International Journal of Psychoanalysis* 59:413–25.

Levenson, E.A. 1972. *The Fallacy of Understanding.* New York: Basic Books.

——. 1981. *The Ambiguity of Change.* New York: Basic Books.

——. 1989. Whatever happened to the cat? Interpersonal perspectives on the self. *Contemporary Psychoanalysis* 25:537–53.

Masterson, J.F. 1981. *The Narcissistic and Borderline Disorders: An Integrated Developmental Approach* New York: Brunner/Mazel.

——. 1988. *The Search for the Real Self.* New York: Free Press.

Menninger, K. 1958. *Theory of Psychoanalytic Technique.* New York: Harper & Row.

Miller, A. 1981. *Prisoners of Childhood.* New York: Basic Books.

Mitchell, S.A. 1986. The wings of Icarus: Illusion and the problem of narcissism. *Contemporary Psychoanalysis* 22:107–32.

——. 1988. *Relational Concepts in Psychoanalysis: An Integration.* Cambridge, Mass.: Harvard University Press.

Modell, A. 1975. A narcissistic defence against affects and the illusion of self-sufficiency. *International Journal of Psychoanalysis* 56:275–82.

Morrison, A.P., ed. 1986. *Essential Papers on Narcissism.* New York: New York University Press.

Ornstein, P.H. 1974. Discussion of the paper of Otto F. Kernberg, "Further contributions to the treatment of narcissistic personalities." *International Journal of Psychoanalysis* 55:241–47.

Ortmeyer, D.H. 1987. Idealization in the transference and countertransference. *Contemporary Psychoanalysis* 23:221–29.

Protter, B. 1985. Toward an emergent psychoanalytic epistemology. *Contemporary Psychoanalysis* 21:208–27.

——. 1988. Reflections. *Contemporary Psychoanalysis* 24:142–55.

Rinsley, D.B. 1982. *Borderline and Other Self Disorders: A Developmental and Object-Relations Perspective.* New York: Jason Aronson.

Rogers, C.R. 1951. *Client-Centered Therapy: Its Current Practice, Implications, and Theory.* Boston: Houghton.

Rothstein, A. 1980. Toward a critique of the psychology of the self. *Psychoanalytic Quarterly* 49:423–55.

Singer, E. 1965. *Key Concepts in Psychotherapy.* New York: Random House.

Spiegel, R. 1987. Reflections on entitlement and idealization. *Contemporary Psychoanalysis* 23:272–77.

Sullivan, H.S. 1940. *Conceptions of Modern Psychiatry.* New York: Norton.

——. 1953. *The Interpersonal Theory of Psychiatry.* New York: Norton.

——. 1954. *The Psychiatric Interview.* New York: Norton.

Tenzer, A. 1987. Grandiosity and its discontents. *Contemporary Psychoanalysis* 23:263–71.

Thompson, C. 1950. *Psychoanalysis: Evolution and Development.* New York: Grove Press.

Witenberg, E.G., ed. 1973. *Interpersonal Explorations in Psychoanalysis: New Directions in Theory and Practice.* New York: Basic Books.

Wolstein, B. 1959. *Countertransference.* New York: Grune & Stratton.

——. 1977a. Psychology, metapsychology, and the evolving American school. *Contemporary Psychoanalysis* 13:126–54.

——. 1977b. From mirror to participant observation, to coparticipant inquiry and experience. *Contemporary Psychoanalysis* 13:381–86.

——. 1983. The first person in interpersonal relations. *Contemporary Psychoanalysis* 19:522–35.

——. 1985. Restructuring psychoanalysis: Toward a convergence of psychology and metapsychology in immediate experience. *Contemporary Psychoanalysis* 21:449–90.

——. 1987. Experience, interpretation, self-knowledge. *Contemporary Psychoanalysis* 23:329–49.

Index